# INSTRUCTIONAL DESIGN
— STEP BY STEP

# INSTRUCTIONAL DESIGN
## — STEP BY STEP

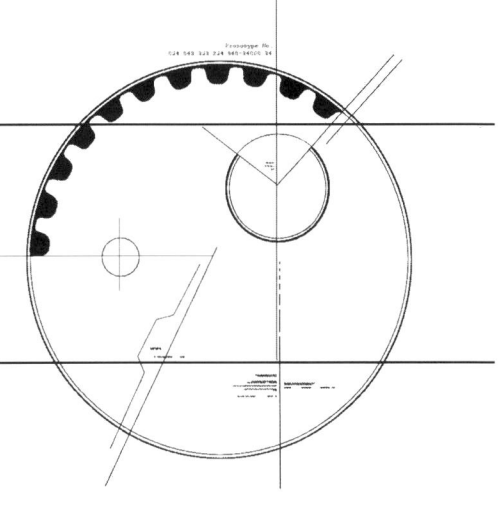

Nine Easy Steps for
Designing Lean, Effective,
and Motivational Instruction

John S. Hoffman, PhD

iUniverse, Inc.
Bloomington

Instructional Design — Step by Step
Nine Easy Steps for Designing Lean, Effective, and Motivational Instruction

Copyright © 2013 John S. Hoffman, PhD

All rights reserved. No part of this book may be used or reproduced by any means, graphic, electronic, or mechanical, including photocopying, recording, taping or by any information storage retrieval system without the written permission of the publisher except in the case of brief quotations embodied in critical articles and reviews.

iUniverse books may be ordered through booksellers or by contacting:

iUniverse
1663 Liberty Drive
Bloomington, IN 47403
www.iuniverse.com
1-800-Authors (1-800-288-4677)

Because of the dynamic nature of the Internet, any Web addresses or links contained in this book may have changed since publication and may no longer be valid. The views expressed in this work are solely those of the author and do not necessarily reflect the views of the publisher, and the publisher hereby disclaims any responsibility for them.

Any people depicted in stock imagery provided by Thinkstock are models, and such images are being used for illustrative purposes only.

Certain stock imagery © Thinkstock.

ISBN: 978-1-4759-8671-6 (sc)
ISBN: 978-1-4759-8672-3 (e)

Library of Congress Control Number: 2013907265

Printed in the United States of America

iUniverse rev. date: 5/13/2013

# Contents

Preface . . . . . . . . . . . . . . . . . . . . . . . . . . . . vii
Acknowledgments . . . . . . . . . . . . . . . . . . . . . . . ix
Introduction and Overview . . . . . . . . . . . . . . . . . . xi

## Part 1. Understanding How Humans Learn . . . . . . . . . 1
1. The Biological Requirements for Learning . . . . . . . . . . 5
2. A Simple Cognitive Model of Learning . . . . . . . . . . . 15
3. Learning Taxonomies and Their Application . . . . . . . . . 45
4. Adult Learning Principles . . . . . . . . . . . . . . . . . . 71
5. Ten Key Teaching Principles . . . . . . . . . . . . . . . . 93

## Part 2. Creating Outstanding Instructional Designs . . . 113
6. Overview of How to Design Training . . . . . . . . . . . . 121
7. Gathering Requirements . . . . . . . . . . . . . . . . . . 155
8. Performing an Instructional Analysis on the Job Outcomes . . . 191
9. Analyzing Complex Procedures . . . . . . . . . . . . . . . 215
10. Identifying the Enabling Content . . . . . . . . . . . . . 247
11. Structuring the Course . . . . . . . . . . . . . . . . . . 267
12. Writing Instructional Objectives . . . . . . . . . . . . . 283
13. Determining the Instructional Delivery System . . . . . . . 309

14. Designing Practice Exercises and Other Instructional Events. . . .341
15. Designing the Prototype or Example Lesson . . . . . . . . . . .377
16. Creating the Formal Design Document. . . . . . . . . . . . . .401

# Part 3. Instructional Design Tips and Traps. . . . . .417
17. Designing Computer Application Training. . . . . . . . . . . .421
18. Twenty Common Training Mistakes, Part 1 . . . . . . . . . . .455
19. Twenty Common Training Mistakes, Part 2 . . . . . . . . . . .479

Summary. . . . . . . . . . . . . . . . . . . . . . . . . . . . . 505

Appendix A: Example Printout of a Template for Microsoft
  Word that Has Been Created Especially for Instructional Analysis  511

Appendix B: Example of an Instructional Analysis . . . . . . . . 513

Appendix C: Example of Using a Structured-English Outline
  to Capture Complex Logic . . . . . . . . . . . . . . . . . . 521

Appendix D: Example of a Content Analysis. . . . . . . . . . . . 535

Bibliography . . . . . . . . . . . . . . . . . . . . . . . . . . 541

Index . . . . . . . . . . . . . . . . . . . . . . . . . . . . . 543

# Preface

This book was written for three audiences:

- those who are relatively new to the field of instructional design
- those who have been tasked with creating training or education who do not have a background or formal education in instructional design
- those who have some background, education, or experience in instructional design who (1) want to expand their skills in certain areas (such as analyzing complex procedures), (2) want a concise summary of the key principles of instructional design, or (3) want a concise, proven, and simple approach to instructional design

In this book, I have tried to distill my thirty-plus years of experience in designing education and training, my university degree in instructional design, and my sitting at the feet of some of the founding fathers of human performance improvement into a simple, straightforward, step-by-step process for designing instruction and training.

This book is not intended as a comprehensive treatment of the field of instructional design. Rather, it is designed to teach a newcomer, in simple, understandable terms, how to design effective, efficient, and successful instruction.

This book is not an academic tome; rather, it is a practitioner's guide. As such, I will be your personal mentor and tutor. I will teach you in the simplest way I know the minimum information and skills you will need to perform systematic instructional design.

The process I teach is not an unproven, abstract, or theoretical musing. I believe it is the quickest, most concise, and most direct way to design effective instruction. I have practiced and refined this approach in numerous real-life projects with many clients on tasks and subject material ranging from the simple to the complex, from soft-skills to the highly technical, covering a wide range of disciplines. In short, in this book, I have condensed all of my wisdom, knowledge, and skill to its most essential elements and have packaged it into a simple step-by-step approach.

The follow-on and companion activity to instructional design is *instructional development*. Instructional development is the set of activities that are required to create the instructional materials that were specified and prescribed by the instructional design document—the blueprints of the training. It is the construction phase of the training project. In instructional development, the course materials are "fleshed out" into their final verbiage and form, based on the course and topic objectives.

Instructional development requires knowledge of such things as how to sequence the instruction, how to identify different types of information, and how to design and write instructional prose, graphics, and treatments accordingly. For a how-to manual on instructional development, see my companion book, *Instructional Development—Step by Step: Six Easy Steps for Developing Lean, Effective, and Motivational Instruction.*

# Acknowledgments

Many people have influenced my thinking, insights, and understanding of instructional design throughout the years. In addition to the fundamentals that I acquired from earning a doctorate degree in instructional design, my insights have been greatly expanded upon by the likes of Joe Harless, Robert Horn, Bob Mager, Ruth Clark, and other giants in the field whose courses, seminars, books, and lectures matured my understanding and skill in human performance improvement. To each of them, I express my sincere gratitude.

I am also grateful to my graduate school mentor, Paul F. Merrill of Brigham Young University, for his original work on structured English analysis that became the basis for my approach to analyzing complex procedures (and simple ones, for that matter).

To the many clients I have worked with during the last three decades, I express my gratitude for the opportunity to test, apply, and refine my approach to instructional design.

Finally, I acknowledge that no book is a solo effort. I am grateful to all of the professionals at iUniverse who have applied their skill and craft to make this book a reality.

# Introduction and Overview

Welcome! You are about to learn how to design instruction and training that is easy to understand, concise, effective, and rewarding. This book has been designed following the same process that I teach in this book. I hope, then, that you will experience firsthand the benefits of following this approach.

In this book, only the minimum, essential information and skills are presented. This will keep you focused on the essential elements—no fluff is included here. After you understand the key principles and practices that make up this cognitive infrastructure, you will have an organized mental framework on which to venture out and assimilate the larger body of information that is available on this subject.

I have divided this book into three parts:

**Part 1** is an overview of some of the basic principles of learning. I present them in plain and simple language; they are not intended to be a comprehensive review of human learning. Rather, I have verbalized some of the key principles that trainers need to know that are relevant to human learning. After all, unless you first understand how humans learn, how can you design instruction that will support that learning process? Part 1 has five chapters.

**Part 2** is a step-by-step approach to instructional design. It begins with an overview of the nine steps of instructional design, which is followed by a detailed discussion of each step in individual chapters. Each of these steps is presented in its simplest terms and is supported by numerous examples, tables, and succinct lists. Part 2 has eleven chapters.

**Part 3** begins with a discussion of designing instruction for computer applications. Because of the unique nature of computers and computer software, a separate discussion is merited on this topic. The principles given in this chapter apply to many other hardware devices. The rest of part 3 discusses twenty common training mistakes. Knowing ahead of time the common pitfalls that even some experienced practitioners make will help you avoid the all-too-frequent mistakes that I see in many instructional materials. Part 3 has three chapters.

At the end of each chapter, I have included a series of checkpoint questions that will test your understanding of the key concepts and techniques found within that chapter. Each question is followed by the correct answer and a detailed explanation. By answering these questions, you will quickly identify any gaps in your understanding, and you will know exactly which material you need to revisit. Some chapters also include hands-on activities that will help you experience firsthand the concepts being discussed.

## Objectives of This Book

This book, having been designed using this process, would not be complete without a formal list of objectives. You can find more detailed objectives at the end of each chapter in the chapter summary.

Upon completion of this book, you should be able to

- list and explain the fundamental principles of human learning;
- describe the overall cognitive learning process, identify where bottlenecks can occur in that process, and explain how to overcome those bottlenecks;

- design effective, lean, and motivational technology-based and non-technology-based training courses and materials by following the nine steps in the instructional design process;
- design blended learning solutions; and
- list twenty common training mistakes; for each mistake, describe the mistake, state the learning principles that were violated, explain how to avoid the mistake, and describe what to do to remedy the mistake.

To finish this introduction, let's discuss what good training feels like from the perspective of those taking the training. Compare this list with how you felt when you took your last training course.

## What Does Good Training *Feel* Like?

If trainers and instructional designers have done their job, taking a course will have all of the following characteristics (as seen from the point of view of the student).

### Learning feels almost effortless:

- Things are so clear that they seem obvious.
- You understand things immediately when they are taught.
- The sequence and flow of the material seem perfectly logical.
- For online instruction, navigation is intuitive and easy to understand.
- Prerequisite knowledge is refreshed as needed.
- Graphics and other media are used appropriately to help teach the information.

### You are given the opportunity to practice what is being taught:

- Practice is frequent and starts with simple practice and builds to more difficult and integrated practice exercises.

**Training feels like it was tailored specifically to meet *your* needs:**

- The material is right on target.
- The training is lean—no irrelevant material is included.

**Training will be motivational and enjoyable to take:**

- Training is engaging and highly interactive.

# PART 1

## Understanding How Humans Learn

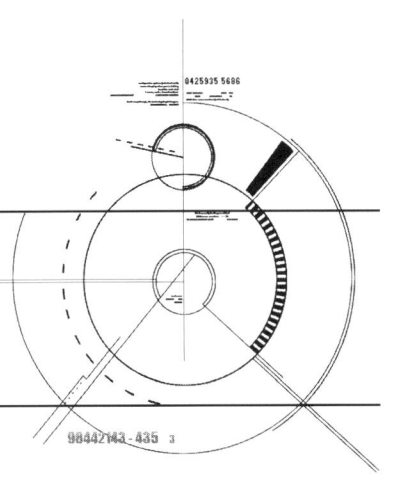

# Overview of Part 1

Part 1 is an overview of how humans learn. It describes the biological requirements for learning, a simple model of learning, ways of classifying learning into types or outcomes, the fundamental principles of human learning, and basic strategies for learning.

After you complete part 1, you should be able to

- explain the biological and cognitive requirements for learning,
- describe the simple model of learning and where learning bottlenecks occur in that model,
- describe the different types of learning and learning outcomes,
- describe the four main learning taxonomies,
- list and explain the fundamental principles of learning, and
- describe Gagne's strategy for instruction.

Part 1 is made up of five chapters.

## Why You Need to Understand How Humans Learn

Sometimes instructional designers are asked by subject matter experts (SMEs) or content developers who are anxious to begin developing training, "Why do I need to understand how humans learn? Why not just jump right in and put some training materials together?"

Imagine that friendly aliens from outer space have landed on earth and that you want to teach them about earthlings and earth life. What would you need to know to be successful?

- how the aliens learn (the methods by which they process and interpret new information and the bottlenecks and limitations that are inherent in those methods)

- what motivates their behavior (so that you could motivate them to want to learn)

Unless you knew this, you would be unlikely to

- be effective or successful in teaching the alien;
- be efficient in your instruction (stimulate learning in the least amount of time, with the least effort, and with the least amount of resources); or
- motivate the alien to learn what you would like to teach it.

## The Fundamental Components of Human Learning

Human learning involves two fundamental processes:

- biological processes (including sensory perception)
- cognitive (mental) processes

As with any process, these processes have bottlenecks and limitations that constrain and limit what you can do at any given moment. However, certain research-based principles and techniques can facilitate and maximize human learning within these processes.

To design successful and effective training, you must understand the biological and cognitive processes involved in learning, the bottlenecks that are built into these processes, and the techniques that you can employ to facilitate and maximize human learning.

In part 1, you will learn the fundamental biological and cognitive processes of learning and key principles of learning and teaching that can be employed to make learning successful and enjoyable. So let's get started!

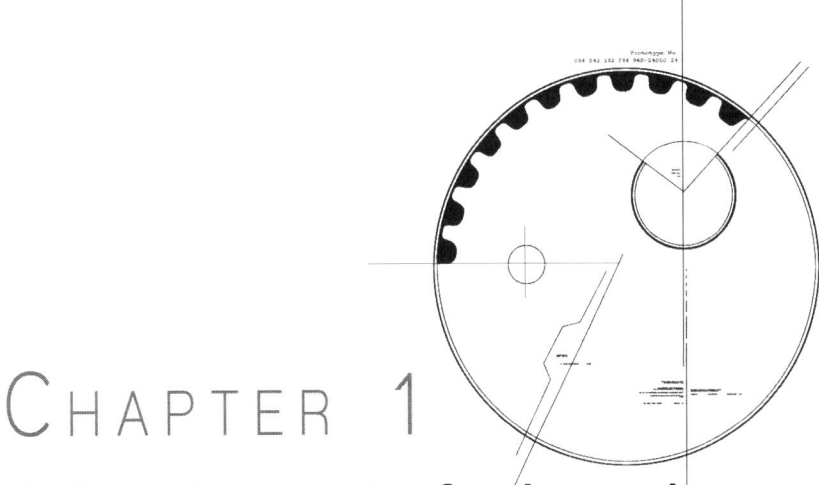

# CHAPTER 1
# The Biological Requirements for Learning

This chapter discusses the biological requirements for learning. It describes what must happen biologically for learning to occur, why biological processes have bottlenecks and limitations, why the "fire hose" approach to training doesn't work, what happens to information that was learned after the learning program has ended, how you can strengthen learning from a biological perspective, and why the brain is different from a computer in how it processes information.

## Activity: Experience for Yourself a Bottleneck to Learning

In this activity, you will experience for yourself one of the bottlenecks to learning. Follow the steps to complete the activity.

1. Set a timer for one minute and a pen and paper. When you are ready to begin, start your timer, read the following words, and try to memorize as many of them as possible. After a minute has passed, immediately write down as many of the words as you can remember.

| | | | | |
|---|---|---|---|---|
| clock | dish | key | pleasant | love |
| her | eyes | plate | tasty | cranky |
| stand | swift | pencil | pain | sad |
| bind | beef | brown | gray | melted |
| zap | solemn | wind | hand | grief |
| tell | phone | branch | time | whistle |
| plane | air | leaf | lie | glove |
| form | pretty | pillow | sharp | sooth |
| explain | dashing | shoe | blue | shower |
| file | control | pen | broken | car |
| float | weight | fork | happy | food |
| chair | green | late | it | heady |

2. Now compare the words you wrote down with the list above.
3. How many items were you able to recall?
4. If the human brain works like a computer, then why were you not able to recall *all* of the items?

## Learning Is Biological, Not Just Intellectual

Learning is often viewed as strictly an intellectual activity—not so! Learning involves the sense organs, such as the eyes and ears. Even the brain itself is a living, biological entity, not just an intellectual capability.

Just like the other organs of the body, the sense organs and the brain are subject to perceptual and processing limitations as well as physical fatigue. Consider these examples:

- What happens when the heart tries to beat faster than it is capable of or to beat in an irregular pattern?
- What happens when the liver is overwhelmed with processing more blood alcohol than it can handle?
- What happens when you are driving down a busy freeway during rush hour in a rainstorm and suddenly all of the cars in front of you start colliding and spinning out of control?

- What happens when an instructor displays slide after slide of densely packed text, spreadsheets, and charts, giving students only a few seconds per slide to assimilate the information?
- Is it reasonable for parents of college students to expect them to be heads down in concentrated study for eight hours with no rest breaks?

## Learning Occurs When New Neural Interconnections Are Made in the Brain

Learning has a biological as well as a cognitive component. Biologically, learning occurs when new neural interconnections (neural pathways between brain cells) are formed in the brain that can later be accessed. A key point you should remember is that it takes time for natural biological processes to *grow* these new neural interconnections and networks.

As an instructor or designer of training, your job is to grow new neural interconnections in the brains of your students—interconnections that represent new skills, knowledge, and attitudes—and to do so in the most efficient and time-effective way.

Up to now, you probably did not see your role as a cultivator of new neural interconnections in students' brains. But you should never forget that learning requires biology. Biology has built-in limitations that require the application of research-based principles to utilize those processes to their maximum capability.

## The "Fire Hose" Approach to Learning Exceeds Human Biological Capacity

You have probably experienced firsthand the fire hose approach to training. This is any training that presents too much material too quickly with too few (or no) learning activities that support and give time for the underlying biological processes to build the new neural interconnections that are required for learning. Perhaps you have been a student in a class in which a subject matter expert gave a "core knowledge dump" slide presentation, in which he or she sped through dozens of slides containing densely packed, detailed information that made perfect sense to the SME but not necessarily to anyone else. If so, were you able to process—let alone remember—all that material?

The fact that learning is biological and not just intellectual is why the fire hose approach to training is ineffective, despite the fact that we see it used every day by well-intentioned trainers and presenters.

Considering our biological limitations, ponder the questions:

**One-trial learning:** Is it enough as an instructor or instructional designer simply to present information to students one time for a few seconds and then expect them to remember it forever thereafter—a notion called "one-trial learning" by researchers?

**More seeds, more water:** Can farmers produce bigger harvests simply by showering the ground with more seeds and more water? Will seeds grow faster simply because a farmer wants the seeds to grow faster?

**Cram, cram, cram:** Will more learning occur when well-meaning instructors or instructional designers try to cram too much material into the time allotted?

## Neural Interconnections Fade Over Time Unless Reinforced or Reused

After information has been learned and new neural interconnections are created, it quickly *fades* (becomes increasingly difficult to recall) in a process called extinction unless that information's neural interconnections are periodically reused and strengthened.

In fact, information doesn't fade from memory at a constant rate. Most of the new information that a person learns is forgotten in the first few days after it was learned, unless that information is refreshed through reviews or applied in exercises or to tasks on the job.

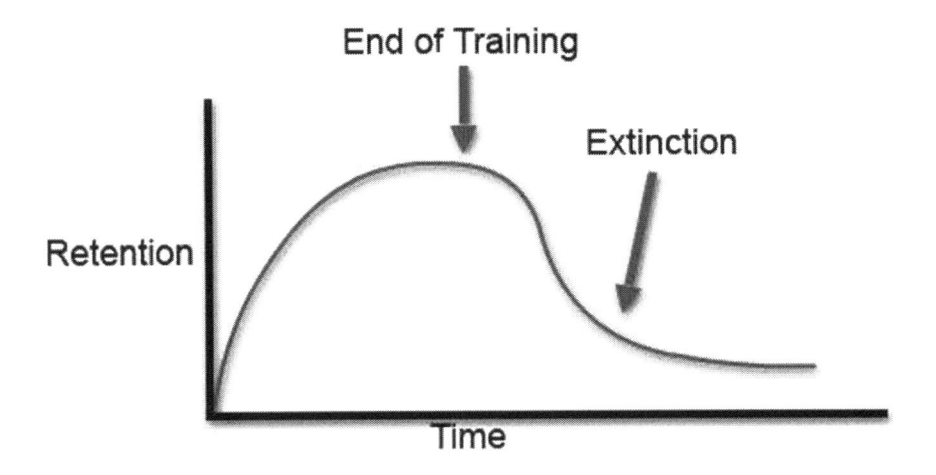

**Figure 1. The memory extinction curve**

That is why periodic reviews and carefully designed practice exercises are essential instructional elements to any training program. And because information fades so quickly during extinction, training must not only *create* new neural interconnections, it must also determine how students will periodically *strengthen* these interconnections *after the training* until the information is regularly applied in real life, such as back on the job, where it will be naturally and frequently reinforced.

## How Can You Strengthen New Neural Interconnections?

Because information fades during extinction, neural interconnections must be strengthened and reinforced *during training* so that they will fade less quickly *after training*.

What can you do to fortify neural interconnections to make them stronger so that they will fade less quickly?

- Either refresh the original material through periodic re-exposure to the information or link the information to other information, thus increasing the richness of the available neural pathways to that information.

*Understanding How Humans Learn*

- Strengthen the pathways to the original neural interconnections through re-exposure to the same material, such as through presenting the same instructional stimulus again, through drill-and-practice techniques, or through reviews and summaries.
- Provide exercises or application activities in which students must use the information to complete an exercise, perform an activity, or complete a task.
- Increase the number or richness of the neural interconnections to the information by using cognitive encoding techniques, such as elaboration, association, advanced organizers, analogies, and examples, or by showing how the information is related to other, already known information.

## Ways in Which the Brain Is Different from a Computer

The human brain is often likened to a computer. For example, in computers, we talk about a central processor, memory, data, and peripherals. These devices have been likened to the brain's cognitive processor and memory and to our peripheral sense organs, such as the eyes and ears, that are connected to the brain.

But believing in this analogy beyond this point will lead to false assumptions that actually deter learning. Computers and humans have very different capabilities, capacities, and processing bottlenecks. For example, the brain is not like a computer, which can soak up endless quantities of knowledge as fast as it can be dispensed.

What are some of the ways in which the brain is *not* like a computer?

- The brain cannot take in, process, or remember vast amounts of fast-streaming information. Computers have no difficulty doing this.
- Human information processing has numerous but often unrecognized bottlenecks and filters that affect or limit processing. Some of these potential bottlenecks and filters include attention, sensory perception, emotional state, cognitive strategies, short-term memory, and previous learning. These will be discussed in detail later in this book.

- Human short-term memory is limited to seven plus-or-minus two items of information without resorting to chunking or some other memory encoding technique. This will be discussed in more detail shortly.
- Memory (neural interconnections) must be biologically grown and then constantly reinforced to endure. This takes time, repetition, and the application of effective instructional techniques. Computers store information almost instantaneously.

# Chapter Summary—
# The Biological Requirements for Learning

This chapter provided an overview of the biological basis for learning. It described what must happen biologically for learning to occur, why biological processes have bottlenecks and limitations, why the "fire hose" approach to training doesn't work, what happens to information that was learned after the learning program has ended, how you can strengthen learning from a biological perspective, and why the brain is different from a computer in how it processes information.

You should now be able to

- describe why learning is biological, not just intellectual;
- describe what actually happens biologically when new learning occurs;
- define the "fire hose" approach to training and explain why it is ineffective;
- define fading and extinction and explain why they occur;
- describe how you can strengthen new neural interconnections in the brain; and
- give three examples of how the brain is not like a computer, and explain the dangers of believing in the brain-computer analogy.

## Check Your Understanding

1. **Which of the following statements about the biological basis for learning are true?**
    A. Learning is completely intellectual—there are no biological processes involved in learning.
    B. Learning occurs when new neural interconnections are formed in the brain that can later be accessed.
    C. Your role as a trainer or designer of training is to cultivate new neural interconnections in students' brains.

D. The biological components involved in learning have built-in limitations that require the application of research-based principles to utilize them to their maximum capability.

2. **Match each concept or idea with its correct definition**

| | |
|---|---|
| Fire hose approach to training | A. The idea that an instructor or training designer can "stuff" as much information as possible into the allotted training time and students will learn more as a result |
| One-trial learning | B. An approach to training in which a subject matter expert (SME) presents far too much information and detail for students to process. Information usually is structured in ways that make sense to the SME rather than in ways that facilitate learning. |
| Core information dump | C. Any training that presents too much material too quickly with too few (or no) learning activities that support and give time for the underlying biological processes to build the new neural interconnections that are required for learning |
| The more information that is presented, the more learning will take place. | D. The idea that students should be able to remember information forever after only one exposure to it |

3. **Which of the following statements about learning are true?**
    A. Memory fades at a constant rate.
    B. The two basic methods to strengthen neural interconnections are to refresh the original material through periodic re-exposure to the information or to link the information to other information, thus increasing the richness of the available neural pathways to that information.

*Understanding How Humans Learn*    13

C. Increasing the number or richness of the neural interconnections to information by using cognitive encoding techniques—such as elaboration, association, advanced organizers, analogies, and examples, or by showing how the information is related to other, already known information—will strengthen learning.

D. The instructor's responsibility is limited to dispensing new information in whatever form the instructor thinks best; then, the student's responsibility is to learn it.

4. **In what ways is the brain different from a computer?**
   A. The brain cannot take in, process, or remember vast amounts of fast-streaming information.
   B. Human short-term memory is limited to nine plus-or-minus two items of information without resorting to chunking or some other memory encoding technique.
   C. Human information processing has numerous but often unrecognized bottlenecks and filters that affect or limit processing, including attention, sensory perception, emotional state, cognitive strategies, short-term memory, and previous learning.
   D. Memory (neural interconnections) must be biologically grown and then constantly reinforced to endure. This takes time, repetition, and the application of effective instructional techniques.

## Answers

1. B, C, and D
2. C, D, B, and A
3. B and C
4. A, C, and D. Human short-term memory is limited to *seven* plus-or-minus two items of information.

# Chapter 2
# A Simple Cognitive Model of Learning

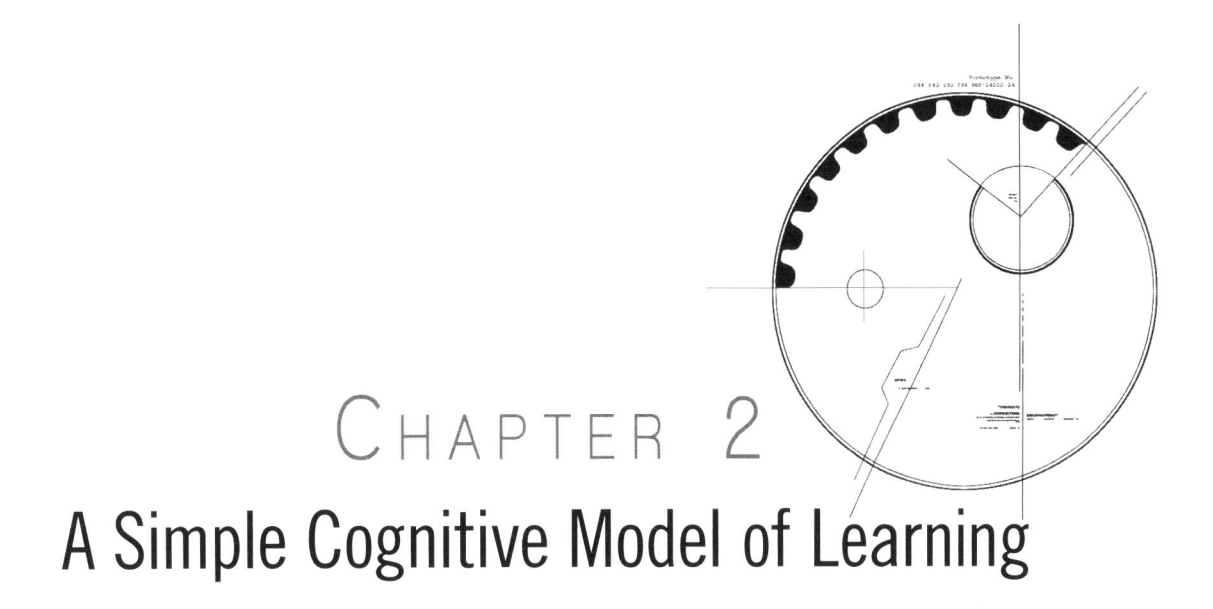

This chapter presents a simple model of learning and explains the cognitive requirements for learning. It describes where bottlenecks in learning processes can occur and what can be done to address those bottlenecks.

## A Simplified Model of How Humans Learn

| Gain Attention | Sensory Perception | Higher-Level Cognition | Memory Storage and Retrieval | Practice with Feedback |
|---|---|---|---|---|

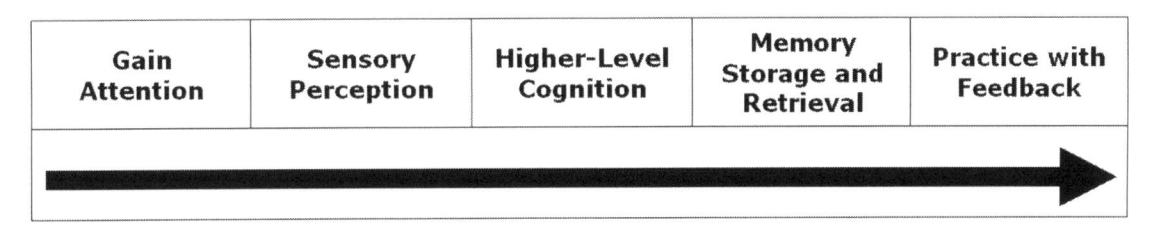

**Figure 2. A simple cognitive model of learning**

For human learning to occur, several perceptual and cognitive events must occur in sequence.

*Understanding How Humans Learn* 15

1. **Gain Attention:** Focusing one's attention on the learning stimulus, such as a slide, text, or computer screen.
2. **Sensory Perception:** Perceiving the learning stimulus with our physical senses, such as eyes or ears.
3. **Higher-Level Cognition:** Processing the learning stimulus in our brain, during which we make sense of it, relating it to what we already know, associating it with other information, and forming new understandings (new neural interconnections).
4. **Memory Storage and Retrieval:** Storing this information for later retrieval (reinforcing the new neural interconnections).
5. **Practice with Feedback:** This simplified model of learning also includes an instructional event—practice with feedback—which is not really an internal learning event but rather an instructional activity that provides learners the opportunity to practice or apply the knowledge and skills that they have learned. This reinforces neural interconnections, clarifies and solidifies conceptual boundaries, and provides an experiential base to learning, all of which improve all aspects of learning and retention.

## Beware of Built-In Bottlenecks in Learning

Bottlenecks can occur at any of the steps in our learning model.

1. **Bottlenecks in Attention**

   Attention is limited to one thing at a time. This explains why there are so many cell phone-related auto accidents. Although we can switch attention back and forth somewhat rapidly between two or more stimuli within certain limitations, expecting students to pay attention to what the instructor is saying while they are trying to read text on the screen, for example, will result in information being lost even before it is perceived.

2. **Bottlenecks in Sensory Perception**

   Each of our senses has its own set of limitations. Some students might be color blind. Acute, high-resolution vision is limited to a very narrow range of field, while peripheral vision is sensitive to motion but poor in resolution. Too many conversations going on at the same time might make it difficult to focus on listening to one. Older students might find it harder to see smaller type sizes.

3. **Bottlenecks in Higher-Level Cognition**

Higher-level cognition is employed when a person is trying to make sense of incoming stimuli. It can be affected by one's emotional state, the quality and variety of one's functioning cognitive strategies, and previous learning. Amusement park rides and fun houses are often designed to overwhelm the senses and the person's ability to interpret the stimuli that they are experiencing.

4. **Bottlenecks in Memory Storage and Retrieval**

To be stored in long-term memory for later retrieval, information must be properly encoded into long-term memory. To the extent that a training designer applies various principles of memory, the more likely it is that students will remember that information. To the extent that they are not applied, or to the extent that students are bombarded with a "fire hose" of information, memory will be overwhelmed and very little will be remembered.

5. **Bottlenecks in Practice with Feedback**

When insufficient or no practice with feedback on performance is provided, extinction quickly takes its toll, concepts are not reinforced and clarified, experiential components to learning are avoided, and retention is greatly reduced.

## Learning Step #1: Gaining Attention

Gaining attention is getting students to mentally and perceptually focus on the desired stimulus.

What are the things that draw a person's attention?

- motion
- novelty
- change in the stimulus

- animation
- multisensory stimulation
- sense of danger or excitement
- color
- unusual or startling sounds or voices
- potential for satisfaction of needs

## Activity: Experience for Yourself the Application of the Principles of Attention

Companies that advertise on television must pay heavy fees for the privilege of enticing people to use their products. To maximize the return on their advertising dollars, commercials are designed to capture your attention and draw your mental focus to their sales pitches. Advertisers know that the first principle of selling, as in learning, is gaining your attention. Unless they capture your attention, their sales message will not even be perceived, let alone mentally processed, and therefore it will have no effect on the viewer.

Experience for yourself the application of the principles of attention. Follow these steps to complete the activity.

1. Turn on your television set and turn off the volume so that you can focus entirely on the visual display.
2. Watch several commercials and note which of the following principles of attention were employed:
   - motion
   - novelty
   - change in the stimulus
   - animation
   - multisensory stimulation
   - sense of danger or excitement
   - color
   - unusual or startling sounds
   - colorful voices
   - fulfillment of biological needs and drives

3. Now repeat steps 1 and 2 with the volume turned up.

## How to Gain Students' Attention in Training

How can you apply the principles of attention to gain students' attention in training?

### Techniques for gaining students' attention for a new course

- Build anticipation through advanced e-mercials (Flash-based animated announcements sent out in advance) or executive pitches in e-mails.
- Provide motivational course lead-ins, such as
  - "What's in it for me?"
  - "Why should I care?"
  - success vignettes, and
  - executive introductions.
- For web-based training (WBT) course lead-ins, consider
  - splash screens (a colorful or dynamic first screen in a course that entices students to proceed into the course),
  - voiceovers (narrated presentations),
  - flash animations,
  - power-person statements (statements from authority figures),
  - music, and
  - graphics.

### Techniques for gaining students' attention for a new unit, module, or topic

- preview or overview the segment—what will students learn and do (the objectives)?
- address relevance of the subject to students
- tie the need to discuss the current topic to the broader goal (provide a transition)
- address why the material is relevant *to students*, not just to the topic under discussion

*Understanding How Humans Learn*

## Maintaining and Directing Students' Attention

After you have gained students' attention, you must maintain it throughout the instruction. Some of the techniques that you can use to direct and maintain students' attention during training include

- relevant graphics and other media,
- emphasis techniques,
- callouts, arrows,
- highlighted areas,
- white space,
- bold text,
- use of color,
- verbal emphasis,
- layout and design,
- appropriate pacing and breaks,
- frequent two-way or multiway interaction, and
- a *variety* of engaging learning activities, such as
  - questions,
  - examples,
  - exercises,
  - stories,
  - case studies,
  - problem scenarios, and
  - games.

## Learning Event #2: Sensory Perception

Before learning can occur, students' senses must detect and register the physical stimulus presented in training. The physical stimuli are the instructional presentations and activities that are presented to students. It includes, for example, the content displayed on a web page or overhead projector, the audio narration that accompanies an online slide show, and the instructor's voice in a live, instructor-led training session.

Usually, you want students to focus their attention on a select portion of the overall instructional stimulus at any given moment. For example, you might want to direct students' attention to a particular part in a complex parts diagram or to a certain button or field in a computer user interface.

When physical stimuli triggers our senses, the resultant stimulation in our sense organs lasts only a few milliseconds before it fades and can no longer be detected, unless the stimuli is constantly refreshed. Therefore, if students do not direct their attention to the stimuli during that time, it will not be further processed.

Instructors, for example, who present a series of complex slides for only a few seconds each cannot expect students to process much of the information on those slides. Humans can only focus on a part of the overall stimulus at a time for further mental processing.

## If the Stimulus is Unclear, Learning Will Be Uncertain

In designing your training materials and presentations, make sure that the instructional stimuli can be easily and clearly perceived. Some examples of unclear instructional stimuli include

- audio narration that is full of noise, plays haltingly, or has a heavy foreign accent,
- cluttered or busy visuals that overwhelm the senses or that do not distinguish key information,
- projected slides that cannot be seen from the back row, and
- text on a computer screen that is too small to be easily read by middle-aged or older students.

## How Can You Facilitate Sensory Perception?

Researchers have identified several principles that influence sensory perception. These include

- grouping (visually breaking scattered stimuli into groups with white space separating the groups; usually similar items are grouped together),
- chunking (breaking information or a stimulus into smaller "chunks"; for example, breaking the format of telephone numbers, xxxxxxxxxxx, into four chunks: x-xxx-xxx-xxxx, to facilitate perception, cognitive processing, and memory),
- closure (for example, the brain's tendency to "close" slightly open circles or lines that are imperfectly drawn or not quite connected),
- Gestalt (holistic perception; seeing and processing a meaningful whole all at once rather than processing each of the components individually; "the whole is greater than the sum of the parts"),
- color usage,
- typography,
- position of the stimulus,
- foreground, and background
- continuity (a tendency to see patterns in things and to perceive things as belonging together if they form some type of continuous pattern),
- perceptual horizon (perceived junction of earth and sky),
- organization,
- contours (how the borders of objects or lines interact with each other and affect perception), and
- familiarity.

Applying these principles when you design your training materials will greatly affect how easily students will perceive your instructional stimuli.

An excellent book on the principles of perception that are relevant to instructional presentations is *Instructional Message Design: Principles from the Behavioral Sciences,* by Malcolm Fleming and W. Howard Levie, Educational Technology Publications, New Jersey, 1978, ISBN 0-87778-104-4.

Although this book is out of print, the principles it teaches are clearly espoused and are still just as powerful today as they were before. Used copies should still be available at online booksellers or at your local library.

## What about Multichannel, Multisensory Stimuli?

Multichannel, multisensory stimuli refers to learning stimuli that are presented simultaneously through dual sensory channels, such as through both aural and visual means at the same time.

Intuitively, it might seem that adding additional sensory channels to the stimuli would automatically increase the likelihood that learning will occur. This has been proven wrong. To have a combined effect, the two sensory stimuli must *complement* each other and avoid dividing or competing for students' attention.

For example, if a presenter narrates a set of slides with narration that is not closely tied to the content of each slide, students will struggle to listen to the presenter at the same time they are reading unrelated text. Audio and graphics should support or enhance the instructional content that is being presented, not divide attention or draw attention away to unrelated material or thoughts.

## Learning Event #3: Higher-Level Cognition

Higher-level cognitive processes deal with how humans

- interpret, process, and understand new information,
- direct their own thinking processes,
- encode information into long-term memory, and
- retrieve information from memory.

The great majority of research-based instructional design principles and techniques have to do with designing and presenting information and instructional activities in ways that facilitate the cognitive processing of that information. For example, instructional design principles specify that different types of information—concepts, facts, processes, procedures, principles, and so forth—require different instructional strategies to facilitate and maximize learning. Teaching a concept, for example, is different from teaching a procedure.

Examples of ways in which you can influence cognitive processing

- refresh prerequisite information just before presenting new information
- go from the familiar to the unknown
- provide advanced frameworks and organizers
- provide periodic reviews or rehearsals of the information

The rest of this book will explain these and other principles and techniques that facilitate higher-level cognition.

## Learning Event #4: Memory Storage and Retrieval

Learning must endure to be used back on the job. But memory is one of learning's greatest bottlenecks.

What can you do to manage this bottleneck?

- Help students manage memory processing by employing organizing techniques such as grouping or providing a meaningful structure.
- Apply well-known memory encoding techniques, such as "Roy G. Biv" to remember the order of the colors of the rainbow.
- Avoid storing noncritical information in memory in the first place.

## Short-Term and Long-Term Memory

It is no coincidence that telephone numbers in the United States were originally created with seven digits. Furthermore, these seven digits were grouped into two strings and separated by a dash. Unfortunately, in some larger cities where more than one area code is used, callers must also dial the area code as part of the number, even to make a local call. Having to remember ten digits pushes the limits of *short-term memory*. Fortunately, callers only have to remember two or three unique area codes for a major city, so that over time, they become embedded and available in *long-term memory*. Callers thus have to memorize only the first digit of the area code for each unique telephone number, if the area codes have different first digits.

What are the characteristics of short-term and long-term memory?

### Short-term memory

- That which is briefly held in conscious thought.
- Has a capacity of seven plus-or-minus two chunks for most people.
- New ideas are linked or associated here with known information from long-term memory to create expanded learning and enriched knowledge networks in the brain.

### Long-term memory

- permanent memory storage
- has an unlimited capacity, but retrieving information from it is a problem if the information is not periodically refreshed or retrieved

## Principles of Memory Facilitation

The principles of memory facilitation have been thoroughly researched and are well known:

- **spaced review:** rehearse critical information repeatedly over time
- **meaning:** make information meaningful
- **organization:** organize and structure information in meaningful ways
- **chunking:** break masses of information into smaller, meaningful chunks
- **concreteness:** choose the concrete over the abstract
- **visualization:** create vivid visualizations of the information
- **attention:** make sure attention is obtained and maintained
- **interference:** recode information to reduce interference from similar information
- **association and elaboration:** relate the unknown to the familiar
- **sequence:** place important information first or last in a sequence

## Activity: Experience for Yourself the Application of a Memory Principle

1. Set a timer for one minute. Start the timer, look at figure 3, and try to remember everything you see.

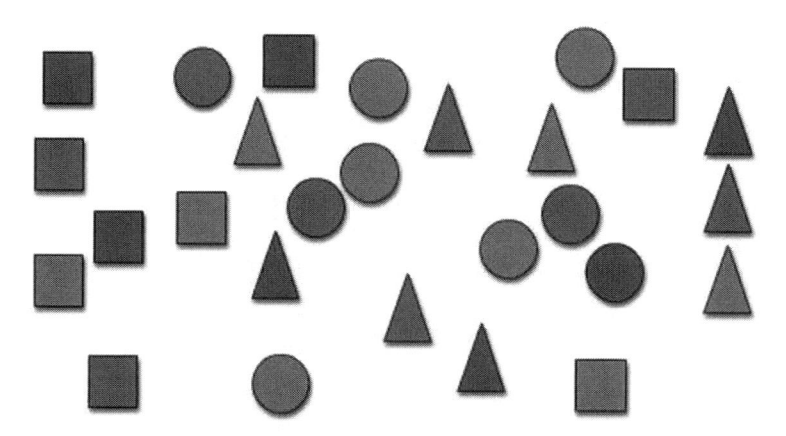

**Figure 3. Memory activity, part A**

2. When the timer rings, close the window and try to re-create exactly what you saw on a piece of paper.//
3. Set the timer again for one minute. Start the timer, look at figure 4, and try to remember everything you see.

**Figure 4. Memory activity, part B**

4. When the timer rings, close the window and try to re-create exactly what you saw on a piece of paper.

Why could you remember the second presentation easier, even though it contains the same identical objects?

In the second presentation, the following memory principles were applied:

- organization (grouping like shapes and colors together, repeated color scheme across rows)
- chunking (grouped objects into three groups)
- meaning (the square shapes containing the objects is itself more meaningful)
- concreteness (a square is easier to remember)
- sequence (put all the colors in same sequence)
- attention (use of white space to group and call attention to three groupings)

## Retrieval of Information from Long-Term Memory

There are two types of information retrieval from long-term memory.

### Recognition memory

**Definition:** Recognizing something you have previously seen or heard when you are presented with the same stimulus later

**Examples**

- recognizing that you have previously seen a picture of a person's face when viewing the same picture among several pictures of unfamiliar faces at a later time
- picking out a suspect from a police lineup
- identifying the five requirements of human learning in a jumbled list of ten items

### Recall memory

**Definition:** Retrieving information from long-term memory without the original stimulus as a cue

**Examples**

- describing the events of an automobile accident at a later time to an insurance agent over the telephone
- remembering the five requirements of human learning with no lists, pictures, or other cues

Which type of memory retrieval is more difficult? Retrieving information using recall memory is more difficult than retrieving information using recognition memory. Also, it is more difficult to train students to store information in memory for later *recall* than to store information that can later be *recognized* when it is presented again.

## Activity: Try Your Hand at Recall and Recognition Memory

**Note:** If you are unfamiliar with the US penny, substitute a familiar coin from your own country's currency.

1. Without looking at a penny, draw what is on the back of that coin. This test requires recall memory.

**Figure 5. Front side of a US penny.**

2. Look at the following four drawings of the back of a penny. Which one is correct? This test requires recognition memory.

**Figure 6. Back side A**

*Understanding How Humans Learn*

**Figure 7. Back side B**

**Figure 8. Back side C**

**Figure 9. Back side D**

The answer is A. You probably found it easier to recognize the back of a penny from the lineup of possible choices than to draw it completely from memory. That is because recognition memory retrieval is easier than recall memory retrieval.

What implications does this activity have for training?

It is more costly and takes more effort to train students to recall information than to train students to recognize previously learned information. Therefore, do not train students to the level of recall memory unless it is absolutely necessary. If recognition memory is fine, then train to that. For example, train students to use a job aid in performing a task so that later they can use that same job aid as a recognition memory device to facilitate retrieval of the information that was learned. Imagine what it would take to train someone to remember a long and complicated procedure from recall memory alone.

## Guidelines for Training to Recognition Versus Recall Memory

Based on this understanding of how memory retrieval works, remember these points when designing your training:

- Training to recall memory is significantly more costly, difficult, and time-consuming to develop, deliver, and take.
- Training someone to perform job tasks using external aids and prompts (such as printed or online job aids) is much faster, easier, and less costly to develop and deliver.
- Because of the above, train to recall only when absolutely necessary!
- Let the job requirements determine the type of recall that you must design into your training.

Here are some job situations for which recall and recognition memory are appropriate:

**Recall memory**

- A heart surgeon is expected to perform surgery from knowledge recalled directly from long-term memory—without the assistance of a step-by-step procedures guide propped open on the patient's chest.
- A person giving a sales presentation or a bank teller interacting with a customer is typically expected to perform customer-facing tasks directly from recall memory, without the help of job aids.

**Recognition memory**

- A back-office administrator entering supply-chain information into an ERP system on a computer terminal could make use of a job aid to perform this task.
- A technician replacing a part on a complex machine might use a repair manual.
- An airplane pilot is required to use take-off and landing checklists because the consequences of forgetting to perform a step or doing one incompletely could be catastrophic.

---

An excellent and very easy to understand book on memory is *Your Memory: How It Works and How to Improve It,* by Kenneth L. Higbee, PhD, 2nd edition, Marlow and Company, New York, 2001, ISBN 1-56924-629-7.

This book not only discusses how human memory works, it also explains mnemonic devices and study-skill techniques that can greatly improve your recall of information.

# Learning Event #5: Practice with Feedback

"Practice with feedback" is asking students to perform the skills that were taught and prescribed by the training objectives and afterwards providing students individual feedback on their performance. The two most common categories of skills that are taught and practiced are motor skills and intellectual skills.

## Motor skills

**Definition:** Skills that involve the use of the body (typically the hands, eyes, and feet) in performing a task. These tasks typically involve some level of hand-eye coordination.

**Examples:** Playing the piano, riding a bicycle, installing a CPU module in a mainframe, and operating a bulldozer are examples of motor skills.

## Intellectual skills

**Definition:** Skills that are mental tasks such as repeating verbatim information, analyzing information and drawing conclusions, recalling a series of steps, and recognizing an instance of a concept.

**Examples:** Discriminating between good and bad loan applications, identifying an instance of an oak tree in a forest, translating from one language to another, and repeating the steps in the company's sales process are examples of intellectual skills.

# Why Is Practice with Feedback a Learning Requirement?

We'll answer this by asking another question: How long will new neurological interconnections in the brain last if they are not directly strengthened, reinforced, and enriched with links to other neurons?

Answer: Not very long. In the last chapter in this book, you learned about the extinction curve. Unless information is rehearsed, refreshed, reviewed, or used in practice, it will fade rapidly over the next few hours and days.

Practice with feedback not only strengthens and reinforces memory, it enriches and refines learning. For example, the saying "You don't know what you don't know until you try to teach it or apply it" is true. Practice also builds self-confidence in students so that they can successfully perform the task. Increasing students' confidence in performing job-related tasks is an important goal of training. For all of these reasons, learning is not complete until it has been firmly entrenched in students' memories and until they can confidently apply the skills they are learning to actual job tasks.

## What Is the *Feedback* Part of Practice with Feedback?

Feedback is information individually given to students after practice on their performance. It is intended to help students refine and improve their performance. It should never demean, belittle, or attack the student and should be provided in an "emotionally safe" environment in which students are not punished for making mistakes. Feedback is different from an end-of-course test or assessment, which is used largely to evaluate whether the student has "passed" the course or not.

Three types of feedback should be given on a student's performance:

- **Adequacy:** Was my performance adequate? Did I get it right?
- **Diagnostic:** What was wrong with my performance?
- **Corrective:** How can I improve my performance?

## Common Questions about Practice with Feedback

The following questions are typically asked about practice with feedback.

### Can practice ever make things worse?

Absolutely. Practice without feedback can actually strengthen the incorrect or unacceptable aspects of the performance because they are practiced over and over again, making them more firmly entrenched in students' minds. For example, piano students practicing a musical score repeatedly over time without ever getting feedback from a teacher will entrench wrong techniques (such as fingering or intonation); those students will find it even harder to correct their performance when feedback is finally provided than if feedback had been provided early on.

### Does feedback always have to be given by a live instructor?

No. Online instruction can give feedback to specific questions posed in the form of an answer button or key. Sometimes feedback is built into the device that students are using to perform the task, such as when focusing a microscope on an object. However, some tasks such as gymnastics lend themselves better to expert human observation, judgment, and feedback.

### When should practice with feedback be given?

Practice with feedback should be given soon after the initial content is taught and before too much other information is taught. For example, as a rule of thumb, in web-based training, practice (exercises, simulations, or checkpoint questions) should be provided after every three to six screens. Additional practice sessions should be provided over time as needed to reinforce memory.

**Should practice with feedback match the
type and level of skill being taught?**

Absolutely. Students should practice the very skills and knowledge they were taught and at the level it was taught. Sometimes instructors or training designers think that they are "stretching" students' minds or knowledge by asking them to perform tasks or intellectual skills that they have not been taught or that are at a higher level of difficulty than what was taught in the instruction. This leads to frustration, confusion, and wasted time on the part of students who are trying to figure out how to perform the practice tasks. Practice is not the place to teach new material, so practice should not ask students to perform tasks (intellectual or otherwise) that were not previously taught. If the instructor's goal is to "stretch" students' minds—to teach students how to reason, perform research, or creatively problem solve on their own—then the instruction should teach students these skills and the practice should match the level of problem-solving or reasoning skills that were taught.

**Should subskills be practiced in isolation before
practicing higher-level skills and scenarios?**

Yes. Complex or difficult tasks should be broken down into component subtasks. These subtasks should be taught and practiced independently before they are integrated with larger, more comprehensive or difficult tasks. For example, algebra and trigonometry should be taught and practiced before learning calculus, how to use a laser level should be taught before learning how to lay out a house foundation, how to brake a car and set the rearview mirrors should be taught before learning how to steer the car and avoid road hazards.

# Chapter Summary— A Simple Cognitive Model of Learning

This chapter presented a simple model of learning and explains the cognitive requirements for learning. It described where bottlenecks in learning processes can occur and what can be done to address those bottlenecks.

You should now be able to

- list and describe the five steps in the simple model of learning;
- describe where learning bottlenecks typically occur in this model and why they occur;
- list and describe the principles of attention;
- describe techniques for getting, maintaining, and directing attention in training;
- explain the limitations of sensory detection and give examples of unclear stimuli;
- list the principles for facilitating sensory processing;
- define multichannel, multisensory stimuli, and describe when it can enhance learning;
- define higher-level cognitive processing and give examples of how it can be facilitated;
- describe the memory bottleneck in learning and general strategies for managing it;
- define and describe short-term and long-term memory;
- list the principles for facilitating memory;
- define and describe the two types of memory retrieval;
- describe when training should be designed for recognition memory versus recall memory;
- define practice with feedback and explain why it is important to learning;
- define and explain the three types of practice feedback; and
- explain when practice can actually make things worse.

## Check Your Understanding

1. **Which of the following is the correct sequence of learning events in the simple model of learning?**

    A.  Sensory perception, gain attention, higher-level cognition, memory storage and retrieval, practice with feedback

    B.  Sensory perception, gain attention, higher-level cognition, practice with feedback, memory storage and retrieval

    C.  Gain attention, sensory perception, higher-level cognition, practice with feedback, memory storage and retrieval

    D.  Gain attention, sensory perception, higher-level cognition, memory storage and retrieval, practice with feedback

2. **Match each learning event in the simple model of learning with its correct definition.**

| | |
|---|---|
| Sensory perception | A. Processing the learning stimulus in our brain, during which we make sense of it, relating it to what we already know, associating it with other information, and forming new understandings (new neural interconnections) |
| Gain attention | B. Activities that provide learners the opportunity to practice or apply the knowledge and skills that they have learned |
| Memory storage and retrieval | C. Storing this information for later retrieval (reinforcing the new neural interconnections) |
| Higher-level cognition | D. Perceiving the learning stimulus with our physical senses, such as eyes or ears |
| Practice with feedback | E. Focusing one's attention on the learning stimulus, such as a slide, text, or computer screen |

3. **True or false? Attention can be divided among two and sometimes three stimuli.**

4. **Which of the following are principles for gaining attention? (Select all that apply.)**
   A. Novelty
   B. Constant stimulus
   C. Unusual or startling sounds or voices
   D. Color
   E. Animation
   F. Monotone narrative voice
   G. Multisensory stimulation
   H. Sense of danger or excitement
   I. Availability of instructional objectives
   J. Change in the stimulus
   K. Potential for satisfaction of biological needs and drives (such as food or sex)
   L. Motion

5. **True or false? One important way to gain students' attention when beginning a new course is to provide motivational lead-ins, such as "What's in it for me?" and "Why should I care?"**

6. **Which of the following are appropriate methods for maintaining and directing students' attention during training? (Select all that apply.)**
   A. Provide relevant graphics and other media
   B. Employ emphasis techniques, such as callouts, arrows, highlighted areas, white space, bold text, use of color, verbal emphasis, and layout and design
   C. Provide appropriate pacing and breaks

D. Threaten students with pop quizzes and final course exams

E. Provide frequent two-way or multiway interaction

F. Provide a variety of engaging learning activities, such as questions, examples, exercises, stories, case studies, problem scenarios, and games

G. Teach interesting but unrelated content

7. **True or false? Stimuli falling on the sense organs only lasts for a few milliseconds before it fades and can no longer be detected unless that stimuli is constantly refreshed.**

8. **True or false? It is possible to facilitate perception through techniques such as grouping, chunking, closure, Gestalt, color usage, typography, position of the stimulus, foreground and background, continuity, perceptual horizon, organization, contours, and familiarity.**

9. **True or false? Adding additional sensory channels to the stimuli automatically increases the likelihood that learning will occur.**

10. **Higher-level cognitive processes are processes that deal with how humans: (Select all that apply.)**

    A. Perceive stimuli with our sense organs

    B. Interpret, process, and understand new information

    C. Direct their own thinking processes

    D. Encode information into long-term memory

    E. Require practice to reinforce what they have learned

    F. Retrieve information from memory

11. **Match each memory principle with its correct explanation.**

| Spaced review | A. Create vivid visualizations of the information. |
|---|---|
| Meaning | B. Recode information to reduce interference from similar information. |
| Organization | C. Relate the unknown to the familiar. |
| Chunking | D. Choose the concrete over the abstract. |
| Concreteness | E. Break masses of information into smaller, meaningful chunks. |
| Visualization | F. Rehearse or review critical information repeatedly over time. |
| Attention | G. Place important information first or last in a sequence. |
| Interference | H. Make information meaningful. |
| Association and elaboration | I. Organize and structure information in meaningful ways. |
| Sequence | J. Make sure attention is obtained and maintained. |

12. **True or false? Short-term memory has a capacity of seven plus-or-minus two chunks of information and is where new ideas are linked or associated with previously learned information retrieved from long-term memory.**

13. **True or false? Recall memory is recognizing something you have previously seen or heard when you are presented with the same stimulus later.**

14. **True or false? It is easier and cheaper to develop and deliver training to the level of recognition memory than recall memory.**

15. **Which of the following statements are the *key* reasons why practice with feedback is important to learning and is an event in our simple model of learning? (Select all that apply.)**
    A. It strengthens and reinforces memory.
    B. It is an important way to assess whether students should pass or fail a course.
    C. It helps students identify "holes" in their learning (aspects of the topic or procedure that they misunderstand, haven't learned, or have learned incorrectly).
    D. It increases students' self-confidence in performing the task.
    E. It makes learning more enjoyable to take.

16. **What are the three types of practice feedback?**
    A. Satisfactory, analytical, corrective
    B. Analytical, positive, negative
    C. Analytical, conceptual, directive
    D. Adequacy, directive, corrective
    E. Adequacy, diagnostic, corrective

17. **Practice without _____ can actually make things worse for learning.**

## Answers:

1. D
2. D, E, C, A, and B
3. False. Attention is limited to one thing at a time, although we can switch attention back and forth somewhat rapidly between two or more stimuli within certain limitations.
4. A, C, D, E, G, H, J, K, and L
5. True

6. A, B, C, E, and F
7. True
8. True
9. False. To have a combined effect, the two sensory stimuli must complement each other and avoid dividing or competing for students' attention.
10. B, C, D, and F
11. F, H, I, E, D, A, J, B, C, and G
12. True
13. False. This is actually the definition of recognition memory. Recall memory is retrieving information from long-term memory without the original stimulus as a cue.
14. True. Training to recall memory is significantly more costly, difficult, and time-consuming to develop, deliver, and take. Because of this, train to recall memory only when absolutely necessary!
15. A, C, and D. Although practice with feedback usually makes learning more enjoyable to take, it is not a key instructional justification for including practice with feedback in our learning model. Many things can make learning more enjoyable to take, but nothing can substitute for practice with feedback. Also, practice with feedback should provide an emotionally safe environment for students to practice. It should not be used as an evaluation tool to determine pass/fail status of students.
16. E
17. The correct answer is "feedback." Practice without feedback can actually strengthen the incorrect or unacceptable aspects of the performance because they are practiced over and over again, making them more firmly entrenched in students' minds.

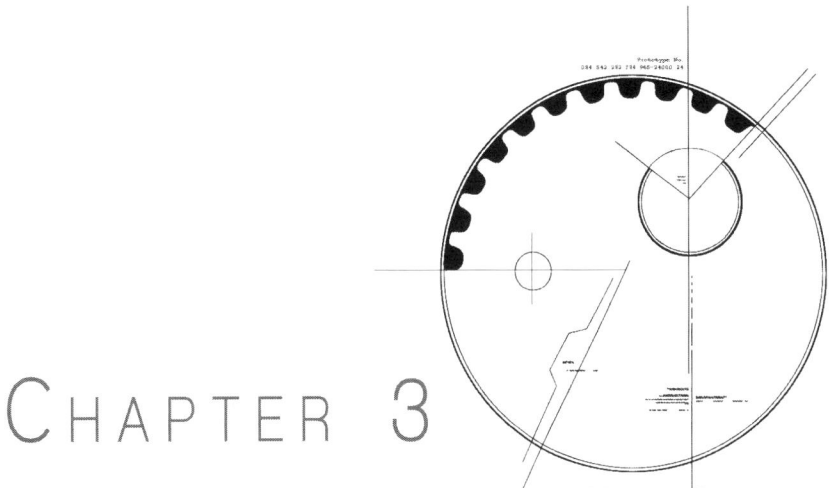

# CHAPTER 3
# Learning Taxonomies and Their Application

This chapter presents ways to classify learning outcomes and content using four different *learning taxonomies* and describes why these classifications are useful.

## What Are Learning Taxonomies and Why Are They Important?

A learning taxonomy is a way to classify learning content or learning outcomes. For example, is the content to be taught on a computer screen or projected slide a concept, procedure, fact, principle, or something else? Is the learning outcome an attitude, a cognitive strategy, or a motor skill? In short, a learning taxonomy describes the types of learning that can be achieved.

Taxonomies, which are nothing more than classification schemes, are useful in many professions. Chemists classify elements on the periodic table. Geologists classify rocks and minerals. Botanists classify plants into detailed hierarchies. If an element, rock, or plant fits into a specific category in the taxonomy, it tells you something useful about its characteristics and qualities.

## Why Learning Taxonomies Are Important

During instructional analysis and design

- the type of learning will determine what *analysis techniques* you should use, and
- the type of learning will help determine what *learning strategies* to employ.

During instructional development

- learning analysis is continued to a more detailed level; the type of learning will help determine what information *presentation strategy* to use.

Researchers in learning have devised several different learning taxonomies. Each has its own application where it is most useful. We will look at four of these taxonomies.

## The Skills, Knowledge, and Attitude (SKA) Taxonomy

This is the simplest of the four taxonomies. It classifies all learning outcomes into three categories.

### Skill

**Definition:** Skills involve the performance of a task that produces an end result.

**Examples**

- Answer customer objections using the ABC methodology.
- Use the ABC ERP software application to send out requests for bids for new orders.

- Analyze a use case to identify potential programming objects.
- Determine the best approach for approaching executives in an enterprise to sell them e-business on demand.

## Knowledge

**Definition:** Knowledge is the understanding, retention, and recall of information (concepts, facts, and so forth).

## Examples

- List all fifty states in the United States.
- Define logical partitions.
- Show the UML representations for objects, messages, classes, and inheritance.
- Identify the parts of a bicycle.
- Describe how data is transferred and transformed from the point of entry to storage in the legacy database system.

## Attitude

**Definition:** Attitudes are a person's feelings toward other people, groups, or things and their effect on that person's behavior.

## Examples

- Voluntarily conform to accessibility guidelines.
- Value the opinions of others on the team.
- Complete all quality checkpoints without error.
- Speak out against sexual harassment when witnessing it in others.
- Submit a suggestion into the suggestion box twice a year.

## Relationship of Skills, Knowledge, and Attitudes to Each Other

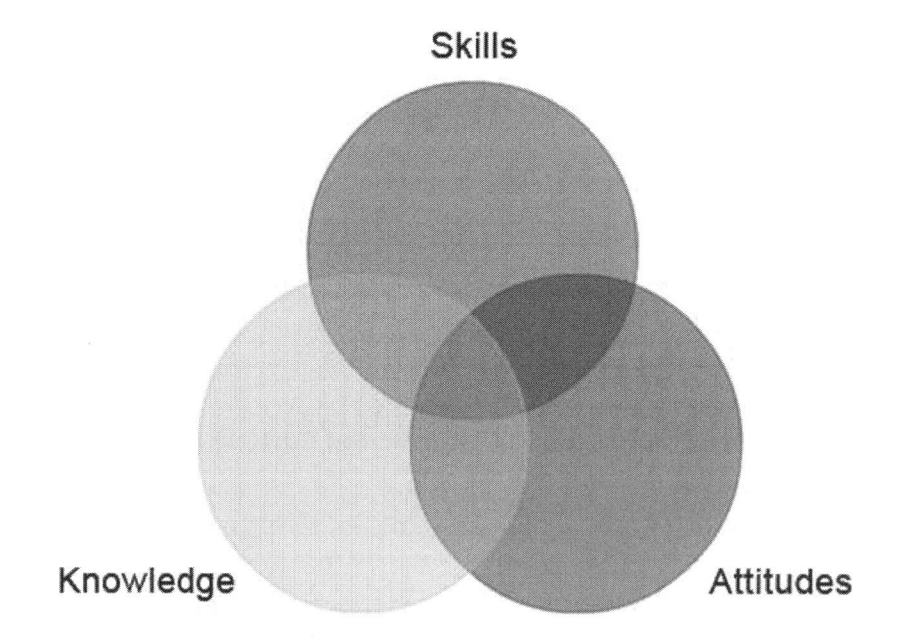

**Figure 10. Relationship of skills, knowledge, and attitude**

Most training involves learning outcomes from two or three categories in the taxonomy.

### Example #1

To perform the *skill* of completing your tax return, for example, you must not only know how to compute your taxes, but you must understand certain *knowledge*, such as tax deductions, capital gains tax, standard deductions, and tax brackets. You must also *value* getting your taxes completed by the due date, which reflects your attitude toward doing your taxes.

### Example #2

In teaching students how to perform a task using a computer application, you must (1) teach them certain *skills*, such as the procedure for installing and configuring the software; (2) teach them certain *knowledge* that they must know to perform the procedure, such as the concepts, facts, and principles to perform the skill intelligently; and (3) teach them to value (have an *attitude* of) a professional result to the extent that they are willing to perform the procedure carefully and correctly.

## The Value of the Skills, Knowledge, and Attitude Taxonomy

The SKA taxonomy is most useful during instructional *analysis* when you are analyzing major learning outcomes and breaking them into their components. Teaching a complex skill, for example, cannot be done all at once. You must first analyze the skill to determine the subskills, concepts, facts, and other knowledge that is necessary to perform the skill. These component skills, knowledge, and attitudes must be taught before you can put them all together and teach the higher-level, more complex steps necessary for successful completion.

Knowing that a learning outcome is a skill, knowledge, or attitude prescribes what type of analysis you must perform to break the outcome into its smaller learning components.

*Skills* are analyzed by breaking them down into their component tasks, subtasks, and steps in a hierarchical fashion and are taught as procedures. This analysis procedure is called a *job* or *task analysis.*

*Knowledge* is analyzed by breaking it down into its component knowledge and is taught using presentation strategies appropriate to the specific type of knowledge (such as concepts, facts, principles). This analysis procedure is called a *content analysis*.

*Attitudes* are analyzed by clearly defining the attitude and identifying its indicator behaviors. This analysis is called an *indicator behavior analysis*.

# Robert Gagne's *Learned Capabilities* Taxonomy

This taxonomy was developed by one of the grandfathers of instructional design, Robert Gagne. It divides learning outcomes (called *learned capabilities* by Gagne) into five distinct categories: intellectual skills, cognitive strategies, verbal information, motor skills, and attitudes. The category of intellectual skills is further subdivided into a hierarchy of skills with discrimination skills at the bottom and higher-order rules at the top.

- **Intellectual skills (hierarchical)**
    - Higher-order rule
    - Rule
    - Defined concept
    - Concrete concept
    - Discrimination
- **Cognitive strategy**
- **Verbal information**
- **Motor skill**
- **Attitude**

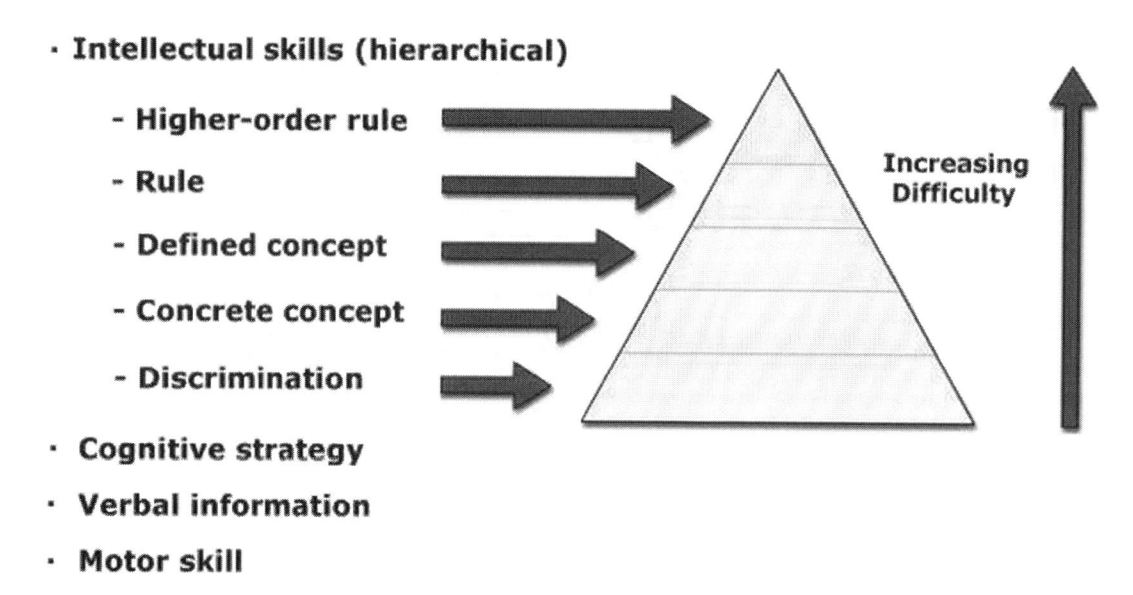

Figure 11. Robert Gagne's learned capabilities taxonomy

## Intellectual skills

As defined by Gagne, these are the capabilities that make symbol use possible. Symbols include such things as the words we use in language, math symbols, or any other symbols. The overall category of intellectual skills is further broken into five subcategories that are hierarchically related: discriminations (at the bottom of the hierarchy), concrete concepts, defined concepts, rules, and higher-order rules (at the top of the hierarchy).

## Higher-order rule

According to Gagne, rules that are combined with other rules into more complex rules.

> Examples of higher-order rules
> - "Algebraic expressions and equations should be written in their simplest (simplified) form."
> - "All sales interactions with clients should progress the engagement forward."
> - "Tax returns must comply with all federal tax codes."

## Rule

A relation between two or more things.

> Examples of rules
> - "Moist air produces rust on iron."
> - "Operating systems cannot cross logical partitions on this system."

## Defined concept

An abstract concept that involves a rule that classifies objects or events.

> Examples of defined concepts
> - mass
> - temperature
> - cousin
> - logical partition
> - sales pipeline

## Concrete concepts

Concepts of physical objects that can be denoted by being pointed out.

Examples of concrete concepts
- chair
- car
- house

## Discriminations

As defined by Gagne: "Telling the difference between variations in some particular object-property."

Example of discriminations
- distinguishing a curved line from a straight line
- telling a defective part from an acceptable part on a moving assembly line
- telling an angry customer's voice on the telephone from a nonangry voice

## Cognitive strategy

According to Gagne, the definition of cognitive strategy is "skills by means of which learners regulate their own internal process of attending, learning, remembering, and thinking."

Examples of cognitive strategies
- strategies that a person uses for problem solving
- methods a person uses for memorizing information
- study strategies used by students

**Verbal information**

Information that is largely verbally described or verbally stated (according to Gagne, you can "tell it" or "state it.")

Examples of verbal information

- describe the causes of the Civil War
- describe situations that are candidates for selling the ABC product
- state how managers should handle a subordinate who is consistently late for work

**Motor skill**

Skills that are performed using certain prescribed movements that are smooth, regular, and precisely timed.

Examples of motor skills

- playing the piano
- replacing a CPU module in a mainframe computer
- riding a bicycle
- driving a car
- molding wood freehand on a lathe

**Attitude**

An internal state that influences the choices of personal action made by the individual.

Examples of attitudes

- choosing educational television programs to watch in your free time instead of sitcoms and reality shows
- choosing healthy foods over fatty and unhealthy foods at the grocery store and in restaurants
- choosing to spend more quality time with your children over playing more video games in your off-work hours

## The Value of Gagne's Taxonomy

Each type of learned capability in Gagne's hierarchy has accompanying instructional strategies for teaching that learned capability. Teaching motor skills, for example, involves a different instructional approach than teaching verbal information or defined concepts.

In addition to specific prescriptions for instruction that are based on the learned capability, the subcategories of intellectual skills—discriminations, concrete concepts, defined concepts, rules, and higher-order rules—form a hierarchy that have the following implications:

- The higher up the learning outcome is in the hierarchy, the more difficult, costly, and time consuming it will be to teach and learn.
- Higher-level intellectual skills must be broken into their component pieces for instruction.

---

The following books are excellent resources for learning more about Gagne's taxonomy:

- *The Conditions of Learning*, 3rd edition, Robert M. Gagne, Holt, Rinehart, and Winston, New York, 1975, ISBN 0-03-089965-6 (this classic is out of print but is available used from online booksellers).
- *The Conditions of Learning: Training Applications,* Karen L. Medsker and Robert M. Gagne, Wadsworth Publishing, 1995, ISBN 0-15-502106-0.

# Benjamin Bloom's Learning Taxonomy, Cognitive Domain

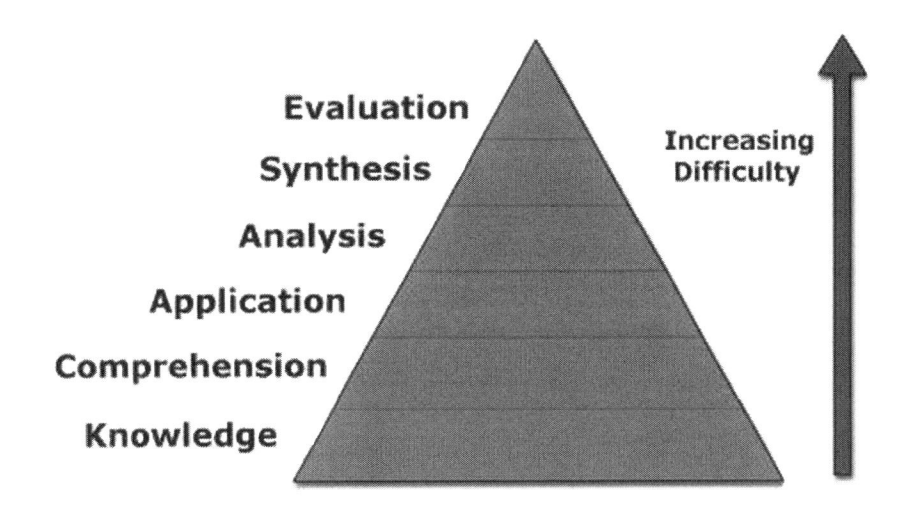

**Figure 12. Benjamin Bloom's learning taxonomy, cognitive domain**

This taxonomy was developed by another educational giant, Benjamin Bloom. We will discuss the cognitive domain part of his overall educational taxonomy, which deals with learning and applying information. This taxonomy, like Gagne's intellectual skills subcategories, is hierarchical. Learning begins at the bottom of the hierarchy with knowledge and continues upward with comprehension, application, analysis, synthesis, and finally evaluation at the top of the hierarchy. As with Gagne's intellectual skills hierarchy, learning outcomes that are higher up in the hierarchy are more difficult, costly, and time consuming to teach and learn.

Here are the entries in this part of his learning taxonomy:

## Knowledge

Verbs that indicate a knowledge-level learning outcome
- defines
- describes
- names

- identifies
- labels
- matches
- recalls
- reproduces

**Comprehension**

Verbs that indicate a comprehension-level learning outcome

- classifies
- restates
- discusses
- explains
- generalizes
- gives examples

**Application**

Verbs that indicate an application-level learning outcome

- applies
- assesses
- charts
- computes
- extends
- instructs
- implements
- solves

**Analysis**

Verbs that indicate an analysis-level learning outcome

- appraises
- diagrams
- compares
- contrasts

- questions
- tests
- discriminates

**Synthesis**

Verbs that indicate a synthesis-level learning outcome
- adapts
- collaborates
- combines
- creates
- designs
- manages
- plans
- models
- revises

**Evaluation**

Verbs that indicate an evaluation-level learning outcome
- appraises
- argues
- judges
- predicts
- rates
- critiques
- interprets
- reframes
- assesses

# Robert Horn's Taxonomy of Information Types

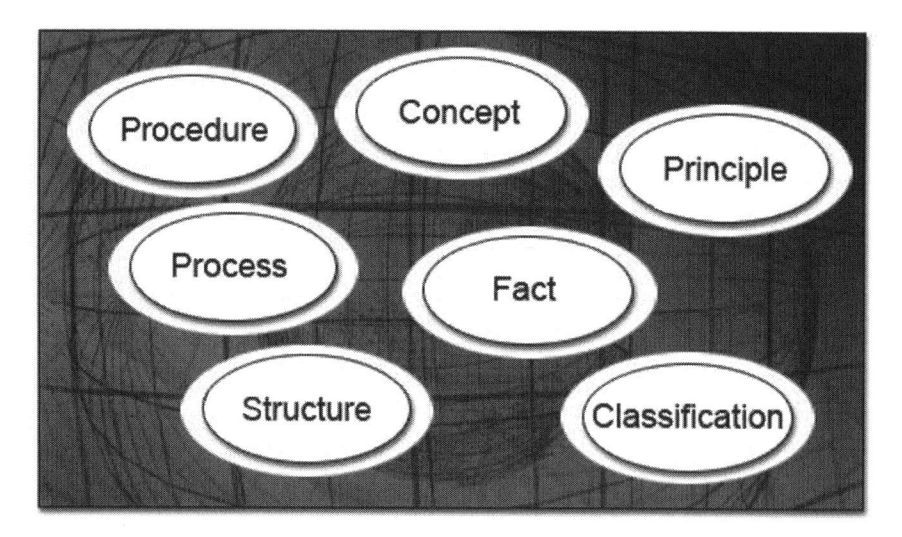

**Figure 13. Robert Horn's taxonomy of information types**

Another researcher and industry practitioner, Robert Horn, has developed a taxonomy for classifying information according to its type. Unlike Bloom's cognitive domain taxonomy and Gagne's intellectual skills taxonomy, this classification scheme is *not* hierarchical in nature. According to Horn, all information, when broken apart into its most elemental components, can be classified into one of seven *types.* Horn has carefully defined each information type and has created detailed prescriptions on how to design, teach, lay out, and present instruction for each type of information. His information types and associated prescriptions are valuable for instructional designers and trainers.

**Procedure**

**Definition:** A step-by-step method for achieving a specified outcome

**Characteristics of procedures**
- begins with a starting state and a set of inputs
- ends with the specified outcome
- tells the student how to do something
- written from the perspective of the student

### Examples of procedures
- how to change a flat tire on a car
- how to create a header in a document
- how to replace the toner in the XYZ copier

## Process

**Definition:** A description of how something functions or works or how things change over time

### Characteristics of processes
- typically composed of major phases, stages, or events
- describes how things evolve as they go from one state to the next
- does *not* tell you how to produce the result
- written for understanding, not to perform

### Examples of processes
- how glass is made
- how a bill becomes law
- how data is transmitted over the Internet
- how SSL encryption works
- what happens when **Enter** is pressed

## Concept

**Definition:** Categories, groups, or classes of objects or ideas that all share certain similar attributes and are given a common label, even though they differ in some way

### Characteristics of concepts
- has a label, a definition, and a description of the common (or critical) attributes
- must have more than one member in the *class* (the set that includes all instances for that concept)

**Examples of concepts**
- chair
- token ring network
- e-business on demand
- context-sensitive menus
- an object (in object-oriented programming)

## Principle

**Definition:** A principle either:
- tells a person what should or should not be done in various circumstances, or
- describes causal or logical relationships, such as what can be concluded in light of the evidence

**Characteristics of principles**
- typically describe policies, rules, heuristics, guidelines, relationships among classes of objects, warnings, requirements for certain conditions to be true, generalizations, and cause-and-effect relationships

**Examples of principles**
- Ohm's law.
- Client rapport improves sales.
- Increasing throughput requires more memory or CPU cycles.
- $E = mc^2$.
- When cooking, never add water to hot oil.

## Fact

**Definition:** Simple assertion or statement that is assumed to be true
- stands on its own
- does not represent classes of objects or ideas as do concepts
- can be product specifications, dates when events occurred, proper names, names of parts, symbols used to represent things, and so forth

### Examples of facts

- Temperature of the sun.
- Speed of a computer bus.
- New Year's Day is January 1.
- Maximum system memory.
- Water is made up of two hydrogen atoms and one oxygen atom.
- Press F9 to invoke spell check.

### Structure

**Definition:** An object, physical or logical, that can be divided into component parts

- typically involves things that you can draw, diagram, represent, or photograph
- tells the student what something looks like and what its parts are

### Examples of structures

- an organization chart
- an exploded view of a bicycle
- the grammatical structure of a sentence
- the parts of the main user interface for XYZ software
- a syntax diagram for a command

### Classification

**Definition:** The assignment of specific items into two or more categories using some kind of sorting criteria

- typically include words such as "types of," "kinds of," "sorts of," and "aspects of"
- differ from facts because their purpose is to show how things are classified, not to state how things are

### Examples of classifications

- types of loans
- the five types of editing functions
- the periodic table

- categories of error codes
- classification of animal life

## How to Classify Information into Its Type

To classify information into its type:

1. Study the definitions and examples given previously of each information type.
2. Determine the *purpose* for presenting this information to students.

For example, if students need to understand:

- how customer orders are received and processed, use a process.
- how to receive and process customer orders, use a procedure.
- which department handles which kind of complaint, use a classification.
- the client's business organization chart, use a structure.
- what e-commerce is, use a concept.
- who must sign off on the sales order, use a fact—unless, that is, certain rules or policies must be followed to determine who must sign off on the order, in which case use a principle.

## Training Usually Requires that Multiple Types of Information Be Taught

Teaching one type of information often requires teaching other types as well. A procedure, for example, might contain some individual steps that require an understanding of certain concepts, principles, processes, classifications, structures, or facts.

If you have been charged with teaching managers how to evaluate an employee's performance, what other types of information might you have to teach as part of your training on this procedure?

The following are only a sample of the possibilities:

- corporate management policies (principles)
- the rating system (classification) along with descriptions of each rating (facts and concepts)
- how to enter the rating into your human resource department's computer application (procedure)

---

Here are some additional resources for learning about Robert Horn's Information Mapping methodology:

- Web site: http://www.infomap.com
- *Mapping Hypertext: The Analysis, Organization, and Display of Knowledge for the Next Generation of On-Line Text and Graphics,* Robert E. Horn, Information Mapping, 1990, ISBN 0-96-255650-5. This book has two pages that describe the various types of information.

# Chapter Summary—
# Learning Taxonomies and Their Application

This chapter presented ways to classify learning outcomes and content using four different *learning taxonomies* and described why these classifications are useful.

You should now be able to

- define learning taxonomies and explain why they are useful in instructional analysis, design, and presentation;
- define each of the categories in the SKA taxonomy and give examples of each;
- explain the interrelationship of skills, knowledge, and attitudes in the SKA taxonomy as it relates to real life training tasks;
- explain the analytical techniques that the SKA taxonomy prescribes to analyze information in each of its three categories;
- define each of the categories and subcategories in Gagne's taxonomy of learned capabilities and give examples of each;
- describe each of the subcategories in the intellectual skills hierarchy and explain why learning outcomes at higher levels in this hierarchy require more time, cost, and effort to teach and learn;
- describe each of the levels in Benjamin Bloom's learning taxonomy (cognitive domain) and give example verbs for each level that describe information that fits into that level;
- define each of the categories and subcategories in Robert Horn's taxonomy of information types and give examples of each;
- describe how to classify information into its type; and
- explain why training usually requires that multiple types of information be taught.

## Check Your Understanding

1. **True or false? Learning taxonomies are important because they help dictate what learning analyses techniques to employ during instructional analysis and what learning strategies and presentation techniques to use in the instruction.**

2. **Classify each of the following learning outcomes as a skill, knowledge, or attitude.**
    A. Describe the value of diversity in the workforce to a large enterprise.
    B. Describe how a bill becomes law.
    C. Use the SSM method of selling in engagements with clients.
    D. Avoid putting other people down who are different.
    E. Configure a large network for optimal performance using a given set of criteria.
    F. List and describe the five requirements for learning.
    G. Calculate the return on investment for a new computer system.
    H. Define return on investment and give two examples.
    I. Voluntarily contribute a white paper to the intellectual capital of the organization.
    J. Sketch the hardware layout of the 2105 Model 800.

3. **Match each SKA learning outcome with the instructional analysis and design strategies that it prescribes.**

| Skills | A. Clearly define it and identify its indicator behaviors. |
|---|---|
| Knowledge | B. Break them down into their component tasks, subtasks, and steps in a hierarchical fashion and teach them as procedures. |
| Attitudes | C. Break it down into its component knowledge and teach them using presentation strategies appropriate to the specific type of knowledge (such as concepts, facts, principles). |

*Understanding How Humans Learn*

4. **Match each learned capability from Gagne's taxonomy with its correct definition.**

| | |
|---|---|
| Cognitive Strategy | A. Information that is largely verbally described or verbally stated (according to Gagne, you can "tell it" or "state it"). |
| Defined Concept | B. The capabilities that make symbol use possible. |
| Higher-Order Rule | C. A relation between two or more things. |
| Discriminations | D. Concepts of physical objects that can be denoted by being pointed out. |
| Motor Skill | E. "Telling the difference between variations in some particular object-property." |
| Concrete Concepts | F. Skills that are performed using certain prescribed movements that are smooth, regular, and precisely timed. |
| Intellectual Skills | G. An abstract concept that involves a rule that classifies objects or events. |
| Rule | H. "Rules ... combined ... into more complex rules." |
| Verbal Information | I. "Skills by means of which learners regulate their own internal process of attending, learning, remembering, and thinking." |

5. **True or false? The higher up the learning outcome is in the Gagne's intellectual skills hierarchy, the more difficult, costly, and time consuming it will be to teach and learn.**

6. **Choose which one of the following pairs of learning outcomes is *higher* on the intellectual skills hierarchy.**

   Pair #1
   (A) Distinguishing between triangles and circles
   (B) Defining the concept of an isosceles triangle

   Pair #2
   (A) Defining the concept of table manners
   (B) Defining the concept of a fork

   Pair #3
   (A) Applying the rules of syntax for the *config* operating system command
   (B) Fine-tuning the performance of a server storage array

   Pair #4
   (A) Completing one's tax return
   (B) Determining which expenses can be deducted

7. **Match each cognitive domain level from Bloom's taxonomy with the list of verbs that describes the level.**

| | |
|---|---|
| Evaluation | A. Appraises, diagrams, compares, contrasts, questions, tests, discriminates |
| Synthesis | B. Applies, assesses, charts, computes, extends, instructs, implements, solves |
| Analysis | C. Appraises, argues, judges, predicts, rates, critiques, interprets, reframes, assesses |
| Application | D. Classifies, restates, discusses, explains, generalizes, gives examples |
| Comprehension | E. Defines, describes, names, identifies, labels, matches, recalls, reproduces |
| Knowledge | F. Adapts, collaborates, combines, creates, designs, manages, plans, models, revises |

8. **Match each type of information from Horn's taxonomy with its definition.**

| | |
|---|---|
| Procedure | A. A description of how something functions or works or how things change over time. |
| Process | B. Either tells a person what should or should not be done in various circumstances, or describes causal or logical relationships, such as what can be concluded in light of the evidence. |
| Concept | C. Simple assertion or statement that is assumed to be true. |
| Principle | D. An object, physical or logical, that can be divided into component parts. |
| Fact | E. A step-by-step method for achieving a specified outcome. |
| Structure | F. The assignment of specific items into two or more categories using some kind of sorting criteria. |
| Classification | G. Categories, groups, or classes of objects or ideas that all share certain similar attributes and are given a common label, even though they differ in some way. |

9. **In determining how to classify a piece of information into its type, what is the key thing you should consider?**
   A. How important the information is to the objectives
   B. Whether it can be further broken down into smaller components
   C. How complex the information is
   D. How the information relates to other information
   E. The purpose for presenting this information to students

10. **Classify the following information into its type:**

    A. What is a bank?

    B. How to spell check a document

    C. How data moves from the web server to the enterprise storage server

    D. The parts of a nuclear power plant core containment building

    E. The types of monarch butterflies

    F. The date that the World Wide Web was invented

    G. Travel expense guidelines

## Answers

1. True

2. A, knowledge; B, knowledge; C, skill; D, attitude; E, skill; F, knowledge; G, skill; H, knowledge; I, attitude; J, knowledge

3. B, C, and A.

4. I, G, H, E, F, D, B, C, and A

5. True

6. Pair #1, B (defining the concept of an isosceles triangle); Pair #2, A (defining the concept of table manners); Pair #3, B (fine-tuning the performance of a server storage array); and Pair #4, A (completing one's tax return)

7. C, F, A, B, D, and E

8. E, A, G, B, C, D, and F

9. E

10. A, concept; B, procedure; C, process; D, structure; E, classification; F, fact; and G, principle

# CHAPTER 4
# Adult Learning Principles

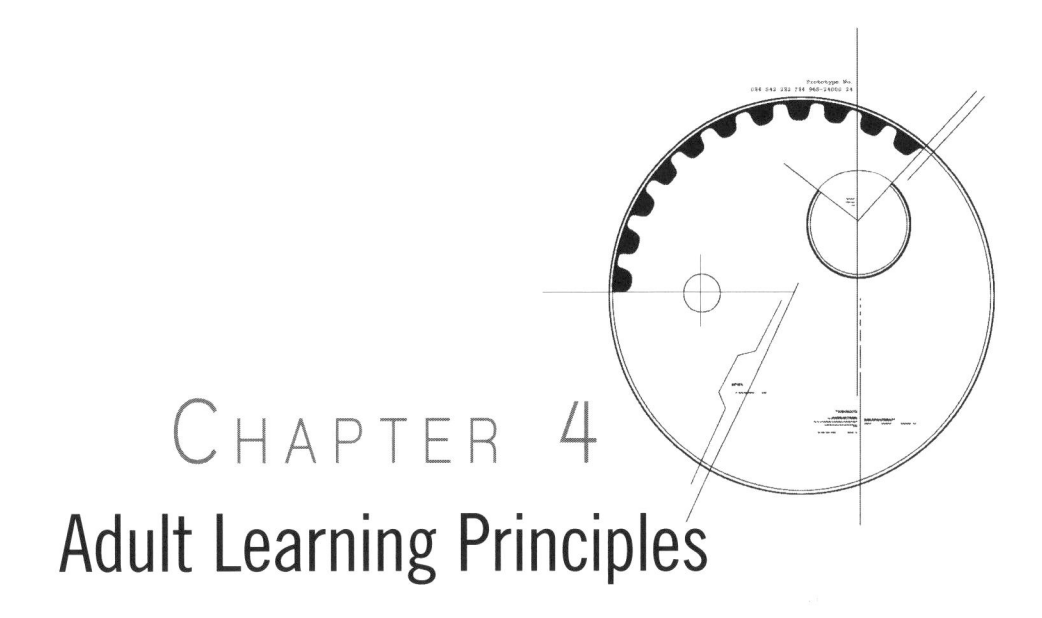

This chapter presents twelve principles of adult learning. Because most corporate and industry training involves adults, they merit special attention in this book.

## Adult Learners

Most formal training programs are targeted at adult learners. Adults typically have to learn new knowledge and skills because of changing requirements and demands in the workplace. Often their livelihoods depend on their success in learning and applying new knowledge and skills. Moreover, in addition to their work life, adults have other demands to worry about and attend to, from their spouses, children, and other sources. As such, adults have the following special needs when it comes to training:

- produce results quickly
- be *shown* how to do things (mentored, explicitly given the steps)

- be taught only what is required to perform their job tasks and roles
- avoid fluff (unnecessary training material or learning events)
- try it out for themselves (practice what they were just taught)
- avoid a time-consuming discovery or research-on-your-own type approach to training (due to constraints on their time and desire for efficiency)

Although many academic theories have been espoused on adult learning, in this chapter, we will present twelve principles of adult learning that will address most if not all of the training needs of your adult learners.

---

The following books are good resources for learning more about adult learning:

- *Understanding and Facilitating Adult Learning: A Comprehensive Analysis of Principles and Effective Practices*, by Stephen D. Brookfield, Jossey-Bass, 1991, ISBN 1-5554-2355-8.
- *Handbook of Adult and Continuing Education*, by Arthur L. Wilson and Elisabeth R. Hayes, Jossey-Bass, 2000, ISBN 0-7879-4998-1.

---

## Principle #1: Learning Should Be Motivated

Adults want to know why they should take or participate in a given training course, why it has value to them, how it will help them in their lives, and why it will be worth the effort. Providing this motivation will help adults set aside time in their busy lives for the training, focus their attention and full mental faculties on the training stimulus, and persist throughout the training until completion.

Here are some ways to motivate adult learners:

- Ask and answer the question: "What's in it for me?"
- Explain the value or relevance of the material to their jobs or lives.
- Provide incentives for learning (with management approval).
- Praise students frequently as they achieve incremental progress.
- Present high-status role models touting the importance, value, or need for this skill.
- Describe stories or examples of how others have benefited from having this skill.
- Make learning fun without sacrificing relevance or focus.
- Provide motivational lead-ins that grab attention, generate interest, and induce excitement.
- Keep training relevant, focused, and lean throughout.
- Vary learning activities.

## Principle #2: Learning Should Be Tailored to Meet Students' Specific Needs

Adults expect that those who created the training did their homework to understand why they have come to class and what specifically they are seeking to attain from the class. Therefore, as the architect of training, you should investigate your audience to find out what their specific training needs are and then design training that will meet those needs.

Among other needs, training for adults should *always* address the overarching need to perform the job tasks that produce the desired new work products or outputs. Therefore, training content should always be designed around and support the performance of these new or modified job tasks. If possible, training should be tailored to specific job roles, and learners should take only the training that is relevant to their job role.

Too often, training content is determined by what one or more subject matter experts believe should be included. This can result in including unnecessary, noncritical material (fluff) in the training. Later in this book, you will learn how to perform a rigorous analysis that identifies the new job tasks that need to be taught. You will also learn how to analytically break these job tasks down into their essential learning components, resulting in training that is not only relevant, but lean and intensely focused on learning the new skills.

The following are some general needs of adult learners:

- acquire specific job skills
- enhance their career
- receive more pay
- do more enjoyable work
- reduce frustration
- make their job life easier
- have a greater sense of accomplishment
- gain greater control
- increase esteem among peers

## Principle #3: Learning Should Focus on Building Skills that Produce Job Outputs

Students do not come to class to be impressed by how much the instructor or course designer knows or to receive an encyclopedic or academic treatment of the subject matter. The only content that should be included should be that which is *required* to perform the necessary job tasks. Everything else should be left out.

The hierarchical instructional analysis technique that will be presented in a later chapter will teach you how to identify these job outcomes, analyze the activities that are required to produce them, break these activities down into tasks and subtasks, and identify the enabling content that students must learn to perform these tasks.

This systematic analysis technique is the only *objective* way of deciding what content to include and whether to include some bit of content that somebody thinks should be in the course.

Subjective methods of deciding what to include in the training are hit-and-miss propositions: they might *miss critical content* that is necessary for learning the new outcomes, and they might *include content that is unnecessary* and thus bloat the size of and dilute the effectiveness of the training.

## Principle #4: Learning Should Be Easy to Transfer to the Real World

Structure the training course around the major tasks users will perform back on the job to produce the new job outcomes. Module and topic titles should reflect the major activities and tasks that a person must perform to produce the job outcomes. The instructional analysis previously mentioned provides that structure. When the course structure—the titles of the modules and topics and their sequencing—reflect required tasks that students will have to perform on the job, students will see the immediate relevance of the course simply by inspecting the course menu or structure.

### Example of How a Course Structure Can Show Relevance to Students

Course title: How to Drive a Car

Course modules and topics

- what you need to know before you get behind the wheel
  - requirements for a driver's license
  - understanding road signs
  - understanding traffic laws
  - basic car safety and maintenance
  - what to do when your car breaks down
  - insurance requirements

- getting behind the wheel—preparing to drive
    - visually checking the car and surroundings
    - setting rearview mirrors
    - buckling seat belts for children and adults
    - adjusting seat and steering wheel position
    - checking locks, parking brake, and transmission
    - starting the car
- safe steering practices
    - backing out
- safe braking practices
- safe parking practices
- emergency car-handling techniques
- defensive driving techniques
- road hazard awareness

## Additional Ways to Help Adults Transfer Learning to the Real World

Here are some additional ways to help adults transfer learning to the real world:

- provide practice that gradually increases in scope, complexity, integration across subskills, and fidelity to the real world
- write procedures and guidelines from the student's perspective
- address students directly in the training materials using second-person active voice
- use numerous examples, analogies, case studies, demonstrations, and problems with worked-out solutions
- provide "how to" job aids (cheat sheets) and train students on using these job aids
- provide a variety of examples of what you are teaching from all major categories of job situations and task variations

- build mental models (such as cause-and-effect) to provide additional task performance adaptability in the real world for problem-solving and other analytical tasks
- provide simulations and "sand boxes" (safe learning environments where students can try things out), where appropriate and cost-justified

## Principle #5: Learning Should Be Relevant

Adult learners do not have patience with material that they perceive is not directly relevant to achieving their learning goals. That is probably why many adults find it very difficult to sit through a college class after they have been in the work force a few years. College courses are typically content-oriented courses. On the other hand, training in business and industry is typically focused on teaching students to produce new work products, not just verbally discourse on a subject.

Why is including irrelevant material so costly and painful to the adult learner?

- It slows down their progress toward their learning goals—they must figure out why the information was included, what to do with it, and how it relates to the main task.
- Sifting through irrelevant information is hard work; it makes learning more difficult, time consuming, and stressful.
- It contributes to information overload (remember the limits of human cognitive processes that were discussed in a prior chapter?).
- It contributes to a loss of motivation and confidence in the training. Students might give up, divert their attention elsewhere, or not work as hard to learn the skills.

How can you ensure relevance in your training?

- Perform a proper training needs analysis during the requirements gathering phase of the training project to identify the true training needs of your audience. This subject will be covered in a later chapter in this book.

- Follow the instructional analysis, design, and development processes presented in this book to ensure that all required information is included in your training and that *only* required information is included in your training.

## Principle #6: Learning Should Occur in an Emotionally Supportive Environment

Adult learners are faced with the daunting task of learning complex new skills with their associated massive amounts of enabling information. Because their jobs are often at stake, this can be emotionally threatening. Furthermore, adult learners will avoid situations that might embarrass them, make them feel stupid or incompetent, or make them look foolish to others. Because of this, you must create a protected learning environment that diminishes these possibilities and that makes learners feel emotionally safe to venture out, interact, try out, practice, make mistakes, contribute insights, and ask questions.

How can you provide an emotionally supportive environment?

- Provide a safe environment for students to learn and practice.
- Provide individual feedback that is factual, private, positive in tone, and never demeaning.
- Praise what the student is doing right and then make suggestions for improvement.
- Let students know that making mistakes will be viewed as a natural and necessary part of learning.
- Don't punish students for asking questions or for asking for information to be repeated.
- Have reasonable expectations and standards.
- Do not make visible or available to superiors or peers students' scores from checkpoint questions and exercises given during the training.

# Principle #7: Learning Should Provide a Clear Context

"Context" describes how the current information is related to the larger framework, topic of discussion, or learning goal. It answers the questions:

- "Why are you telling me this?"
- "Why do I need to know this?"
- "How does this relate to the previous material, the course structure, or the task that I thought I was learning?"
- "How will this help me learn this new job task?"

Without a context, learners wonder how the current information fits into what has already been presented. As you learned previously, memory retrieval is much stronger when information can be organized into meaningful frameworks or sequences. Showing learners how this slide, screen, or presentation fits into the framework that you previously presented or to the content that they were just taught will help them make sense of the information, process it more thoroughly, and retrieve it more confidently.

How to provide context

- Include transitional slides, screens, titles, paragraphs, and sentences.
- Provide advanced organizers and organizing logical frameworks.
- Provide the big picture up front and then refer to it again at transition points and show where you are at in the big picture.
- Provide objectives and overviews.
- Answer the questions
  - "Why are you telling me this?"
  - "Why do I need to know this?"
  - "How does this relate to the previous material, the course structure, or the task that I thought I was learning?"
  - "How will this help me learn my new job task?"

# Principle #8: Learning Should Simplify Complexity and Emphasize Key Points

Not all knowledge is equal. Some key knowledge enables a person to understand how to effect changes in the real world. Consider the following examples of key knowledge:

- the concept of compound interest in finance
- key selling strategies and techniques
- the problem-solving model used by expert service engineers
- principles of defensive driving
- Ohm's law in electronics

Help learners to simplify complexity and distinguish key information from other information

- Give key information more attention.
- Make key information **stand out** in the presentation—visually, semantically, structurally, and organizationally.
- Use the foreground/background principles of perception and place the key information in the foreground.
- Reference or point to details.
- Preview your presentation or topic by referencing key information.
- Provide periodic summaries in which you review key information.
- Provide exercises that explicitly require the application of key information.

## Principle #9: Learning Should Provide the Proper Environment for Practice

Adults are eager to try out new skills. They want to know for themselves how well they are progressing in acquiring a new competency. Intuitively, they know that they must practice what is being taught to really master the skill and feel confident in performing it.

What is a proper environment for practice? It is an environment that provides

- an emotionally and physically safe place where students can practice new skills without negative consequences and without compromising their personal safety;
- the proper tools, equipment, and physical facilities to practice;
- protection from embarrassment, scrutiny by management, or potential damage to costly equipment;
- meaningful exercises that practice both enabling skills and higher-level integrative skills (if integrative skills have been taught at this point in the course); these exercises should match the level of complexity given in the instruction;
- a sufficient number of meaningful tasks to practice;
- exercises that are identical with or that simulate actual job tasks, if this level of instruction has been given at that point in the course; and
- meaningful exercise guidance, supervision, support, and individual feedback.

## Principle #10: Learning Should Have Variety and Be Appropriately Paced

Learning requires variety and pacing to maintain attention, reduce mental and physiological fatigue, stimulate human interest, and make training more humane. But avoid arbitrary interruptions that do not directly support these purposes.

To pace training and keep it fresh, provide

- a suitable pace for your particular audience;
- frequent breaks;
- multisensory stimulation, such as the use of color, graphics, animation, music, voice, and typographical variations;
- changes in learning activities, such as group work, self-study, exercises, checkpoint questions, simulations, games, videos, role-plays, quizzes, and demonstrations;
- human interest elements that are relevant to what is being taught, such as "war stories," examples, role models, competitions, and games; and
- frequent but meaningful student interaction.

## Principle #11: Learning Should Build Students' Confidence in Performing the Task

People who are not confident in their ability to perform a task are reluctant to perform that task and are likely to avoid situations where they are required to do so. This works against the transfer of the skills that were learned in training to the workplace.

How can you build students' confidence in performing a task?

Provide practice that

- is first demonstrated,
- increasingly matches real life,
- is private to the student,
- allows repetition of practice until proficiency is reached,
- provides a representative range of conditions likely to be encountered in real life, and
- has interim milestones.

Focus on

- performance improvement, not aptitude,
- gains, not shortfalls (showing how far along the student is in the progression),
- reinforcement and review of key principles and mental models, and
- specific feedback given in a supportive way.

## Principle #12: Learning Should Be Worth the Effort

Adult learners are pressured to increase productivity, take on increasing responsibilities, do more with fewer resources, and account for every minute of their time. Because of this, adult learners naturally ask themselves, "Will the benefits I expect to get from this training significantly outweigh the time and energy that will be required to take it?"

Why might students view the training as not worth the effort? Students might say things about the training such as

- "It wasn't tailored to my specific job needs—too general to be of much help."
- "It was just an information dump—I cannot afford to sift, sort, and piece together information and figure out how to do it myself."
- "The delivery technology required too much learning just to take the training."
- "It was poorly designed and written."
- "There was too much irrelevant or unimportant information."
- "It was focused on teaching information, not new skills and tasks."

# Chapter Summary—Adult Learning Principles

This chapter presented twelve principles of adult learning. Because most corporate and industry training involves adults, they merit special attention in this book.

You should now be able to state and describe each of the following principles of adult learning and explain how to apply them in training:

- Learning should be motivated.
- Learning should be tailored to meet students' specific needs.
- Learning should focus on building skills that produce job outputs.
- Learning should be easy to transfer to the real world.
- Learning should be relevant.
- Learning should occur in an emotionally supportive environment.
- Learning should provide a clear context.
- Learning should simplify complexity and emphasize key points.
- Learning should provide the proper environment for practice.
- Learning should have variety and be appropriately paced.
- Learning should build students' confidence in performing the task.
- Learning should be worth the effort.

## Check Your Understanding

1. **When it comes to training, adults have which of the following needs? (Select all that apply.)**
    A. Produce results quickly
    B. Be shown how to do things
    C. Be taught only what is required to perform their job tasks and roles
    D. Avoid fluff
    E. Avoid a time-consuming discovery or research-on-your-own-type approach to training

2. **To motivate adult learners, you must answer the question for them, "What's in it for ____?"**

3. **Training should be ____ to meet the needs of adult learners and should *always* address the overarching need to perform job ____ that produce the desired new work products or outputs.**

4. **What is wrong with the subjective method of deciding what to include in the training? (Select all that apply.)**
   A. It can result in including content that is unnecessary.
   B. It results in a course that is lean and efficient.
   C. It might miss critical content that is necessary for learning the new outcomes.
   D. It produces a course in which everyone is happy with the end result.
   E. It impresses students with how much the instructor or the course designer knows.
   F. It can bloat the size of and dilute the effectiveness of the training.

5. **Which of the following techniques are ways to help adult learners transfer learning to the real world? (Select all that apply.)**
   A. Require that students practice skills at a higher level ("stretch" themselves) than they have been taught in the instructional materials.
   B. Write procedures and guidelines from the student's perspective.
   C. Use numerous examples, analogies, case studies, demonstrations, and worked problems.
   D. Provide practice that gradually increases in scope, complexity, integration across subskills, and fidelity to the real world.
   E. Provide a variety of examples of what you are teaching from all major categories of job situations and task variations.
   F. Provide practice exercises only for concepts, facts, and other intellectual knowledge.

G. Build mental models (such as cause-and-effect) to provide additional task performance adaptability in the real world for problem-solving and other analytical tasks.

H. Provide simulations and "sand boxes" (safe learning environments where students can try things out), where appropriate and cost-justified.

6. **Why is including irrelevant material so costly and painful to the adult learner? (Select all that apply.)**

   A. It slows down their progress towards their learning goals—they must figure out why the information was included, what to do with it, and how it relates to the main task.

   B. Sifting through irrelevant information is hard work; it makes learning more difficult, time consuming, and stressful.

   C. It requires that students think more deeply about the subject matter.

   D. It contributes to information overload (remember the limits of human cognitive processes that were discussed in a prior chapter?).

   E. It contributes to a loss of motivation and confidence in the training. Students might give up, divert their attention elsewhere, or not work as hard to learn the skills.

   F. It takes up more space.

7. **True or false? Adult learners avoid situations that might embarrass them, make them feel stupid or incompetent, or make them look foolish to others.**

8. **Which of the following techniques are ways to provide an emotionally supportive learning environment? (Select all that apply.)**

   A. Provide a safe environment for students to learn and practice.

   B. Let students know that making mistakes will count against them on their final score.

   C. Have reasonable expectations and standards.

D. Criticize students for asking that information be repeated.

E. Do not make visible or available to superiors or peers students' scores from checkpoint questions and exercises given during the training.

F. Provide individual feedback that is factual, private, positive in tone, and never demeaning.

G. Firmly criticize what the student is doing wrong and then make suggestions for improvement.

9. **Which of the following techniques are ways to provide a clear context during training? (Select all that apply.)**

   A. Provide human interest stories and sidebars.

   B. Provide the big picture up front and then refer to it again at transition points and show where you are at in the big picture.

   C. Provide advanced organizers and organizing logical frameworks.

   D. Provide objectives and overviews.

   E. Provide exercises that simulate job performance.

   F. Include transitional slides, screens, titles, paragraphs, and sentences.

   G. Answer the questions "Why are you telling me this?" "Why do I need to know this?" "How does this relate to the previous material, the course structure, or the task that I thought I was learning?" and "How will this help me learn my new job task?"

10. **Which of the following techniques are ways to distinguish key information? (Select all that apply.)**

    A. Give it more attention.

    B. Make it stand out in the presentation—visually, semantically, structurally, and organizationally.

    C. Use the foreground/background principles of perception and place the key information in the foreground.

    D. Provide periodic summaries in which you review key information.

    E. Provide transitional slides, screens, titles, paragraphs, and sentences.

F. Provide exercises that explicitly require the application of key information.

G. Answer the questions "Why are you telling me this?" "Why do I need to know this?" "How does this relate to the previous material, the course structure, or the task that I thought I was learning?" and "How will this help me learn my new job task?"

11. **True or false? Practice should provide a sufficient number of meaningful exercises that practice both enabling skills and any higher-level integrative skills that have been taught; these exercises should match the level of complexity given in the instruction.**

12. **Which of the following techniques are ways to pace training and keep it fresh? (Select all that apply.)**

    A. Give frequent but meaningful student interaction.

    B. Design into the training frequent changes in learning activities, such as group work, self-study, exercises, checkpoint questions, simulations, games, videos, role-plays, quizzes, and demonstrations.

    C. Give frequent breaks.

    D. Provide multisensory stimulation, such as the use of color, graphics, animation, music, voice, and typographical variations.

    E. Present three days of solid lecture followed by a day of lab exercises before doing an activity or exercise.

    F. Provide a suitable pace for your particular audience.

    G. Provide human interest elements that are relevant to what is being taught, such as "war stories," examples, role models, competitions, and games.

13. **True or false? To build students' confidence in performing a task, demonstrate the task and then provide practice that increasingly matches real life, is private to the student, allows repetition of practice until proficiency is reached, provides a representative range of conditions likely to be encountered in real life, and recognizes the accomplishment of interim milestones.**

14. **From the perspective of the student, what are some reasons that training might not be worth the effort? (Select all that apply.)**
    A. "It was tailored to my specific job needs."
    B. "It was just an information dump—I cannot afford to sift, sort, and piece together information and figure out how to do it myself."
    C. "The delivery technology required too much learning just to take the training."
    D. "It was poorly designed and written."
    E. "It provided too much irrelevant or unimportant information."
    F. "It focused on teaching information, not new skills and tasks."
    G. "It was too easy to take."

15. **Match each violation of an adult learning principle with the principle it violates.**

| | |
|---|---|
| Including a topic in the course without telling students why it is important. | A. Learning should be tailored to meet students' specific needs and be focused on building skills that produce job outputs. |
| Teaching students how to cut 2 x 4 boards and nail them together but not how to create walls when they will be required to create walls on the job. | B. Learning should occur in an emotionally supportive environment. |
| Students want training on how to close sales but training focuses on traits that make a good salesperson. | C. Learning should provide a clear context. |
| Students are forced to show their work before the class and are made light of when they have wrong answers. | D. Learning should be motivated. |
| The course proceeds from unit one through unit ten and never tells students within each unit how the material fits into the overall course. | E. Learning should be easy to transfer to the real world. |

16. **Match each violation of an adult learning principle with the principle it violates.**

| | |
|---|---|
| Students are shown complicated, busy slides and the instructor gives equal emphasis to every detail. | A. Learning should build students' confidence in performing the task. |
| Students are given few opportunities to practice. | B. Learning should simplify complexity and emphasize key points. |
| Learning the online user interface to take the training takes thirty to fifty minutes. | C. Learning should have variety and be appropriately paced. |
| Students are given the most realistic, difficult exercises to complete immediately after their initial exposure to the teaching material. | D. Learning should provide the proper environment for students to practice. |
| The training consists of a page turner. | E. Learning should be worth the effort. |

## Answers

1. A, B, C, D, and E
2. The correct answer is "for me." Adults want to know why they should take or participate in a given training course, why it has value to them, how it will help them in their lives, and why it will be worth the effort.
3. The correct answer is "tailored" and "tasks."
4. A, C, and F.
5. B, C, D, E, G, and H
6. A, B, D, and E
7. True
8. A, C, E, and F
9. B, C, D, F, and G

10. A, B, C, D, and F
11. True
12. A, B, C, D, F, and G
13. True
14. B, C, D, E, and F
15. D, E, A, B, and C
16. B, D, E, A, and C

# Chapter 5
# Ten Key Teaching Principles

This chapter presents ten key teaching principles that add to the twelve adult learning principles discussed in the last chapter. These teaching principles are fundamental to all instruction; they apply to every learning situation and audience.

## Principle #1: Support the Cognitive Learning Process in Your Topic or Lesson Design

| Gain Attention | Sensory Perception | Higher-Level Cognition | Memory Storage and Retrieval | Practice with Feedback |
|---|---|---|---|---|

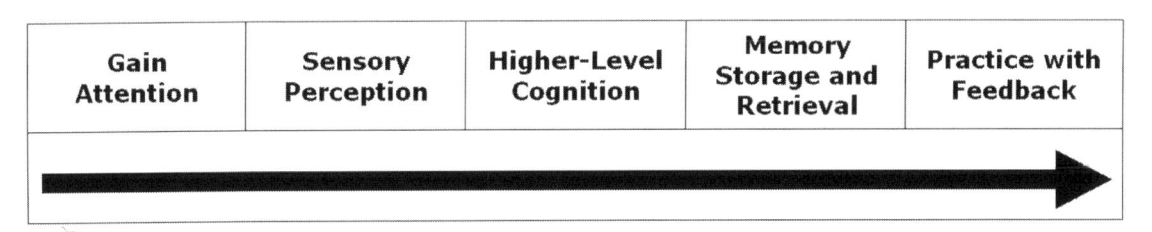

**Figure 14. A simple cognitive model of learning**

In a previous chapter, we presented a simple model of learning with its five learning components: gain attention, sensory perception, higher-level cognition, memory storage and retrieval, and practice with feedback.

Robert Gagne, one of the grandfathers of instructional design, has devised a general prescription for designing instructionally sound training materials called the eight *events of instruction.* These events of instruction support the cognitive learning process represented in our simple model of learning. They represent the flow or sequence of instructional events that must be presented in the training to support the underlying cognitive learning process. Typically, they are applied at the lowest unit of instruction, such as in a topic within a course, but they are valid for teaching any chunk of information, even within a topic.

### Gagne's Eight Events of Instruction

1. **Gain attention:** Get students to focus on the instruction being presented.
2. **Stimulate recall of prerequisite information:** Review prerequisite information that students must understand before they will be able to understand what you are about to present.
3. **Present the stimulus:** Present the new information or material to be learned.
4. **Guide thinking:** Provide cognitive strategies, organizers, emphasis techniques, and so forth to facilitate cognitive processing, learning, and retention.
5. **Elicit performance:** Have students practice the skill and knowledge you are teaching.
6. **Provide feedback:** Provide individual feedback on each student's performance.
7. **Provide generalizing experiences:** Help students generalize, transfer, and apply concepts, procedures, and practices to the real world or to a broader application.
8. **Assess performance:** Provide an assessment to measure how well the student can perform the task or the objectives.

# Principle #2: Manage Channel Capacity and Accommodate Biological Limitations

Channels are the different sensory methods by which we can take in new information. As we discussed previously, each sensory channel has certain biological and cognitive limitations. Instructional designers must become aware of and respect these limitations.

## Ways to manage channel capacity and accommodate biological limitations

- Avoid presenting competing or conflicting information in visual and aural channels
  - Attention is limited; be careful when dividing it across channels.
  - For example, it is difficult to visually decipher and read a complex slide while listening to the instructor briefly talk about things that are only remotely related to the slide before quickly jumping to the next slide.
- Avoid information (channel) overload and information dumps
  - You can create a bottleneck anywhere in the simple model of learning by, for example, presenting too much raw sensory information too quickly to be processed.

## Additional ways to manage channel capacity and accommodate biological processes

- Pace training, provide ample breaks, and provide variety, practice, and frequent interaction.
- Chunk information, simplify it, emphasize key information, layer information.
- Eliminate unnecessary information, teach to recall only when necessary, and provide job aids (such as procedure guides and cheat sheets).
- Support transfer to long-term memory.
- Avoid ten-hour teaching days for classroom instruction.
- Remember that the instruction has to grow new neural interconnections in students' brains. This is a biological process that takes time and is subject to fatigue.

## Principle #3: Provide Overviews and Frameworks

*Overviews* provide a high-level preview of what is to be covered. They are always appropriate at the unit, module, topic, or lesson levels and typically include objectives as part of the overview. Overviews can range from one or more sentences that preview the information and relate it to what has already been covered to a whole topic that overviews an entire course.

*Frameworks* are advanced organizers and provide a logical or physical model or structure that organizes the information at a high level.

### Examples of frameworks

- a simplified view of the whole object (such as a graphic of a bicycle with labeled parts) for instruction that teaches a structure (parts of a whole)
- a graphic that is used to organize the discussion, such as the one used in this book to present our simple cognitive model of learning
- familiar organizing schemes, such as numbered lists, part-whole, and hierarchies ("Here are the six steps to the Super Sales Process" or "Here is a flowchart of the approval process")
- a concrete analogy or metaphor that is used to organize or relate new information (relating the brain to a computer)

## Principle #4: Teach Prerequisite Information First

Although this principle is common sense, it is often unintentionally violated in poorly designed instruction or in training that was quickly thrown together without any kind of systematic analysis of the content or training outcomes. This principle can be violated in three ways:

- Prerequisite information is left out altogether (overlooked).
- Prerequisite information is presented in the instruction at a later point than where it is first required.

- Prerequisite information *was* previously taught but so much time has passed that it is unlikely that students will remember the information, and no refreshing of the information was provided just before the new information was taught (this is what causes many students to stumble in math class).

## The Importance of Prerequisite Information

Failing to teach prerequisite information first is especially important in highly structured or hierarchical subjects such as math or programming. It is important in teaching any content in which one piece of information builds on another. One way to avoid violating this principle is to always define new concepts, terms, and other jargon before they are used to teach new material.

## How to Identify Prerequisite Information

Prerequisite information is determined by a systematic analysis of the content and should not be left to an ad hoc approach, which often fails to identify *all* of the prerequisite information that is required or teaches prerequisite content too late in sequence of material in the lesson or course. Systematic content analysis and sequencing of material in a lesson will be taught in later chapters in this book.

Leaving the identification of prerequisite information to subject matter experts (SMEs) is a risky proposition. Subject matter experts are so close to and familiar with the subject matter that they have great difficulty identifying enabling information—it is second nature to them and is no longer in their consciousness.

## Principle #5: Teach Enabling Skills and Content Right before They Are Needed

Enabling skills and content are prerequisite skills and content that must be taught and understood before a person can learn new information or a new skill. For example, before you can understand the concept of "mother-in-law," you must understand the enabling concepts of "mother," "marriage," "spouse," and "related."

## Example of enabling content for a procedure

<u>How to change a tire</u>

1. Pull over to a safe and appropriate location
2. Locate the tools and spare tire
3. Jack up the car
4. Remove old tire
5. Mount new tire
6. Lower the car

<u>Enabling skills and content</u>

- identifying safe locations
- identifying appropriate locations
- recognizing and locating tools and spare tire
- jacking up the car
- loosening lug nuts
- tightening lug nuts
- lowering the car

## What to do if the same piece of enabling content is needed in more than one place

- If it is needed in only two or three places, teach it the first time it is needed, then refresh or remind students about it in the other instances.
- If it is needed in multiple places, consider teaching it before or at the beginning of the lesson, unit, or course along with other similar information.

- If you have a large body of related enabling content that is best taught together (such as networking concepts for a course in network problem determination), then teach it up front as its own unit or topic and provide sufficient reviews and practice to store the information in students' long-term memories.

## Principle #6: Present Information According to Its Type

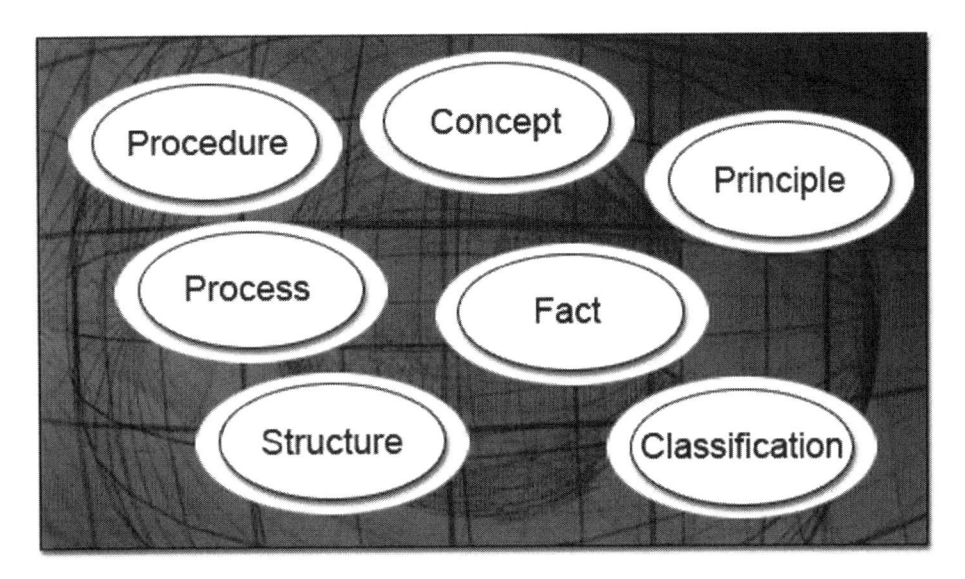

Figure 15. Robert Horn's taxonomy of information types

In a previous chapter on learning taxonomies, we discussed Robert Horn's taxonomy of seven information types (see the graphic below). Each type of information has research-based recommendations for facilitating learning of that type.

Teaching a concept, for example, requires specific instructional prescriptions that are different from teaching a process or a procedure. These prescriptions are based on years of research and study; therefore, leverage this knowledge and apply these specific instructional strategies for each type of information that you teach in your training.

## Examples of instructional strategies for two types of information

### Example A: How to Enter an Invoice (Procedure)

describe **what** the procedure does, **when** the procedure is used, and any **requirements** for performing it

**provide the steps** of the procedure and teach any required **enabling content** for each step:

How to enter an invoice

1. Invoke the XYZ app
2. Click *Enter Invoice*
3. Enter the invoice data
4. [And so forth]

**give a demonstration** of the procedure

**have students practice** the procedure and **provide feedback**

### Example B: What is a Zifferbocker? (Concept)

**teach enabling concepts and facts that students do not know**

What is a mammal?

What is an axleberry tree?

What is the Amazon?

**define the concept**

A zifferbocker is a three-legged Amazonian mammal that eats exclusively moss, sleeps in the day in axleberry trees, and has three stomachs.

**provide examples** (instances) of the concept

**provide nonexamples** (noninstances) of the concept

**provide close-in nonexamples of the concept** (that have some but not all of the required attributes) and explain why they are instances or noninstances of the concept

**Have students practice classifying previously unencountered instances and noninstances** of the concept and provide feedback.

## Principle #7: Teach from the Known to the Unknown

Always start with where your students are in their skills, knowledge, and attitudes and build from there. Relate the new information to what they already know. To help students learn, teach from the

- known to the unknown,
- simple to the complex, and
- concrete to the abstract.

### Examples of teaching from the known to the unknown

### known to the unknown

- The Z506 processor not only has a standard instruction set, but a special instruction set designed for …
- A computer file system organization is similar to that of a standard office file cabinet and folders …

### simple to the complex

- A triangle is a …. An isosceles triangle is a …

### concrete to the abstract

- An object in computer programming is like an object in real life (recliner chair) that is an instance of a larger class (the class of chairs).

**How to teach from the known to the unknown**

- Identify what students already know by identifying the entry-level skills, knowledge, and attitudes during audience analysis so that you know where to start (audience analysis will be discussed in a later chapter in this book).

- Relate the unknown to the known through analogies, similes, and metaphors.

- Provide organizing structures that add meaning to the information, such as frameworks, structures, diagrams, and organizing graphics.

- Use the technique of elaboration to drill down from high-level overviews, frameworks, and structure diagrams to successive levels of detail in the presentation.

## Principle #8: Provide Generous Examples and Illustrations

An example is often worth a thousand words. Examples help students

- materialize abstract words and ideas;
- identify the boundaries of concepts and ideas;
- see how the information that was just presented—the rule, principle, definition, principle, procedure, concept, and so forth—is applied to real instances;
- increase the number and richness of neural interconnections that are associated with that information; and
- remember the information, because examples are often more concrete and understandable than abstractions or descriptions; many concepts and ideas are just fuzzy mental images until they are made concrete through examples.

## How to provide generous examples and illustrations

Follow these guidelines

- Give examples for every important new piece of information.
- Err on the side of providing too many examples.
- Provide examples that match the complexity of the information you are teaching; for example, if you are teaching how to address client objections, provide several scenarios that illustrate the handling of client objections.
- Provide a variety of examples that will broaden students' understanding of the information.
- Concepts require that you provide both examples and nonexamples to thoroughly establish the concept's boundaries.

## Additional ways to provide examples

- Verbal descriptions: "Examples of mammals are …"
- Graphics: "The following graphic shows an example of a token ring network."
- Demonstrations: "Watch me enter an invoice."
- Scenarios or short stories: "Mary was at her second sales call. The customer asked why the price was so high. Mary …"

## Principle #9: Periodically Review Key Information

One-trial learning—one brief exposure to a large amount of information—is not a very effective instructional technique. Spaced reviews, which are periodic reviews of previously presented information, are important in learning. Neural connections need to be strengthened through repetition, recall, elaboration, and use; otherwise, extinction quickly takes its toll (see previous chapters).

What is repetition? Repetition does not mean repeating entire lessons or presentations at the same level of detail. If properly spaced, reviews can be at successively higher levels and can touch on just the key concepts, principles, procedures, and so forth that you previously presented. Key information can also be captured and reviewed in job aids and other summary forms.

The time students are in training ("seat time") is precious because of the high cost of developing and delivering the training and because employees are away from normal productive work. It would be easy, therefore, to discard reviews and the refreshing of previously learned information as an unneeded luxury or as an indication that the training is somehow flawed. This would be a serious mistake. For long-term retention of learning, periodically refreshing the information is a must. Relying on students' jobs to exercise everything that they have learned immediately after training is almost always unrealistic and flawed.

**When should you refresh information?**

- the next time it is needed again as enabling content
- when you are using it as a framework or advanced organizer, before transitioning to the next element of the framework
- at the conclusion of topics, lessons, and units of instruction
- as an integral part of exercises, discussions, and activities
- once or twice more during the course if not otherwise reviewed by any of the above techniques

## Principle #10: Take the Viewpoint of Your Students

Training should be personal and feel more like mentoring than a formal learning program. As the instructional designer, you should be an advocate of your students and try to see things from their life and work situations.

**How to take the viewpoint of your students**

- Understand who your students are and what their needs and goals are through requirements gathering and audience analysis (techniques that will be discussed in later chapters in this book).
- Write directly to students (second-person active voice) and avoid passive or impersonal grammatical forms.
- Avoid a stiff, clinical, or a sterile corporate style of writing.
- Talk to students as if you were a mentor by their side.
- Imagine yourself in the shoes of your students and try to visualize what would be most valuable to them to learn during training and what they would find most useful to take back with them from training (such as job aids, reference material, and so forth).
- Be an advocate of your students.

# Chapter Summary—Ten Key Learning Principles

This chapter presented ten key teaching principles that add to the twelve adult learning principles discussed in the last chapter. These teaching principles are fundamental to all instruction; they apply to every learning situation and audience.

You should now be able to state and describe each of the following teaching principles and explain how to apply them in training:

- support the cognitive learning process in your topic design
- manage channel capacity and accommodate biological limitations
- provide overviews and frameworks
- teach prerequisite information first
- teach enabling skills and content right before it is needed
- present information according to its type
- teach from the known to the unknown
- provide generous examples and illustrations
- periodically review key information
- take the viewpoint of your students

1. **Match each of Gagne's Events of Instruction with its correct definition**

| | |
|---|---|
| Gain attention | A. Present the new information or material to be learned. |
| Stimulate recall of prerequisite information | B. Have students practice the skill and knowledge you are teaching. |
| Present the stimulus | C. Provide an assessment to measure how well the student can perform the task or the objectives. |
| Guide thinking | D. Provide individual feedback on each student's performance. |
| Elicit performance | E. Get students to focus on the instruction being presented. |
| Provide feedback | F. Help students generalize, transfer, and apply concepts, procedures, and practices to the real world or to a broader application. |
| Provide generalizing experiences | G. Review prerequisite information that students must understand before they will be able to understand what you are about to present. |
| Assess performance | H. Provide cognitive strategies, organizers, emphasis techniques, and so forth to facilitate cognitive processing, learning, and retention |

2. **Which of the following statements are ways to manage channel capacity and accommodate biological processes? (Select all that apply.)**

   A. Have students remember and process fifteen chunks of information all at once in short-term memory.

   B. Pace training, provide ample breaks, and provide variety, practice, and frequent interaction.

C. Teach for ten or eleven hours in the classroom to take advantage of students' time away from work and cover more material.

D. Chunk information, simplify it, emphasize key information, layer information.

E. Eliminate unnecessary information, teach to recall only when necessary, and provide job aids (such as procedure guides and cheat sheets).

F. Present different, noncomplementary information simultaneously in two channels.

G. Support transfer to long-term memory.

H. Cover as much information in the time as possible.

3. **True or false? Frameworks are advanced organizers and provide a logical or physical model or structure that organizes the information at a high level.**

4. **Which of the following statements are ways in which the principle "teach prerequisite information first" can be violated? (Select all that apply.)**

   A. Too few graphics were included in the instruction.

   B. So much time has passed since the prerequisite information was taught that it is unlikely that students will remember the information.

   C. Prerequisite information is included as optional reading.

   D. Prerequisite information is presented in the instruction at a later point than where it is first required.

   E. No topic or lesson summary was included.

   F. Prerequisite information is left out altogether.

5. **True or false? Enabling skills and content are skills and content that are taught after the prerequisite content; it expands students' knowledge and transfers learning to the work place.**

6. **Research has provided unique instructional strategies for teaching each of Horn's seven types of information. For example, the instructional strategy shown below is appropriate for teaching ____.**

   **Instructional Strategy**

   1. Teach enabling concepts and facts that students do not know
   2. Define the concept:
   3. Provide examples (instances) of the concept.
   4. Provide nonexamples (noninstances) of the concept.
   5. Provide close-in nonexamples of the concept.
   6. Have students practice classifying previously unencountered instances and noninstances of the concept and provide feedback.

7. **True or false? One of the techniques to relate the unknown to the known is through analogies, similes, and metaphors.**

8. **Which of the following statements are reasons why examples help students learn? (Select all that apply.)**
   A. They materialize abstract words and ideas.
   B. They identify the boundaries of concepts and ideas.
   C. They see how the information that was just presented—the rule, principle, definition, procedure, concept, and so forth—is applied to real instances.
   D. They increase the number and richness of neural interconnections that are associated with that information.
   E. They help students remember the information because examples are often more concrete and understandable than abstractions or descriptions.

9. **True or false? If training designers were to err on one side or the other, they should err on the side of providing too many examples.**

10. **True or false? "Periodically review key information" means to present the identical instructional presentation that was first presented to students periodically over time.**

11. **True or false? Good training should be personal and feel more like mentoring than a formal learning program.**

12. **Match each description with the learning principle that it violates.**

| | |
|---|---|
| A dirt rodent is a rat-like creature that lives underground; birds also are part of the animal family. | A. Teaches from the abstract to the concrete in the sequencing of information across the two sentences. Violated the principle: Teach from the known to the unknown. |
| One creates a footnote by pressing F12 and completing the fields in the popup box. | B. Teaches prerequisite information much later than where it is first required. Violated the principle: Teach prerequisite information first. |
| Super dynamic DRAM is a CMOS double-plated silicon wafer with HiT2 coating on each plate …. A silicon wafer is a computer chip made from silicon. | C. No examples and nonexamples were provided. Violated the principle: Provide generous examples and illustrations. |
| A bicycle is made up of a seat, a frame, two wheels, and a handlebar. | D. Wrong lesson sequence—doesn't follow Gagne's sequence of Events of Instruction. Violated the principle: Support the cognitive learning process in your topic or lesson design. |
| An equilateral triangle is a triangle with three equal sides [several more paragraphs] …. A triangle is … | E. Talks in third person voice instead of second-person voice. Violated the principle: Take the viewpoint of your students. |
| Lesson design: Teach concepts, then explain why they are important, then teach the enabling information, then tie it all together in an overall framework, then summarize what was taught, then practice classifying new instances of the concepts. | F. This is a structure type of information and should therefore be taught with the help of a labeled visual diagram. Violated the principle: Present information according to its type. |

**Answers**

1. E, G, A, H, B, D, F, and C
2. B, D, E, and G
3. True
4. B, D, and F
5. False. Enabling skills and content are prerequisite skills and content that must be taught and understood before a person can learn new information or a new skill.
6. The correct answer is "concepts."
7. True
8. A, B, C, D, and E
9. True
10. False. Repetition does not mean repeating entire lessons or presentations at the same level of detail. If properly spaced, reviews can be at successively higher levels and can touch on just the key concepts, principles, procedures, and so forth that you previously presented. Key information can also be captured and reviewed in job aids and other summary forms.
11. True
12. C, E, A, F, B, and D

# PART 2

## Creating Outstanding Instructional Designs

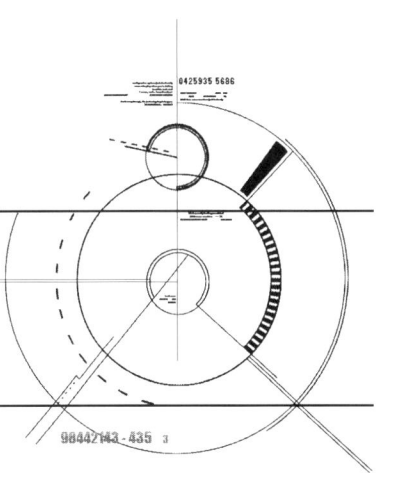

# Overview of Part 2

Part 2 is a succinct course on instructional design. It describes a nine-step process for performing instructional design and explains key analysis techniques. It provides guidance on gathering requirements, performing instructional and content analyses, writing instructional objectives, structuring and sequencing the course, choosing an instructional delivery system, designing practice exercises and other instructional events, designing training prototypes and example lessons, and writing an instructional design document—the architectural plans for the training.

After you complete part 2, you should be able to

- define instructional design,
- state and describe each of the eight steps of instructional design,
- perform requirements gathering,
- perform an instructional analysis,
- perform a content analysis,
- structure and sequence a course,
- write sound instructional objectives,
- determine the instructional delivery system,
- design practice exercises and other instructional events,
- design and create the prototype or example lesson, and
- create the formal instructional design document.

Part 2 is made up of eleven chapters.

## What Is Instructional Design?

Instructional design is:

- A serious profession and well-established field within the overall education profession
- A systematic method for creating effective, lean, and motivational training

The focus of this book will *not* be on the profession of instructional design, but on the instructional design *methodology* that this field practices. This methodology is a structured and systematic procedure for applying sound learning principles to create successful, cost-effective, and lasting learning. It is the shortest and most effective path to outstanding training.

The reason for this is because instructional design prescribes only those techniques and activities that are absolutely required to assure successful learning results. Moreover, the training that is prescribed by instructional design will be both effective and lean—it will contain *all* of the required content and instructional activities to achieve the results *and nothing more*.

The output of instructional design is a design document, which is a plan or *blueprint* for creating the instructional materials and activities and building the course. Content developers, graphic artists, authoring-language software experts, and others use this plan to guide and direct their efforts. In other words, training developers build the course from this plan.

In designing training, instructional designers perform activities that are similar to those performed by architects. They

- identify the needs and budget of the owner,
- analyze requirements to determine what is required to address those needs,
- design a floor plan and structure that will address those needs,

- create blueprints and sequence of construction activities, and
- oversee construction to ensure compliance to plans.

## Why Not Just Jump into Development?

Why take all this time and disciplined effort to create training? Why not just get a group of subject matter experts together and let them create the training materials? Although this ad hoc approach to creating training materials is popular, it suffers from some serious drawbacks. For example, how would you know

- what specific information and learning activities are needed? (Even SMEs differ from one another in what they think should be included.)
- what could have been left out of the training? (Again, how can this be determined objectively?)
- if the course is sequenced and structured for optimal learning? (It might even run the risk of making learning more difficult.)
- whether it could have been developed more efficiently and for less cost?

In fact, taking an ad hoc approach to training could lead to end results like the following:

- "A camel is a horse designed by committee."
- The 160-room Winchester Mystery House in San Jose, California, which was continually added onto for years, but is impossible to navigate without experienced guides and special maps because no master plan was ever created or followed (see http://www.winchestermysteryhouse.com).
- A fire hose or information dump training course.

## What Skills Will You Need?

A common belief about creating training is that it is a highly creative enterprise. Although creativity certainly has its place in activities such as creating outstanding graphics, creating interesting case studies and exercises, creating meaningful student interaction and involvement, and getting students' attention, most of what instructional designers do in instructional design is *analytical* in nature—collecting data, analyzing data, and creating detailed training blueprints that are based on that data.

Instructional designers use several techniques to gather data, analyze it, and design the course, including:

- **requirements gathering** techniques (including audience analysis),
- **instructional analysis** (outcome analysis or job/task analysis),
- **content analysis**, a technique for determining the enabling content—the required skills and knowledge necessary to carry out the steps in the procedures identified by the instructional analysis,
- techniques for **structuring and sequencing** the course,
- techniques for **determining and writing instructional objectives,**
- techniques for **determining the instructional delivery system,**
- techniques for **designing practice exercises and other instructional events,**
- techniques for **designing prototypes and example lessons,** and
- techniques for **creating an outstanding instructional design document.**

In reviewing this list, you might rightly conclude that creating training is more like doing engineering work than creating a great work of art.

What are the skills and attitudes you will need to design good training?

**Skills and attitudes you will need to implement instructional design methodology**

- a desire to understand how humans learn
- a desire to understand and apply well-known, proven principles of learning and teaching
- analytical reasoning and problem-solving ability
- the ability to handle complexity, uncertainty, and incomplete information
- the discipline necessary to rigorously follow instructional design methodology
- an ability to deal with things at both high levels and detailed levels
- attention to detail
- excellent teaming and communication skills
- great persistence

# Chapter 6
# Overview of How to Design Training

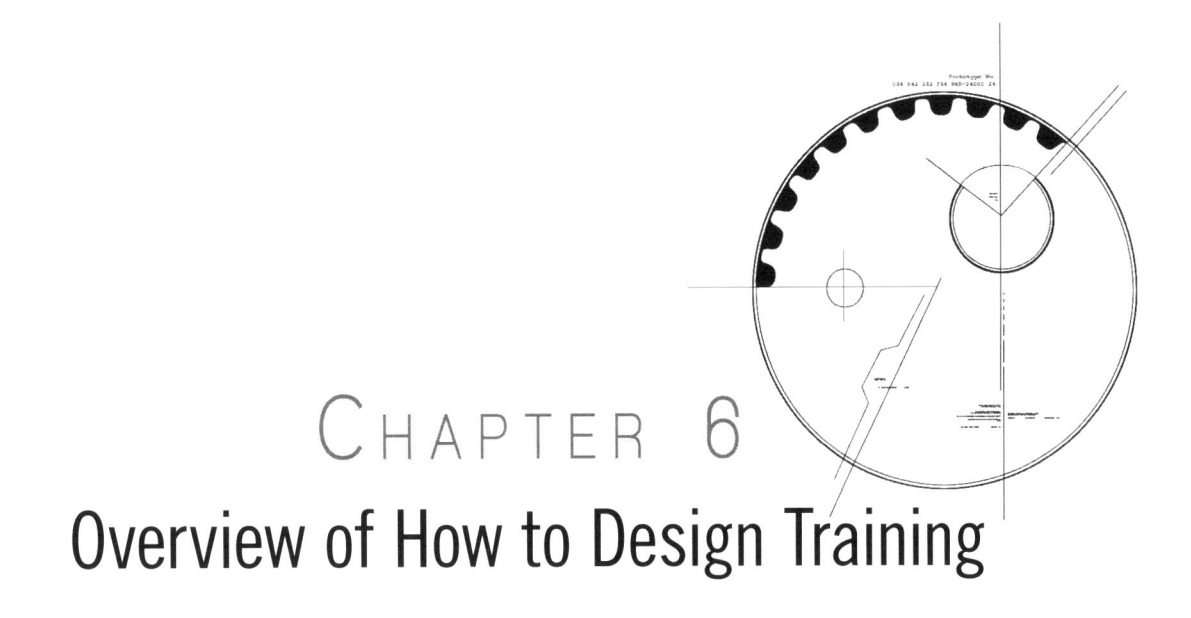

This chapter presents an overview of the instructional design process. It describes the major activities involved in designing training, including gathering requirements, performing instructional and content analyses, structuring the course, specifying objectives, choosing an instructional delivery system, designing practice exercises and other instructional events, designing a prototype lesson or topic, and creating the design document.

## Overview of the Instructional Design Process

Designing instructionally sound training is no accident. It is accomplished through a disciplined, systematic approach that involves an understanding of the training needs and audience, a careful analysis of the subject matter, and the application of the principles of learning to the structuring and presenting of information. The outcome of instructional design is the instructional design document—the architectural plan for developing the training.

**The nine steps of the instructional design process are**

1. **Gather training requirements:** Determine the purpose of the training, the training outcomes, the training audience, and any project constraints and parameters.]

2. **Perform an instructional analysis on the job outcomes:** Hierarchically analyze the training outcomes to determine the major outcomes, activities, tasks, subtasks, and steps that must be performed to produce those outcomes.

3. **Identify the enabling content**: Hierarchically analyze the information (concepts, facts, procedures, principles, and so forth) that must be understood to perform the activities, tasks, and subtasks identified in the instructional analysis; identify the locations in the instructional analysis where that information must be understood.

4. **Structure the course:** Determine the instructional modules, units, topics, and lessons that will be presented to students and their sequencing.

5. **Write formal objectives:** Write properly composed statements that describe what students will be able to perform or produce after taking an instructional module, unit, topic, or lesson.

6. **Determine the instructional delivery system:** Determine the set of technologies and methods by which you will deliver the training to the students.

7. **Design practice exercises and other instructional events:** Identify the type and number of practice exercises and the other instructional events and activities that are required to bring students' skill and knowledge up to the levels specified in the instructional objectives and determine where to place those instructional events in the course.

8. **Design the prototype or example lesson:** For online training, create the look and feel and navigational elements for the course (if not already defined) and create a working prototype (topic). For instructor-led training, create any required shell or template documents for the presentation materials (such as a slide template) and create an example lesson or topic. For both types of instruction, create a style guide document of design, presentation, and writing standards that will be followed in creating the training materials.

9. **Create the design document:** Create the formal instructional design document or blueprint that details how the training will be structured, developed, and presented; this document includes, among other things, all of the instructional activities that will be included in the training and detailed descriptions of the course content.

## Step 1. Gather Training Requirements

*Training requirements* are the collection of information that instructional designers need to know before beginning the design process, such as

- what the training sponsors want the training to do for their business or organization, including the business performance problem or issue that is to be solved by training;
- project constraints or parameters, such as budget, deadlines, and availability and willingness of subject matter experts to participate;
- who will be taking the training (target audience);
- what they bring with them in knowledge, attitudes, and skills;
- what their work environment, roles, and responsibilities are;
- what they want the training to accomplish for them;
- the tasks and outcomes they will have to perform or produce back on the job that this training is to teach; and
- the feasibility and appropriateness of possible training delivery systems.

**Note:** A *training delivery system* is the method used to deliver the training, such as web-based training, classroom training, self-study workbook, online performance support, online remote synchronous instructor-led training, and so forth.

Engineers charged with building a bridge across a river need to collect and understand certain information before they perform an engineering analysis and create a bridge design, such as

- traffic flow requirements,
- the weight and composition of vehicles that will cross the bridge,
- the span across the river,
- the depth of the water,
- the soil conditions on shore and on the river bottom,
- the bedrock depth, and
- anticipated weather extremes.

Likewise, instructional designers need to know certain critical information *before* they perform an instructional analysis and create their training designs.

## Why Is Requirements Gathering Necessary?

Training designers who design training without first gathering requirements are like doctors who write prescriptions and prescribe treatments without first talking to their patients and gathering the information that is needed to make a correct diagnosis. Such doctors would likely treat the wrong problem—and possibly even nonexistent problems—and thus fail to heal the patient. Ponder these questions:

- Would you pay a doctor to treat you who did not examine you and question you about your illness?
- Would you drive across a bridge over the Mississippi River that had been hastily constructed without any consideration for gathering the engineering information that was needed to ensure a safe bridge design?

Novice trainers often feel pressured to immediately begin development of training materials as soon as they receive a request or a mandate to develop training. Experienced designers know that they cannot just shoot arrows into the fog and hope to hit desirable targets. They know that they cannot design effective training when the target is obscured by ignorance of the answers to fundamental training requirements questions.

**Questions that you should feel comfortable answering before you design your training**

- Do you know the business issues or performance gaps that training is supposed to resolve?
- Do you believe that training is the right solution and will resolve these gaps or issues? What evidence do you have for that conclusion?
- Do you know how your client will be evaluating the success of your training project?
- Do you know who is going to be trained and what their work environment is like?
- Do you know what tasks students must perform and what outcomes students must produce back on the job as a result of training?
- Do you know what skills, knowledge, and attitudes students bring to the training?
- Do you know the parameters and constraints that you must work under as you develop the training?

## How Are Requirements Gathered?

Requirements are gathered by asking specific questions of those who are qualified and authorized to address those questions. Instructional designers schedule and conduct requirements gathering meetings with the client and the client's team. If requirements are gathered by someone other than the instructional designer, as is often suggested, the information gathered may be incomplete and lack the clarity and focus that is needed.

What are some of the skills and values needed to gather requirements?

- a knowledge of the requirements information that *must* be gathered to design effective training
- the ability to ask questions in a nonthreatening way, draw out information, and probe to clarify general or vague information
- the ability to guide the discussion and keep it focused on gathering key information
- the ability to uncover, identify, and specify training outcomes and their detailed activities and tasks *during the call*, based on the information that is provided by the subject matter experts and others

Instructional designers typically use a *requirements gathering template* to guide their requirements gathering sessions. This template lists the detailed questions that should be asked during the requirements gathering interviews. By using a standard template, you will avoid forgetting to ask important questions or forgetting the responses that were made to those questions. More information on requirements gathering will be provided in a later chapter in part 2.

## Step 2. Perform an Instructional Analysis on the Job Outcomes

The next step in instructional design is to perform an instructional analysis on the job outcomes that students are expected to accomplish as a result of the training. Instructional analysis, also known as job/task analysis, is the process by which the job outcomes that were identified during requirements gathering are hierarchically analyzed and broken down into their component parts (suboutcomes, activities, tasks, subtasks, and steps). The result of instructional analysis is a hierarchical diagram or outline that shows the job outcomes at the top of the hierarchy with the successive component layers underneath.

Figure 16 is a conceptual view of an instructional analysis:

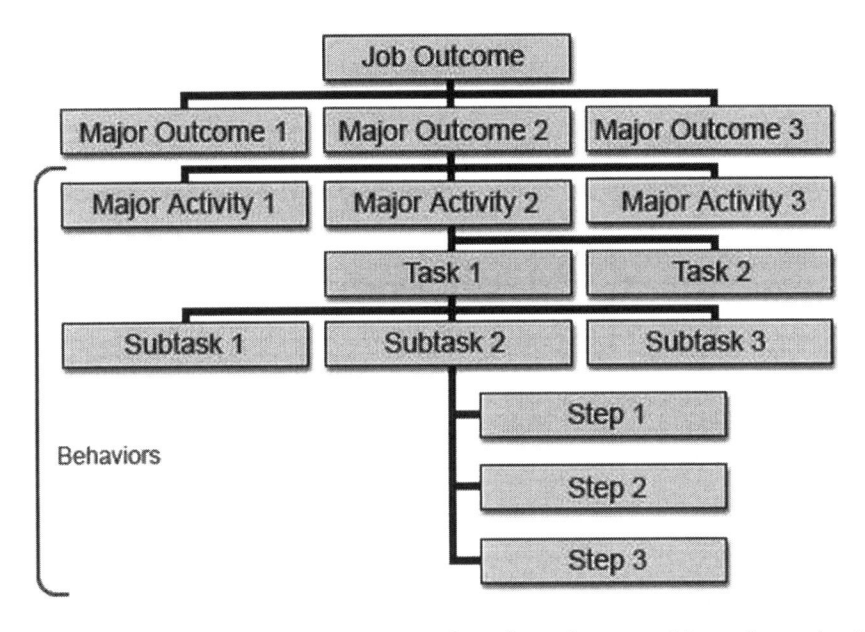

Figure 16. A conceptual example of an instructional analysis

### What to do if your training does not involve the teaching of any tasks or procedures?

If your training is only going to teach nonskill knowledge (such as concepts, processes, principles, facts, and so forth)—that is, your training is not going to teach students how to produce specific job outcomes or work products—then skip this step and continue the instructional design process with step 3. In step 3, you will perform a content analysis to break the conceptual content into its component parts.

## How Is Instructional Analysis Performed?

Instructional designers typically use a tool such as the outline function of a word processor to document and create this hierarchy, although org chart-type structures can be drawn when the overall analysis is not too complex.

The following is a simplified example of an instructional analysis that was created using the outline function of a word processor application.

**Properly parked car in parallel or diagonal parking space**

1. Park the car in a parallel parking space.
   1.1 Park the car in a parallel parking space between two other cars.
      1.1.1 Pull your car alongside the vehicle in front (about two to three feet away) until your front bumpers are even
      1.1.2 Slowly pull backward into the parking space at about a 45-degree angle until your front door is even with the back bumper of the car alongside.
      1.1.3 Turn the wheel sharply in the opposite direction, clear the bumper, and continue moving back until you are just in front of the car behind
      1.1.4 Pull the car forward and straighten the wheel until the car is centered in the parking space
   1.2 Park the car in a parallel parking space that has no other cars immediately in front or back
      1.2.1 Gradually steer the car into the space as you pull forward.
2. Park the car in a diagonal-entry parking space.
   2.1 As your bumper clears the car to the right, turn the wheel to the right
   2.2 Slowly pull in, watching both sides of your car, until you are fully in the space.

The instructional designer creates the hierarchy by working interactively with the SME, asking numerous questions to identify, document, validate, and drill down to successive levels of detail in the hierarchy.

## What To Do if No Subject Matter Experts (SMEs) Are Available

If no SMEs are available—either internal or external to the company or organization—and good study and source material exist that can teach the instructional designer how to perform the task, then the instructional designer can study this material, become a substitute SME for the purpose of developing the training, and perform the analysis solo.

If no SMEs are available but master performers can be observed performing this task in the job environment, then the instructional designer can "shadow" the expert on the job and learn how to perform the task in that manner. The instructional designer would become a substitute SME and perform the instructional analysis solo. The instructional designer would be wise to ask the master performer to validate the final instructional analysis hierarchy and task steps.

If no SMEs or master performers are available and no good source material is available to learn the task, then training might have to be postponed until SMEs become available or be outsourced if the tasks are not proprietary or sensitive in nature. Alternately, depending on the nature of the tasks that you need to teach, generic training courses might already exist and be available on the market that could be of some value to your students.

## Why Is Instructional Analysis Important?

Although instructional analysis is intellectually demanding and can be arduous and time consuming to perform on complex or difficult tasks, it is one of the most important design tasks in the instructional design process. The output of the instructional analysis—the task hierarchy—is the foundation and structure on which all other subsequent design activities are tied, including content analysis, course structuring, course sequencing, and determining instructional objectives.

### Example of how the instructional analysis helps to structure the course

The higher-level entries in the instructional analysis often become the organizing structure for modules and topics. If a job outcome is broken down into Activity A and Activity B, and Activity A has three tasks and Activity B has four, then the course structure would probably include these entries:

Module X: Title for Activity A

Topic 1. Title for task 1

Topic 2. Title for task 2

Topic 3. Title for task 3

Module Y: Title for Activity B

Topic 1. Title for task 1

Topic 2. Title for task 2

Topic 3. Title for task 3

Topic 4. Title for task 4

Instructional analysis tells you what *behaviors* (activities, tasks, subtasks, and steps) are required to produce the new job outcomes or work products. How can you teach someone to produce those outcomes if you do not know the action steps that are required to produce them?

## Step 3: Identify and Analyze the Enabling Content

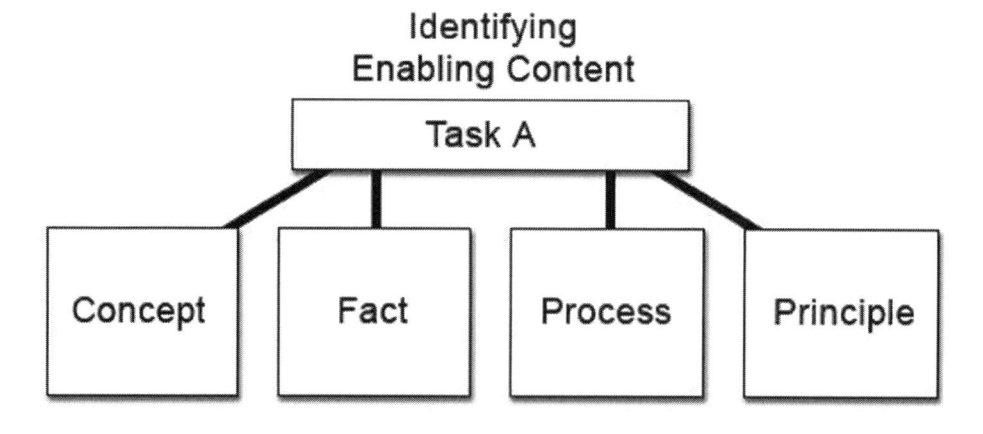

**Figure 17. A conceptual example of identifying enabling content for a task**

Enabling content is the knowledge and subskills students must learn to perform the tasks that produce the job outcomes. For example, the enabling content and enabling skills for "adding page numbers to a document in a word processor" might be "What are page numbers?" "What is a footer?" "What is a page?" "Which menu option contains this function?" "How do I display menus?" and so forth.

Enabling content is systematically identified and analyzed using a procedure called *content analysis*. During content analysis, each low-level step in the instructional analysis is analyzed to determine what students must know or be able to do to complete that step. This information is then added to the hierarchy at the point where it is needed. Color coding the enabling content makes it easy to distinguish it from the procedural content in the instructional analysis. After content analysis is performed, information that students already know when they come to training is deleted from the list of enabling content (you do not need to teach information that students already know).

Here is an example of enabling content that has been imbedded in a portion of an instructional analysis (**Note:** text enclosed in square brackets [ ] is the enabling content):

## Example of enabling content imbedded in a procedure

Use ping with the host name to verify that you can communicate with several of the other hosts on the same network

> Ping returns with "unknown host" response
>
>> Diagnose name resolution problem [Concept: Network name resolution and how it works; file names on local hosts where names are found; Name Servers—what they are and how to tell if they are "up" and functioning]
>>
>>> Verify that the host name is listed in the /etc/hosts file on the local host

Verify that the IP address of the Domain Name server is listed in the /etc/resolv.conf file on the local host

Verify that the Name Server is functioning [If not obtained locally, obtain from the customer]

Ping returns with "Network is unreachable"

Diagnose routing problem [Covered previously under architecture and protocol of networks]

Ask the customer to verify that the IP address and subnet mask of the local host are correct [Covered previously under IP addressing]

Ask the customer to verify that all hosts on the local network are using the same subnet mask [Get subnet masking information from the customer and then individually compare it to the nodes to make sure it is correct using DMIT]

Ask the customer to verify that the default (gateway) router IP address is correct [Get default router IP address information from customer and individually compare it to the nodes to make sure it is correct using DMIT]

If problem is not resolved, call the next level of support

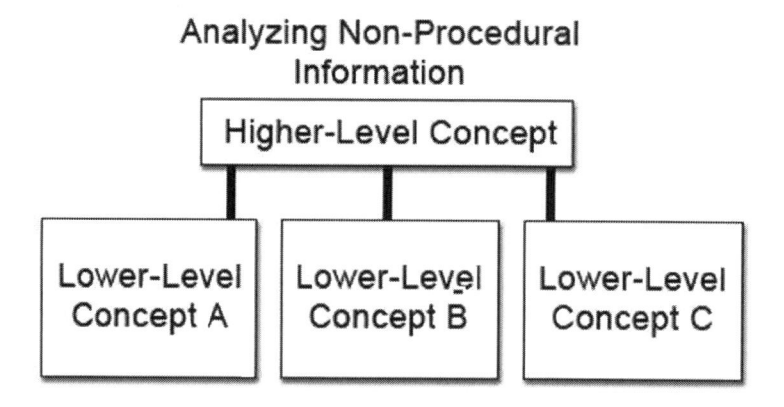

**Figure 18. A conceptual example of identifying enabling content for nonprocedural information**

Sometimes, if a group of related enabling content is large and is required in many places in the instructional analysis, it is useful to pull that enabling content together and teach it upfront in a course module of its own. The content in this situation is analyzed hierarchically to organize and break higher-level information into its lower-level components.

Here is a partial example of how this was done for a network problem determination course (only the top three levels of the analysis are shown).

  Networking concepts
    Definition of a network
      Collection of interconnected hosts that share information
    Network control
      Why network control is necessary
      Types of network control
    Network cabling [How to recognize cable type and connector]
      Why you need to know about network cables
      Types of network cables
    Network topologies
      Network topologies
    ISO model
      The ISO model and how it functions
      Software suites that use the ISO model
    Types of networks
      LANs
      WANs

Due to space limitations, we cannot show the entire analysis. The following outline is the lower-level content analysis for the "Network Control" section of the content analysis displayed above:

  Network control
    Why network control is necessary
    Types of network control
      Hierarchical network (e.g., RTLL, CSAM, BRL/TRU)
        One central host that controls the entire network

      One host (system) within the network controls all the data flow across the network
      Requires adapter cards
    Peer-to-peer network (TCP/IP, BDL, ZAQ201, ZPPN)
      All the hosts in the network are equal (peers to each other) and equally control the network
      No central controlling host required; each peer has its own network control program
      Network control program must be running in each peer
      SS/6000Z SPs are peer-to-peer
      Requires adapter cards
    Net-centric network (e.g., GGL, frame relay)
      Does not require a host
      No network operating system
      Any host can be attached to this type of network
      Requires some kind of box to attach to the network (e.g., 4698, router, etc.)

## Why Is the *Systematic* Identification of Enabling Content Important?

Content analysis is a systematic procedure. Every step of every task is analyzed to determine what the enabling content and subskills are that students must know to perform that step. Then, enabling content that the target audience already knows is deleted from the content analysis. What is left is the body of content that *must* be taught in the course and *nothing more*! No unnecessary information is included. This approach has the following advantages:

- It avoids a free-for-all approach as to what information to include in the course, which invariably leads to bloated courses that teach unnecessary information and consume unnecessary training resources and student seat time.

- The instructional analysis and content analysis together provide an *objective method* for determining what content should be included and not included in the course. This makes it easy to resolve disputes among SMEs who might each *feel* that they know what should be taught.

- Because the analysis is *systematically* conducted (*every* task and step is analyzed), no critical enabling content is left out. A nonsystematic approach runs a high risk of overlooking important enabling content. This creates stumbling blocks to learning.
- It identifies the typical location *where* the enabling content should be taught in the flow and structure of the course.
- Enabling information common to many tasks can be easily identified and logically presented upfront in a separate instructional module in the course.

## Step 4: Structure the Course

Structuring the course is determining the makeup and sequence of the instructional modules, units, topics, and lessons along with their associated exercises, tests, and other instructional activities. Online courses are typically structured into modules and topics; instructor-led courses are typically structured into units and lessons.

The highest two or three levels of the combined instructional and content analysis usually become the modules and topic titles or the unit and lesson titles. This is another major benefit of performing instructional and content analysis. There is a natural mapping from the output of the final analysis to the structure and content of the course, as shown in figure 19:

**Instructional analysis + Content analysis → Course structure**

Outcome: Car properly parked in parallel or diagonal parking space

1. Park the car in a parallel parking space.
   - 1.1 Park the car in a parallel parking space between two other cars.
     - 1.1.1 Pull your car alongside the vehicle in front (about two to three feet away) until the bumpers are even.
     - 1.1.2 Slowly pull backward into the parking space at about a 45-degree angle until your front door is even with the back bumper of the car alongside.
     - 1.1.3 Turn the wheel sharply in the opposite direction, clear the bumper, and continue moving back until you are just in front of the car behind.
     - 1.1.4 Pull the car forward and straighten the wheel until the car is centered in the parking space.
   - 1.2 Park the car in a parallel parking space that has no other cars immediately in front or back
     - 1.2.1 Gradually steer the car into the space as you pull forward.
2. Park the car in a diagonal-entry parking space.
   - 2.1 As your bumper clears the car to the right, turn the wheel to the right.
   - 2.2 Slowly pull in, watching both sides of your car, until you are fully in the space

Course 4218: How to Park a Car

Unit 1. Types of parking spaces
  Topic 1. Parallel parking spaces
  Topic 2. Diagonal parking spaces
Unit 2. Parallel parking between two cars
  Topic 1. Pulling up alongside the car ahead
  Topic 2. Angling the car into the space
  Topic 3. Positioning the car in the space
Unit 3. Parallel parking a car with no cars around
  Topic 1. Steering the car into a parallel space
Unit 4. Diagonal parking a car
  Topic 1. Positioning the car alongside the car behind
  Topic 2. Steering the car into the diagonal space

**Figure 19. A conceptual example of structuring a course**

Sometimes there is not enough content for each high-level entry in the analysis to become its own unit or topic. In that case, use judgment to group entries that have the same parent and are at the same level together into the same unit or topic until you have sufficient content.

Figure 20 shows how two entries in the instructional analysis hierarchy were combined into one topic in the course structure:

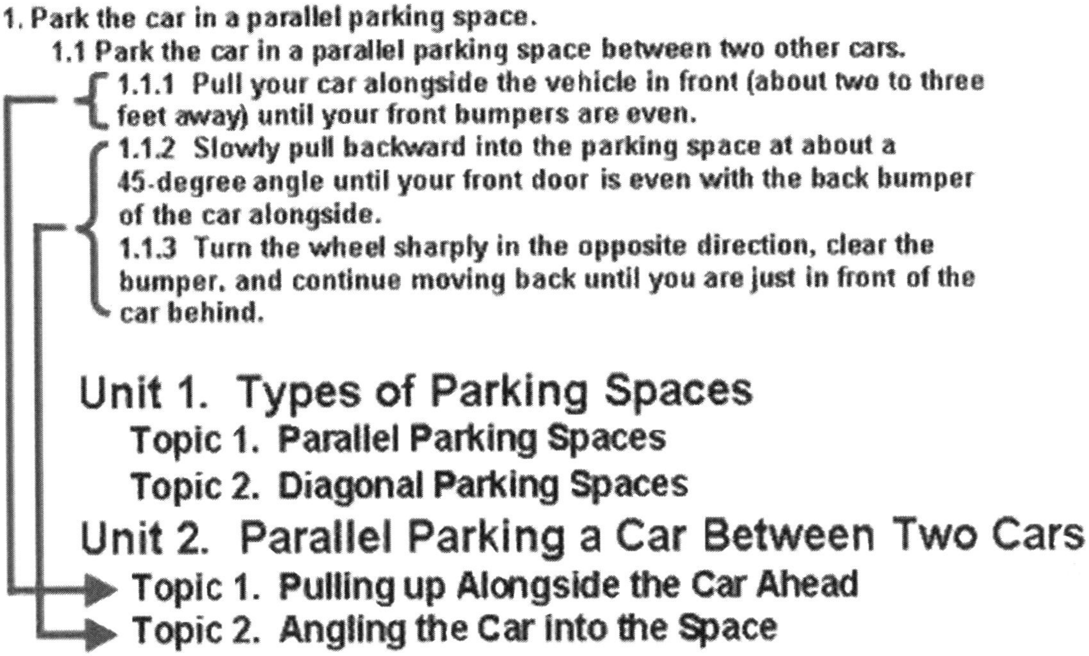

1. Park the car in a parallel parking space.
   1.1 Park the car in a parallel parking space between two other cars.
      1.1.1 Pull your car alongside the vehicle in front (about two to three feet away) until your front bumpers are even.
      1.1.2 Slowly pull backward into the parking space at about a 45-degree angle until your front door is even with the back bumper of the car alongside.
      1.1.3 Turn the wheel sharply in the opposite direction, clear the bumper, and continue moving back until you are just in front of the car behind.

## Unit 1. Types of Parking Spaces
   Topic 1. Parallel Parking Spaces
   Topic 2. Diagonal Parking Spaces

## Unit 2. Parallel Parking a Car Between Two Cars
   Topic 1. Pulling up Alongside the Car Ahead
   Topic 2. Angling the Car into the Space

**Figure 20. Example showing how a course structure is derived from the instructional analysis**

## Why Is Structuring the Course Based on the Instructional and Content Analyses Important?

When a course is structured to reflect the highest level entries in the instructional and content analyses, the course outline will automatically reflect the major activities and tasks required to produce the new job outcomes. Why? Because an instructional analysis, by definition, determines what those major activities and tasks are.

Structuring a course in this manner has the following benefits:

- The course structure (course outline) that is presented to students reflects the major activities and tasks that students will have to perform back on the job to produce the new job outcomes. Thus, students will see the relevance of the course and its content just by reviewing the course structure alone. Perception of relevance is essential for getting and maintaining motivation.

- Students will see that the course is structured to facilitate transfer back to the job. They will see that the course is not just a collection of loosely related or quickly thrown together conceptual information with bits and pieces of procedures that leave it to students to figure out how to apply the information back on the job to create real work products. Rather, they will see that the course structures and presents information in the way that tells them exactly *how* to perform the new tasks back on the job.

## Step 5: Write Formal Instructional Objectives

Objectives are structured statements of what students should be able to do as a result of taking the training. Complete objectives describe the behavior to be exhibited, any tools or conditions for performing the action, and the criteria for evaluating the behavior. Often, the criterion is assumed to be "perform the task successfully and accurately" and is not stated in the objective. The following is an example of two instructional objectives:

After completing this unit, you should be able to

- describe from memory the steps of the procedure for performing an audience analysis, and
- perform an audience analysis using a requirements template.

### The three important uses of instructional objectives

Instructional objectives are used

- by instructional developers who design and write detailed content presentations to design presentations and keep content properly focused,
- to communicate to the sponsors of the training what the training outcomes will be, and
- to communicate to students at the time of training what they will be expected to do as a result of the training.

Objectives are usually written for each major structuring division in a course, including the course level, the module (or unit) level, and the topic (or lesson) level.

## Why Didn't We Write Objectives Earlier in the Process?

Well-intentioned educators might insist that objectives should be determined upfront in the design process before anything else and that objectives drive all other design activities. The truth is that you do not know what the major activities, tasks, subtasks, steps, and enabling content are until *after* you have performed an instructional and content analysis.

If you write objectives without knowing the tasks and content that students must know as *objectively* determined by instructional and content analyses, then you are writing objectives for content that you or others *guess* or *feel* should be included in the course. All of the problems associated with the ad hoc method of instructional design follow (these were we previously discussed in this chapter).

Moreover, objectives are usually written for each module or topic in the course, and the course structure is based on the instructional and content analyses.

On the other hand, after performing instructional and content analysis, you know every required task and every piece of required enabling content. At that point, it is an easy matter to write appropriate objectives for each of the tasks and enabling content. And by waiting until the course has been structured, objectives can be written for each instructional module and topic in the course where they logically belong.

## Step 6: Determine the Instructional Delivery System

After you have performed instructional and content analyses, structured the course, and written the instructional objectives, you are ready to determine the instructional delivery system.

An instructional delivery system is the set of technologies and communication methods by which the training is delivered to and taken by the students.

**Examples of instructional delivery systems**

- classroom delivery by an instructor
- satellite delivery to a learning center
- web-based training
- Web Lectures (narrated PowerPoint presentations) delivered over the Internet
- computer-based training (CBT) distributed physically on computer disk or media
- web conference delivered over the Internet
- online wizards, coaches, help, and electronic performance support systems (EPSS)
- computer, machine, and staged simulations
- hardcopy self-study workbooks, reference materials, and job aids
- mentoring and on-the-job training
- collaborative online classroom environments
- virtual online worlds

A *blended learning solution* is a training delivery system in which more than one training method or technology is used to deliver the training. Typically, at least one of the delivery methods is technology based. Different parts of the training or curriculum are delivered using different technologies or delivery methods. For example, you might create a training program in which students first listen to a Web Lecture, then take an interactive web course, then attend a live instructor-led workshop.

Determining an instructional delivery system is not a mechanical process. Many different factors must be weighed and taken into consideration before making a final decision.

# Step 7: Design Practice Exercises and Other Instructional Events

Training is not training unless it provides practice with feedback and other instructional events. *Practice with feedback* consists of exercises and test questions that practice the skills and subskills specified in the instructional objectives. *Instructional events* are learning strategies and activities that are built into the training that are specifically designed to facilitate and promote learning.

## Examples of instructional events and activities

- presenting information that was designed and developed using sound instructional design principles and techniques
- answering questions
- performing individual exercises
- solving problems
- taking quizzes and exams
- participating in group discussions and exercises
- interacting within a case study on a computer
- using tools or new equipment
- role-playing with fellow students
- watching a video
- viewing an animation or Flash sequence
- playing an instructional game
- watching demonstrations
- observing expert performers
- going through an online simulation
- teaching others
- completing a mentorship
- making presentations

- writing a paper
- performing real work (usually, in a protected, "safe" environment)
- interacting with a virtual world

This step in the instructional design process consists of three activities:

- identify *where* instructional events are needed in the course
- determine *what* each event will be (its type, such as an exercise or quiz)
- *design* (write specifications for) the instructional event

In practice, this consists of systematically reviewing each instructional segment (subtopic, topic, module, and course) in light of a specific set of guidelines (that we will provide) to determine where instructional events should occur and what they should be. These events are then documented in the course structure document and later in the formal instructional design document.

## Step 8: Design and Create the Prototype or Example Lesson

Now that the course content is defined, the course structure determined, the delivery system chosen, and the practice exercises and other instructional events designed, the next step in instructional design is to design a proof-of-concept—an example topic or lesson. The general steps for designing and creating a proof-of-concept are slightly different, depending on the type of delivery system that you have chosen.

For an online or technology-based training delivery system

- design the user interface (look-and-feel and navigational elements) for the training delivery system,
- create a style guide of standards to be used in creating content,

- build a working prototype with real or dummy content for a unit or topic,
- test the prototype with users from the target audience and solicit feedback, and
- present the prototype to sponsors for approval.

For a non-technology-based training delivery system

- design the standard elements that will appear in a unit or lesson,
- create a style guide of standards to be used in creating content,
- create any templates that are required (such as for slides to be shown in a classroom environment),
- create an example unit or lesson using the templates and following the style-guide standards,
- test the prototype with users from the target audience and solicit feedback, and
- present the prototype to sponsors for approval.

## Step 9: Create the Design Document

An instructional design document is a formal blueprint for the training. Just as the blueprints for a building tell the construction engineers and tradesmen exactly what to build and how to build it, the instructional design document details and communicates to the instructional developers exactly what should be developed and how it should be packaged. It also defines the structure of the course and the appearance (look and feel) of the training from the student's point of view. Finally, it shows the sponsors exactly what the training will accomplish and what deliverables will be created.

**Typical entries in a design document**

- executive summary
- sign-off page
- overall business goal
- justification for training
- job outcomes targeted for training
- target audience
- course prerequisites and curriculum fit
- overall course description (including delivery mechanism)
- technology requirements
- course objectives
- course structure (units, lessons, topics)
- course agenda
- prototype, look-and-feel, or example lesson
- course style guide or development specifications
- unit, lesson, and exercise descriptions, objectives, and specifications
- evaluation and assessment procedures and criteria

The instructional design document should be concise and to the point. Its purpose is not to impress others with the depth of knowledge possessed by the designer. Rather, it should be a concise blueprint for the development of training.

# Chapter Summary—
# Overview of How to Design Training

This chapter presented an overview of the instructional design process. It described the major activities involved in designing training, including gathering requirements, performing instructional and content analyses, structuring the course, specifying objectives, choosing an instructional delivery system, designing practice exercises and other instructional events, designing a prototype lesson or topic, and creating the design document.

You should now be able to

- give a high-level overview of the instructional design process,
- define each of the nine major steps for designing effective instruction
    1. Gather training requirements,
    2. Perform an instructional analysis on the job outcomes,
    3. Identify the enabling content,
    4. Structure the course,
    5. Write formal objectives,
    6. Determine the instructional delivery system,
    7. Design practice exercises and other instructional events,
    8. Design and create the prototype or example lesson,
    9. Create the design document, and
- for each step in the process, state the purpose of that step, describe at a high level how it is carried out, and explain why that step is important.

**Check Your Understanding**

1.  **Match each of the nine steps of the instructional design process with its correct step description.**

    | Step 1 | A. Structure the course |
    |---|---|
    | Step 2 | B. Create the design document |
    | Step 3 | C. Perform an instructional analysis on the job outcomes |
    | Step 4 | D. Design the prototype or example lesson |
    | Step 5 | E. Gather requirements |
    | Step 6 | F. Identify the enabling content |
    | Step 7 | G. Write formal objectives |
    | Step 8 | H. Determine the instructional delivery system |
    | Step 9 | I. Design practice exercises and other instructional events |

2.  **True or false? The ad hoc method of instructional design is a disciplined, systematic approach that involves an understanding of the training needs and audience, a careful analysis of the subject matter, and the application of the principles of learning to the structuring and presenting of information.**

3.  **True or false? Training requirements is the collection of information that instructional designers need to know *before* beginning the training design process.**

4.  **What is the *best* way to gather requirements?**
    A. Send out a questionnaire containing requirements gathering questions to the client and ask that they return them to you with their completed answers.
    B. Get a group of subject matter experts (SMEs) together in a meeting and ask them to tell you what needs to be in the training.

C. Present what you think should be in the training to a group of subject matter experts (SMEs) and get their feedback.

D. Schedule a requirements gathering session with the client and appropriate subject matter experts (SMEs), ask specific questions during the meeting as prompted by the requirements gathering template, ask follow-up questions to probe for more information, and record your answers in the template.

E. Randomly call up workers on the telephone who belong to the target audience and conduct phone interviews.

5. _____ (also known as job/task analysis) is the process by which the job outcomes that were identified during requirements gathering are hierarchically analyzed and broken down into their component parts (suboutcomes, activities, tasks, subtasks, and steps).

6. **What is the correct top-down hierarchy of levels of an instructional analysis?**
   A. Job outcome, major activity, major outcome, major task, step, subtask
   B. Job outcome, major task, major activity, major outcome, subtask, step
   C. Job outcome, major outcome, major activity, major task, subtask, step
   D. Major outcome, job outcome, major activity, major task, subtask, step
   E. Major activity, job outcome, major outcome, major task, subtask, step
   F. Major task, job outcome, major activity, major outcome, subtask, step

7. **What should you do if your training does not involve the teaching of any tasks or procedures?**
   A. Gather more training requirements information, as training always involves the teaching of at least one task or procedure.
   B. Ask the subject matter experts how they apply the information back on the job.
   C. Write instructional objectives and go on from there with the instructional design process.

*Creating Outstanding Instructional Designs*   147

D. Combine the training with related training that does include the teaching of tasks or procedures.

E. Skip instructional analysis and go on to content analysis.

8. **Which of the following actions should be considered if no subject matter experts are readily available for you to perform the instructional analysis? (Select all that apply.)**

   A. If good source material exists that can teach you how to perform the task, then you could study this material, become a substitute SME for the purpose of developing the training, and perform the analysis solo.

   B. If master performers are available who could be observed performing the task in the job environment, you could "shadow" the expert on the job and learn how to perform the task in that manner.

   C. If no source material is available to learn the task and no master performers are available to be shadowed, then you might have to postpone training until SMEs become available or outsource the training if the tasks are not proprietary or sensitive in nature.

   D. If the tasks that you need to teach are generic in nature, you might be able to find existing training courses for purchase that would be of value.

9. **Instructional analysis tells you what \_\_\_\_ are required to produce the new job outcomes or work products.**

10. **\_\_\_\_ \_\_\_\_ is the knowledge and subskills students must learn to perform the tasks that produce the job outcomes and is systematically identified using a procedure called \_\_\_\_ \_\_\_\_.**

11. **True or false? During content analysis, each low-level step or task in the instructional analysis is analyzed to determine what students must know or be able to do to complete that step or task.**

148  *Instructional Design — Step by Step*

12. **True or false? After content analysis is performed, information that students already know when they come to training is added to the list of enabling content.**

13. **After making your first pass through a content analysis, what should be done if you have a group of related enabling content that is large and is required in many places in the instructional analysis?**
    A. Pull that enabling content together and teach it upfront in a course module of its own.
    B. Repeat the teaching of the enabling content at each place that it is required.
    C. Teach enabling content only where it is first required.
    D. Teach the procedures first, then the enabling content.
    E. Make the enabling content a prerequisite for taking this course.

14. **Why is the *systematic* identification of enabling content important? (Select all that apply.)**
    A. It avoids a free-for-all approach as to what information to include in the course, which invariably leads to bloated courses that teach unnecessary information and consume unnecessary training resources and student seat time.
    B. The instructional analysis and content analysis together provide an *objective method* for determining what content should be included and not included in the course. This makes it easy to resolve disputes among SMEs who might each *feel* that they know what should be taught.
    C. When the content analysis is *systematically* conducted (*every* task and step is analyzed), no critical enabling content is left out. A nonsystematic approach runs a high risk of overlooking important enabling content. This creates stumbling blocks to learning.
    D. It gives the course designer a wide choice of topics to include or not include in the course.

E. It identifies the typical location *where* the enabling content should be taught in the flow and structure of the course.

F. Enabling information common to many tasks can be easily identified and logically presented upfront in a separate instructional module in the course.

15. \_\_\_\_ **the course is determining the makeup and sequence of the instructional modules, units, topics, and lessons along with their associated exercises, tests, and other instructional activities.**

16. **True or false? The highest two or three levels of the combined instructional and content analysis usually become the modules and topic titles or the unit and lesson titles.**

17. **What should you do if there is not enough content for each high-level entry in the analysis to become its own unit or topic?**

    A. Accept the fact that some units and topics will be very brief.

    B. Group entries without regard to their location in the hierarchy together into the same unit or topic until you have sufficient content.

    C. Group entries that have different parents together into the same unit or topic until you have sufficient content.

    D. Group entries that have the same parent and are at the same level together into the same unit or topic until you have sufficient content.

    E. Ask the subject matter expert what content to include in a unit or topic.

18. **Why is structuring the course based on the instructional and content analyses important? (Select all that apply.)**

    A. The course outline will reflect the tasks that students will have to perform back on the job to produce the new job outcomes. Thus, students will see the *relevance* of the course and its content just by reviewing the course structure alone.

B. It reflects what the subject matter experts agree is the best way to structure the course.

C. The prototype or example lesson that is developed next can be created in no other way.

D. Students will see that the course presents information in the way that tells them *how* to perform the new tasks back on the job.

19. **True or false? The three main elements of instructional objectives are the behavior to be exhibited, the audience, and the criteria for evaluating the action.**

20. **Who uses instructional objectives? (Select all that apply.)**
    A. Instructional developers, to design and write detailed content
    B. Computer authoring application technical experts, to know how to program the delivery of the course
    C. The sponsors of the training, to learn what the training deliverables and outcomes will be and what the training will look like
    D. Students, to know what they will be expected to do as a result of the training

21. **Why aren't objectives written upfront, before any instructional analysis is performed? (Select all that apply.)**
    A. Because the objectives aren't needed until the course prototype or example lesson is created.
    B. Writing objectives for content that has not been *objectively* determined by instructional and content analyses is nothing more than writing objectives for content that you or others *guess* or *feel* should be included in the course. All of the problems associated with the ad hoc method of instructional design would follow.

C. Objectives are usually written for each module or topic in the course, and the course structure is based on the instructional and content analyses.

D. You do not know what the major activities, tasks, subtasks, steps, and enabling content are until *after* you have performed an instructional and content analysis.

22. **True or false? An instructional delivery system is the set of teaching strategies employed by a live instructor or by the training materials to teach the content of a course.**

23. **True or false? Designing practice exercises and other instructional events consists of (1) identifying *where* instructional events are needed in the course, (2) determining *what* each event will be, and (3) *designing* (writing specifications for) the instructional event.**

24. **To create a working prototype for technology-based training, such as a web-based training course, the instructional designer must design or define which of the following? (Select all that apply.)**

    A. The slides that will be presented by an instructor in front of a classroom

    B. The look-and-feel of the user interface

    C. The navigational buttons and functions

    D. A style guide containing the layout and writing standards that should be followed

25. **True or false? An instructional design document performs the same basic purpose as an architectural blueprint in the construction industry.**

**Answers**

1. E, C, F, A, G, H, I, D, and B
2. False. This is a definition of the systematic design of instruction.
3. True
4. D
5. The correct answer is "Instructional analysis."
6. C
7. E
8. A, B, C, and D
9. The correct answer is "behaviors."
10. The correct answer is "Enabling content" and "content analysis."
11. True
12. False. After content analysis is performed, information that students already know when they come to training is deleted from the list of enabling content.
13. A
14. A, B, C, E, and F
15. The correct answer is "Structuring."
16. True
17. D
18. A and D
19. False. The three main elements of instructional objectives are the behavior to be exhibited, any tools or conditions for performing the action, and the criteria for evaluating the behavior.
20. A, C, and D
21. B, C, and D

*Creating Outstanding Instructional Designs*

22. False. An instructional delivery system is the set of technologies and communication methods by which the training is delivered to and taken by the students.
23. True
24. B, C, and D
25. True

# CHAPTER 7
# Gathering Requirements

This chapter presents information on how to gather training requirements, the first step in the instructional design process.

## Where We Are at in the Instructional Design Process

This chapter discusses step 1 in the instructional design process: Gather requirements.

1. **Gather requirements**
2. Perform an instructional analysis on the job outcomes
3. Identify the enabling content
4. Structure the course
5. Write instructional objectives
6. Determine the instructional delivery system
7. Design practice exercises and other instructional events

8. Design the prototype or example lesson
9. Create the formal design document

**Overview of How to Gather Requirements**

As discussed in the last chapter, information designers need training requirements upfront to proceed with design; these requirements are typically gathered through interviews with the client and with the client's stakeholders and subject matter experts. The purpose of gathering requirements is to clearly identify the target for the training—what the outcomes will be and who will be expected to produce those outcomes.

Gathering requirements is a six-step process:

1. Clarify the training request.
2. Determine and validate the business problem to be solved by training.
3. Identify, categorize, and describe the target audience.
4. Identify and begin analysis of the job outcomes to be produced by students back on the job.
5. Determine training delivery system constraints and possibilities.
6. Gather general project-related information.

We will look at each of these steps in the rest of this chapter.

**Step 1: Clarify the Training Request**

The first step in gathering requirements is to clarify the training request—that is, to understand who is making the request, why they are making the request, and what their role is within the organization. This gives you a clear understanding of who the sponsors are, what has been requested, and why it is being requested. To clarify the training request, ask the following questions:

- What exactly is the request?
- Who made it and what is their title and role?
- Why did they request it (what prompted it)?
- Who are the other stakeholders?
- What are their deadlines?
- How will they be evaluated on this project?
- What is the political environment?
- What is their organizational and authority structure?

## Step 2: Determine and Validate the Business Problem to Be Solved by Training

Training is created for a purpose—to solve business or organization problems and needs. In step 2, you identify the specific business or organization problems that training is expected to solve within the context of the organization's overall business goals. You also determine how the sponsor will know when the problem has been corrected or the business need has been fulfilled. State these findings in business terms, not educational terms.

One of the first things that you should determine from the answers to these questions is if training is intended to close an identified business gap or deficiency, or whether it is intended to meet a new, future, anticipated need. The answer to this question determines the next set of questions you should ask.

### Questions to ask if training is intended to close a business gap or deficiency

- What are job incumbents not producing or accomplishing that motivated the request for training?
- What should job incumbents be producing or accomplishing that they are currently not producing?
- What worth do those accomplishments have to the business?
- What will happen if those accomplishments are not achieved?

**Questions to ask if training is intended to meet a new, upcoming or future need**

- What will job incumbents be required to produce or accomplish?
- Why are those accomplishments important and worthwhile to the business?
- What will happen if those accomplishments are not achieved?

**Validate That Training Will Solve the Business Problem or Need**

For training intended to close business gaps or deficiencies, it is not enough to clearly identify the employee performance gap or deficiency that the sponsor wants to solve. You must perform additional detective work to determine if training is the right solution and will indeed close the performance gap.

Training is often the first suggestion that managers and executives make when they feel a performance-related organizational pain point. If employees are not meeting expectations, it must be because they lack knowledge or skills they need to perform their jobs. However, experts in human performance, such as Robert F. Mager and Thomas F. Gilbert, have identified many possible reasons why workers might not be performing to expectations.

**Other reasons why a performance gap or issue might exist**

- Unclear expectations.
- Inadequate resources.
- Quality of performance is not visible (no feedback).
- Desired performance is punishing.
- Poor performance is rewarding.
- Could do it in the past but have forgotten.
- There are obstacles in the way of performance.

So how can you make the determination if training is the right solution? The answer is by conducting a *performance analysis* on the problem or performance gap.

---

The classic and easy-to-read book on analyzing performance problems is *Analyzing Performance Problems, or You Really Oughta Wanna*, 3rd edition, Robert F. Mager and Peter Pipe, The Center for Effective Performance, Atlanta, Georgia, 1997. It is available from http://www.cepworldwide.com.

---

## Clarifying Fuzzy Business and Training Goals

Sponsors do not always state their business problems and training goals in precise terms. In fact, their requests are often "fuzzy" or broadly stated, meaning their goals do not adequately describe the precise behaviors they want their employees to perform. Consider the following examples of fuzzy goals:

- "Employees need to be more customer-oriented."
- "Employees need to know how to use the application."
- "Our salespeople need to be motivated to embrace our new methodology."

These goals are too broad to be useful in designing training.

How can you recognize fuzzy goals? According to Mager, ask yourself: "Is there a single behavior or class of behaviors that will indicate the presence of the alleged performance, about which there would be general agreement." If the answer is yes, you have a well-defined goal; if the answer is no, then you have a fuzzy goal that needs further analysis. Another way of asking this question is, "How will I know one when I see one?"

Goal analysis is the technique that is used to analyze fuzzy goals into well-defined goals.

---

The classic and easy-to-read book on goal analysis is *Goal Analysis: How to Clarify Your Goals so You Can Actually Achieve Them,* 3rd Edition, Robert F. Mager, The Center for Effective Performance, Atlanta, Georgia, 1997. It is available from http://www.cepworldwide.com.

---

## Step 3: Identify, Categorize, and Describe the Target Audience

The next step in gathering requirements is to identify the target audience—the people who are going to be trained. Knowing your audience will help you create audience-appropriate instructional stimuli and will be useful in making later design decisions such as

- the type of training delivery system to use (live classroom, virtual classroom, the web, and so forth),
- what enabling skills and knowledge students already possess when they come to training (these don't need to be taught as part of the training),
- how much time students can devote to training and when they can take the training (during work hours or after hours),
- how to motivate students during training,
- age-related considerations that can have implications on type size and other issues, and
- job aids (online help, "cheat sheets," or printed summary sheets) that could be feasibly used in students' job environments.

### Questions you should ask about the audience

- Who is the audience for this training?
- What are the major subgroups of the audience?
- How many are internal and external to the organization or company?
- How many people are in each group?
- What relevant skills, knowledge, and attitudes do they already have?
- What relevant experience do they have?
- What are their learning styles and preferences?
- How have they traditionally been trained?
- What motivates them and turns them off?
- How are they evaluated?
- What is their experience and comfort level with technology and online training?
- Where are they located and how are they distributed?
- What are their job titles, major job duties, and responsibilities?
- What is their job environment like (including their physical environment, time constraints, expected throughput, and so forth)?
- What relevant tools do they have to do their job?
- What are their relevant demographics?

### Step 4: Identify and Begin Analysis of the Job Outcomes to be Produced by Students Back on the Job

*Job outcomes* are outputs, such as work products, decisions, plans, and other specific accomplishments, that are produced on the job and are valued by the business or organization. In step 4 of requirements gathering, you identify the job outcomes that students need to produce back on the job that they are currently not producing or that they will need to produce. During requirements gathering, job outcomes are identified and analyzed into their highest-level components (major outcomes or major activities).

Job outcomes, or simply *outcomes* for short, are nouns or noun phrases, not verbs. They are the *outputs* or *results* of behavior, *not* the behaviors that produce the outputs. To identify job outcomes during requirements gathering, ask the client team to visualize what students will finally produce back on the job that is of value to the organization that they are not currently producing or will need to produce in the near future. At this point, do not focus on what students will do to produce those outcomes. That will come later. Your goal in this step is to clearly and precisely identify and document the specific outcomes.

Because this step is somewhat tricky to master, we will discuss how to craft properly written job outcomes in detail in this chapter. First, though, you need to understand why we are identifying outcomes instead of skills.

## Why Does Instructional Analysis Begin with Job Outcomes Instead of Skills?

Some educators believe that training design should begin with the identification of the skills and knowledge that employees need to master. Why, then, are we identifying job outcomes instead? This is a very important question, and you should feel comfortable answering it and defending this position.

- When you think about it, companies and organizations do not pay employees simply to sit around being *capable* of achieving and producing valued outcomes, even if those employees possess great knowledge and skills. They pay employees because of what they *produce* or *accomplish* on the job that has value to their organization.

- Behaviors are the stepping-stones that produce outcomes. Only by (1) identifying the outcomes and (2) drilling down in the instructional analysis to determine the behaviors (tasks and steps) that are required to produce those outcomes will you ensure that your training will not just teach isolated knowledge and skills, but the very behaviors that will produce job outcomes that address the organization's pain points and performance needs.

- Outcomes are what is truly valued by a business or organization—not capability. Your focus must therefore be on identifying the desired outcomes that are lacking or needed. Only then will you be ready to perform an instructional analysis on those outcomes to determine the specific behaviors (actions) that are required to produce those outcomes. Similarly, only after you perform the instructional analysis will you be ready to perform a content analysis to determine the specific subskills and knowledge that students must possess to perform those behaviors.

- Looking at it another way, how would you know what knowledge and skills to teach unless you first know the outcomes? It is only by identifying and analyzing the *outcomes* using instructional and content analysis that you determine the specific skills and knowledge that should be taught. Any other course of action would simply be an educated guess as to what skills and knowledge to include in the course.

- Suppose, however, that you do start your analysis with skills and knowledge. Even if you assume that you have correctly identified the right skills and knowledge to teach, how will your students know how to *apply* it back on the job to produce valued outcomes? They would be left on their own to generalize and transfer their knowledge from the training to the job environment. Research has shown that students are not very successful in doing this if they have not been taught the specific behaviors that they will have to perform back on the job.

## Characteristics of Job Outcomes

Job outcomes are stated as nouns and noun phrases. Noun phrases are nouns with modifiers before or after the noun.

Examples of noun job outcomes

- contract
- report
- presentation
- widget
- sales

- profits
- solution
- decision

Examples of noun phrase job outcomes

- painted house
- accessible web page
- running network after a crash
- findings from analysis
- widget after quality check (or quality-checked widget)
- decision on sales approach
- instructional designers who can produce good instructional designs
- servers in optimum operating condition 24 x 7
- copier in operating order

## What Job Outcomes Are Not

Novices at identifying job outcomes often confuse job outcomes with subject matter statements and behavior or skill statements. Remember, outcomes are nouns or noun phrases, not verbs or subject matter statements.

### Examples of subject matter statements that are *not* job outcomes

- principles of selling
- fundamental concepts of electricity
- TCP/IP Protocol
- types of insurance

**Examples of behavior or skill that are *not* job outcomes**

- sell more widgets
- fix a broken television
- write accessible computer user interfaces
- prepare for sales call
- resolve customer complaints
- give employee feedback
- determine who should be promoted

Novices also confuse job outcomes (noun and noun phrases) with past-tense verb phrases. Although the differences can be subtle, it is important to distinguish the two. Past-tense verb phrases should be avoided.

The following table shows how past-tense verb phrases can be rewritten as job outcomes (noun or noun phrases):

| Past-tense verb phrase | Phrase rewritten as a job outcome (noun or noun phrase) |
| --- | --- |
| "Employees properly managed" | "Productive employees who comply with all business guidelines and policies" |
| "Hardware fixed" | "Running hardware after problem" |
| "Widgets sold" | "Widget sales" |
| "Software bug fix applied" | "Software with bug fix applied," or "Updated software" |
| "Defects recorded" | "Completed quality record with defects recorded" |

## How to Determine if a Statement Is a Job Outcome

Apply the following tests to a statement to determine if it is a job outcome:

- If the first word is a verb (or a word used as a verb), then it is probably not a job outcome.

- If the first word is a noun or noun phrase, then it might be a job outcome.

- Ask yourself, "Does this statement describe a resultant state or condition, or does it describe activities or tasks that are to be performed?" If the statement describes a state or condition and it is not a past-tense verb phrase, then it is an outcome.

- Be sure to read and analyze the *entire* phrase, not just part of it.

## Types of Job Outcomes

Joe Harless, one of the founding fathers of human performance improvement who engineered extensive and well-thought-out methods for analyzing and improving human performance, identified three types of job outcomes, or *accomplishments* (as Harless likes to call them): normal, off-normal, and emergency. Do not forget to consider all three types of outcomes when you are identifying job outcomes.

The following table defines each of the three types of job outcomes and gives examples of each:

**Types of Job Outcomes (Accomplishments)**

|  | **Normal** | **Off-Normal** | **Emergency** |
|---|---|---|---|
| **Definition** | Produced routinely on the job. | Not produced on a predictable basis, but still part of the job. | • For situations that have severe consequences<br><br>• These accomplishments must be produced very quickly to restore status to normal or to minimize the effects. |
| **Examples** | • Sales reports<br>• Widgets that meet specifications<br>• Rated employees<br>• Presentations at major industry conferences<br>• Decision to invest or not invest | • Working part after identified defect<br>• Counseled employee after business code violation<br>• Car with mounted spare tire after a flat | • Strategy to protect assets after stock market crash<br>• Defibrillated employee after heart attack<br>• Restored and protected network after hacker intrusion |

## Incorporating Standards in Job Outcomes

In the workplace, it might not be acceptable for an employee simply to produce widgets, reports, or other work outcomes. Employers typically want employees to produce widgets, reports, and work outcomes that meet specified quality and performance standards. Therefore, in identifying and writing job outcomes, you should include any required standards in the outcome statement or document the standards in a footnote.

The following table explains the types of standards that can be incorporated in job outcome statements:

**Incorporating Standards in Job Outcome Statements**

| Type of Standard | Examples |
| --- | --- |
| **Accuracy** | - Widget ready to be shipped with no defects<br>- Sales call with all five sales points made<br>- Manufactured widget within proper tolerances |
| **Time** | - Manager with report in possession before project deadline<br>- Trained employees before new system deployment<br>- Successfully completed customer service call within target call duration |
| **Productivity** | - Five orders by end-of-day<br>- Twenty or more completed calls per shift<br>- Two completed topic scripts per week |
| **Safety** | - Completed lab procedure with no safety violations<br>- Factory with no OSHA safety violations in the last six months<br>- Secured computers with log on passwords |

## Real-Life Examples of Job Outcomes

Study the following outcome statements, taken from actual course design documents, to see how all of the elements of well-crafted job outcomes have been incorporated.

**Examples of Outcome Statements**

| From a course on: | Outcome statement |
|---|---|
| Instructional design | "Training that is instructionally sound, lean, effective, and motivational" |
| Corporate forecasting | "Unbiased, accurate, and timely hardware forecasts at the appropriate level of detail that are convincingly communicated" |
| IBM RS/6000 SP I/O problem determination | "Working RS/6000 SP after I/O problems and changes" |
| Servicing IBM RS/6000 and pSeries Enterprise Servers | "Satisfied customer with entry-level and midrange RS/6000 and pSeries enterprise servers properly installed, upgraded, and serviced" |
| IBM RS/6000 SP Network Administration | "Working RS/6000 SP network after networking problems and changes" |
| IBM OS/2 Warp Server for e-business Networking | "Network with OS/2 Warp Server for e-business properly installed, configured, tuned, and administered" |

## Identifying Job Outcomes

To identify job outcomes during requirements gathering, ask the client to visualize what students will finally produce back on the job that is of value to the organization that they are not currently producing or that they will need to produce in the near future. Ask questions such as

- "What will students be expected to accomplish or produce back on the job as a result of this training?"
- "What work products will students be responsible for creating?"
- "What results are employees paid to produce?"

If the client responds with statements that are skills or tasks, ask follow-on questions such as

- "Why do students need those skills?"
- "Why do students need to perform those tasks?"
- "When employees do these things, what do they ultimately produce or accomplish that has value to the company or organization?"

## Analyzing Job Outcomes to Their First Few Levels

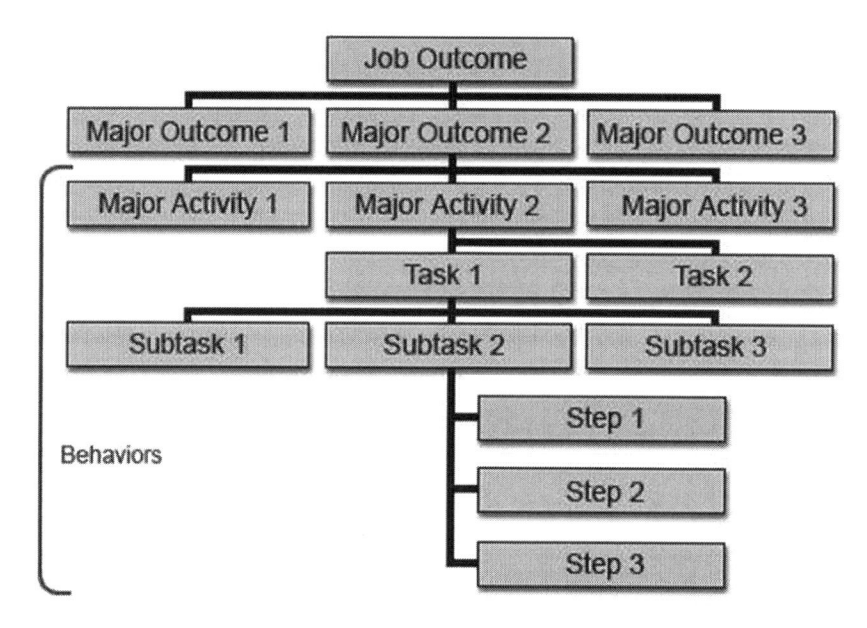

**Figure 21. A conceptual example of an instructional analysis**

During requirements gathering, you should analyze each job outcome to determine the next level's components in the instructional analysis hierarchy.

If the job outcome is comprised of several major accomplishments, break it down into the major outcomes or accomplishments that make up the overall job accomplishment.

**Examples of breaking a job outcome into major outcomes**

- twenty sales of XYZ product per month
  - list of new prospective clients
  - decisions regarding which clients to pursue
  - decisions regarding sales strategy
  - clients who have closed a sale after a sales presentation
- web server that meets demand, thwarts attacks, and enforces security
  - web server that responds within standards after peak demand
  - unharmed web server after attack by hackers
  - web server that responds only to authorized users

If the job outcome does *not* have major subaccomplishments, break it down into the major activities that produce the job accomplishment.

**Examples of breaking a job outcome into major activities**

- order cooked and on plate
  - receive and interpret order
  - determine cooking order
  - cook order items
  - place and arrange items properly on plate
- functioning Websphere portlet
  - determine portlet functional requirements
  - design portlet code and portlet API
  - code portlet
  - test and debug portlet

## Why instructional analysis is only carried out to the first level or two during requirements gathering

Instructional analysis is too time consuming to perform completely during requirements gathering. To complete the full analysis typically requires extensive interaction with highly specialized subject matter experts who are unlikely to be in attendance at the requirements gathering work session. The complete instructional analysis is performed immediately after requirements gathering, often on a different occasion and with one or more client SMEs.

## Step 5. Determine Training Delivery System Constraints and Possibilities

In step 5 of the requirements gathering process, you ask questions about the types of training delivery platforms that are feasible for delivering the training. Your goal in this step is *not* to determine the training delivery platform; rather, your goal is to uncover what the *possibilities* are. Final decisions on delivery platform will occur later in the instructional design process, after further analysis.

You should gather information in each of the following areas that can affect training delivery decisions.

### Identify technical issues for technology-delivered training

- availability of and connection speed to the web or network
- the minimum system hardware and software platform that students have
- any server and client software that is already installed that could be used to deliver training (such as web browsers with Flash plug-ins installed)

### Determine delivery needs of students

- general computer experience and sophistication
- experience with different training delivery technologies

- when students will be able to take training—during work time or off hours
- whether students are mobile or desk side
- desirability of various delivery options, such as web-based, live synchronous, download and play, CD ROM, and instructor-led
- motivation level of students for the tasks to be trained
- language and translation considerations

**Determine geographic distribution of students**

- centrally located or dispersed?
- local, national, or international?

**Determine organizational and business issues**

- company or organizational security issues (sensitivity of the information)
- organizational experience with new delivery technologies
- organizational or managerial mandates regarding accessibility, style issues, and so forth
- facilities requirements
- administration requirements
- ownership and maintenance issues
- internal political issues
- level of funding
- life expectancy of the training
- availability of training—24 x 7 or otherwise

## Step 6. Gather General Project-Related Information

The final step in requirements gathering is to gather general project-related information, such as

- deadlines
- budget for
  - requirements gathering
  - design
  - development
  - delivery (including administration and maintenance)
- availability and commitment of SMEs
- available resources (for design, development, and delivery)
  - authoring and delivery tools
  - instructors (if needed)
  - subject matter experts
- exit and success criteria for the project
- project players and contact information
- available source material
- certification, translation, and accessibility requirements

This information defines project constraints and parameters and helps ensure that the training will be acceptable to the business or organization.

## Requirements Gathering Templates

Conducting requirements gathering is much easier when a requirements gathering template is used. This template is a structured document or spreadsheet that contains the sequence of questions that should potentially be asked during requirements gathering. Requirements gathering templates provide the following benefits:

- The same template can be used across many projects, thus ensuring a consistent level of quality in requirements gathering.
- Questions are prompted so that they are not overlooked.
- The correct order and sequence of questions is maintained.
- Space is provided for recording the answers.
- Information can be edited in place during requirements gathering and later to create polished text for the final training requirements report.
- The structure of the template can help structure the formal training requirements report.

Most training organizations develop their own detailed and structured requirements gathering template. This ensures that all of the information that is important to the organization is gathered.

Here is a simple example of a requirements gathering template:

## Training Requirements Template

### Introduction

The following list of questions can be used as a guide for collecting training requirements or as a preparatory checklist for those who will be providing requirements information to instructional designers.

### What Is the Training Request?

- What is the request (what are they asking you to do)? [Reproduce their request as accurately and as completely as possible; this is very important.]
- Who made the request?
- What is their title and organizational role (what are they responsible for)?

- What are the overall business goals of their organization (what does their organization do that is of value to the company; what are they trying to achieve as an organization; how does their organization fit into the larger organization)?
- Were any other persons involved in initiating or sponsoring this request (who else is sponsoring or pushing the need for this training beside the requester; e.g., higher-level management)? If so, answer each of the above questions for each stakeholder.
- Why is this person (or group) making this request (is it to solve a deficient performance on the part of job incumbents, or to train job incumbents in anticipation of an upcoming new program, product, or application)? [See the next section for additional detail about these two possibilities.]

**Who Is the Target Audience?**

- What major audience groupings will receive the training?
- For each major audience grouping
  - how many people are in each group (list by geographies, if important)?
  - where are they located (what is their geographic distribution)?
  - what are their major job duties and responsibilities (describe what they typically do and are responsible for in their job)?
  - how have they traditionally been trained to do their job?
  - what motivates them, and what "turns them off?"
  - what relevant entry-level skills, knowledge, and job experience do they already have?
  - what learning styles and preferences, if any, do they have?
  - what is their comfort level and experience with technology and technology-based training?
  - what are their relevant demographics (age, experience in the company, and so forth)?

## Is Training to Close a Performance Gap or to Prepare for an Upcoming New Program, Product, or Job Performance?

- Is training to close a performance gap or to prepare for an upcoming *new* program, product, or job performance?
- For training designed to close business gaps
  - what are job incumbents *not* producing or accomplishing on the job that motivated the request for training, or what should job incumbents be producing or accomplishing on the job that they are currently *not* producing? [describe the deficiency in the job incumbent's performance]
  - why are those employee accomplishments of worth to the business (include what will happen if those accomplishments are not achieved)?
  - what evidence exists that the business need or problem can be met or addressed through training?
  - have other potential causes of performance gaps been eliminated (or identified as contributing causal factors), such as lack of tools or resources on the job, lack of authority, unclear expectations, lack of feedback on performance, performance is punished, performance goes unrewarded, and performance is socially unacceptable?
  - have participants performed these skills in the past, and, if so, could they perform these skills if they had sufficient motivation?
  - if training is not the complete solution, then what part does training play in the total solution?
- For training designed to meet upcoming or anticipated needs
  - what will job incumbents be required to produce or accomplish?
  - why will those employee accomplishments be important and worthwhile to the business (include what will happen if those accomplishments are not achieved)?

**What Will Job Incumbents Produce Back on the Job as a Result of This Training?**

- What should course participants be able to produce or accomplish *back on the job* as a result of this training? To what level or standard of accomplishment? [Important! This is probably the most important question on this checklist, as it serves as the basis for all subsequent training analysis and design, yet it is often the most difficult to ferret out and compose during requirements gathering. Outcomes are not verbs, verb phrases, or even skills; they are nouns and noun phrases since they represent outcomes or accomplishments—they are what tasks and skills produce.]

- How confident do participants need to be at the end of training in their ability to produce these accomplishments?

- [Optional, if time permits and situation is appropriate]: What are the major tasks required to accomplish those outcomes, along with their importance, frequency, rate of performance, complexity, and consequences for performing and not performing those tasks to standard?

**What Are the Characteristics of the Job Environment?**

- What is the job environment like physically, socially, and organizationally?
- What do performers say they are rewarded and punished for on the job?
- What tools and resources are available on the job?
- What constraints, if any, exist in the job environment?

**How Will the Success of This Project Be Measured?**

- How will the success of this course be measured (this project will be deemed a success if _____)?

## How Will Training and Students Be Evaluated?

- How will the training be evaluated?
- How will course participants be evaluated? (Will students be tested? If so, when and how will the tests be administered? Will test scores be tracked or recorded?)

## How Will Administration and Tracking Be Handled?

- How will course participants enroll in this training?
- Will prerequisites be verified and enrollment restricted?
- Are there any other administration, tracking, or enrollment requirements?

## What Implementation and Delivery Requirements Are Known at This Time?

- How will the training be rolled out (as pilot, as phases, or what)?
- Who will identify and enroll students for the pilot and T3?
- Who will provide instructors (if required) for this course?
- How many instructors will be needed?
- Who will own this course after development (be responsible for managing the course through its entire lifecycle, from updating through sun setting)?

## Are There Any Special Global Considerations for This Project?

- Are there any special global considerations for this project, such as translation requirements, document formatting and printing requirements, cultural considerations, and financial arrangements?

## What Are the Project Constraints?

- What are the project deadlines and how firm are they (include pilot course, if applicable, and final)?
- What is the approximate project budget?

- What media and delivery systems are and are *not* available, feasible, or practical?
- What up-front demands must be met (such as the use of a specific media or delivery method)?
- Are there any special project priorities?
- Are there any organizational politics that might affect this project?
- Are there any organizational or personal "hot buttons" to avoid?
- Are there any safety regulations that must be followed?
- Are there any security or authorization procedures that must be followed?
- Are there any company policies that must be followed that affect this project?
- Are there any government regulations that must be met or adhered to on this project?
- Are there any union considerations or requirements that should be taken into account?

## What Resources Are Available for Developing the Training?

- Who are the subject matter experts (SMEs) or accomplished performers?
- What is their availability?
- What incentives do they have for responsive participation?
- What other resources are available, who will provide them to the instructional designer, and how current and relevant are they to the project at hand?
    - prerequisite training (to the course being developed)
    - existing or related training
    - manuals, guides, job aids, check sheets, wall charts, or other relevant documentation
    - online sources of information, such as databases and web sites
    - reports documenting the business problem
    - organization charts and documents explaining the goals of the business

- marketing literature and presentations, specification documents, and prototypes
- human sources of information

## What Are the Major Risks and Project Exposures?

- What are the project's major risks, challenges, and exposures?

## Who Are the Team Members and What Are Their Roles?

- For each team member, provide the following
  - name
  - role in this project (client, management stakeholders, subject matter expert, expert performer, instructional designer, project manager, content developer, graphic artists, editor, programmer, and so forth)
  - contact information (external telephone, tie line number, Notes address, Internet address, physical location, and so forth)
  - other relevant information, as applicable

# Chapter Summary—Gathering Requirements

This chapter presented information on how to gather training requirements, the first step in the instructional design process.

You should now be able to

- list the six steps of the requirements gathering process;
- describe how to clarify training requests;
- describe how to determine and validate the business problem to be solved by training;
- describe how to validate that training will solve the business problem or need;
- list seven reasons why a performance gap or issue might exist other than a lack of training;
- describe how to identify fuzzy business or training goals and statements;
- describe how to identify, categorize, and describe the target audience;
- define job outcomes and describe what type of grammatical structures they can be;
- give five reasons why instructional analysis begins with job outcomes instead of skills;
- provide several examples of noun and noun-phrase job outcome statements;
- distinguish job outcomes from subject matter statements and behavior or skill statements;
- distinguish job outcomes from past-tense verb phrases;
- describe what tests you can perform to determine if a statement is a job outcome;
- define the three types of job outcomes;
- list the four types of standards that are used in job outcome statements and provide examples of each;
- construct properly worded job outcome statements;

- describe how to identify job outcomes during requirements gathering;
- describe how to analyze job outcomes to their first few levels;
- describe how to determine training delivery system constraints and possibilities;
- describe the general project-related information that should be gathered during requirements; and
- explain the value of using a requirements gathering template.

## Check Your Understanding

1. **Match each step in the requirements gathering process with its correct definition.**

   | | |
   |---|---|
   | Step 1 | A. Identify, categorize, and describe the target audience |
   | Step 2 | B. Determine delivery system constraints and possibilities |
   | Step 3 | C. Identify and begin analysis of the job outcomes to be produced by students back on the job |
   | Step 4 | D. Clarify the training request |
   | Step 5 | E. Gather general project-related information |
   | Step 6 | F. Determine and validate the business problem to be solved by training |

2. **Which of the following tasks are completed in step 2 of requirements gathering, "Determine and validate the business problem to be solved by training?" (Select all that apply.)**
   A. Clarify the training request.
   B. Identify the *business* problems that training is expected to solve.
   C. Determine how the sponsor will know when the problem has been corrected or the business need has been fulfilled.
   D. Determine if training is intended to close an identified business gap or deficiency, or whether it is intended to meet a new, upcoming need.

E. Validate that training will indeed close the performance gap or fill the upcoming need.

F. Clarify fuzzy business and training goals and requests.

3. **True or false? Training is the right solution for all types of employee performance problems.**

4. **Which of the following are fuzzy goals or statements that need further analysis and clarification? (Select all that apply.)**
    A. "We need to improve employee morale."
    B. "We need to teach staff how to use the ABC function of the new HR application to file their weekly timesheets."
    C. "Employees on the assembly line need to improve quality."
    D. "Our college students need to develop better study skills."
    E. "We need to land more deals and increase profits."
    F. "Employees need to be taught how to talk to customers on the telephone."

5. **Which of the following are reasons why information needs to be gathered about the training audience? (Select all that apply.)**
    A. It helps identify the enabling skills and knowledge students already possess when they come to training that you do not need to teach as part of the course.
    B. It helps provide information on what motivates students.
    C. It helps structure the course.
    D. It helps determine any special considerations that should be taken into account for this particular audience, such as type size considerations.
    E. It helps determine how much time students can devote to training and when they can take the training.
    F. It helps determine what kind of job aids, if any, are feasible for students' job environments.

6. **True or false? During requirements gathering, job outcomes are only analyzed to their first or second level.**

7. **Why does instructional analysis begin with identifying and analyzing job outcomes instead of skills? (Select all that apply.)**
   A. Because employees are paid to produce results (outputs) that have value to the business, not to sit around being capable of achievement.
   B. By analyzing the identified job outcomes, you identify the specific behaviors (tasks and steps along with their enabling content) that produce the desired job outcomes; thus, you know exactly what you must teach in your training, and you avoid teaching extraneous behaviors, skills, and knowledge.
   C. It provides the only objective way to determine what should be taught in the course.
   D. It enhances transfer of learning to the job place because it teaches the very behaviors that are required to produce those results on the job.

8. **Which of the following are characteristics of job outcomes? (Select all that apply.)**
   A. They are verbs or verb phrases.
   B. They are nouns or noun phrases.
   C. They describe the *outputs* or *results* of behavior, *not* the behaviors that produced the outputs.
   D. They describe the behaviors that job incumbents do on the job.
   E. They represent outcomes the training audience is not currently producing or will need to produce in the near future.
   F. They are any statement that describes what the sponsors want training to achieve.

9. **Which of the following are subject matter statements and therefore are *not* job outcomes? (Select all that apply.)**
   A. Principles of accounting
   B. Object-oriented programming

C. 25% higher widget sales

D. ABC copier machine problem-determination principles

E. On-time monthly sales reports

10. **Classify each of the following into a noun, noun phrase, or a skill (behavior).**

    A. Produce a spreadsheet of last month's sales figures

    B. Satisfied customer after complaint

    C. Solution for improving network performance

    D. Improve motivation in employees

    E. ERP application with completed orders

    F. Write code with no errors

    G. Apply managerial policies

    H. Sales

11. **Which of the following are past-tense verb statements and therefore are *not* job outcomes? (Select all that apply.)**

    A. Team project completed

    B. Product XYZ produced within tolerances

    C. Satisfied customer after service call

    D. Solution for improving network performance

    E. Sales figures turned in by monthly deadline

    F. Order-entry application with completed orders

12. **Which of the following are job outcomes? (Select all that apply.)**

    A. FDA meat packaging standards

    B. Strategy for beating the competition

    C. Answer customer calls

D. 95% worker productivity

   E. Performance evaluation interviews conducted

   F. Order entered into the ABC application

   G. Document with proper formatting and style

   H. Pleasant bank teller

   I. Sales increased

13. **According to Joe Harless, what are the three types of job outcomes?**

    A. Daily, weekly, infrequent

    B. Usual, unusual, out of scope

    C. Frequent, infrequent, emergency

    D. Normal, off-normal, emergency

    E. Entry-level, intermediate, mastery-level

    F. Novice, semiskilled, guru

14. **For each one of the following job outcomes, indicate which type of standard was used (accuracy, time, productivity, or safety).**

    A. Annual tax return with no errors

    B. Sellable toy widget with no lead paint

    C. Weekly time sheet with 50 billable hours

    D. New running computer application before customer rollout

    E. 90% sales call closure rate

    F. Accessibility checklist for ABC software application with all checklist items in compliance

    G. Service calls with average hold time of less than 90 seconds

15. **What should you do if you are trying to identify job outcomes with your client's requirements gathering team but they react by naming various skills that they want employees to learn?**

    A. Analyze the skills to determine what should be taught in the course.

    B. Ask the team to identify the tasks that need to be performed back on the job.

    C. Ask the team to reflect on what they needed to know when they were learning how to do the job.

    D. Ask the team to prioritize the skills.

    E. Ask the team why students need those skills and what they will produce with them that is of value to the company.

16. **During requirements gathering, job outcomes are analyzed into ___ ___ or ___ ___.**

17. **True or false? During requirements gathering, the training delivery platform is selected.**

18. **True or false? General project-related information is gathered during requirements to understand project deadlines, development budgets, availability of subject matter experts (SMEs), the criteria by which the project will be evaluated, who the team players are, what source material is available, and any special requirements for certification, translation, and accessibility.**

## Answers

1. D, F, A, C, B, and E

2. B, C, D, E, and F. The first choice, clarify the training request, is part of step 1 of the requirements gathering process. All of the other tasks are performed in step 2.

3. False. Training can only solve performance gaps and fill performance needs if job incumbents are not performing due to a lack of knowledge or skill. Performance gaps can exist for many other reasons, such as unclear expectations, inadequate resources, quality of performance is not visible (no feedback), desired performance is punishing, poor performance is rewarding, forgetting how to perform the task, and obstacles exist in the way of performance. In these cases, performance problems should be directly addressed through nontraining performance-improvement interventions.

4. A, C, D, E, and F. Regarding the second to the last statement: How many more deals? What kind of deals? How much profit?

5. A, B, D, E, and F

6. True

7. A, B, C, and D

8. B, C, and E

9. A, B, and D

10. #1, skill; #2, noun phrase; #3, noun phrase; #4, skill; #5, noun phrase; #6, skill; #7, skill; and #8, noun. You could change skill statements #1, #4, #6, and #7 into noun phrases (outcomes) if you stated them, respectively, as: "spreadsheet of last month's sales," "employees with improved motivation," "code with no errors," "managers who understand managerial policies" (or equivalently, "employees who are managed in accordance with policy").

11. A, B, and E

12. B, D, G, and H. A is a subject matter phrase, not an outcome of behavior. C is a skill or behavior. E is a past-tense verb phrase (an outcome would be "rated employees"). F is a past-tense verb phrase (an outcome would be "orders in ABC application" or "ABC application with orders entered." H

is an outcome, but it is a fuzzy outcome that should be further clarified. I is a past-tense verb phrase (an outcome would be "higher sales").

13. D

14. A, accuracy; B, safety; C, productivity; D, time; E, productivity; F, accuracy; and G, time

15. E

16. The correct answer is "major outcomes" and "major activities."

17. False. Your goal in requirements gathering is to uncover what the *possible* and *feasible* delivery platforms or methods are. Final decisions on delivery platform occur later in the instructional design process, after further analysis.

18. True

# Chapter 8
# Performing an Instructional Analysis on the Job Outcomes

This chapter is the first of two chapters that discuss how to perform an instructional analysis on the job outcomes identified in requirements gathering. Instructional analysis is the second step in the instructional design process (see part 2 introduction). The output of instructional analysis is the skeleton on which the rest of instructional design is based. Because of the importance of this task, we will discuss how to perform instructional analysis for simple job tasks in this chapter and how to perform instructional analysis for complex job tasks in the next chapter.

## Where We Are at in the Instructional Design Process

This chapter discusses step 2 in the instructional design process: Perform an instructional analysis on the job outcomes.

1. Gather requirements
2. **Perform an instructional analysis on the job outcomes**
3. Identify the enabling content
4. Structure the course
5. Write instructional objectives
6. Determine the instructional delivery system
7. Design practice exercises and other instructional events
8. Design the prototype or example lesson
9. Create the formal design document

## Instructional Analysis

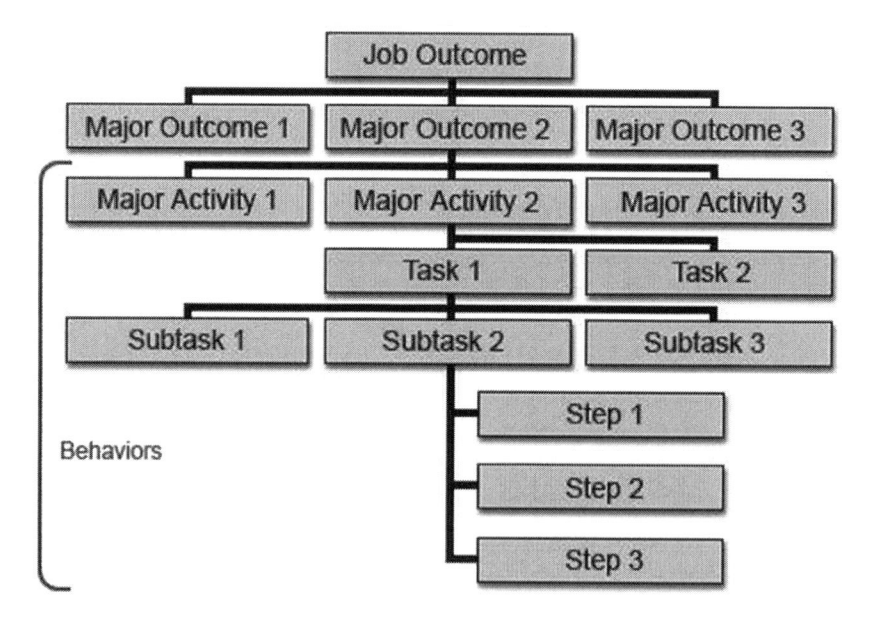

Figure 22. A conceptual example of instructional analysis

In step 2 of the instructional design process, you complete the instructional analysis that you began during requirements gathering. As you recall, instructional analysis, also called job/task analysis, is the process by which job outcomes are analyzed and broken down into the major outcomes, major activities, tasks, subtasks, and steps that produce those outcomes.

The final work product of instructional analysis is a hierarchical breakdown of the major outcomes and behavior components that produce the job outcomes. For small, simple job outcomes, this hierarchy might be only a few pages long. For large, complex, highly technical job outcomes, the resulting hierarchy might be fifty or even seventy-five pages long.

Here is a simplified example of an instructional analysis:

**Properly parked car in parallel or diagonal parking space**

   1. Park the car in a parallel parking space.
      1.1 Park the car in a parallel parking space between two other cars.
         1.1.1 Pull your car alongside the vehicle in front (about two to three feet away) until your front bumpers are even
         1.1.2 Slowly pull backward into the parking space at about a 45-degree angle until your front door is even with the back bumper of the car alongside.
         1.1.3 Turn the wheel sharply in the opposite direction, clear the bumper, and continue moving back until you are just in front of the car behind
         1.1.4 Pull the car forward and straighten the wheel until the car is centered in the parking space
      1.2 Park the car in a parallel parking space that has no other cars immediately in front or back
         1.2.1 Gradually steer the car into the space as you pull forward.
   2. Park the car in a diagonal-entry parking space.
      2.1 As your bumper clears the car to the right, turn the wheel to the right
      2.2 Slowly pull in, watching both sides of your car, until you are fully in the space.

During instructional analysis, an instructional designer interacts with one or more knowledgeable subject matter experts (SMEs) or expert performers, preferably face-to-face, but in virtual work sessions if necessary, to drill down the analysis. In this chapter, we will show you tools and techniques for capturing the hierarchical logic and flow of an instructional analysis.

## How to Perform an Instructional Analysis

To perform an instructional analysis, carry out the following three steps:

1. Identify the job outcomes that students will be taught to produce during training and their first level components (the major outcomes or major activities); this step should have been completed during requirements gathering (see the previous chapter).

2. Push each level of the hierarchy down to the next (more detailed) component level:
   - For each major outcome, ask "What are the major activities a master performer performs to produce this outcome?"
   - For each major activity, ask "What are the major tasks a master performer performs to complete this activity?"
   - For each higher-level task, ask "What are the subtasks that a master performer performs to complete this task?"
   - For each lower-level task, ask "What are the major steps an expert performer performs to perform this task?"
   - For each higher-level step, ask "What are the detailed steps an expert performer performs to carry out this step?"

3. Continue pushing the analysis down to lower levels until you reach outcomes, activities, tasks, subtasks, and steps that students already know how to produce or perform; in other words, drill down the hierarchy until you reach a point at which entry-level skills are listed.

## Instructional Analysis in Practice

In theory, instructional analysis appears simple and easy. In practice, it takes skilled interaction to tease information out of the minds of master performers, including information that might not even be in their consciousness. Moreover, it takes great judgment and skill to make sense of the SME's information, craft consistent entries across levels in the hierarchy, word appropriate titles for the entries in the hierarchy, and place them in their proper sequence.

**Example of how judgment and skill are required in performing instructional analysis**

For example, suppose the job outcome is "Car with mounted spare after flat tire." The SME might rattle through a series of actions, but it would be up to you as the instructional designer to organize them into activities, tasks, and steps. For example, you might organize the first level of your analysis into the following step entries:

1. Jack up the car.
2. Using the tire wrench, remove the lug nuts.
3. Pull the tire off the car.
4. Place the new tire on the car.
5. Tighten the lug nuts.
6. Lower the car.

Then you would drill down each of these entries until you reach the assumed entry-level skills and knowledge of the students. For example, you might determine that students already know how to perform the step "Pull the tire off the car," so you do not need to analyze this step any further because it is an assumed entry-level skill. However, step 2, "Using the tire wrench, remove the lug nuts" would likely need further analysis. Some students might not know to keep the tire in slight contact with the ground while the lug nuts are being loosened or might not know how to use a tire iron.

## Tools for Conducting an Instructional Analysis

The output of an instructional analysis is, by definition, a hierarchical breakdown of the job outcomes into successively more detailed components. This requires a way to capture and document hierarchical information. For very simple tasks, this can be done with paper and pencil, whiteboard, or sticky notes. For more complex tasks, you need a computer application that has the capability to capture hierarchical representations and allows easy editing, copying, and printing of the analysis.

Although flowcharting software is one possible way to capture procedural information, flowcharts become unwieldy and difficult to understand for large or complex tasks. Probably the best tool for conducting instructional analysis is a word processor possessing excellent outline functions, such as

- outline, normal, and print views;
- indentation (each level of indention represents a lower level in the hierarchy; eight to ten levels is usually sufficient); and
- the ability to
    - collapse and expand parent entries individually or by level;
    - move entire levels left, right, up, and down; and
    - add and remove numbering.

## Using the Outline Function of a Word Processor in Conducting an Instructional Analysis

### Anatomy of an indented hierarchy

- Each line or contiguous group of lines is an action step or a decision step.

- Procedure flow is from top to bottom, left to right, just as a normal outline is read.

- Indented lines are subordinate steps of the procedure that provide layering or more detail.

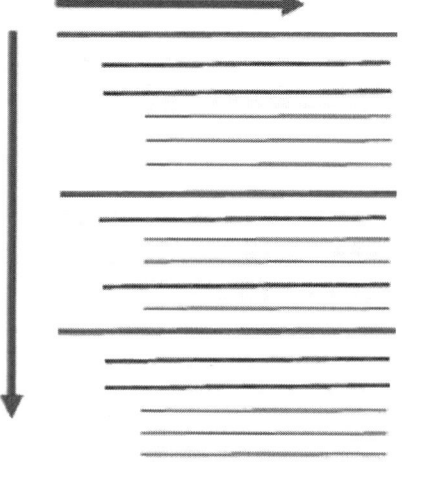

**Figure 23. A conceptual view of an indented hierarchy**

An indented outline is one of the most effective ways of representing large amounts of hierarchical information. Each level of indention from left to right represents the next lowest level in the hierarchy. Indention also shows what is subordinate to what. In an indented outline, the logic flows from top to bottom and left to right in the outline, as depicted by the arrows in figure 23.

Here is an example of an incomplete hierarchical outline for the job of chef at a diner:

  Orders on plates ready to take to patrons
    Receive and interpret orders
      Display list of orders on computer screen
        Click the Display Orders button
      Display details for the next two or three orders in the queue
        Click the next order in the queue
        Hold down the Shift key and click an order
        Click the Display Details button
      Interpret order details
        Interpret waitress abbreviations and writing
        Interpret menu codes
    Determine cooking order
      Mentally group items together by cooking time
      Within each group, mentally group by cooking method (frying or baking)
    Cook order items
      Begin cooking items that have the longest cooking time
        Cook fried items
        Cook grilled items
        Cook microwave items
        Cook baked items
      Repeat for the next group of items to cook
    Place and arrange items properly on plate
      Arrange food in pleasing manner on plate
        Keep food items separated on the plate
        Add garnishments
        Avoid soiling the edges of the plate

Here is an example of an incomplete hierarchical outline for driving a car:

  Car at destination with no safety or traffic violations
    Enter the car.
      If the door is locked, unlock the door.
        Put the key in the keyhole.
        Turn the key clockwise until the lock knobs on the door lift.
        Open the door.
        Sit down in the driver's seat.
      Adjust the mirrors.
        Adjust the sideview mirrors.
        Adjust the rearview mirrors.
    Start the car.
      Put the key in the ignition.
      Turn the key clockwise until the car starts.
      Release the key.
  And so forth.

**Why the outline functions of a word processor are so valuable to instructional analysis:**

One useful outline function is the ability to collapse the outline to any given level in the hierarchy (for example, to only show the first three levels of the outline). For large, complex tasks, this makes it easy to check flow and logic for a given level in the hierarchy without being distracted by lines and lines of intervening, underlying details.

Another useful feature is the ability to collapse all of the lower-level entries underneath an entry and move the entire collapsed section to another part of the hierarchy or change its level of indention.

Another useful function is the ability to switch to Print view and print a polished, formatted outline of the instructional analysis to place in reports and instructional design documents.

All of these functions make it easy to edit your analysis "on the fly" and create iterative refinements of your analysis as you work with your SMEs.

## Using Word Processing Templates

Most word processors support the use of templates. When a new document is created using a template, the template's formatting is automatically applied to the document. For example, a template used for instructional analysis might include paragraph styles with different levels of indentation, font selections, and other formatting.

Microsoft Word is a word processor that has an Outline view that supports levels of indentation and includes a number of powerful outline functions.

Appendix A contains an example printout of a template for Microsoft Word that has been created especially for instructional analysis.

### Instructions on using the instructional analysis template for Microsoft Word

Store the Instructional Analysis Outline.dot template in the same location where other templates are stored in Microsoft Word (see the application's online help documentation). When creating a new document for instructional analysis, select New and select the template in the task box in the section, New from Template. Instructions on how to use the outline functions of Microsoft Word are contained in the template itself (see appendix A).

## Getting Information Out of the Heads of Subject Matter Experts

Subject matter experts and master performers often know their area of specialization so well that they have difficulty mentally slowing down to consciously identify detailed procedure steps at the level of precision required by an instructional analysis. Many steps are obvious to them, are processed unconsciously, are carried out automatically, or are processed so fast that they are not even conscious of how they arrived at a result, decision, or conclusion.

Moreover, sometimes SMEs are reluctant to share their knowledge and tricks of the trade that they have developed through years of study and work experience because to do so might decrease the scarcity or importance of those skills within their organization, diminish their status among their peers, or even threaten their job security.

**Tips on how to deal with uncooperative or guarded SMEs**

- Try to set SMEs at ease by assuring them that their jobs and status within the organization are not being threatened. This is perhaps best handled *indirectly* by pointing out the positive benefits of their sharing their knowledge and expertise, such as spending less time tutoring and mentoring others, being freed to focus on higher-level problems and challenges in their work, having greater consistency and quality in the deliverables that are produced by the organization, and the ability to hire new staff and quickly bring them up to speed in response to fluctuating delivery requirements.

- Explain upfront that instructional analysis will take significant time and commitment. Provide a best-estimate of that time.

- Explain that many of the things that seem obvious to them are not at all obvious to novice learners. "Sometimes we are too close to the forest to see the trees."

- Explain why they are *not* getting together to discuss or debate what the course should cover (including their favorite content) or to create a course outline (refer back to the first two chapters in this module for the rationale on why this is the case). Instructional analysis is different from the way SMEs usually create training. It will seem strange to them that you want to drill down a detailed behavioral hierarchy. Help them understand why.

- Help SMEs understand the benefits of doing the instructional analysis, especially how the time spent upfront will be paid back multiple times over when the course is actually developed (materials created) because the required content is already identified and structured. The upfront investment also pays high dividends in the instructional effectiveness and leanness of the training.

- If all else fails, appeal to the SME's manager or higher authority. If this fails, you might have to find another SME.

## Anatomy of an Instructional Analysis Work Session

You will need the following resources to perform an instructional analysis:

- subject matter experts or master performers who know all of the details of how to produce the job outcomes—knowledgeable SMEs are a must!
- a way for both you and your SMEs to view the analysis document as it is being crafted—an overhead video projector works well for live work sessions, and a screen-sharing application works well for virtual work sessions
- sufficient time with the SMEs to conduct the analysis—depending on the complexity of the job outcome, this might range from an hour to several weeks

In a typical work session, you will perform two basic activities:

- ask question after question of the SMEs (the questions that were listed as step 2 of instructional analysis given previously in this chapter)
- process that information by summarizing what was said, validating it, organizing it, simplifying it, crafting entries in the analysis document, and editing existing entries as you gain additional insight into the required components, steps, or logic flow

### How you can validate the information given by the SME during instructional analysis

SMEs do not always give complete information in an answer to a question. This does not mean that they are deliberately withholding information. It might mean that they simply need additional questioning to prompt their memory or to stimulate their thinking about other possibilities. That is why you must try to *understand* and *make sense* of the information you receive from your SMEs *at the time it is given.* If you do not understand what a SME is saying, ask questions until you do.

One way, for example, to validate the information you receive from a SME is to ask the SME to review all of the next-lower-level entries that the SME has provided for a drilled-down entry to see if they are complete and accurate and then prompt the SME to see if he or she can think of any others.

For example, if the entry is a task and the SME has identified several subtasks that make up the task, you might ask questions such as "Are there any other subtasks that we have missed that are a part of this task, or have we identified all of them?" "Are the subtasks that I have written accurate and clearly stated?" "Should any of these subtasks be combined because they are logically part of the same entity?" "Are all of the subtasks at the same level of detail?"

## The Importance of Choosing Knowledgeable SMEs

One of the greatest challenges in any training endeavor is finding knowledgeable SMEs who are available to lend their knowledge and expertise. The quality of your final course content will be no better than the quality of the content provided to you by your SMEs. The old saying "garbage in, garbage out" certainly applies here.

In choosing SMEs for training to resolve performance gaps for existing job outcomes, select SMEs who are accomplished performers—that is, who have proven track records for producing the targeted job outcomes accurately, efficiently, and perhaps more quickly than others. Job tasks are often complex, not well documented, in the heads of a few top performers, or are themselves in the process of being defined (such as for new, upcoming tasks). Accomplished performers frequently know the most effective ways to perform the tasks, including shortcuts, efficiencies, and insights that only come with experience. They are proven performers.

If you begin your instructional analysis work session and realize that your SME is unknowledgeable, go back to your sponsors and request a SME who is an accomplished performer—a "Top Gun" in their field.

## What if You Discover That a Major Process Is Undefined?

Suppose you try to analyze a procedure only to find out that it cannot be broken down because it has not yet been defined by the department, business, or organization. What should you do?

For example, suppose you identify the task "Make an accurate forecast of product demand," and you want to analyze it into its component parts (subtasks or steps) but your SMEs inform you that there is wide disagreement about how the task should be performed and there is no "official" or sanctioned way for doing it. What should you do?

### What to do if a major process, task, or procedure is undefined?

- If the process is undefined because it resides in the heads of accomplished performers and has never been documented, then proceed with the instructional analysis if you can tease the information from them using the techniques we have already discussed. Have the newly documented information reviewed by other accomplished performers and try to reach consensus on the newly documented process.
- If the process is undefined because there is widespread disagreement among SMEs on how to perform the process, then consider asking the sponsor to offload the responsibility from you for getting the appropriate SMEs together to define and document an agreed-upon process.
- If you as an instructional designer are skilled in process reengineering, you can offer your services to lead a process reengineering effort, given client and project management approval and additional funding.
- If none of the above is possible, then you might have to settle for one of the following resolutions:

- remove any work products that rely on performers carrying out this process, task, or procedure from the training objectives or goals of the course
- release the training in phases
- postpone training development until the information becomes available

## An Example of an Instructional Analysis

The Word template previously given uses numbered entries for the individual elements of the hierarchy. Numbered entries make it easier for SMEs to communicate with you when you are conducting the instructional analysis. SMEs can reference an entry that needs to be changed by a specific number. The numbers also indicate the specific location and depth of that entry within the hierarchy.

For example, 3.6.1.5 is an entry at the fourth level in the hierarchy because it has four numbers separated by decimal points. The first number, 3, tells you that this item is the third entry at the first level. The second number, 6, tells you that this entry is a child entry beneath the third entry and is at the second level in the hierarchy and so on. This is a military numbering scheme.

When the analysis is complete, the numbers can easily be removed in Word by selecting the entire analysis (*CTRL+A*) and clicking *Format*, *Bullets and Numbering*, and *None*.

Here is a simple example of an instructional analysis for an actual training project (see appendix B for a more complete example):

204  *Instructional Design — Step by Step*

# Working SS/6000Z SP Network After Networking Problems and Changes

**1 Understand the customer's request**

   1.1 Ask the customer the following questions:
      1.1.1 How would you describe the problem you are having?
      1.1.2 Is this a new network?
         1.1.2.1 Has the network ever worked?
      1.1.3 Have there been any recent network changes?
         1.1.3.1 Have there been any new network hardware additions, subtractions, or relocations?
         1.1.3.2 Have there been any configuration changes in IP addressing, network software, and network-related APARs?
      1.1.4 Have you already performed any problem determination?
         1.1.4.1 Have you checked cables?
         1.1.4.2 Have you checked that the network is properly cabled to network components?
         1.1.4.3 Have you done any sniffer traces?
         1.1.4.4 Have you checked the adapter configurations?
      1.1.5 Do you know what is causing the problem?
         1.1.5.1 Why do you think that is the problem?
      1.1.6 Does the problem only affect a single node or does it affect multiple nodes?
      1.1.7 Has anyone else worked on the problem?
      1.1.8 Is the problem intermittent or solid?
      1.1.9 What do you want me to do?

**2 Gather information specific to the network type**

   2.1 Ask the customer what type of network he has
      2.1.1 If the customer has token ring network
         2.1.1.1 How big is the ring?

2.1.1.1.1 Are you running a multiple MAU (or CAU or token-ring hub) network?
2.1.1.2 What type of cabling are you using?
2.1.1.2.1 If Type 1
2.1.1.2.1.1 Probably indicates a hub or CAU network
2.1.1.2.2 If Type 5
2.1.1.2.2.1 Probably indicates a MAU network
2.1.1.3 Does your network have a beaconing condition?
2.1.1.3.1 Yes, the network has a beaconing condition
2.1.1.3.1.1 Does the customer have the appropriate cabling diagrams to help determine where the break is?
2.1.1.3.1.1.1 Yes, the customer has the appropriate cabling diagrams
2.1.1.3.1.1.1.1 Check the cabling at the appropriate locations in the network
2.1.1.3.1.1.2 No, the customer does not have the appropriate cabling diagrams
2.1.1.3.1.1.2.1 Refer to the token ring problem determination guide
2.1.1.3.2 No, the network does not have a beaconing condition
2.1.1.3.2.1 Is the problem affecting a single node or multiple nodes?
2.1.1.3.2.1.1 Problem is affecting a single node
2.1.1.3.2.1.1.1 Perform single-node problem determination (see below)
2.1.1.3.2.1.2 Problem is affecting multiple nodes
2.1.1.3.2.1.2.1 Perform multiple-node problem determination (see below)
2.1.2 Customer has Ethernet network
2.1.2.1 Determine the type of Ethernet cabling and topology
2.1.2.1.1 Ask the customer if they have a thin net or UTP cabling and topology
2.1.2.1.1.1 If the customer has thin net
2.1.2.1.1.1.1 Topology is a bus
2.1.2.1.1.2 If the customer has UTP
2.1.2.1.1.2.1 Topology is a star
2.1.2.2 Ask the customer if he is having a performance problem
2.1.2.2.1 If the customer is having a performance problem (a large number of collisions)
2.1.2.2.1.1 Limit scope of hardware problem determination and consider having the customer bring in a systems performance consultant

  2.1.2.2.2 If the customer is not having a performance problem
   2.1.2.2.2.1 Is the problem affecting a single node or multiple nodes?
    2.1.2.2.2.1.1 If the problem is affecting a single node
     2.1.2.2.2.1.1.1 Perform single-node problem determination (see below)
    2.1.2.2.2.1.2 If the problem is affecting multiple nodes
     2.1.2.2.2.1.2.1 Perform multiple-node problem determination (see below)
 2.1.3 Customer has GDDI or ZTM network
  2.1.3.1 Is the problem affecting a single node or multiple nodes?
   2.1.3.1.1 If the problem is affecting a single node
    2.1.3.1.1.1 Perform single-node problem determination (see below)
   2.1.3.1.2 If the problem is affecting multiple nodes
    2.1.3.1.2.1 Perform multiple-node problem determination (see below)

## 3 Diagnose problems that only affect a single node

 3.1 Check the error log for errors on the failing adapter
  3.1.1 If there are errors
   3.1.1.1 Follow the problem determination procedures in the maintenance documentation
  3.1.2 If there are no errors
   3.1.2.1 Continue with the next task
 3.2 Use the mcnft command to determine if the adapter is properly configured?
  3.2.1 If adapter is not properly configured
   3.2.1.1 Run advanced diagnostics to verify that the adapter is properly functioning
  3.2.2 If adapter is properly configured
   3.2.2.1 Continue with the next task
 3.3 Use ping to verify that the local adapter is functioning
  3.3.1 If local adapter is functioning
   3.3.1.1 Use DMIT to verify and correct as needed the configuration options (verify with the customer the IP address, netmask, hardware config as appropriate)
   3.3.1.2 Continue with the next task
  3.3.2 If local adapter is not functioning
   3.3.2.1 Run advanced diagnostics to verify that the adapter is properly functioning
    3.3.2.1.1 Follow the procedures in the maintenance documentation

3.4 Verify the cabling from the adapter to the network component

   3.4.1 Verify that the adapter has been physically connected to the appropriate network component

   3.4.2 Verify the physical integrity of the cable

**[Analysis continues from here—see appendix B for a more complete example]**

# Chapter Summary—
# Performing an Instructional Analysis on the Job Outcomes

This chapter is the first of two chapters that discuss how to perform an instructional analysis on the job outcomes identified in requirements gathering. Instructional analysis is the second step in the instructional design process (see part 2 introduction). The output of instructional analysis is the skeleton on which the rest of instructional design is based. Because of the importance of this task, we discussed how to perform instructional analysis for simple job tasks in this chapter, and we will discuss how to perform instructional analysis for complex job tasks in the next chapter.

You should now be able to

- define instructional analysis and draw its hierarchical structure and major components,
- list and explain the three major steps for conducting an instructional analysis,
- explain why, in practice, judgment and skill are required to perform an instructional analysis,
- list the tools that can be used for conducting an instructional analysis and why an indented outline is probably the best choice,
- describe how different levels of indention are used in an indented outline to represent the different levels of the instructional analysis,
- describe the benefits of using a word processing template that has been specifically designed for instructional analysis,
- describe strategies for dealing with uncooperative or guarded SMEs,
- list the resources required for performing instructional analysis and describe what happens during the analysis,
- explain why knowledgeable SMEs must be obtained to conduct a high-quality instructional analysis,

- describe what you should do if, during instructional analysis, you discover that a major process is undefined, and
- explain why automatic line numbering should be used in an indented outline during instructional analysis.

## Check Your Understanding

1. **Which of the following are characteristics of instructional analysis? (Select all that apply.)**

    A. It breaks job outcomes into major units, major topics, concepts, and facts.

    B. It is hierarchical in structure and form.

    C. It includes the behaviors that are necessary to produce the job outcomes.

    D. It is the foundation on which all subsequent instructional design is based.

    E. The outcome of instructional analysis is a hierarchical breakdown of job outcomes into major outcomes, major activities, tasks, subtask, and steps.

2. **True or false? The three major steps of instructional analysis are (1) identify the job outcomes that students will be taught to produce, (2) analyze each level of the hierarchy down to the next level, and (3) repeat step 2 until all branches of the hierarchy are analyzed down to the point at which entry-level skills are listed.**

3. **Why does instructional analysis take skill and judgment on the part of the instructional designer? (Select all that apply.)**

    A. To draw information out of the minds of master performers

    B. To make sense of the SME's information

    C. To craft consistent entries across levels in the hierarchy

    D. To word appropriate titles for the entries in the hierarchy

    E. To place entries in their proper sequence

4. **The best tool for conducting instructional analysis is the ____ function of a ____ ____.**

5. **What does the level of indentation in an indented outline instructional analysis indicate?**
    A. The sequence in which the SME gave the information
    B. How important that entry is in the instructional analysis
    C. The beginning of a new paragraph in the analysis
    D. Information that is unrelated to the information above it
    E. Entries of the same level that are all related to a common parent, regardless of where they are located in the hierarchy
    F. The level of hierarchy of the entry and what the entry is subordinate to

6. **True or false? Word processing templates are useful because they automatically lead you through the steps of the analysis.**

7. **Which of the following techniques are good tips for getting information out of the heads of SMEs? (Select all that apply.)**
    A. Point out the benefits to them personally of participating.
    B. Provide a realistic estimate of their time commitment.
    C. Explain why you are not getting them together to reach consensus on course content.
    D. Threaten them directly that you will go to their manager or supervisor if they do not cooperate.
    E. Explain the benefits of performing an instructional analysis.

8. **In addition to a tool for capturing hierarchical analysis, what other resources are essential for performing an instructional analysis? (Select all that apply.)**

    A. Subject matter experts or master performers

    B. Ample snacks available in the room

    C. A way for both you and your SMEs to view the analysis document as it is being crafted

    D. A whiteboard

    E. Sufficient time with the SMEs to conduct the analysis

    F. A third party moderator to make final decisions in disputes over content

9. **True or false? As it applies to instructional analysis, "garbage in, garbage out" means the quality of the final instructional analysis depends on the quality of the information that is given by the SMEs.**

10. **True or false? What to do if you discover that a major process is undefined depends on many factors, including if the process can be well defined by the SMEs, if there is widespread disagreement among SMEs on the process, your level of process reengineering skill, and the implications for altering the training objectives, postponing training, or releasing training in phases.**

11. **True or false? Numbering is used in an instructional analysis so that branching statements can reference the line numbers to which they point.**

## Answers

1. B, C, D, and E
2. True
3. A, B, C, D, and E
4. The correct answer is "outline" and "word processor."
5. F
6. False. Templates automatically apply preconfigured formatting to the document, such as formatting for each level of entry in the hierarchy.
7. A, B, C, and E
8. A, C, and E
9. True
10. True
11. False. Numbered entries make it easier for SMEs to communicate with you when you are conducting the instructional analysis because they can reference an entry that needs to be changed by a specific number. The numbers also indicate the specific location and depth of that entry within the hierarchy. Numbers are *not* used to indicate the destination of branching statements because the references become invalid when new steps are added or deleted from the procedure and the procedure entries are automatically renumbered.

# CHAPTER 9
# Analyzing Complex Procedures

This is the second chapter that discusses how to perform an instructional analysis on the job outcomes identified in requirements gathering. In this chapter, you will learn a specialized technique for capturing and analyzing complex job procedures—procedures that have complex, branching logic with many decision steps.

## Analyzing Complex Procedures: A Special Challenge

In analyzing job outcomes into major outcomes, major activities, and tasks, you will encounter two kinds of tasks: simple procedures and complex procedures. *Simple procedures* are straightforward tasks that involve a sequence of action steps and no decision steps in which the logic jumps from one point to another point in the procedure. This is the case with many simple clerical, administrative, and repetitively performed procedures, such as entering data into a computer from a customer application form or baking a cake by following a recipe.

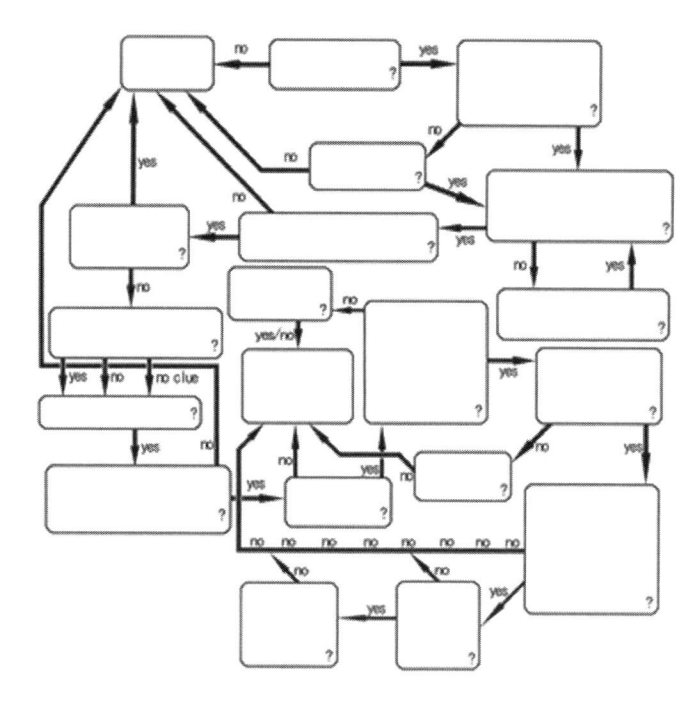

**Figure 24. A conceptual example of a complex procedure**

However, many tasks have decision steps in which the logic branches to another point in the procedure upon certain conditions. For example, a procedure might specify that if a customer has a Gold Account, provide expedited service, but if the customer has a Silver Account, provide normal service. Higher-paid jobs often require employees to make complex judgments or perform procedures that involve multiple decisions and complex logic. For example, the procedure for creating a market strategy for a business might involve the analysis of multiple market factors, each of which could alter the final strategy.

*Complex procedures* are procedures that have a relatively large number of decision steps that branch to other steps, to other subprocedures, or even to other procedures. The branched-to logic might itself contain multiple imbedded decision points, making the logic even more convoluted and difficult to follow. Many if not most real-life job procedures that you will analyze are complex procedures.

Capturing complex logic from SMEs is a daunting task. It requires not only excellent interaction, questioning, and analysis skills, but also the use of specialized techniques. Both of these areas will be discussed in detail in the remainder of this chapter.

## Action Steps and Decision Steps

Complex procedures are made up of two types of steps: action steps and decision steps.

*Action steps* tell the performer to take some kind of action. Examples of action steps include

- "Click the Delete key,"
- "Attach the bolt to the chassis,"
- "Compute the tax on the purchase," and
- "Insert the operator key into the machine console."

*Decision steps* ask the performer to answer a question, make a decision, or choose among alternatives depending on real-life conditions. Examples of decision steps include

- "Click one of the following options,"
- "Is the widget in stock?"
- "Is the customer's credit score above 400?" and
- "What kind of outage is the customer reporting?"

Decision steps are branching points in the flow of the logic. Depending on the condition or answer to a question, a different series of steps or actions are subsequently taken.

## Traditional Methods Are Inadequate for Capturing and Documenting Complex Procedures

Traditional methods for capturing and documenting procedures include

- **step-by-step descriptions**, which typically involve numbered steps written in prose style or step-action tables,
- **flowcharts**, which use symbols that are connected by directional lines showing the flow of the logic,
- **indented Outlines,** which, as we have already seen, work nicely for capturing simple procedures, and
- **hybrids**, which are custom versions or variations of these three methods that are often employed in customer engineer service manuals and other technical documents.

These methods have serious drawbacks, though, when you try to use them to capture complex procedures.

### The problem with using step-by-step descriptions to capture complex procedures

Numbered steps work well for simple, linear flows, but the numbering scheme breaks down when decision steps and branching are involved and you need to insert a new step in the flow, thus causing the steps to be renumbered.

Consider the following procedure:

… [steps before]

  25. Click xyz.

  26. Type Dallas1 in the Location field.

  27. Process the file using the ZZZ application.

  28. Did any error messages appear?
    28.1 If yes, go to step 29.
    28.2 If no, go to step 54.

29. Which error message appeared?
   29.1 If error 100, go to step 15.
   29.2 If error 200, reconfigure the program and go to step 200.
   29.3 If error 300, go to step 70.

... [steps after]

What happens if you later need to insert a step between steps 8 and 9 (not shown)? All of the branching references (such as the one in step 28, "If yes, go to step 29") now point to the wrong step number (they are off by one step). This is true for any entry that branches to a step anywhere after the inserted step. Because edits are inevitable when you are capturing and refining a complex procedure, this method is impractical.

### The problem with using flowcharts to capture complex procedures

Flowcharts become unwieldy and difficult to comprehend as they grow in size and complexity. They are difficult to piece together when they span multiple pages. It is not visually apparent which level in the hierarchy a given entry is at, and it is difficult to see the big picture because you cannot collapse levels of detail. This makes it difficult to check your logic at any given level in your instructional analysis.

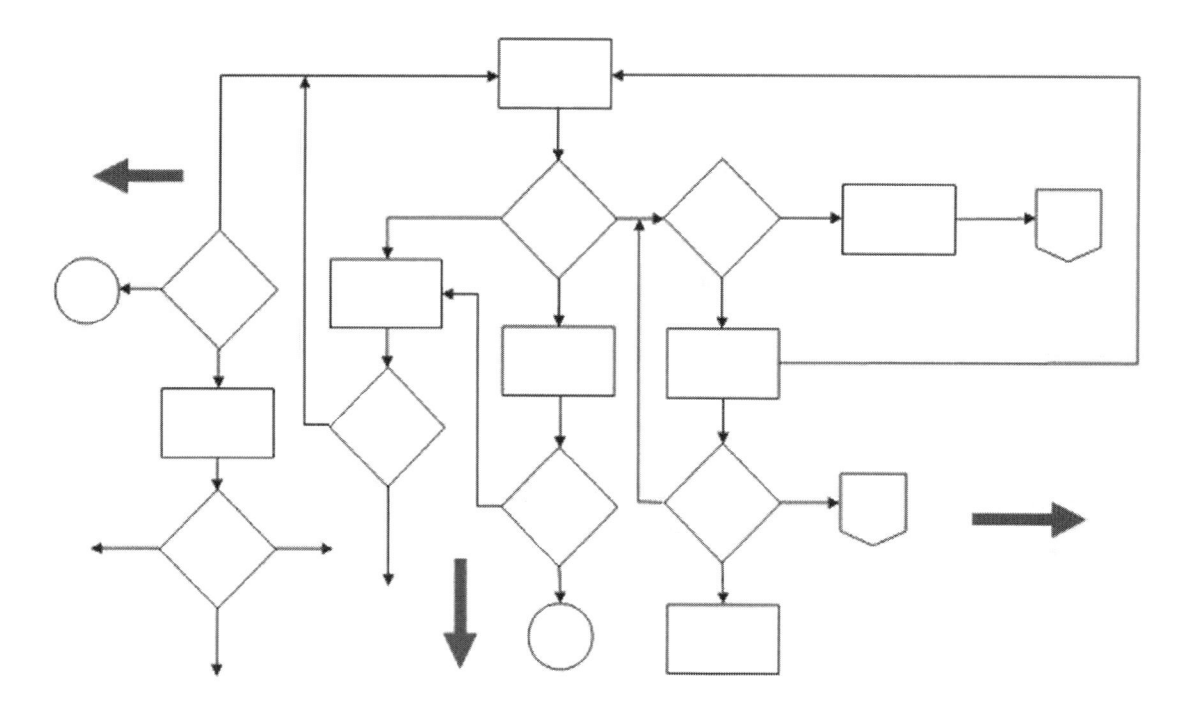

**Figure 25. The problem with trying to capture complex procedures with flowcharts**

## The problem with using indented outlines to capture complex procedures

Indented outlines, without additional modification, have the same problem with branching as numbered steps. If a new step is added or a step is deleted, the renumbering of the steps invalidates the branching references. If the entries are not numbered, then there is no way to identify branching destinations unless they are labeled. However, if this technique is modified in a way that we will discuss in the rest of this chapter, it will then become a powerful tool for capturing complex procedures.

Hybrids, because they are variations of these techniques, suffer from the same drawbacks as the other techniques for capturing complex procedures.

## Issues That Must Be Resolved to Capture Complex Procedures

The following issues must be resolved by any method that is used to successfully capture complex procedures:

- layering of steps
  - An action or decision step might itself be a high-level procedure that must be broken down into an entire subprocedure or series of steps and decisions.
- extensive branching from decision steps
  - The flow of the procedure is redirected to continue at some other point in the procedure depending on conditions that are present.
- maintenance of procedure documentation
  - The procedure must be able to be modified (such as adding or deleting a step) without invalidating one or more of the branching destination references.
- collapsing the logic so that only the higher levels are visible or so that only a particular logical path is visible
  - This function temporarily reduces the complexity of the procedure so that you can check the overall logical flow at a given level and drill down to lower levels of detail while maintaining context of where you are in the procedure.

## A list of capabilities that a tool for capturing complex logic should have

- provides for extensive branching
- supports the layering of information
- provides the ability to collapse subordinate (more detailed) levels of logic to facilitate checking the logical flow for accuracy and completeness
- makes it easy to copy and transfer the analysis results to other tools that are used to build job aids, online coaches, or electronic performance support systems (EPSS)
- requires little training to master the tool and technique

# Capturing Complex Logic Using Structured-English Outlines

The solution to the problem of capturing complex logic is to use a word processor that has indented outline capability and functions, such as Microsoft Word, and a technique adapted from computer programming that we will call *structured-English indented outlines*. This technique enhances the indented outline that we have already discussed with structured English syntax for controlling and directing the flow of logic in a procedure.

Structured English syntax consists of key words and phrases that are used to change or end the flow of logic in a procedure. If you are familiar with programming structures in computer science, these structures provide for branching, looping, subroutines, and termination in a procedure.

The technique uses six statements that assist in directing logic flow and two other statements (the last two) that are used for other purposes. Each of these statements will be explained in more detail below:

- goto
- label
- case
- continue the procedure
- subroutine
- end of procedure
- result
- note

## The *Goto* and *Label* Keywords

The *goto* statement is used to branch (redirect the flow of logic) to another point in the procedure. It consists of the keyword *goto* followed by a unique label in square brackets. Note that the square brackets are part of the actual syntax. The following is an example of the *goto* statement:

**Goto [label 001]**

This statement indicates that the flow of the procedure continues with the one entry in the indented outline that has the label **[label 001]**. Thus, *goto* and *label* work together and always appear in pairs in the procedure.

The *label* keyword creates a unique identifier, such as **[label 125]**, that is different from all other labels in the procedure. It appears before an entry in the hierarchy and remains permanently attached to that entry regardless of any editing to the procedure that occurs before or after the entry. Note that the square brackets are part of the actual syntax. The following is an example of the *label* statement:

> **[label 027]** Multiply the result of the computation by 1.10 to compute the price that you can offer the customer.

The *label* statement is attached to the entry in the hierarchy that is the destination of a corresponding *goto* statement.

**Example of how *goto* and *label* keywords are used together to redirect the flow of logic in a procedure**

… [steps before]

  50 Subtract the division's costs from revenue to get the division's gross profit.
  51 **[label 001]** Subtract taxes from the gross profit.
  52 Write the result on the corresponding profit line in the report.
  53 Determine the next division's revenue, costs, and taxes.
  54 **Goto [label 001]**

… [steps after]

When line 54 is reached in the procedure, the flow of logic (execution) is redirected to the statement that has the same label as that in the *goto* statement (in this case, line 51). Because you are using labels instead of step numbers to reference the destination of *goto* statements, and because the labels are permanently

*Creating Outstanding Instructional Designs*

attached to that entry in the outline, the *goto* references remain accurate even when later editing might insert a new step immediately after step 50.

## The *Case* Statement

As mentioned previously, complex procedures consist of two types of steps: action steps and decision steps. Decision steps are branch points in the procedure where one of several conditions might exist that require different actions. These conditions reflect the varying conditions that a performer might encounter in real life. For example, a decision step might be, "What type of credit card does the customer want to use to purchase the item?" The *case* statement is used to test for and handle these varying conditions.

The following example shows how the *case* statement is constructed in an indented outline:

Question

   **Case A:** Condition A
   Do ABC

   **Case B:** Condition B
   Do DEF

   **Case C:** Condition C
   Do GHI

**Example of a *case* statement**

   9 [steps before]

   10 What color is the error indicator light?

   11 **Case A:** Red
      11.1 Turn the control knob to position 100.

   12 **Case B:** Blue
      12. 1 Turn the control knob to position 200.

   13 **Case C:** Green

       13.1 Turn the control knob to position 300.

   14 Fill the paper tray with the proper forms.

   15 Push the start button on the printer.

[additional steps after]

This case statement begins with a question in line 10 and ends with the last indented entry underneath the last **Case** condition—in this case, line 13.1. Each possible answer to the question is indicated with **Case A**, **Case B**, **Case C**, and so forth, followed by one possible answer (condition) to the question.

Actions that should be taken for each answer are listed in entries that are indented under that answer or condition and are only performed if that condition exists. For example, when line 10 is reached in the procedure, if the error indicator light is green, the action "Turn the control knob to position 300" is performed next.

After all *indented* actions are taken underneath a particular case condition, the flow of the logic continues with the next entry in the hierarchy that is not subordinate to *any* of the Case conditions (in this example, the flow continues with lines 14, 15, and so on). For example, if the indicator light is blue, then line 12.1 is performed ("Turn the control knob to position 200") followed by line 14 ("Fill the paper tray with the proper forms"), line 15 ("Push the start button on the printer"), and so on.

## Case and Goto Are Sometimes Used Together

Sometimes *case* and *goto* statements are used together to branch to different places in a procedure depending on the conditions. For example, a procedure for making ice cream might branch to different places in the procedure depending on the flavor of ice cream that is being made.

Here is an example of how these two statements are used together:

   75 What color is the error indicator light?

     76 **Case A:** Red

        76.1 Turn the control knob to position 100.
        76.2 **Goto [label 125]**

     77 **Case B: Blue**

        77.1 Turn the control knob to position 200.
        77.2 **Goto [label 130]**

     78 **Case C: Green**

        78.1 Turn the control knob to position 300.
        78.2 **Goto [label 135]**

If the indicator light is red, then the statement "Turn the control knob to position 100" is performed, after which the logic flow continues with the entry in the outline that has the label **[label 125]**.

## Two-Option Conditionals

If decision points or questions have only two possible options, then you can choose between using a *case* statement with two **Case** options or using an *if-then-else* statement.

Compare the following examples of the two logic structures

### Example case statement

   10 Is your current speed above the speed limit?

     11 **Case A:** Yes

        11.1 Slow down.

     12 **Case B:** No

        12. 1 Drive at a safe speed.

### Example if-then-else statement

10 **If** your current speed is over the speed limit:

11 **Then** Slow down.

12 **Else** Drive at a safe speed.

The *if-then-else* statement has the following syntax:

**If** [Condition]

**Then** [Action to be taken if condition is true]

**Else** [Action to be taken if the condition is false]

Which one you use is really a matter of preference. However, if you use the case statement for two-option conditionals, then all of your conditional statements in your indented outline will have the same syntax. You can also easily edit the statement later if you determine that there are more than two possible answers to the conditional question.

## The *Continue the Procedure* Statement

The *continue the procedure* statement is used where no action needs to be taken at that point in the procedure; it indicates that the procedure should continue with the next logical step in the indented outline, as indicated by the top-down, left-to-right reading of the hierarchy. This statement is often used in *case* statements where some options do not require any actions.

In the example below, if the error indicator light is blue, then no action needs to be taken, and the *continue the procedure* statement in line 77.1 does nothing other than to end the *case* statement and continue the flow with the first statement after the *case* statement—line 79. However, if the indicator light is red or green, then specific action to position the control knob needs to be taken before continuing with line 79.

75 What color is the error indicator light?

76 **Case A:** Red

   76.1 Turn the control knob to position 100.

   76.2 **Goto [label 125]**

77 **Case B: Blue**

   77.1 **Continue the procedure**

78 **Case C: Green**

   78.1 Turn the control knob to position 300.

   78.2 **Goto [label 135]**

79 Turn the power switch on the generator to the "on" position.

Why not just skip the *continue the procedure* statement altogether, as it does not require any action?

### Why the *Continue the procedure* statement is necessary

Without this statement, you would not know why an option in a case statement that did not have any statements underneath it was left without any entries. It might be left vacant because

- you overlooked it when you performed the analysis—you forgot to drill down this path in the logic,
- your current version is a working draft, and you have not yet drilled down that option, or
- this option simply does not require any action at all.

How would you know which of the three possibilities is the case? You would not know unless you enter a statement that does nothing but inform you that the logic for this path has already been considered and no actions are necessary.

## The *Subroutine* Statement

A *subroutine* is a self-contained subprocedure with a beginning and an end that is referenced (invoked or jumped to) from multiple places in the procedure. The *subroutine* statement indicates that the named subroutine should be performed at that point in the flow of logic. For example, a subroutine to print a document might be referenced in several places in a procedure where the logic requires the printing of a document.

Subroutines are useful because they need only be written once rather than duplicated in their entirety wherever they are repeatedly used in a procedure. They also make maintenance of their logic much easier because changes need only be made in one place in the procedure flow.

The following statements show how the *subroutine* statement is used:

 10 Do ABC.

 11 Do DEF.

 12 **Subroutine:** Compute profit on investment.

 13 Do GHI.

 14 Do JKL.

 15 **Subroutine:** Compute profit on investment.

 16 Do MNO.

In this example, after line 11 is performed, the next step that should be performed is the first step in the subroutine entitled *Compute profit on investment*. After line 14 is performed, this same subroutine is called and performed once again.

## How Subroutine Procedures Themselves Are Defined in the Analysis

To understand how subroutines work, you must distinguish between the *subroutine* statement and the subroutine itself. The subroutine statement is the statement that invokes the subroutine. The subroutine itself is a block of logic that is usually placed at or near the end of the indented outline. The subroutine logic is visually distinguished and contained within the following beginning and ending statements:

    500 **Subroutine Begin:** [name of the subroutine]

    ...

    [logic or steps of the subroutine]

    ...

    547 **Subroutine End:** [name of subroutine]

### Example of a subroutine

A print subroutine might look like the following block of logic at the end of the indented outline:

    100 **Subroutine Begin:** Print a document
       100.1 Turn the power on to the computer.
       100.2 Load the required paper in the printer.
       100.3 Press CTRL+P on your keyboard.
       100.4 Select the desired options.
       100.5 Press Enter or click OK.
    101 **Subroutine End:** Print a document

## How the Flow of Logic Is Passed to and from a Subroutine

Consider the following example subroutine for printing a document:

    100 **Subroutine Begin:** Print a document
       100.1 Turn the power on to the computer.
       100.2 Load the required paper in the printer.

100.3 Press CTRL+P on your keyboard.

100.4 Select the desired options.

100.5 Press Enter or click OK.

101 **Subroutine End:** Print a document

When this subroutine is invoked, the first line that is performed is line 100.1. The last line that is performed is line 100.5. After the last line of this subroutine is performed, the flow of logic continues with the line that follows the original calling subroutine statement in the parent procedure.

**Example of how the flow of logic is passed to and from a subroutine**

For example, suppose our print subroutine is called in the procedure flow with the following lines:

20 Click *Create Report* in the toolbar.

21 **Subroutine:** Print a document

22 File the report in the department directory.

When line 21 is reached in the logic flow, the Print a document subroutine is performed in its entirety, after which the logic flow automatically returns and continues with the next statement—line 22—that follows the invoking *subroutine* statement in line 21.

**How the *subroutine* statement is like and unlike the *goto* statement**

The *goto* statement is a one-way jump from the point of origination. There is no automatic return in the logic flow back to the line after its point of invocation as with the *subroutine* statement. You might wonder why, then, a returning *goto* statement could not be used for this purpose at the end of the subroutine's logic. The reason why is because the subroutine is invoked from more than one place in the parent procedure, so a final *goto* statement in the subroutine

*Creating Outstanding Instructional Designs* 231

would return the flow of logic to the correct place for only *one* of the invoking subroutine statements.

## The *End of Procedure* Statement

This is the easiest of all the structured English flow control statements to understand. This statement simply indicates the end of a procedure. It is necessary because complex procedures can have multiple ending points. For example, if a procedure contains a decision step that branches to three different and independent sets of actions that must be performed to complete the procedure, then each set of actions would conclude with an *end of procedure* statement.

Consider the following example, which contains two *end of procedure* statements:

> 100 What color is the error indicator light?
> 101 Case A: Red
>   101.1 Turn the control knob to position 100.
>   101.2 **End of procedure:** How to handle error light indications
> 102 Case B: Blue
>   102.1 Turn the control knob to position 200.
> 103 Case C: Green
>   103.1 Turn the control knob to position 300.
> 104 Flip the temperature sensor switch to the decrease position.
> 105 **End of procedure:** How to handle error light indications

In this example, if the indicator light is red, then the control knob is turned to position 100 and the procedure ends. If the indicator light is blue or green, the control knob is turned to the corresponding position, after which the temperature sensor switch is flipped to the decrease position. At that point, the procedure ends.

## The *Result* and *Note* Statements

The *result* and *note* statements do not control the flow of logic in an indented outline. They are used for convenience. The *result* statement is used to identify and distinguish the result or results of performing the previous step's action. It tells what should happen in real life when the action is taken. This feedback lets performers know if they took the right action and if their actions were successful. For example, what should happen in real life when the user presses the *Enter* key? What should happen in real life when the performer flips the toggle switch on the machine's control panel from *A* to *B*?

There are two forms of the *result* statement: one for a single result, and one for multiple results. A single result has the following syntax:

> **Result:** [description of the result of taking the previous action]

Multiple results have the following syntax:

> **Results**
>
>> [Description of the first result]
>> [Description of the second result]
>> [Description of the third result]
>> [And so forth]

### Example of Single Result Feedback

> 10 Click *Actions, Login.*
>> 10.1 **Result:** The ABC Application Logon window appears.

### Example of Multiple Results Feedback

> 10 Click Logon.
>> 10.1 Results
>>> 10.1.1 The *ABC Application News Topics – Local window* appears.
>>> 10.1.2 The main menu for XYZ appears in a PCOMM session window.

The *Note* statement is used to document any explanatory notes that are important for the performer to know in a step of the procedure. It has the same dual syntax as the *result* statement.

## Using Structured-English Indented Outlines to Capture Complex Logic

You have now learned the mechanics of how to use the following eight statements in a structured-English indented outline to capture complex procedures:

- goto
- label
- case
- continue the procedure
- subroutine
- end of procedure
- result
- note

Perfecting this technique will require some practice on your part. You will likely learn faster if you work with an experienced mentor on several real-life projects. Once you have mastered this technique, you can use it to capture any kind of procedural information, from simple to extremely complex. In fact, after you have seen its benefits and power, you just might begin using it in all of your instructional analyses, regardless of complexity. The instructional analyses produced by this technique are compact, concise representations of the logic of real-life procedures—in all their complexity and glory—and all this using a simple word processor!

Here is a partial real-life example of using structured-English indented outlines to capture complex logic (see appendix C for a more complete example):

## 4 Take a call

4.1 Make yourself available to take calls

    4.1.1 Do one of the following:

        4.1.1.1 Press *AutIn* on the telephone

            4.1.1.1.1 Result: The *AutIn* green light shines

        4.1.1.2 Click *Avail* in SDPhone

            4.1.1.2.1 Result: The *AutIn* green light shines

4.2 Listen for an incoming call

    4.2.1 When a call arrives, you will hear a beep and a whisper

        4.2.1.1 Examples of whispers:

            4.2.1.1.1 "Software"

            4.2.1.1.2 "AIX"

            4.2.1.1.3 "Rational"

            4.2.1.1.4 "Return caller"

4.3 Introduce yourself and ask if this is a new or existing call

    4.3.1 Say, "My name is [your first and last name]. Is this for a new or existing call?"

4.4 Is this for a new or existing call?

    4.4.1 How to decide if it is new or existing, if the caller does not know:

        4.4.1.1 If the caller is calling on an issue or request that he or she has previously made to ABC SERVICE CENTER, a PMR should have already been created, so it is an existing call

        4.4.1.2 If the caller is calling with a new request that he or she has not previously made to ABC SERVICE CENTER, then it is a new call

            4.4.1.2.1 The new request could be for anything, such as:

            4.4.1.2.2 Service for a software product

            4.4.1.2.3 A request for TSR

            4.4.1.2.4 A request to talk to a duty manager

    4.4.2 Case A: New Call

        4.4.2.1 Ask the caller, "May I have your customer number or serial number?"

        4.4.2.2 Did the caller provide one or both of the following: a customer number or serial number?

        4.4.2.3 Case A: Yes

            4.4.2.3.1 Record on paper or in MS Notepad the information

        4.4.2.3.2 Continue the procedure
    4.4.2.4 Case B: No
        4.4.2.4.1 Record on paper or in MS Notepad that the customer could not provide a customer number or serial number
  4.4.3 Case B: Existing Call
    4.4.3.1 Ask the caller, "May I have your PMR number and branch?"
    4.4.3.2 Verify the PMR number with the customer
        4.4.3.2.1 Example: Say "Thank you, that's PMR xxxxxx, branch xxx?"
    4.4.3.3 Record on paper or in MS Notepad the information

**[analysis continues from here—see appendix C for a more complete example]**

## Additional Tips for Working with SMEs to Capture Complex Procedures

Capturing complex logic is an intellectually demanding and arduous task, both for you and your SMEs. The following tips, based on much experience, will help your analysis sessions to be more productive and successful:

- Minimize SME distractions. SMEs should be dedicated to the analysis task, not answering e-mails on their laptops or answering cell phone calls while you are trying to interact with them.

- Back up your work frequently. Wait no longer to back up your work than the amount of work you are willing to lose and have to re-create.

- Create new versions of the file from time to time when you are doing the analysis so that you will have prior versions to refer to if your system crashes, your file becomes corrupted, or you discover later that you have inadvertently deleted part of the analysis.

- Take short breaks at least hourly. Ask your SMEs to take care of personal business during these breaks, at lunch, and before and after work.

- Don't expect SMES to work more than eight hours a day. Analysis work is mentally exhausting, and the quality of your analysis will decrease if you push your own and your SMEs' mental stamina and focus.

## Teaching Complex Procedures

Straightforward, complex procedures with minimal branching can easily be taught using traditional teaching methods, such as classroom or online. However, teaching highly complex procedures with convoluted or deep logic can present many challenges.

One of the best ways to address the latter situation is to use an online coach, intelligent tutor, help system, or electronic performance support system (EPSS) in which the logical flow of the procedure can be built right into the tool. These systems present the procedure to performers one step (or a few) at a time and automatically branch the procedure flow to the right place at decision points.

The performer invokes the support tool when it is appropriate to perform the procedure on the job and follows the steps as prompted to perform the task. This approach works well if students are not required to memorize the steps of the procedure outright and if the job environment is conducive to allowing the performer to follow an online wizard or coach.

### Benefits of presenting complex procedures using an online coach, tutor, help system, or EPSS

- Branching is handled automatically and seamlessly by the application (for example, using hypertext links).
- Decision support (context-sensitive help) can be attached to each instructional screen.
- Prompts can appear in a stay-on-top window on students' screens, thus allowing students to perform real work while learning and following the procedure.
- If the same decision question appears repeatedly throughout the procedure, the coach can capture the performer's answer, remember it,

and apply it to subsequent decisions where the same question is asked. The result is the performer is never asked the same question again in the procedure. For example, if the procedure repeats the decision step "Is the caller a Gold Customer or a Silver Customer?" in several places throughout the procedure, the online coach can capture the answer to this question the first time it is posed and apply that answer automatically to the other places in which this question is asked.

- An online coach or EPSS can be used as an effective problem-solving resource when students get stuck in a procedure that they are trying to perform by memory alone.

- The online coach simulates having a master performer (expert) by your side leading you through the procedure one step at a time, providing your additional support to perform actions and make decisions wherever you need it or ask for it.

# Chapter Summary—Analyzing Complex Procedures

This chapter is the second chapter that discusses how to perform an instructional analysis on the job outcomes identified in requirements gathering. In this chapter, you learned a specialized technique for capturing and analyzing complex job procedures—procedures that have complex, branching logic with many decision steps.

You should now be able to

- define complex procedures and explain the challenges involved in capturing them;
- define and describe the two types of steps that can be found in complex procedures;
- list traditional methods for documenting procedures and explain why they are inadequate for capturing complex procedures;
- describe the four main issues involved in capturing complex procedures;
- list the eight statements used in the structured-English indented outline method for capturing complex procedures and what tool is used;
- describe the use and syntax of the Goto and Label statements;
- describe the use and syntax of the Case statement;
- describe why the Case and Goto statements are often used together;
- describe two ways of representing two-option conditionals;
- describe the use and syntax of the Continue the Procedure statement;
- describe the use and syntax of the Subroutine statement;
- describe how subroutines are defined in the body of the indented outline;
- describe how the flow of the logic is passed to and from a subroutine;
- explain the use and syntax of the End of Procedure statement;
- explain the use and syntax of the Result and Note statements;

- apply structured-English representations in indented outlines to capture complex procedures;
- describe several tips for working with SMEs to capture complex procedures; and
- describe why an online coach, intelligent tutor, help system, or electronic performance support system (EPSS) is a powerful way to present complex procedures.

**Check Your Understanding**

1. **True or false? The difference between simple procedures and complex procedures is complex procedures have one or more decision points that branch to different sets of actions.**

2. **Indicate which of the following statements are action steps and which are decision steps.**
    - A. Glue the leg assembly onto the chair.
    - B. Choose one of the following materials: …
    - C. Is the profit below 10%?
    - D. Click Enter.
    - E. Is the customer a senior citizen?
    - F. Get the report approved by the appropriate manager.
    - G. Which of the following symptoms are displayed?

3. **True or false? Traditional methods of capturing procedures, such as step-by-step descriptions and flowcharts, are not well suited to representing complex procedures.**

4. **A tool for capturing complex procedures should have which of the following essential capabilities? (Select all that apply.)**
   A. Layering of steps
   B. Support for branching from decision steps
   C. The ability to color-code text to represent different kinds of content
   D. Easy editing of the procedure without disturbing decision branch destinations
   E. Spreadsheet capabilities
   F. The ability to collapse layers of logic to make it easier to validate the flow of logic at a given level

5. **Structured-English indented outlines capture complex logic using which of the following sets of keywords or phrases?**
   A. Branch to, case, procedure continue, subprocedure, end of procedure, feedback, tip
   B. Branch to, option case, continue, subroutine, end, action result, decision note
   C. Goto, case, number, continue, subprocedure, task end, step result, note
   D. Goto, label, case, continue the procedure, subroutine, end of procedure, result, note
   E. Jump, jump destination, decision point, no action, end, result, feedback

6. **The ____ statement is used to branch (redirect the flow of logic) to another point in the procedure, and the ____ statement is used to indicate the destination of this statement.**

7. **True or false? The *case* statement has the following syntax:**
   **Case:** Lead question
   **Option A:** Condition A
       Logic if condition A exists

> **Option B:** Condition B
>> Logic if condition B exists
>
> **Option C:** Condition C
>> Logic if condition C exists

8. **True or false? Sometimes *case* and *goto* statements are used together to branch to different places in a procedure, depending on the conditions.**

9. **True or false? An *if-then-else* statement is equivalent to a two-option *case* statement.**

10. **Which of the following statements are true about the *continue the procedure* statement? (Select all that apply.)**
    A. It is used where no action needs to be taken at that point in the procedure.
    B. It indicates that the procedure should continue with the next logical step in the indented outline, as indicated by the top-down, left-to-right reading of the hierarchy.
    C. It is used to continue the procedure where it has been abruptly halted by the *pause* statement.
    D. It is used to continue the action given in the previous step.
    E. It is often used in *case* statements where some options do not require any actions.

11. **True or false? A *subroutine* is a self-contained subprocedure with a beginning and an end that is referenced (invoked or jumped to) from multiple places in the procedure.**

12. **True or false? Subroutines are usually defined at or near the end of the procedure in a structured-English indented outline using the following syntax:**

   **Subroutine Begin**

   ...

   [logic or steps of the subroutine]

   ...

   **Subroutine End**

13. **How does the *subroutine* statement differ from the *goto* statement? (Select all that apply.)**

   A. The *goto* statement is a one-way jump from the point of origin.

   B. The goto statement is used for branching to multiple destination points from a single goto statement.

   C. The goto statement has no automatic return in the logic flow back to the line after its point of invocation, as with the *subroutine* statement.

   D. The goto statement passes control only if certain conditions are met.

   E. The goto and subroutine statements do not differ—they are interchangeable.

14. **True or false? The *end of procedure* statement is necessary because complex procedures can have multiple ending points.**

15. **True or false? The *result* and *Note* statements help control the flow of logic in a structured-English indented outline.**

16. **True or false? Probably the best way to master using structured-English indented outlines to capture complex procedures in an instructional analysis is to work alongside a proficient mentor on several projects in which this technique is used.**

17. **Which of the following are recommended tips for working with SMEs to capture complex procedures? (Select all that apply.)**

    A. Provide free sodas and snacks.

    B. Don't expect SMEs to work more than eight hours a day.

    C. Minimize SME distractions.

    D. Back up your work frequently.

    E. Create new versions of the file from time to time when you are doing the analysis so that you will have prior versions to refer to if needed.

    F. Take short breaks at least hourly.

    G. Have your SMEs follow you in a stretching exercise routine every two hours.

18. **True or false? One of the best ways to present complex procedures is to use an online coach, intelligent tutor, help system, or electronic performance support system (EPSS) in which the logical flow of the procedure can be built right into the tool.**

## Answers

1. True
2. A, action step; B, decision step; C, decision step; D, action step; E, decision step; F, action step; and G, decision step.
3. True
4. A, B, D, and F
5. D
6. The correct answer is "goto" and "label."
7. False. The correct syntax is
   Question
   **Case A:** Condition A
       Do ABC

  **Case B:** Condition B
   Do DEF
  **Case C:** Condition C
   Do GHI

8. True
9. True. The use of one or the other is a matter of preference.
10. A, B, and E
11. True
12. False. The subroutine must be named for it to be referenced. The correct syntax is

    **Subroutine Begin:** [name of the subroutine]
      ...
      [logic or steps of the subroutine]
      ...
    **Subroutine End:** [name of subroutine]

13. A and C
14. True
15. False. These keywords are used for convenience only. The *result* statement is used to identify and distinguish the result or results of performing the previous step's action. The *Note* statement is used to document any explanatory notes that are important for the performer to know in a step of the procedure. They both have the same syntax.
16. True
17. B, C, D, E, and F
18. True

# CHAPTER 10
# Identifying the Enabling Content

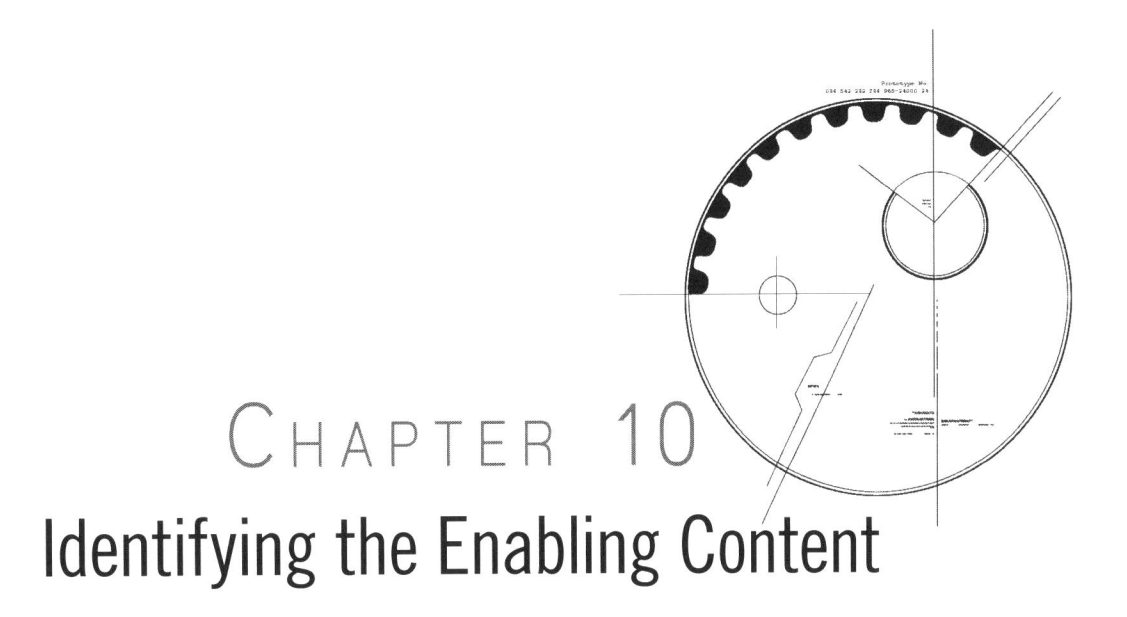

This chapter discusses how to identify the enabling content that is required to intelligently perform the steps that you identified in the instructional analysis. Identifying the enabling content is the third step in the instructional design process (see the introduction to part 1). The output of this step is an instructional analysis (structured-English indented outline) that has been enhanced with the required enabling content.

## Where We Are at in the Instructional Design Process

This chapter discusses step 3 in the instructional design process: Identify the enabling content.

1. Gather requirements
2. Perform an instructional analysis on the job outcomes
3. **Identify the enabling content**
4. Structure the course

5. Write instructional objectives
6. Determine the instructional delivery system
7. Design practice exercises and other instructional events
8. Design the prototype or example lesson
9. Create the formal design document

## What Is Enabling Content and Why Is It Needed?

As we discussed previously, *enabling content* is the knowledge (concepts, facts, principles, and so forth) and basic skills that performers must possess to carry out the activities, tasks, subtasks, and steps that were identified in the instructional analysis. For example, the enabling content for "Adding page numbers to a document in a word processor" is "What are page numbers?" "What is a footer?" "What is a page?" "Which menu option contains this function?" "How do I display menus?" and so forth.

Instructional analysis identifies the behaviors (steps) that produce the desired job outcomes. As we discussed in the last chapter, these steps can either be action steps or decision steps. However, to perform each step successfully or make each decision intelligently almost always requires an understanding of certain concepts, principles, and facts, and possibly the ability to perform certain actions.

Take, for example, the simple action of pressing the *Enter* key on a computer keyboard. Although this action might be intuitive to you, someone who does not already understand the enabling information and skills required to perform this step would have to learn the following concepts and skills:

- a computer keyboard
- a computer key
- how to recognize the Enter key
- how to press a key
- how to know if you have successfully pressed a key

**Example of a decision step and its enabling content:**

A step in a procedure for applying for a house loan might be "Choose the type of loan that you want." However, most first-time borrowers do not know how to do this. They need to understand certain information, such as

- what are the different types of loans that I can choose from (fixed rate, variable rate, balloon, and so forth)?
- what are the characteristics of each type of loan and its advantages and disadvantages?
- how do the loans differ in important characteristics such as required down payment, interest charged, early payoff penalties, and so forth?
- where can I obtain each type of loan?
- what is the best way to choose which loan is best suited for me?

If borrowers did not understand this information and did not know how to make the best choice of loan, then they could not carry out this decision step intelligently and the resulting outcome might be very consequential based on this one step alone.

## Enabling Content Is Tied to the Specific Behaviors It Supports

Let us pause to consider the approach that we are taking so far in instructional design. After we gathered requirements and identified the job outcomes that have value to the business that we need to teach, we analyzed those job outcomes and determined the specific on-the-job behaviors that are required to produce those outcomes. In identifying the enabling content, we determine the enabling content that a performer must know to perform each behavior (step). Why didn't we just identify the required content upfront by asking a group of qualified SMEs to tell us what we should teach? Why bother with systematically identifying the enabling content for each step? Is that not tedious and unnecessary?

The answer is that a SME-consensus approach, although frequently employed in creating new courses, risks one or both of the following: (1) including content in the course that is *not* needed, resulting in a bloated, unfocused course, or (2) failing to include content in the course that *is* needed, resulting in an instructionally ineffective course. The only objective and sure way to know what concepts, principles, processes, and facts you must teach is to first identify the behaviors (actions) that are required to produce the desired job outcomes and then to identify, one behavior step at a time, what a person must know or be able to do to carry out those behaviors. In short, course content is tied to specific behaviors; conceptual content is not identified in isolation.

Suppose a subject matter expert insists that a particular concept or topic should be taught in a course that you are developing, but you do not recognize that concept or topic as belonging to the body of enabling content you identified.

**What to do if a SME wants to include a concept or topic that is not enabling content?**

Ask the SME to show or tell you *where* in the instructional analysis hierarchy the information is needed to perform a step or make a decision. If they cannot show you, and it is not part of the enabling content that you identified, then students do not need to know that information to produce the desired job outcomes. It might be useful information for students in a particular job role, but it does not belong in the course. It belongs in another course or in some other place in the curriculum.

## Using Content Analysis to Identify Enabling Content

Enabling content is systematically identified using a procedure called *content analysis*. In content analysis, each low-level action or decision step in the instructional analysis is analyzed to determine what students must know or be able to do to complete that step. This information is then added to the instructional analysis at or underneath that step, right where it is required. The enabling content is often color coded to make it easy to distinguish it from the procedural content in the enhanced instructional analysis.

## Example of how enabling content is imbedded in an instructional analysis

Note: The bulleted list of items under each step of the following procedure is enabling content.

This example assumes that the audience for this course are teenagers who have never changed a tire on a car. Notice that some enabling content—such as "What are lug nuts?"—is needed in more than one place. We will discuss what to do with repeated enabling content later.

1. Jack up the car.
    What is a car?
    What is a jack?
    Where is the jack located?
    How do you remove the jack?
    How do you position the jack under the car?
    How do you operate the jack?
    What does it mean to jack up the car?

2. Using the tire wrench, remove the lug nuts from the tire.
    What is a tire?
    What is a tire wrench?
    What are lug nuts?
    Why the tire should be in slight contact with the ground when removing the lug nuts
    How do you use a tire wrench to remove lug nuts?

3. Pull the tire off the car.
    What is a tire?
    How do you remove the tire from the car after the lug nuts have been removed?

4. Place the spare tire on the car.
    What is a spare tire?
    Where is the spare tire located?
    How do you remove the spare tire from its location?
    What to do if the spare tire is too heavy to lift

5. Using the tire wrench, tighten the lug nuts.
   What are lug nuts?
   How are lug nuts started on the hub bolts?
   Why the tire should be in slight contact with the ground when tightening the lug nuts
   How to use the tire wrench to tighten the lug nuts
   What order to tighten the lug nuts
   How to tell when the lug nuts are tight enough

6. Using the tire wrench, lower the car.
   What is a car?
   What is a tire wrench?
   How to use a tire wrench to lower the car
   What does it mean to lower the car?

Then, to complete the content analysis, information that students already know when they come to training (entry-level skills and knowledge) is deleted from the list of enabling content because you do not need to teach information that students already know. Of course, to make this decision correctly, you must know who your audience is and what their entry-level knowledge and skills are. This information should have been gathered during requirements gathering. Information that you delete should be kept in a separate list for later validation of your assumed entry-level skills and knowledge.

**Example of deleting entry-levels skills and knowledge from the Content Analysis**

This example assumes that the audience for this course are teenagers who have never changed a tire on a car.

1. Jack up the car.
   ~~What is a car?~~
   What is a jack?
   Where is the jack located?
   How do you remove the jack?

    How do you position the jack under the car?
    How do you operate the jack?
    ~~What does it mean to jack up the car?~~

2. Using the tire wrench, remove the lug nuts from the tire.
   ~~What is a tire?~~
   What is a tire wrench?
   What are lug nuts?
   The importance of making sure that the tire is in slight contact with the ground when removing the lug nuts
   How do you use a tire wrench to remove lug nuts?

3. Pull the tire off the car.
   ~~What is a tire?~~
   How do you remove the tire from the car after the lug nuts have been removed?

4. Place the spare tire on the car.
   ~~What is a spare tire?~~
   Where is the spare tire located?
   How do you remove the spare tire from its location?
   What to do if the spare tire is too heavy to lift?

5. Using the tire wrench, tighten the lug nuts.
   What are lug nuts?
   How are lug nuts started on the hub bolts?
   The importance of making sure that the tire is in slight contact with the ground when tightening the lug nuts
   How to use the tire wrench to tighten the lug nuts
   What order to tighten the lug nuts
   How to tell when the lug nuts are tight enough

6. Using the tire wrench, lower the car.
   ~~What is a car?~~
   What is a tire wrench?
   How to use a tire wrench to lower the car
   ~~What does it mean to lower the car?~~

*Creating Outstanding Instructional Designs*    253

## How to Perform a Content Analysis

To perform a content analysis, carry out the following steps:

1. Locate the steps for one of the tasks in the hierarchy. Task steps are found at the lowest levels in your hierarchical instructional analysis. Start at the top of the hierarchy and drill down a path of descendants until you reach the lowest level. There you will find the series of steps that are required to carry out the parent task that is shown at the next highest level in the hierarchy.

2. For each step, ask, "What must a person understand or be able to do to perform this step?" Write down that information in the hierarchy under or next to the entry.

3. Drill down the next branch in the hierarchy and repeat these steps. Continue the analysis until all of the tasks and steps have been analyzed.

4. Save your current version of the analysis document with all enabling content identified. This version is a backup that can be referenced later after carrying out step 5 if you make an error in judgment on students' entry-level skills and knowledge.

5. Cross out or delete the information that students already know (entry-level knowledge and skills). Enter this information in a separate list for later validation.

If, during content analysis, you discover that a task step is really a task in its own right that was not drilled down previously, then complete the instructional analysis for that task and perform the content analysis on those steps.

### What you need to conduct a content analysis

- A completed instructional analysis (job outcomes analyzed down to step-by-step tasks or procedures).
- Knowledgeable SMEs.
- An undisturbed environment in which to work (virtual or real).

- A way for both you and your SMEs to view the analysis document as it is being crafted—an overhead video project works well for live work sessions, and a screen-sharing application works well for virtual work sessions.
- Sufficient time with the SMEs to conduct the analysis.

## Tips for Analyzing Individual Steps to Identify Their Enabling Content

The following tips will help you analyze individual task steps to determine their enabling content:

- Look at all the nouns in the sentence. Nouns often represent concepts. For example, in the sentence "Change the level of indention of a bullet list entry in Microsoft PowerPoint," the underscored noun and noun phrases prompt the enabling content entries "What is a level of indention?" "What is a list?" "What is a bullet list?" "What is Microsoft PowerPoint?"
- Examine the verbs. They often identify required enabling skills. For example, in the sentence "Change the level of indention of a bullet list entry in Microsoft PowerPoint," the verb indicates the enabling content entry, "How do you change the level of indention?" If this is not an entry-level skill, then it should be further analyzed as part of the instructional analysis, after which a content analysis should be performed on each of the steps of this new task.
- For decision steps, will the performer already know how to intelligently make the decision (entry-level knowledge or skill), or will that step have to be further analyzed into a procedure on how to make the decision?
- For decision steps, pause and think about the decision to identify logically connected prerequisite knowledge or skills. For example, in the decision step "Determine if the applicant's credit history is acceptable," the enabling content would include, among other things, "What is a credit history?" "How is the applicant's credit history obtained?" and "What is an acceptable credit history?"
- After you have done all you can to analyze the enabling content for a step using the above tips, ask the SMEs to review your list and see if there is anything else that a person would have to know or be able to do to carry out that step.

# What If Enabling Content Is Repeatedly Required in the Instructional Analysis?

If the same enabling content is needed in several individual steps in a task, such as the concept "return on investment" in an accounting task, then that content should be taught once somewhere before the first step in which it is needed.

If a large amount of logically related enabling content is required throughout the instructional analysis, such as a detailed understanding of concept of a computer network in a course on network problem determination, then that content should be organized and taught as a whole before it is first needed. This often takes the form of a module or topic of its own placed upfront in the course flow that teaches purely conceptual information.

Here is an example of how enabling content that was needed throughout a course on network problem determination was organized into a conceptual hierarchy in the instructional analysis and mentally tagged to be taught as a separate module upfront in the course (see appendix D for a more complete example):

---

1 Fundamental network concepts
  1.1 Networking concepts
    1.1.1 Definition of a network
      1.1.1.1 Collection of interconnected hosts that share information
        1.1.1.1.1 Systems interconnected with wires or fibers
        1.1.1.1.2 Wires and fibers are attached to system adapter cards and other network components (hubs, routers, and switches)
        1.1.1.1.3 Signals are transmitted through the wires using specific hardware and software protocols (data packaging and signaling standards)
        1.1.1.1.4 Data moves through the physical network using these network protocols
    1.1.2 Network control
      1.1.2.1 Why network control is necessary

1.1.2.2 Types of network control
  1.1.2.2.1 Hierarchical network (e.g., RTLL, CSAM, BRL/TRU)
    1.1.2.2.1.1 One central host that controls the entire network
    1.1.2.2.1.2 One host (system) within the network controls all data flow across the network
    1.1.2.2.1.3 Requires adapter cards
  1.1.2.2.2 Peer-to-peer network (TCP/IP, BDL, ZAQ201, ZPPN)
    1.1.2.2.2.1 All the hosts in the network are equal (peers to each other) and equally control the network
    1.1.2.2.2.2 No central controlling host required; each peer has its own network control program
    1.1.2.2.2.3 Network control program must be running in each peer
    1.1.2.2.2.4 SS/6000Z SPs are peer-to-peer
    1.1.2.2.2.5 Requires adapter cards
  1.1.2.2.3 Net-centric network (e.g., GGL, frame relay)
    1.1.2.2.3.1 Does not require a host
    1.1.2.2.3.2 No network operating system
    1.1.2.2.3.3 Any host can be attached to this type of network
    1.1.2.2.3.4 Requires some kind of box to attach to the network (e.g., 9125, router)
1.1.3 Network cabling [how to recognize cable type and connector]
  1.1.3.1 Why you need to know about network cables
    1.1.3.1.1 Each topology specifies valid cable types
    1.1.3.1.2 To check the physical integrity of the cable and connector
  1.1.3.2 Types of network cables
    1.1.3.2.1 Type 1
      1.1.3.2.1.1 Best wire but bulky and expensive
      1.1.3.2.1.2 Black box connector (like the old token ring)
    1.1.3.2.2 Type 5 (STP: Shielded Twisted Pair)
      1.1.3.2.2.1 Next best wire but fairly expensive
      1.1.3.2.2.2 RJ-45 connector
    1.1.3.2.3 UTP: Unshielded twisted pair
      1.1.3.2.3.1 Cheap but susceptible to noise
      1.1.3.2.3.2 RJ-45 connector
    1.1.3.2.4 Coax
      1.1.3.2.4.1 Strong and shielded but uncommon (used mainly for thin net)

       1.1.3.2.4.2 Requires termination
          1.1.3.2.4.2.1 Termination requires 50 Ohm terminators
       1.1.3.2.4.3 BNC
    1.1.3.2.5 Fiber

**[analysis continues from here—see appendix D for a more complete example]**

---

## Enabling Content Can Be Any Type of Information

Enabling content could be any type of information—concepts, facts, principles, procedures, processes, classifications, and structures. For example, a decision step "Determine if the applicant's credit history is acceptable" has the following types of information in the identified enabling content:

- "Who is an applicant?" (concept)
- "What is a credit history?" (concept)
- "How is the applicant's credit history obtained?" (procedure)
- "What is an acceptable credit history?" (business rule, which is a principle)
- "How do you determine if the credit history is acceptable?" (procedure)

If you identify a procedure as one of the enabling information entries, you should ask yourself if the performer already knows how to perform this procedure (is it an entry-level skill?). If so, then simply identify it as enabling content; you do not need to analyze it further. If not, then you should continue performing instructional analysis on that procedure until you reach the entry-level skills.

## What Is the Final Result of a Content Analysis?

You have completed the content analysis when you have an instructional analysis (structured-English indented outline) that has been enhanced in the following ways:

- Every step of every procedure has been analyzed to determine its enabling content.
- The identified enabling content has been listed in the hierarchy at the point at which it is needed, preferably using a different color or type of font to distinguish it from the procedural information.
- The only remaining *procedure* type of enabling content that remains are assumed entry-level skills. All other procedures have been further analyzed to determine their detailed steps and the enabling content for those steps.
- A version of the analysis document has been saved after performing the above actions and before performing the remaining actions listed below. This version is a backup that can be referenced later if you need to see where enabling content originally was identified before you delete any of it or move it.
- Entry-level knowledge and skills have been struck through or removed from the hierarchy and placed in a separate document for later validation. If you later discover that your audience does not know some of the things you thought they knew, you will have to add this enabling content back into the hierarchy at the appropriate places using your backup version.
- Enabling content that is required in multiple places has been pulled out and placed upfront before the first step that requires it. The repeated entries have been removed from their other locations in the hierarchy.

Your resulting enhanced hierarchical analysis has now identified all of the content that you need to teach in your course! Nothing more is needed and nothing should be taken away. This is quite an accomplishment. In addition, as you will see, you have also performed most of the legwork for structuring the course (packaging and sequencing of the information into modules and topics). This is another one of the powerful benefits of using this approach to instructional design.

# Chapter Summary—Identifying the Enabling Content

This chapter discussed how to identify the enabling content that is required to intelligently perform the steps that you identified in the instructional analysis. Identifying the enabling content is the third step in the instructional design process. The output of this step is an instructional analysis (structured-English indented outline) that has been enhanced with the required enabling content.

You should now be able to

- define enabling content and explain why it is needed,
- explain why enabling content is tied to specific behaviors,
- explain what you should do if a SME wants to include a concept or topic that is not enabling content,
- define content analysis and give an overall description of how it is performed,
- explain why enabling knowledge and skills are struck through or deleted from the content analysis,
- list and describe the five steps for performing a content analysis,
- list and explain several tips for analyzing step instructions to determine their enabling content,
- explain what to do if enabling content is repeatedly required in an instructional analysis,
- list the seven types of enabling content, and
- describe how you know when you have completed content analysis.

## Check Your Understanding

1. \_\_\_\_ \_\_\_\_ **is the knowledge and basic skills that performers must possess to carry out the activities, tasks, subtasks, and steps that were identified in the instructional analysis.**

2. **True or false? Decision steps do not have enabling content.**

3. **Enabling content is tied to:**
   A. A concept
   B. A topic or lesson
   C. The general body of knowledge about a topic
   D. A specific behavior
   E. The highest level in the instructional analysis hierarchy

4. **What should you do if a SME wants to include a concept or topic that is not enabling information?**
   A. Ask the SME why it is important.
   B. Add the topic to the course.
   C. Tell the SME that you will add it to the list of topics that will be added later after you have completed the rough draft if there is sufficient space in the course.
   D. Ask the SME to show or tell you where in the instructional analysis hierarchy the information is needed to perform a step or make a decision.
   E. Go back and reanalyze the behaviors in the instructional analysis.

5. **True or false? Content analysis is a procedure for systematically identifying the entry-level skills and knowledge that students bring to the training.**

6. **Match each step number in the procedure for conducting a content analysis with its description.**

| Step 1 | A. Save your current version of the analysis document with all enabling content identified. |
|---|---|
| Step 2 | B. Drill down the next branch in the hierarchy and repeat these steps. Continue the analysis until all of the tasks and steps have been analyzed. |
| Step 3 | C. For each step, ask, "What must a person understand or be able to do to perform this step?" Write down that information in the hierarchy under or next to the entry. |
| Step 4 | D. Locate the steps for one of the tasks in the hierarchy. |
| Step 5 | E. Cross out or delete the information that students already know (entry-level knowledge and skills). Enter this information in a separate list for later validation. |

7. **Why is entry-level knowledge and skills struck through or removed from the content analysis?**
   A. Because it will be taught in a subsequent course
   B. Because it is content students already know coming into the training
   C. To keep the course from growing too large
   D. Because it is content that will be collected and taught in conceptual units at the beginning of the training
   E. To separate content that is more complex so that it can be taught later in the course

8. **Which of the following resources do you need to conduct a content analysis? (Select all that apply.)**
   A. A large supply of sticky notes
   B. Knowledgeable SMEs

Creating Outstanding Instructional Designs

C. A way for both you and your SMEs to view the analysis document as it is being crafted

D. A completed instructional analysis

E. Sufficient time with the SMEs to conduct the analysis

F. An undisturbed environment in which to work (virtual or real)

9. **In analyzing a step of a task during content analysis, ____ often represent enabling concepts and ____ often indicate enabling skills.**

10. **Which of the following guidelines are tips for analyzing decision steps of a task during content analysis? (Select all that apply.)**
    A. Ask yourself if the performer already knows how to intelligently make the decision. If not, then identify the steps for making the procedure.
    B. Pause and think about the decision to identify logically connected prerequisite knowledge or skills.
    C. Ask the SME if the decision is difficult to make.
    D. Ask the SME what the possible outcomes of the decision are.
    E. Ask the SME to rate the procedure on a scale of low, medium, or high level of difficulty.

11. **True or false? If a large amount of logically related enabling content is required throughout the instructional analysis, then that content should be organized and taught as a whole before it is first needed.**

12. **True or false? Enabling content is always concepts, facts, principles, or classifications.**

13. **True or false? Content analysis is complete when you have identified and listed the enabling content for every step in the instructional analysis, a backup copy of this version of the analysis has been saved, the entry-level knowledge and skills have been removed from the enhanced analysis document and placed in a separate list of assumed entry-level skills and knowledge, and repeated enabling content has been pulled out, grouped, and placed upfront or before it is first needed in the analysis document.**

## Answers

1. The correct answer is "Enabling content."
2. False. Both action and decision steps must be analyzed to determine their enabling content.
3. D
4. D
5. False. Content analysis is a procedure for systematically identifying *enabling* skills and knowledge. Enabling skills and knowledge minus the entry-level skills and knowledge must be taught during the training.
6. D, C, B, A, and E
7. B
8. B, C, D, E, and F
9. The correct answer is "nouns" and "verbs."
10. A and B
11. True
12. False. Enabling content can be any of the following types of information: concepts, facts, principles, procedures, processes, classifications, and structures.
13. True

# CHAPTER 11
# Structuring the Course

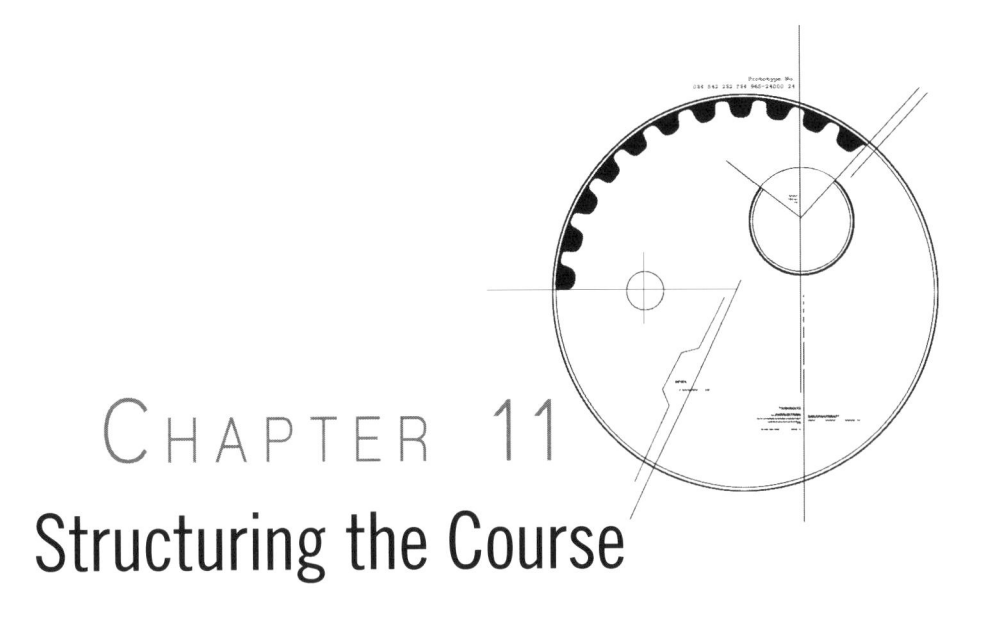

This chapter discusses how to structure a course. Structuring a course is the next step in the instructional design process. It is performed after you have completed your instructional and content analyses (see the previous chapters in part 2 for a discussion of those techniques).

## Where We Are at in the Instructional Design Process

This chapter discusses step 4 in the instructional design process: Structure the course.

1. Gather requirements
2. Perform an instructional analysis on the job outcomes
3. Identify the enabling content
4. **Structure the course**
5. Write instructional objectives

6. Determine the instructional delivery system
7. Design practice exercises and other instructional events
8. Design the prototype or example lesson
9. Create the formal design document

## What Is Course Structuring?

Structuring a course is dividing up (chunking) and sequencing the tasks and enabling content that were previously identified into courses, units, lessons, and topics.

Training courses consist of structured instructional sequences that typically include overviews, the presentation of new information, exercises, learning activities, quizzes, summaries, and so forth. These instructional sequences are typically organized into modules and topics (for technology-based training) or into units and lessons (for live virtual or classroom training).

So how can you use the instructional and content analyses to package training into instructional modules and topics in a way that makes sense? As you will see, structuring the course is a relatively easy task to perform when you previously completed sound instructional and content analyses.

Here is an example of structuring a course from the instructional and content analyses:

**Note:** In figure 26, the content analysis is not shown.

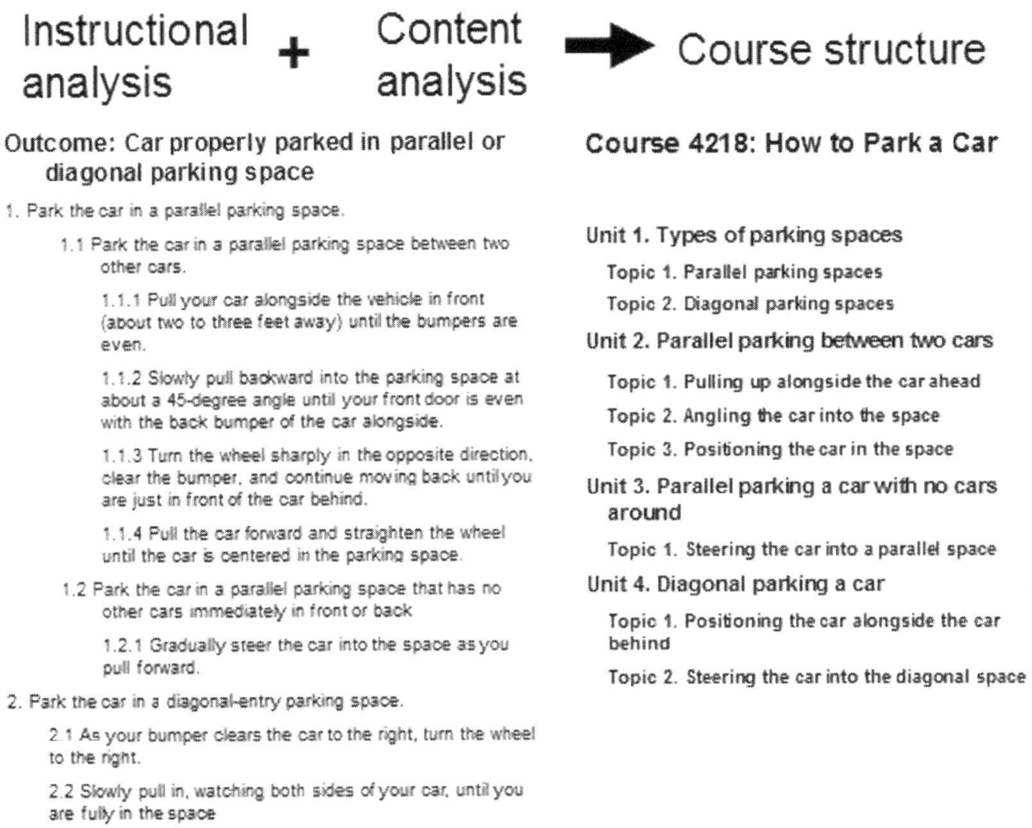

**Instructional analysis + Content analysis → Course structure**

Outcome: Car properly parked in parallel or diagonal parking space

1. Park the car in a parallel parking space.
    1.1 Park the car in a parallel parking space between two other cars.
        1.1.1 Pull your car alongside the vehicle in front (about two to three feet away) until the bumpers are even.
        1.1.2 Slowly pull backward into the parking space at about a 45-degree angle until your front door is even with the back bumper of the car alongside.
        1.1.3 Turn the wheel sharply in the opposite direction, clear the bumper, and continue moving back until you are just in front of the car behind.
        1.1.4 Pull the car forward and straighten the wheel until the car is centered in the parking space.
    1.2 Park the car in a parallel parking space that has no other cars immediately in front or back
        1.2.1 Gradually steer the car into the space as you pull forward.
2. Park the car in a diagonal-entry parking space.
    2.1 As your bumper clears the car to the right, turn the wheel to the right.
    2.2 Slowly pull in, watching both sides of your car, until you are fully in the space

**Course 4218: How to Park a Car**

Unit 1. Types of parking spaces
  Topic 1. Parallel parking spaces
  Topic 2. Diagonal parking spaces
Unit 2. Parallel parking between two cars
  Topic 1. Pulling up alongside the car ahead
  Topic 2. Angling the car into the space
  Topic 3. Positioning the car in the space
Unit 3. Parallel parking a car with no cars around
  Topic 1. Steering the car into a parallel space
Unit 4. Diagonal parking a car
  Topic 1. Positioning the car alongside the car behind
  Topic 2. Steering the car into the diagonal space

**Figure 26. A conceptual example of structuring a course**

## Overview of Structuring a Course

The procedure for structuring a course has four steps. Each of these steps will be discussed in greater detail in the rest of this chapter.

1. Identify and group common or related enabling information in your combined instructional and content analysis.
2. Make the *highest-level* major activities, tasks, and grouped or related enabling content in the analysis the top-level units or modules in the course.

3. Make the *second-highest-level* activities, tasks, and grouped or related enabling content in the hierarchy the next level topics or lessons in the course.

4. Adjust and refine the course structure using sound instructional judgment.

## Step 1. Identify and Group Common or Related Enabling Information

The first step in structuring a course is to review the combined instructional and content analysis to see if common or related enabling content is required in several places throughout the analysis. For example, for the task of changing a tire on a car, students need to know how to identify and use a tire iron in several steps of the task; specifically, to identify and remove the tire iron from the trunk, to loosen the lug nuts when removing the flat tire, and to tighten the lug nuts when installing the spare tire. Common enabling content is often best taught upfront, somewhere before the first place in the course where it is needed. Remember, enabling content can be knowledge or skills.

The same principle applies to related enabling content, which is content that is all conceptually related to or a part of a subject or topic. For example, in a course that teaches service technicians how to fix problems with computer networks, knowledge of various networking concepts is required throughout the course. Because this information is highly interrelated, it makes sense to pull it out and teach it as an integrated module or topic upfront in the course. Because the information is so highly interrelated, it is best learned as an integrated whole so that the rich interrelationships can be easily demonstrated and understood.

Here is an example of *common* enabling content for a worker at a fast food restaurant:

**Note:** In the example below, enabling content is in the indented text; notice that some enabling content is common (the same) across different tasks.

Greet customers at the drive through window.
> Welcome customer.
> Speak clearly and in a friendly tone of voice.
> Give customer drive-through instructions.

Greet customers at the dine-in counter.
> Smile.
> Welcome customer.
> Speak clearly and in a friendly tone of voice.

Greet customer at table in full-service dining area.
> Smile.
> Welcome customer.
> Speak clearly and in a friendly tone of voice.

Here is an example of *related* enabling content for a computer network engineer (the content is all related to each other, but none is common or identical):

**Note:** In the example below, enabling content is indented.

Design a computer network
> Determine network performance standards
>> Network performance standards
>
> Determine network topology
>> Network topologies
>
> Determine network protocol
>> Network protocols
>
> Determine network operating system
>> Network operating systems

*Creating Outstanding Instructional Designs*

## Step 1. Decision Table

The following decision table summarizes the first step in the procedure for structuring a course (read the table from left to right and top to bottom):

| Is there significant common or related enabling information in the instructional and content analyses? | Would that information be taught best as a whole somewhere before it is first used? | Action |
|---|---|---|
| Yes | Yes | Group that information and determine where to teach it. |
|  | No | Teach the enabling content the first place it is needed and review and refresh it (as appropriate) at subsequent points where it is needed. |
| No | Continue to the next step in the course structuring procedure. | |

**Factors to consider in determining if common or related enabling content should be taught as a whole**

- Is it required in many places (used repeatedly)?
- Do several or most aspects of a particular topic show up as enabling content?
- If yes, would it be better understood if it were taught as an integrated subject?
    - **Caution:** be careful not to add new information in teaching the topic that was not identified as enabling content.

- Is each piece of enabling content better taught at the point where it is needed?
- Regardless of which approach you take, always teach enabling content *before* it is required, not after, and refresh individual pieces of enabling content that were previously taught if significant time has gone by before they are needed again.

## Step 2. Map the Highest-Level Activities, Tasks, and Grouped Enabling Content in the Analysis to Modules or Units in the Course

The highest level activities or tasks in your hierarchical instructional analysis and the high-level groupings of enabling content are mapped to the highest-level instructional chunks in your course—typically course modules or units.

For example, consider the following combined instructional and content analysis (only the top level of tasks and grouped enabling content are shown):

> Networking concepts
> Install a computer network
> Configure a computer network
> Diagnose and fix networking problems

These high-level entries become the modules or units in your course, as shown in the following course structure:

> Module 1. Networking Concepts
> Module 2. Installing a Computer Network
> Module 3. Configuring a Computer Network
> Module 4. Diagnosing and Fixing Networking Problems

## Step 3. Map the Second-Highest Level of Activities, Tasks, or Grouped Enabling Content to Topics or Lessons in the Course

The entries in your hierarchical analysis that are immediate children of the ones you identified in the previous step become the next level of chunked instructional information in the course.

For example, consider the following instructional and content analysis (only the top two levels of tasks and grouped enabling content are shown):

>Networking concepts
>>What is a network?
>>Network topologies
>>Network protocols
>>Network operating systems
>>Network performance standards
>
>Install a computer network
>>Install the network infrastructure
>>Install the network clients and servers
>>Install the network operating system and client software
>
>Configure a computer network
>>Configure the network servers
>>Configure the network clients
>>Test the network configuration

Here's how the highest two levels in the example analysis map to the course structure:

Module 1. Networking Concepts
>Topic 1. Definition and Overview of Networks
>Topic 2. Network Topologies
>Topic 3. Network Protocols
>Topic 4. Network Operating Systems
>Topic 5. Network Performance Standards

Module 2. Installing a Computer Network
  Topic 1. Installing the Network Infrastructure
  Topic 2. Installing the Network Clients and Servers
  Topic 3. Installing the Network Operating System and Client Software
Module 3. Configuring a Computer Network
  Topic 1. Configuring the Network Servers
  Topic 2. Configuring the Network Clients
  Topic 3. Testing the Network Configuration
  Topic 4. Configuring the Network Servers
  Topic 5. Configuring the Network Clients
  Topic 6. Testing the Network Configuration

The following figure shows another example of how a course structure was created from the analysis:

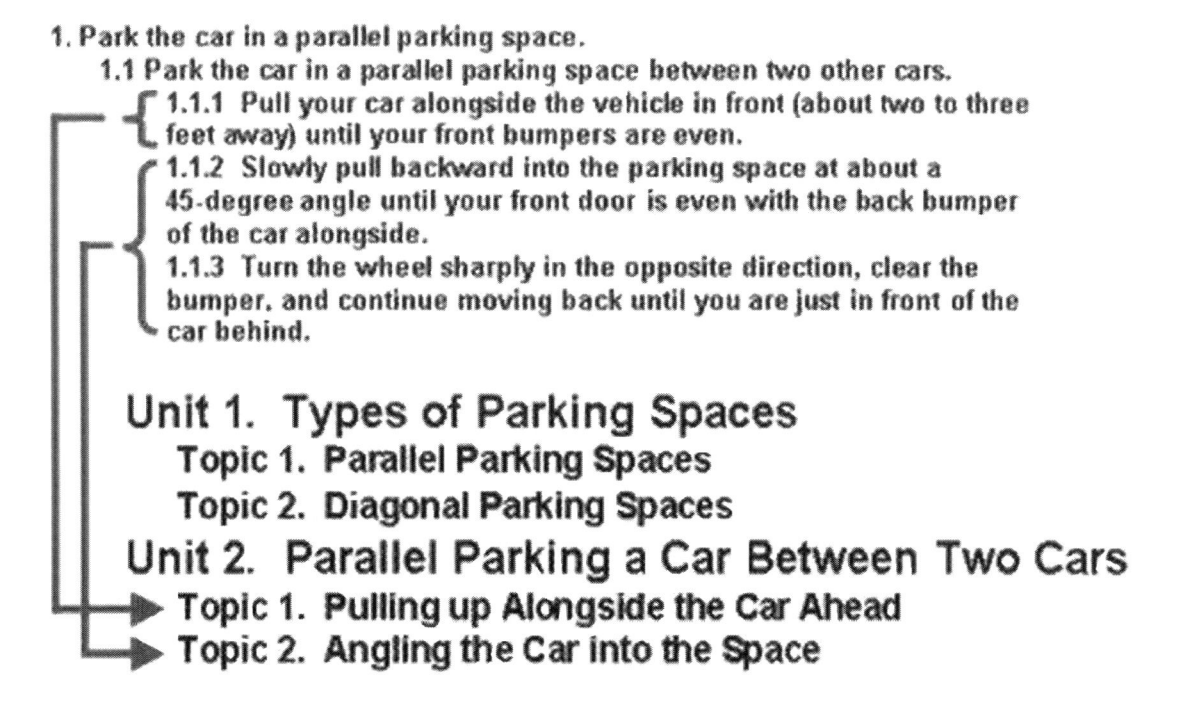

1. Park the car in a parallel parking space.
   1.1 Park the car in a parallel parking space between two other cars.
      1.1.1 Pull your car alongside the vehicle in front (about two to three feet away) until your front bumpers are even.
      1.1.2 Slowly pull backward into the parking space at about a 45-degree angle until your front door is even with the back bumper of the car alongside.
      1.1.3 Turn the wheel sharply in the opposite direction, clear the bumper, and continue moving back until you are just in front of the car behind.

### Unit 1. Types of Parking Spaces
  **Topic 1. Parallel Parking Spaces**
  **Topic 2. Diagonal Parking Spaces**
### Unit 2. Parallel Parking a Car Between Two Cars
  **Topic 1. Pulling up Alongside the Car Ahead**
  **Topic 2. Angling the Car into the Space**

**Figure 27. An example of how the course structure is derived from the instructional analysis**

## Step 4. Adjust and Refine the Course Structure

The final step in structuring the course is to refine the course structure dictated by the last two steps. Refinement is necessary to add introductory (overview) and summary modules and topics, to adjust the size of modules and topics to make them a reasonable size, to teach steps out of sequence to accommodate special instructional circumstances (a description of such cases is beyond the scope of this book), and to make sure that the sequence of modules and topics teaches prerequisite information before the information on which it relies.

To adjust and refine the course structure

1. Combine units or topics to keep the length of each fairly consistent,
2. Break lengthy units or topics into two,
3. Add overviews and summaries as appropriate,
4. Create exceptions to normal structuring to accommodate special instructional circumstances, as dictated by learning and instructional design principles (such as "backward chaining"), and
5. Do a final check to make sure that the flow and sequence of modules and topics is instructionally sound (taught in a logical flow with prerequisite modules and topics coming before their corresponding subsequent modules and topics).

**Here's how the course structure from the previous example was adjusted and refined (adjustments are shown in bold text):**

Module 1. Networking Concepts
  Topic 1. Definition and Overview of Networks
  Topic 2. Network Topologies
  Topic 3. Network Protocols
  Topic 4. Network Operating Systems
  Topic 5. Network Performance Standards
Module 2. Installing a Computer Network
  **Topic 1. Overview of Installing a Network**
  Topic 2. Installing the Network Infrastructure

Topic 3. Installing the Network Clients and Servers

Topic 4. Installing the Network Operating System and Client Software

Module 3. Configuring a computer network

**Topic 1. Overview of Configuring a Computer Network**

Topic 2. Configuring the Network Servers

Topic 3. Configuring the Network Clients

Topic 4. Testing the Network Configuration

Topic 5. Configuring the Network Servers

Topic 6. Configuring the Network Clients

Topic 7. Testing the Network Configuration

## The Benefits of Structuring the Course from the Analysis

Hopefully, you can now better understand why performing instructional and content analysis is so important—these analyses not only identify the tasks and enabling content that must be taught in the course, they also provide the skeleton for how the course is structured. What could be more logical than structuring a course into chunks that correspond to the same major tasks and activities that are required to produce the desired job outcomes or work products back on the job (with grouped enabling content modules and topics inserted where appropriate)?

When courses are structured from the combined analysis, students reviewing the course structure (table of contents or course contents page) can immediately see the relevance of the course material to what is important to them—learning how to produce the new job outcomes. The major tasks and conceptual content areas that must be mastered to produce the new job outcomes are right there before their eyes. When students perceive that the course is highly relevant to their needs, it greatly enhances their motivation.

Furthermore, because the course structure matches the major behaviors that must be performed to produce the new job outcomes, it is easier for students to transfer and apply their newly acquired knowledge and skills to the job. Research has shown that transfer of knowledge to the job is a difficult task for most students and, unless it is explicitly taught, is likely to fail in significant ways.

# Chapter Summary—Structuring the Course

This chapter discussed how to structure a course. Structuring a course is the next step in the instructional design process. It is performed after you have completed your instructional and content analyses (see the previous chapters in part 2 for a discussion of those techniques).

You should now be able to

- define course structuring;
- list the four steps to structuring a course;
- describe what common or related enabling information is and why it is often grouped and taught together;
- explain the decision logic for deciding if common or related enabling content should be grouped and taught together;
- describe how to map the highest-level activities, tasks, and grouped enabling content in the instructional and content analyses to the modules or units in the course;
- describe how to map the next highest-level activities, tasks, and grouped enabling content in the instructional and content analyses to the topics or lessons in the course;
- list and describe the five steps for adjusting and refining the course structure; and
- describe the benefits of structuring the course from the instructional and content analyses.

**Check Your Understanding**

1. \_\_\_ \_\_\_ **is dividing up (chunking) and sequencing the tasks and enabling content that was previously identified into courses, units, lessons, and topics.**

2. **Match each step in the course structuring procedure with its correct step description.**

| Step 1 | A. Adjust and refine the course structure using sound instructional judgment. |
|---|---|
| Step 2 | B. Make the next level tasks in the hierarchy the next level topics or lessons in the course. |
| Step 3 | C. Identify and group common or related enabling information in your combined instructional and content analysis. |
| Step 4 | D. Make the top-level major activities or tasks in the analysis the top-level units or modules in the course. |

3. **Classify each of the following chunks of related enabling content into electrical concepts, plumbing concepts, or building structural engineering. Note: Each of these three enabling concept areas would be taught in the course as a separate module or topic.**

   A. Methods of strengthening cement footings
   B. Electrical codes
   C. Soldering copper pipes and fittings
   D. Stud spacing requirements for load-bearing walls
   E. Wiring electrical three-way switches
   F. Electrical safety procedures
   G. Requirements for securing natural gas piping
   H. Load bearing requirements for roof
   I. Providing proper electrical grounding for residential wiring
   J. Sizing residential waste water and vent pipes

4. **True or false? Identical enabling information that is repeated in several places throughout the analysis is a potential candidate for being pulled out and taught upfront.**

5. **True or false? Related enabling information that is scattered in several places throughout the combined instructional and content analysis is a potential candidate for being pulled out and taught upfront as an integrated whole.**

6. **In structuring the course, make the *highest-level* major activities, tasks, and grouped or related enabling content in the analysis the top-level ___.**

    A. Exercises and quizzes in the course

    B. Sections in the course

    C. Units or modules in the course

    D. Overviews in the course

    E. Topics or lessons in the course

7. **In structuring a course, make the second-highest level of activities, tasks, or grouped enabling content to topics or lessons in the course ___.**

    A. Exercises and quizzes in the course

    B. Units or modules in the course

    C. Overviews in the course

    D. Sections in the course

    E. Topics or lessons in the course

8. **Why is it necessary in step 4 of creating a course structure to refine the course structure? (Select all that apply.)**

   A. To combine units or topics to maintain a fairly consistent length of units and topics

   B. To break lengthy units or topics into two

   C. To add overviews and summaries as appropriate

   D. To create exceptions to normal structuring to accommodate special instructional circumstances

   E. To do a final check to make sure that the flow and sequence of modules and topics is instructionally sound

   F. To adjust the structure for errors made in prior steps

9. **What are some of the benefits that follow from structuring a course based on the combined instructional and content analysis? (Select all that apply.)**

   A. The course structure represents the same major tasks and activities that are required to produce the desired job outcomes or work products back on the job.

   B. Students reviewing the course structure (table of contents or course contents page) can immediately see the relevance of the course material to what is important to them.

   C. Students can pick and choose which modules and topics they want to take.

   D. Students are taught common or related enabling content in integrated units or topics.

   E. Students perceive that the course is highly relevant to their needs, which greatly enhances their motivation.

   F. It is easier for students to transfer and apply their newly acquired knowledge and skills to the job.

**Answers**

1. The correct answer is "Course structuring."
2. C, D, B, and A
3. A, building structural engineering concepts; B, electrical concepts; C, plumbing concepts; D, building structural engineering concepts; E, electrical concepts; F, electrical concepts; G, plumbing concepts; H, building structural engineering concepts; I, electrical concepts; and J, plumbing concepts.
4. True
5. True
6. C
7. E
8. A, B, C, D, and E
9. A, B, D, E, and F

# CHAPTER 12
# Writing Instructional Objectives

This chapter discusses how to write instructional objectives. Writing objectives is the next step in the instructional design process and is performed after you have performed instructional and content analyses and structured the course (see the previous chapters in part 2 for a discussion of these techniques).

## Where We Are at in the Instructional Design Process

This chapter discusses step 5 in the instructional design process: Write instructional objectives.

1. Gather requirements
2. Perform an instructional analysis on the job outcomes
3. Identify the enabling content
4. Structure the course
5. **Write instructional objectives**

6. Determine the instructional delivery system
7. Design practice exercises and other instructional events
8. Design the prototype or example lesson
9. Create the formal design document

## What Are Instructional Objectives?

Instructional objectives are statements of what students should be able to do after the training. The following are examples of simple instructional objectives:

- list and describe how to perform each of the steps of the procedure for performing an audience analysis
- perform an audience analysis using a requirements template
- assert the need to perform an audience analysis when challenged

Objectives are sometimes classified into three types.

### Three types of objectives

In the example given in the text, the first objective is a knowledge objective, the second is a skill objective, and the third is an attitudinal objective. This classification is based on the skills, knowledge, and attitude (SKA) taxonomy.

Instructional objectives are important components of instructional design because they help content developers write course materials that directly support the achievement of the objectives. They describe in specific terms what students should be able to do or produce after completing the training and thus provide developers direction on what content to create.

## When Should Instructional Objectives Be Written During Instructional Design?

Some educators believe that instructional design should begin with the identification of the training objectives by democratic vote or dictation by a group of course developers and subject matter experts. Some models of instructional design even place the creation of training objectives upfront in the instructional design process. While this may have a certain intuitive appeal ("What do we want students to know and be able to do when they leave the course?"), it is premature to start design by defining instructional objectives.

Why is this so?

In pondering this question, first review the nine steps in the instructional design process. Ask yourself, "At what point in this process do I know what to teach for each module and topic?"

### The Nine Steps in the Instructional Design Process

1. Gather requirements
2. Perform an instructional analysis on the job outcomes
3. Identify the enabling content
4. Structure the course
5. Write instructional objectives
6. Determine the instructional delivery system
7. Design practice exercises and other instructional events
8. Design the prototype or example lesson
9. Create the formal design document

The answer is, only after step 4.

## Why it is premature to begin instructional design by defining instructional objectives

The reason you do not begin instructional design by defining instructional objectives upfront is because you do not know what major activities, tasks, subtasks, steps, and enabling content students must learn to produce the desired job outcomes until *after* you have performed an instructional and content analysis.

"But," you might ask, "don't I need to know what the course has to accomplish upfront?" The answer is, you do not need to know the specific instructional objectives of the course upfront; instead, you need to identify the desired *job outcomes or accomplishments* that students will be expected to produce after training. Job outcomes are identified during the requirements gathering (see chapter 2) phase of the instructional design process.

Although you might think that we are just splitting fine definitions of terminology here, this is not the case. Job outcomes describe tangible *work products* (such as a marketing plan) and intangible *work results* (such as a decision to invest or not invest in a particular new line of business)—not the skills, knowledge, and attitudes that are required to produce them, which is typically the level at which instructional objectives are written. Job outcomes are nouns and noun phrases (chapter 2); in stark contrast, objectives always include a behavior (verb).

The focus in the early stages of design should be on identifying and clarifying the work products and accomplishments that have value to the organization that will justify the cost and investment in training, not with the identification of general skills, knowledge, or competencies that some group of people think students ought to know. These work products and accomplishments are then systematically analyzed to determine the specific behaviors (major activities, tasks, and steps) and enabling content that are required to produce them. This rigorous approach to analysis produces lean, effective instruction.

Instructional objectives are written only *after* the specific behaviors and enabling content have been identified and structured into the modules and topics of the course. Until then, you do not know the specific skills and information you should teach that will produce those outcomes, because it has not yet been systematically identified.

## The Three Components of an Instructional Objective

Formal instructional objectives, as described by Robert Mager, an expert in the field of human performance improvement, should have three components:

- **Performance:** An action verb or verb phrase describing the performance (behavior) that students will exhibit to show that they have mastered the objective
- **Conditions:** The conditions under which students will exhibit this behavior
- **Criteria:** The criteria for satisfactory performance

## Examples of Instructional Objectives

Consider the following three instructional objectives:

Example #1. Perform requirements gathering using the approved departmental template with all criteria specified in the template satisfied.

Example #2. Using Horn's classification scheme, classify the following chunks of information into their correct type.

Example #3. Without any aids, correctly list all nine steps in instructional design.

An analysis of these objectives into their corresponding components is given in the following table. **Note:** As shown in objectives #2 and #3, the three components can be stated in any order when writing the objective.

|  | **Example #1** | **Example #2** | **Example #3** |
|---|---|---|---|
| **Performance** | perform requirements gathering | classify the following chunks of information | list all nine steps in instructional design |
| **Conditions** | using the approved departmental template | using Horn's classification scheme | without any aids |
| **Criteria** | with all criteria specified in the template satisfied | into their correct type | correctly |

## Objectives for a Course Are Typically Written at Many Different Levels

Objectives are usually written for each of the structured levels of the course—for example, at the course level, the module level, and the topic level. Course-level objectives are the most broad and encompassing, while topic-level objectives are the most specific and narrow. Each lower-level objective should support at least one higher-level objective.

### Course objectives

- statements describing what students will produce back on the job (the outcomes)
- high-level instructional course objectives

**Module or unit objectives**

- high-level unit objectives
- written at a more detailed level than the course level
- objectives specific to that module

**Topic or lesson objectives**

- low-level topic objectives
- written at a more detailed level than the unit level

## Overview of How to Write Objectives

The procedure for writing objectives consists of five steps:

1. Choose a level in the course to write the objectives (course, unit, or topic)
2. Write the **performance** (observable behavior) that you expect students to exhibit using nonfuzzy verbs
3. Add the **conditions** under which students will exhibit the performance
4. Add the **criteria** by which students will be judged as having exhibited adequate performance
5. Validate and edit each objective for conciseness, precision, and clarity

## Step 1. Choose a Level in the Course to Write the Objectives (Course, Module, or Topic)

Because objectives are specific to an instructional sequence or chunk of instruction, first decide at which level you want to begin writing your objectives. Write the objectives for this level (course, module, or topic) and then choose another level to write objectives.

It is usually best to begin at the lowest level in the course and work your way up to higher levels. It is easier to collapse more detailed objectives into higher-level objectives than write higher-level objectives that adequately summarize detailed objectives that have not yet been written.

# Step 2. Write the Performance That You Expect Students to Exhibit Using Nonfuzzy Verbs

The performance is the specific behavior that students will manifest to indicate mastery of the objective. It is impossible to tell if students have learned something until they do something that demonstrates acquired learning, such as carrying out a procedure, making decisions, or performing an intellectual skill. The performance describes what students will do after the instructional sequence that will provide evidence that they have acquired the desired skills, knowledge, or attitude.

Choosing precise verbs that accurately describe the desired indicator behavior is a critical part of writing objectives. Fuzzy verbs do not adequately describe the desired performance.

Fuzzy verbs that often show up in objectives include "know," "understand," and "appreciate." How can you know if students know, understand, or appreciate something? You cannot unless you prescribe concise indicator verbs, such as "state," "list," "write," "recite," "code," "present," "build," "contrast," and "distinguish."

**Verbs appropriate to each level in Bloom's taxonomy**

### Knowledge
- defines, describes, names, identifies, labels, matches, recalls, reproduces

### Comprehension
- classifies, restates, discusses, explains, generalizes, gives examples

### Application
- applies, assesses, charts, computes, extends, instructs, implements, solves

### Analysis
- appraises, diagrams, compares, contrasts, questions, tests, discriminates

### Synthesis

- adapts, collaborates, combines, creates, designs, manages, plans, models, revises

### Evaluation

- appraises, argues, judges, predicts, rates, critiques, interprets, reframes, assesses

## Avoid Writing Performance Capabilities in Place of Actual Performances

In writing objectives, be sure to write actual performances that students are expected to exhibit after the training, not capabilities for performing.

The following table shows how each statement of capability should be rewritten using specific performances.

| Replace these statements of capabilities ... | with specific performances |
|---|---|
| Be able to debug faulty code | Debug the following code containing ... |
| Be able to recite the five requirements for learning | Recite the five requirements for learning |
| Be able to apply good principles of design | Design a course using the principles of sound instructional design |
| Be able to handle client objections to closing the sale | Follow the WIN procedure for handling the following categories of client objections to closing the sale ... |
| Be skilled in forecasting channel demand | Correctly forecast channel demand each quarter within 5% of actuals following company-approved techniques |

# Step 3. Add the Conditions Under Which Students Will Exhibit the Performance

Conditions are the environments, tools, and constraints under which students will be required to exhibit the specified performance.

The following questions will help you identify the conditions for an objective:

- What will students be given to help them perform (tools, templates, job aids, forms, and so forth)?
- What constraints will students be placed under?
    - What will students *not* be given?
    - How will the environment in which students perform be constrained?
- What are the circumstances and environments in which students will perform?
    - Under what real-life job conditions will students perform?

**Examples of conditions**

Conditions describing what students will be given

- Using the accessibility checklist, ...
- Given a scientific calculator, ...
- Using the loan application form, ...
- Using the ABC Point of Sale Terminal Quick Reference, ...

Conditions describing constraints or what students will not be given

- Without using a calculator, ...
- From memory, ...
- Without access to peer support, ...
- Without any other resources, ...

Conditions describing circumstances or environments

- In a simulated irate customer face-to-face scenario, …
- In a close-the-sale role-play with the instructor, …
- Presented with a broken computer network, …
- Given an opportunity to make a sale, …

## Step 4. Add the Criteria by Which Students Will Be Judged as Having Exhibited Adequate Performance

Criteria are the standards by which students' performance will be judged as meeting the objective. Without criteria, how would you know what depth, skill level, or complexity that students' performance must achieve? For example, how effective would it be for a college professor to give an exam in which she asked students to write a 500-word essay on a particular topic if she did not have any criteria for judging the adequacy of the essay? Objectives are like mini tests in which students are asked to perform specific behaviors under specific conditions and meet specific criteria. Without criteria, how would you know if students' performance was adequate?

For example, consider the objective, "Play Chopin's Nocturne in E-Flat Major." Without criteria, how would you know if the performance was adequate? The criteria defines the *level* of performance that must be achieved: "Play Chopin's Nocturne in E-Flat Major without any mistakes and using proper fingering, expression, and intonation, receiving a total score of 8 out of 10 as judged by a panel of three piano instructors using the provided evaluation checklist." This is a specific level of performance.

Criteria also provide benchmarks by which you and the sponsors of training can objectively demonstrate that the training achieved what it set out to achieve. This is valuable information that helps show that the sponsor's training investment was wisely used.

## Examples of types of criteria

### Speed

- within five seconds
- before the project due date

### Accuracy

- without any mistakes
- with no software bugs
- in a way that meets ISO 9000 requirements

### Quality

- with each of the items on the following checklist satisfactorily completed
- in compliance with all items on the accessibility checklist for web sites

## Step 5. Validate and Edit Each Objective for Conciseness, Precision, and Clarity

To accomplish this step

- validate the objective to make sure that your main intent has been accurately captured and specified,
- clarify any vague components (performance, conditions, criteria) in the objective, and
- edit the objective for clarity and conciseness.

The following table provides examples of how objectives have been rewritten for this purpose:

| Problem objective | Rewritten version |
|---|---|
| **Inaccurate main intent** Describe the nine steps for designing instruction ... | **Accurate main intent** Perform the nine steps for designing instruction ... |
| **Vague components** Write compact code ... | **More clear and precise** Write Java code for doing X in 1,000 lines of code or less ... |
| **Wordy and vague** Students should be able to demonstrate a thorough understanding of XYZ by convincing the instructor of their knowledge ... | **More clear and concise** State the three main characteristics of XYZ and give two examples of each ... |

# The Relationship between Objectives and Course Content, Exercises, and Tests

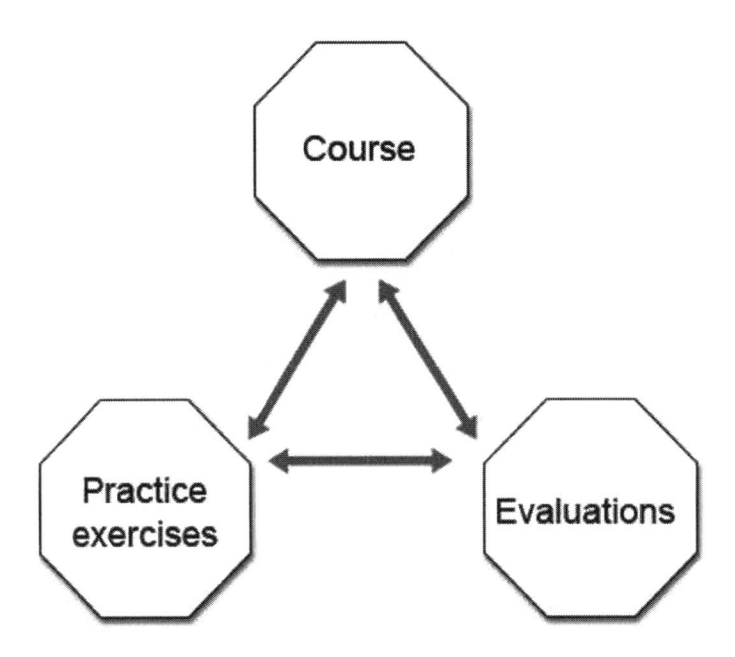

**Figure 28. Objectives should match the course content, practice exercises, and evaluations**

You should have a unity between your objectives and the course content, exercises, tests, and other instructional elements. Specifically, this means that

- the **course** should only include lesson material that is required to achieve the objectives;
- the **practice exercises** should test the specific behaviors specified in the objectives;
- the **evaluations, postcourse tests**, and **performance assessments** should match the performance, conditions, and criteria stated in the corresponding objectives; and
- other instructional activities are used in the course, such as **demonstrations**, **simulations**, and so forth.

Tests, for example, should not test performances and behaviors that were not taught nor expect higher levels of performance than those that were taught. This principle is commonly violated in many professor-authored college tests in an effort to create a better—albeit artificial—spread of scores.

The following table has course elements that do and do not match the objective:

| Objective | Course elements |
|---|---|
| Draw a diagram of each of the five network topologies with each major component identified and labeled. | Lesson content<br><br>The importance of networks<br><br>Network speeds<br><br>Network topologies |
| | Practice exercise<br><br>List the five network topologies and explain their major components |
| | Test<br><br>Draw a diagram of each of the five network topologies with each major component identified and labeled |

Analysis of the course elements in the table

- Under lesson content, "The importance of networks" and "Network speeds" do not support the objective and should be removed unless there are other objectives to that effect. The topic "Network topologies" does directly support the objective and is therefore matched to the objective.

- The practice exercise specifies a different performance (listing and explaining) than the one prescribed by the objective (drawing and labeling) and is therefore mismatched.

*Creating Outstanding Instructional Designs*

- The test specifies the same performance (drawing and labeling) of the same object (network topologies) and is therefore correctly matched to the objective.

Objectives flow naturally from the course structure if that structure was based on the combined instructional and content analysis.

The following table shows an example of how objectives flow naturally from the course structure (**Note:** enabling content is shown in **bold** text).

| Analysis document | Topic 1 objectives |
|---|---|
| **Topic 1. Mowing the lawn**<br><br>Check the mower's gasoline and oil levels and replenish as needed.<br>- **How to check the fluid levels**<br>- **How to replenish fluids**<br><br>Prime the mower.<br>- **How to prime the mower**<br><br>Set engine control to run.<br>- **What is the engine control?**<br>- **How to set the control**<br><br>Pull starter cord to start mower.<br>- **What is the starter cord?**<br>- **How to pull the starter cord**<br><br>And so forth | - Using the supplied power mower, mow the front lawn at the proper height and with a proper mowing pattern.<br>- Correctly assess the engine's fluid levels and replenish fluids as necessary to their proper fill levels.<br>- Prime the mower the correct number of times.<br>- Set the engine control to the run position before starting.<br>- Correctly identify the engine control and its settings |

## Objectives Are Meant for Communication

Keep the following in mind as you create your objectives:

- The instructional objectives you create are meant to be used by the course developers who must shape course materials and content to match the objectives.

- Most educators also believe there is value in presenting the objectives to students as well. Objectives written for students, however, are often simplified versions of high-level course objectives meant to give students a better idea of what the course is about. Many students will not read long or detailed lists of technical instructional objectives.
    - Some designers present objectives to students using the three categories of the skills, knowledge, and attitude (SKA) taxonomy: skill objectives, knowledge or enabling objectives, and attitudinal objectives. This is a preference on the part of the course designer.
    - Other designers like to present objectives to students as a hierarchy with each course-level objective broken into module and topic objectives in an indented fashion.
    - Yet other designers present course-level objectives upfront and save presenting module and topic-level objectives to their respective modules and topics.

- The *conditions* component of the objective is often left out if there are no unusual or specific conditions required.

- The *criteria* component of the objective might also be left out if it is implied or is known by the readers of the objectives (but be careful in making this assumption!).

- The *performance* component of the objective is never left out.

---

An excellent book on this topic is *Preparing Instructional Objectives*, 3rd edition by Robert F. Mager, The Center for Effective Performance, Atlanta, Georgia, 1997. It is available from http://www.cepworldwide.com.

# Chapter Summary—Writing Instructional Objectives

This chapter presented how to write instructional objectives. Writing objectives is the next step in the instructional design process and is performed after you have performed instructional and content analyses and structured the course (see the previous chapters in part 2 for a discussion of these techniques).

You should now be able to

- define instructional objectives and describe why they are important;
- explain when instructional objectives should be written during instructional design and defend your assertion;
- list and describe the three components of instructional objectives;
- provide three examples of well-written instructional objectives;
- explain why instructional objectives are written at each level in a course structure;
- list the five steps in the procedure for writing instructional objectives;
- explain what it means to choose a level in the course to write objectives;
- define fuzzy verbs and explain how to write nonfuzzy performances;
- give examples of verbs that are appropriate for each of the levels in Bloom's learning taxonomy;
- define the *performance* component of objectives and identify objectives that have performance capabilities instead of actual performances in them;
- define the *conditions* component of objectives and state three questions that you should ask to help define conditions;
- define the *criteria* component of objectives, explain why it is important, and give three categories of criteria with examples of each;
- explain how to validate and edit objectives for conciseness, precision, and clarity;
- describe the relationship that should exist between objectives and course content, exercises, tests, and other course elements;

- given a set of objectives, identify matched and mismatched course elements;
- describe how objectives are created from the course structure document that is based on the combined instructional and content analysis; and
- describe how objectives should be communicated and when it is appropriate to leave out various components of objectives.

## Check Your Understanding

1. \_\_\_ \_\_\_ are statements of what students should be able to do after the training.

2. **Consider the following early activities in instructional design:**
    1. Gather requirements
    2. Perform an instructional analysis on the job outcomes
    3. Identify the enabling content
    4. Structure the course

    **After which activity do you know what content to teach for each module and topic in the course?**
    - A. After activity 1
    - B. After activity 2
    - C. After activity 3
    - D. After activity 4

3. **What should be defined very early in the instructional design process?**
    - A. The desired new job outcomes, work products, and accomplishments that students need to acquire
    - B. The instructional objectives for the course

C. The structure of the course

D. The learning activities that you need to put into the course for students to learn

E. The specific content that should be put into the course

F. The skills, knowledge, and attitudes that need to be taught in the course

4. **According to Robert Mager, which of the following are the three components of instructional objectives?**

    A. Action, conditions, time

    B. Action, time, performance constraints

    C. Behavior, conditions, criteria

    D. Behavior, environment, criteria

    E. Performance, conditions, criteria

    F. Performance, environment, criteria

5. **Classify each of the following components of objectives into performance, conditions, or criteria:**

    A. Code a Java applet

    B. that correctly computes mortgage interest on home loans

    C. using the Websphere development environment

    D. Given a foot-long piece of rope,

    E. correctly tie a sheepshank knot

    F. in three seconds or less

    G. Change the design template used by the following Microsoft PowerPoint presentation to the XYZ template

    H. in 30 seconds or less

    I. without using the Help function

6. **What is missing from the following objectives (performance, conditions, criteria)?**

    A. Explain the meaning of love.

    B. Using any resources available on the Internet, 400 lines of functioning web crawler code without bugs

    C. The twelve principles of adult learning

    D. Operate the ABC machine.

    E. Distinguish good code from bad.

    F. Understand the principles of networking.

    G. Write a 500-word essay from memory on the rise and fall of the Roman Empire

    H. Rules of good grammar

7. **Instructional objectives are usually written for each _____ of the course structure.**

8. **Identify the correct sequence of steps in the procedure for writing instructional objectives.**

    | Step 1 | A. Add the criteria by which students will be judged as having exhibited adequate performance. |
    | --- | --- |
    | Step 2 | B. Validate and edit each objective for conciseness, precision, and clarity. |
    | Step 3 | C. Write the performance that you expect students to exhibit using nonfuzzy verbs. |
    | Step 4 | D. Add the conditions under which students will exhibit the performance. |
    | Step 5 | E. Choose a level in the course to write the objectives (course, unit, or topic). |

9. **True or false? In writing instructional objectives, it is usually best to write high-level objectives first and then write lower-level objectives.**

10. **Which of the following are fuzzy verbs? (Select all that apply.)**
    A. State
    B. Appreciate
    C. List
    D. Describe
    E. Know
    F. Explain
    G. Match
    H. Understand
    I. Draw

11. **What is wrong with the description of the *performance* in the objective, "Be able to handle client objections to closing the sale"?**
    A. It does not describe which specific categories of client objections students should be able to handle.
    B. It describes a performance capability rather than an actual performance.
    C. The verb "handle" is too vague.
    D. No criteria or conditions are given.

12. **Which of the following questions will help you identify the conditions for an objective? (Select all that apply.)**
    A. What are the circumstances and environments in which students will perform?
    B. How will the environment in which students perform be constrained?
    C. What is the criteria by which students' performance will be judged?

D. What will students be given to help them perform (tools, templates, job aids, forms, and so forth)?

E. What will students *not* be given?

F. What constraints will students be placed under?

G. What is it that students must do?

H. Under what real-life job conditions will students perform?

13. **What are the two most important reasons why you should include criteria in your instructional objectives? (Select the two that apply.)**

    A. Without criteria, you would not know the depth, skill level, or complexity that students' performance must achieve.

    B. Criteria make it easier to write course tests.

    C. Criteria tell the sponsor how smart students will be at the end of the training.

    D. Criteria are the key way to show that standardized testing has been implemented in the course.

    E. Criteria provide benchmarks by which you and the sponsors of training can objectively demonstrate that the training achieved what it set out to achieve.

14. **What are the three main categories of criteria in objectives?**

    A. Functionality, speed, tolerance measurements

    B. Time, quality, completeness

    C. Time to completion, number of units completed, checklist compliance

    D. Accuracy, speed, quality

    E. Accuracy, time, level of professionalism

15. **After you have written your objective, you should validate and edit each objective for conciseness, precision, and clarity by: (Select all that apply.)**

    A. Making sure that the performance has been written as a capability.

    B. Making sure that your main intent has been accurately captured and specified.

    C. Choosing a verb that is broad enough to capture an entire class of behaviors.

    D. Clarifying any vague components (performance, conditions, criteria) in the objective.

    E. Rewriting the objective for clarity and conciseness as needed.

16. **Which of the following course elements should match the objectives in terms of what they ask students to learn or do? (Select all that apply.)**

    A. The course content

    B. The practice exercises

    C. The course tests, evaluations, and performance assessments

    D. The within-topic checkpoint questions

    E. Other instructional activities, such as demonstrations, simulations, and so forth

17. **Consider the following objective:**

    "Given a list of ten objectives with one or more missing components, identify the missing components for each objective."

    **Which of the following course elements match this objective?**

    A. Content within a lesson: The three components of an objective

    B. Content within a lesson: Identifying performances

    C. Content within a lesson: Identifying conditions

    D. Content within a lesson: Identifying criteria

E.  Practice exercise: Revise each of the following ten poorly written objectives to make them instructionally sound objectives.

F.  Course test: Write instructional objectives for the following ten behaviors.

G.  Course test: For each of the following ten objectives in the table below, identify the missing components, if any, for each objective by checking the appropriate cell or cells to the right of each objective.

18. **True or false? Objectives that are presented to students should always be identical to instructional objectives in the design document.**

19. **Which component of an instructional objective should *always* be explicitly stated in the objective?**
    A. The conditions
    B. The enabling components
    C. The criteria
    D. The prerequisite components
    E. The performance

## Answers

1. The correct answer is "Instructional objectives."
2. D
3. A
4. E
5. A, performance; B, criteria; C, conditions; D, conditions; E, performance; F, criteria; G, performance; H, criteria; I, conditions
6. A, conditions; B, performance and conditions; C, performance, conditions, and criteria; D, conditions and criteria; E, conditions and criteria; F, performance, conditions, and criteria; G, performance and conditions; H, performance, conditions, and criteria

7. The correct answer is "level."
8. E, C, D, A, and B
9. False. It is usually best to begin with the lowest-level objectives and work up to writing higher-level objectives.
10. B, E, and H
11. B
12. A, B, D, E, F, and H
13. A and E
14. D
15. B, D, and E
16. A, B, C, D, and E
17. A, matches; B, matches; C, matches; D, matches; E, does not match; F, does not match; and G, matches
18. False. Objectives written for students are often simplified versions of high-level course objectives meant to give students a better idea of what the course is about. Many students will not read long or detailed lists of technical instructional objectives.
19. E

# CHAPTER 13
# Determining the Instructional Delivery System

This chapter discusses how to determine which technology or method you will use to deliver training to students. This is the next step in the instructional design process. It is performed after you have completed the instructional and content analyses, structured the course, and written the instructional objectives (see the previous chapters in part 2 for a discussion of these topics).

## Where We Are at in the Instructional Design Process

This chapter discusses step 6 in the instructional design process: Determine the instructional delivery system.

1. Gather requirements
2. Perform an instructional analysis on the job outcomes
3. Identify the enabling content

4. Structure the course
5. Write formal objectives
6. **Determine the instructional delivery system**
7. Design practice exercises and other instructional events
8. Design the prototype or example lesson
9. Create the formal design document

## What Is an Instructional Delivery System?

After you have performed instructional and content analyses, structured the course, and written the instructional objectives, you are ready to determine the instructional delivery system.

An instructional delivery system is the set of technologies and methods by which you will deliver the training to the students. Traditional delivery methods, such as instructor-led classroom delivery and on-the-job training, have been around for ages. However, technology is always advancing, providing new ways to deliver training to students. Examples of training delivery methods include

- classroom delivery by an instructor;
- satellite delivery to a learning center;
- web-based training;
- Web Lectures (narrated PowerPoint presentations) delivered over the Internet;
- computer-based training (CBT) distributed physically on computer disk or media;
- web conference delivered over the Internet;
- online wizards, coaches, help, and electronic performance support systems (EPSS);
- computer, machine, and staged simulations;
- hardcopy self-study workbooks, reference materials, and job aids;

- mentoring and on-the-job training;
- collaborative online classroom environments; and
- virtual online worlds.

## Choosing a Delivery System

Deciding which method or methods to use to deliver the training is a complex decision involving many factors. Some organizations standardize all training delivery on a subset of possible delivery methods, thus narrowing down the range of possible choices. Others have created worksheets or elaborate prescriptions for making delivery system decisions.

In choosing a delivery system for your training, you must weigh many factors. Choosing a delivery system requires balancing the students' and organization's delivery needs and constraints with the delivery methods and technologies that would be most suitable for the instructional goals and course content. There is no easy or mechanical process that will remove all judgment in selecting an effective delivery system.

*For that reason, no procedure for doing so will be presented here.* Rather, we will present some of the most important factors that you should consider in making this decision and discuss IBM's current model for choosing delivery systems that match the instructional content and objectives.

## Audience Considerations in Choosing a Delivery System

In choosing a delivery system, you should consider several factors related to the audience of the training—the students themselves.

### How many students need to be trained?

Creating highly interactive technology-based training incorporating lots of media treatments (graphics, animations, and so forth) is resource intensive and generally not cost-effective for small numbers of students. The return on investment for resource-intensive technology-based delivery systems generally increases as the number of students increases. If you have a small number of students, you should probably consider less expensive and less elaborate delivery systems.

Also, classroom-delivered instruction might be cost effective for a one-time rollout to a handful of students but cost prohibitive for training large numbers of students simultaneously at different locations. You might also be limited by the number of instructors who are available to teach.

### How are students distributed geographically?

If students are centrally located, such as in the same city or building, it is more practical and less costly to get them together for classroom, collaborative, or one-on-one instruction than it would be if they were scattered geographically across a wide region. Travel and living expenses generally prohibit bringing a large number of geographically dispersed students to a central location for training.

Students who are widely distributed geographically are probably best served with a delivery system that can provide training directly to each student, such as some form of technology-based training or self-study training.

### What methods of training are students already familiar and comfortable with?

Avoid introducing a new training delivery system when an existing or familiar one would do the job. Using a training delivery system that students are already familiar with and comfortable with removes a potential barrier for students to take the training and avoids the need to motivate and teach students how to use a new system.

On the other hand, if the current methods are unsuitable for teaching the required content and outcomes or for reaching a geographically dispersed audience, you might consider introducing an appropriate new training delivery system if other factors, such as cost and organizational acceptance, are not a problem.

## When can students take the training and how much time can they devote to it each time?

Students in the real world have real-world demands. Training takes dedicated time out of their already busy schedules. For example, sales agents might be busy meeting with clients and marketing teams during regular work hours.

Furthermore, students might be unable to dedicate a full day out of their schedule to training. They might only have one- or two-hour blocks of time available sporadically and unpredictably.

In these situations, on-demand, self-directed forms of delivery in which students can take training whenever they want it, 24/7, and pause and resume training at will, would be more suitable.

## Where will students take the training?

Will students take the training at their desk (using a computer, for example), in transit using their laptop computer, or at home, using hardcopy training materials, or will they be required to go to a learning resource center or classroom facility to take the training?

The answer to this question depends in part on the availability of computers or other technology at these locations, on understanding the students' work demands and environment, and on understanding the training facilities that are available to the organization.

For mobile workers who are always on the go, higher-end media might pose a problem because of the larger file sizes and longer download or replication times that are required. In this case, a DVD disk or other computer media distribution method might be used.

### What are students' motivations to learn this content?

If students have low motivation to learn the material, you might need to consider a delivery system that provides a higher level of student interaction and richer media treatments.

### What are students' preferred learning styles?

A group of engineers might prefer an analytical approach to the material, which requires reading, self-study, and the completion of practice problems. On the other hand, a group of salespeople might prefer live demonstrations, slide presentations, and verbal interaction with an instructor and other students.

Additionally, some students might be more visually oriented; others might be more aural. While student preference is generally not a critical factor in choosing a delivery system, it should be considered and accommodated where it makes sense.

## Organizational, Logistical, and Sponsor Factors in Choosing a Delivery System

In choosing a delivery system, you must also be aware of any constraints, policies, and limitations imposed by the organization and sponsors for whom you are developing the training.

### Training development and delivery budget

Budget is one of the most influential factors in choosing a delivery system. Smaller budgets generally mean simpler, less costly, less media-and-technology-rich delivery systems.

Because of this, budget should be one of the first factors you should consider, because it can immediately narrow the list of fundable delivery systems.

## Organizational standards and policies

Has the organization already standardized on certain training delivery systems? If so, are exceptions allowed, or will you be required to choose an approved delivery method?

Is there a move in the organization away from instructor-led training and toward technology-based training?

If workers are unionized, does the union have any restrictions that affect how training is delivered?

## Maintenance requirements and course life span

How will the training be updated and maintained over time? Is funding in place to provide for updates, or will individual departments or units have to maintain their own training materials?

In the latter case, you might need to choose a delivery method that the organization has the required in-house expertise to make updates to. Flash-based training, for example, requires sophisticated skills to modify.

Moreover, it is easier to cost-justify courses that are more expensive to develop and maintain if they have a longer life span than courses that have a shorter useful life span. How quickly will the information in the course become outdated?

## Accessibility and translation requirements

Will the training have to be translated? If so, then costs and space requirements of translated text (which is physically much longer in some languages) must be taken into account in choosing a delivery system. Higher-end media, such as graphics, Flash files, audio, and video, generally cost more and are more difficult to translate.

Another issue is, to what degree will the training materials be required to be accessible to those with disabilities or impairments? Some forms of training are easier to make accessible than other forms.

## LMS Integration requirements

Will the training need to be integrated into the organization's learning management system (LMS) for student enrollment, delivery, and tracking? If so, for example, you might need to choose development and authoring tools that are SCORM compliant.

## Management and administration requirements

How will students enroll in the course? How will the course be administered? For instructor-led classroom delivery, who will prepare and send out student materials for each class? Do student completion and test scores need to be tracked and reported?

Some delivery systems, such as those that are integrated with an LMS, can automate many of these tasks.

## Availability of subject matter experts for development

Some forms of delivery might require more development time on the part of subject matter experts (SMEs). For example, web-based training with simulations might require detailed SME involvement, whereas classroom instruction might require that the instructor fill in details or give demonstrations.

## Availability of instructors for delivery

By definition, instructor-led training, whether it is live or virtual, requires an instructor. If you choose this form of delivery, are there sufficient instructors available to meet delivery schedule demands, and can their salaries and travel-and-living expenses be funded?

## Development window and training deadlines

How much time do you have to develop the training? Generally, technology and media-rich training delivery methods require longer development windows than other methods of delivery. Do not choose a delivery system for which you do not have sufficient time to develop the training.

## Subject Matter and Learning Outcome Considerations in Choosing a Delivery System

In choosing a delivery system, you must also consider the content of the course and what type of interaction is required to accomplish the training objectives.

### Types of learning objectives and outcomes

Learning outcomes involving psychomotor skills (skilled movement involving hand-eye coordination, for example, such as operating a lathe) would benefit from instruction in which these skills can be demonstrated and practiced. Video, Flash animations, simulations, and live instructor-led training would be likely candidates for this type of subject matter.

Training outcomes that require the handling of complex interpersonal interactions might be best delivered using role-based scenarios, simulations, and group or individual practice with instructor observations and feedback. Live or virtual classroom or technology-based training with interactive simulations would be potential candidates, among others.

Training outcomes that involve information awareness-type outcomes could be delivered using a low-cost, low-tech system, such as Web Lectures (narrated PowerPoint presentations), Internet QuickViews (tabbed web page presentations), and hardcopy training materials.

## Complexity of the content

Teaching service technicians how to repair supercomputers is considerably more ambitious than teaching sales staff how to follow an order-entry procedure. Complex content involving complex decision making, for example, might benefit from technology such as a wizard, decision support system (DSS), or electronic performance support systems.

Other complex content might best be taught through traditional classrooms and labs in which students can interact continuously with an instructor, be taught subtle distinctions, and be personally observed and mentored.

## Level of interactivity required to achieve mastery

How much interaction is required to teach the content and achieve the desired learning outcome? Some forms of training, such as Web Lectures and static hardcopy training, have little or no interactivity. Other forms of training, such as live instructor-led training, web-based training, and simulations, can provide a high level of interactivity.

Learning pure facts such as sales information might not require much interactivity beyond drill-and-practice exercises and embedded checkpoint questions. On the other hand, learning to play the piano or learning algebra both require a high degree of interactivity during training to master.

## Skill level

Learning objectives dictate the degree to which students must demonstrate the objective's performance. The skill of closing a sales deal, for example, can be taught to the level of simple awareness of the principles for closing a sale, to closing sales with assistance, to closing sales consistently without assistance.

Higher levels of skill mastery generally require more interactivity and sophistication on the part of the delivery system to provide realistic practice with feedback, true-to-life scenarios and simulations, and careful observations and critiques of students' performance.

Lower-level outcomes, such as awareness outcomes, can be accomplished with much less sophistication and functionality in the delivery system.

## Technology Considerations in Choosing a Delivery System

In choosing a delivery system, you must also consider technology requirements.

### Hosting availability and cost

For web-based or server-based training, is a hosting server available to host the training program? If so, will the budget support the required ongoing hosting costs?

### Download and response time

If students must download an entire course before starting the training, what is the download time, and is it acceptable to students?

If training is interactive over the Internet or a network, what is the response time for student interactions, and is it satisfactory?

### Technical support personnel required

Technology-dependent training, such as virtual classroom and web-delivered training, require skilled technical staff both to develop the training and later to solve technical issues as they arise during pilot and delivery.

### Availability and cost of authoring and development tools

Does the organization have access to the development applications and corresponding licenses? If not, will the budget support acquiring them?

If developers do not have expertise in using the tools, how will they be trained in their use, and who will pay for this training?

**If new training technology is used, the time and effort required by students to learn the new technology**

Learning a new training delivery system is overhead on the part of students—they are not learning the desired new skills; rather, they are learning how to use the tool that will teach them the new skills.

New technology means new user interfaces to learn, new navigational systems to master, and new styles of training delivery with which to become familiar. If the overhead on the part of students to learn the new system is too high, they will be discouraged from taking the training.

Moreover, for sophisticated new systems, you might need to create a training module just to teach students how to use the new technology, thereby adding to students' training time, time away from the job, and development costs.

**Students' access to the technology**

Do students already have the technology required to take the training (such as a computer), or will new technology have to be purchased and provided to students, which would increase training costs?

Remember too that higher-end media and high-tech delivery systems generally require more sophisticated hardware and software.

## Blended Learning Solutions

A *blended learning solution* is a training delivery system in which more than one training method or technology is used to deliver the training. Typically, at least one of the delivery methods is technology based. Different parts of the training are delivered using different technologies or delivery methods. For example, you might create a training program in which students first listen to a Web Lecture, and then take an interactive web course, and then attend a live instructor-led workshop.

Blended learning solutions can also apply at the curriculum level in which different courses and curriculum elements are delivered in different ways.

**When to consider a blended learning solution**

- Are there major upfront units that teach largely conceptual (nonprocedural) enabling information? If so, consider breaking these components off into technology-based interactive training components that do not involve a live instructor or collaboration with other students.
- Do you have a large, geographically dispersed audience? If so, consider all or some technology-based components.
- Is a classroom too expensive or impractical? If so, and if face-to-face is not required for the learning outcomes, then consider appropriate nonclassroom interventions.
- Will the audience have trouble taking time away from their jobs for classroom training? If so, then consider a blended learning solution in which a classroom is used, if at all, only for the subset of learning outcomes that require it and nonclassroom solutions are used for the balance of the training.
- Do different parts of the audience require different training outcomes? If so, then consider a blended learning solution in which more collaborative and interactive solutions are used for those who need a deeper level of training and mentoring.
- Would the training objectives best be taught using differing methods, each of which is matched to a specific type of objective? If so, then consider a blended learning solution in which training objectives are matched to the level of interaction and to the technology that would best serve those objectives.

## Advantages of Blended Learning Solutions

Blended learning solutions have the following advantages, where they are used appropriately:

### Training delivery methods are matched to the training delivery factors

For example, training content that requires a high degree of expert-student interaction can be delivered using a highly interactive delivery system (such as instructor-led training), while awareness-type content can be delivered using a less interactive form of training (such as a Web Lecture).

Delivery methods can be chosen for each solution component that matches the level of interaction (computer-to-student, student-to-student, and instructor-to-student) required by the training design.

### Training can be more economical to deliver

For example, if classroom training is required to teach certain content but other content can be taught through web-delivered, self-paced QuickViews, classroom time might be significantly reduced, saving on travel and living expenses, facilities costs, and students' time away from productive work.

Or live virtual classroom delivery might be used for the instructor-led content and web-based for the rest, eliminating travel and living costs entirely.

### Technology-delivered components are often delivered on demand

Technology-delivered components are often delivered in an on demand fashion, making training available 24/7 whenever it is needed, including during off hours when it will not impact students' work schedules.

Additionally, students can take these components at their own pace, providing more time to absorb the information and allowing students to repeat the training as needed.

## Technology-delivered portions of training ensure consistency of training

The consistency of training is better assured for technology-delivered, on demand solution components because technology-based self-study courses are delivered with perfect consistency every time they are presented.

Instructor-led training can be presented with high variability across instructors and course delivery sessions.

## Differing needs of audience subgroups can be addressed

The differing needs of large, diverse audiences can often be met through blended learning solutions. For example, "Top Gun" service technicians might receive highly interactive classroom training from a variety of subject matter experts, while less highly skilled technicians might be offered technology-delivered self-paced training.

## The Disadvantages of Blended Learning Solutions

All of the advantages of a blended learning solution do not come without a cost. The following list explains some of the disadvantages of blended learning solutions:

### They are more complex.

Blended learning solutions typically involve the following issues:

- They require multiple delivery technologies and platforms.
- They require more complex design documents.
- User interfaces must be designed.
- Larger style guides must be created due to the details of technology.
- Multimedia elements must be designed and scripted.
- Navigational options and alternate paths through the training must be defined.

- Additional accessibility concerns must be addressed.
- Additional standards compliance issues must be addressed.
- Tools must be investigated and acquired.
- Technology platforms, issues, and their limitations must be investigated.
- More complex development is required because of additional tools, technologies, media, and testing.
- They require more sophisticated project management and costing and sizing.
- They require multiple teams with more specialists.

**They are more work to develop.**

Development of training is often more difficult because

- technology-based training is harder to design, develop, test, and deliver due to the increase complexity (see the first cost factor given above); and
- the quality and instructional effectiveness of technology-based training must be high to avoid replicating ineffective instruction across the entire audience.

**They can increase students' apprehension.**

For self-paced technology-based solution components, students

- might be apprehensive about not having a live instructor,
- might feel that the training is unfriendly or impersonal,
- might miss spontaneous, lively discussions with the instructor and interaction and networking with other students,
- might miss the personalized attention and individual feedback to overcome learning hurdles, and
- often drop out of the training more frequently than with instructor-led training.

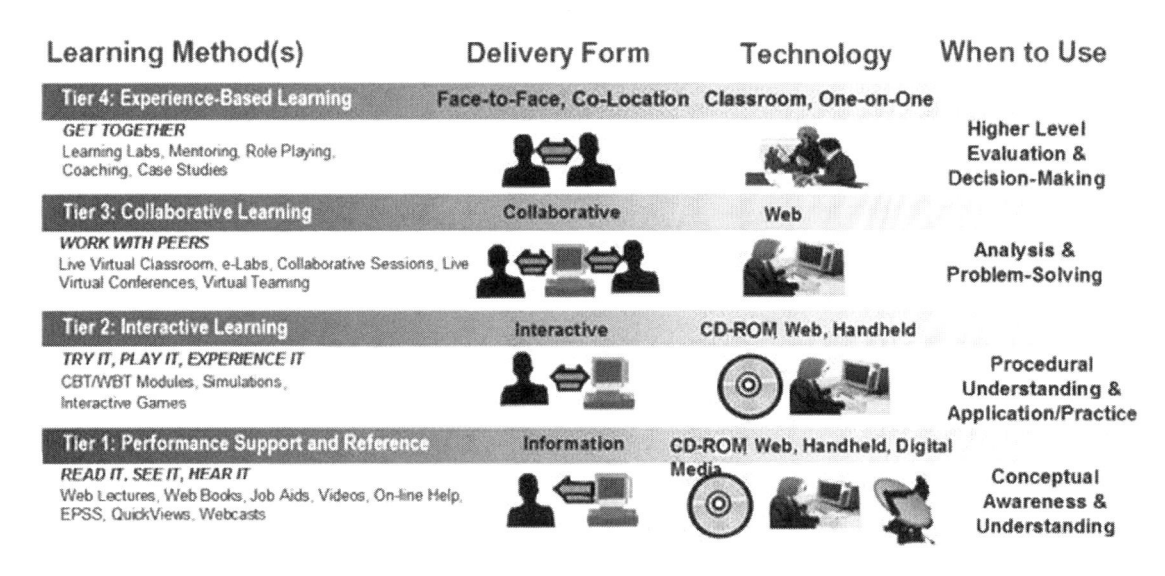

## IBM's 4-Tier Blended Learning Model

| Learning Method(s) | Delivery Form | Technology | When to Use |
|---|---|---|---|
| **Tier 4: Experience-Based Learning**<br>GET TOGETHER<br>Learning Labs, Mentoring, Role Playing, Coaching, Case Studies | Face-to-Face, Co-Location | Classroom, One-on-One | Higher Level Evaluation & Decision-Making |
| **Tier 3: Collaborative Learning**<br>WORK WITH PEERS<br>Live Virtual Classroom, e-Labs, Collaborative Sessions, Live Virtual Conferences, Virtual Teaming | Collaborative | Web | Analysis & Problem-Solving |
| **Tier 2: Interactive Learning**<br>TRY IT, PLAY IT, EXPERIENCE IT<br>CBT/WBT Modules, Simulations, Interactive Games | Interactive | CD-ROM Web, Handheld | Procedural Understanding & Application/Practice |
| **Tier 1: Performance Support and Reference**<br>READ IT, SEE IT, HEAR IT<br>Web Lectures, Web Books, Job Aids, Videos, On-line Help, EPSS, QuickViews, Webcasts | Information | CD-ROM Web, Handheld, Digital Media | Conceptual Awareness & Understanding |

Copyright (c) 2000 IBM Corporation, used with permission

**Figure 29. The IBM 4-Tier Blended Learning Model**

One example of a model that ties together the learning requirements and the delivery system is *IBM's 4-Tier Blended Learning Model*. This model specifies a delivery method or methods that are driven by the learning requirements.

**Note:** This model is intended only as a general guide to be used with judgment and with due consideration for all of the delivery factors given earlier in this chapter. Typically, different parts of the training or curriculum are delivered using a different tier's methods, as dictated by the different learning outcomes.

## How IBM's 4-Tier Blended Learning Model Maps to Bloom's Taxonomy:

**Benjamin Bloom's learning taxonomy, cognitive domain mapped to IBM's model**

T4 { Evaluation
     Synthesis

T3 [ Analysis

T2 [ Application

T1 { Comprehension
     Knowledge

↑

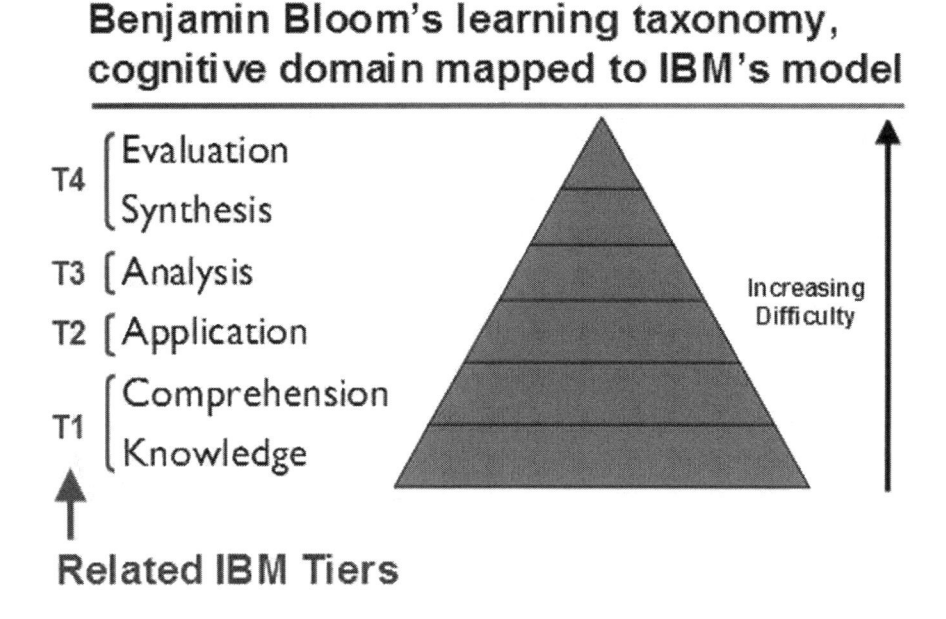

**Related IBM Tiers**

Increasing Difficulty

**Figure 30. How IBM's 4-Tier Blended Learning Model maps to Bloom's taxonomy**

## Tier 1: Performance Support and Reference

Tier 1 learning in the IBM 4-Tier Blended Learning Model is "read it, see it, hear it." The overall learning strategy is to learn from direct exposure to information. This level of training includes performance support, reading, and reference materials, whether they be delivered online or in print form. The main technologies for delivering Tier 1 learning are the Internet, web and handheld devices, CD-ROMs, DVDs, and other digital media.

Select Tier 1 delivery when you are striving to achieve conceptual awareness and understanding for information such as new corporate directives or policies, product updates, product awareness training, new product launches, facts, verbal information, concepts, or other "pure" information. This tier corresponds to the

*Knowledge* and *Comprehension* tiers in Benjamin Bloom's learning taxonomy. Note that Tier 1 training has no learning interaction between the student and an instructor, the materials, or other students (simple navigation does not count as a learning interaction).

Examples of Tier 1 training include

- Web Lectures (PowerPoint presentations with audio and a delivery interface);
- web books and QuickViews (reference or reading material delivered over the web in a structured format);
- web conferences, web meetings, and web casts in which visual and text information is shared in real time over the web with or without audio and with little or no student interaction;
- noninteractive Flash presentations (such as simple animations or slide-show-type presentations);
- videos;
- online job aids, performance aids, and online help; and
- electronic performance support systems.

## Tier 2: Interactive Learning

Tier 2 learning in the IBM 4-Tier Blended Learning Model is "try it, play it, experience it." The overall learning strategy is to learn from interaction with the technology. This level of training includes interactive learning, simulations, and games. The main technologies for delivering Tier 2 learning are multimedia: CD-ROMs, DVDs, and web and handheld devices.

Tier 2 training has two-way interaction between the student and the training application but no direct interaction between the student and an instructor or other students. It uses techniques such as interactive presentations, exercises, quizzes, simulations, and interactive games.

Select Tier 2 training when you are striving to achieve procedural understanding and application and practice or to teach complex concepts, principles, processes, structures, and classifications. This tier corresponds to the *Application* tier in Benjamin Bloom's learning taxonomy.

Examples of Tier 2 training include

- computer-based training,
- web-based training (WBT),
- CD-ROM-based or DVD-based training,
- interactive exercises,
- interactive simulations,
- interactive games,
- interactive web pages, and
- coaching by the training application.

## Tier 3: Collaborative Learning

Tier 3 learning in the IBM 4-Tier Blended Learning Model is "work with peers: discuss it and practice it with others." The general learning strategy is to learn from collaboration with others. This level of training includes any kind of collaborative learning. The technologies for delivering Tier 3 training are those technologies that support collaborative learning, such as web virtual classrooms, interactive collaborative satellite training, and virtual collaborative worlds. Collaborative technologies are generally synchronous (live), but they can be asynchronous (threaded) collaborative environments as well.

Select Tier 3 training when you need to teach analysis and problem-solving objectives that involve collaboration; when collaboration and interaction with fellow students and the instructor are needed, but not face-to-face; and when live classroom delivery is not feasible or cost effective and a virtual classroom delivery is suitable. This tier corresponds to the *Analysis* tier in Benjamin Bloom's learning taxonomy.

Examples of Tier 3 training include

- online chat rooms, team rooms, and support for instructor interaction;
- live virtual classroom environments (such as Lotus Sametime virtual classroom);
- collaborative sessions, live virtual conferences, and virtual teaming (for example, over the web with or without the use of a telephone); and
- e-labs (access to labs over the web with support for collaborative teamwork).

## Tier 4: Experience-Based Learning

Tier 4 learning in the IBM 4-Tier Blended Learning Model is "experience-based learning." The overall learning strategy is to learn from face-to-face (collocation) interaction. Tier 4 learning requires that students be physically located together so that they and the instructor can interact freely, such as in a classroom. Face-to-face learning activities and interactions are typically part of the training design. This tier corresponds to the *Synthesis* and *Evaluation* tiers in Benjamin Bloom's learning taxonomy.

Use Tier 4 learning when

- you need to teach higher-level evaluation- and decision-making-type objectives;
- learning strategies that rely on face-to-face experiences with peers and mentors are required;
- developing people skills for which human interaction in a classroom setting is needed, such as skills that involve understanding nuances or nonverbal cues;
- instructor flexibility is required to address student-specific needs or to accommodate special needs that cannot be anticipated and addressed in advance; and
- hands-on labs are needed to teach tasks using actual physical hardware and simulations are a poor, costly, or inadequate substitute.

Examples of Tier 4 training include

- classroom instruction,
- onsite labs,
- personal mentoring,
- role-playing,
- coaching, and
- instructor-directed and monitored case studies.

## Is the Latest Technology a Panacea for Training?

Using a technology-based delivery system does not mean that training will automatically be better or more effective. The rules of learning have not changed just because you change your delivery vehicle. All of the principles of learning and sound instructional design still apply, as do the procedures for designing and developing sound instruction. Technology has been changing for years, but the human machine remains relatively constant in its biological learning capacity and limitations. Delivery system fads come and go. What is popular today might not be popular tomorrow.

The one constant you should remember is that effective learning depends on good instructional design and development. It is better to have a rough course that has quality design and effective instructional events than a polished, sexy course that has all the technology bells and whistles but is poorly designed and does not provide the needed instructional events. As Ruth Clark, an expert in human performance improvement, stated, "It's not the medium, but rather the instructional methods that cause learning." Clark also said, "Technology can deliver more sensory data than the human nervous system can process."

## Key strengths of technology in relation to training delivery systems

The following are potential strengths of technology-delivered training:

- Although technology-delivered training can be more expensive to develop, the cost of delivery per student is often significantly less than non-technology-based training over a large numbers of students.
- Technology can provide certain learning experiences on demand, remotely, and without the involvement of an instructor.
- Technology can deliver certain types of interactions, events, or presentations that would otherwise be difficult to provide, such as a complex business enterprise simulation that would be impossible or impractical to provide in the real world.
- Technology can deliver a consistent presentation every time a student takes the training.
- Technology can provide a high degree of interaction between students and the training application, instructor, or other students.
- The training application can be designed to adapt to students' learning styles, job roles, preferences, or other factors.
- Technology often supports a wide array of media presentations.

## Considerations for Designing and Delivering Technology-Based Training

You should review the following considerations when choosing a technology-based training solution:

### Technology must be in place and be functioning at the time it is needed.

Examples of required technology are

- networking infrastructure and connectivity,
- server-side hardware and software,
- general client-side hardware and software (including requirements such as CPU speed, memory, operating system level, and so forth),

- storage and hosting requirements,
- power upgrades to the facility to handle the additional power load at the site, and
- specialized hardware and software that must be on students' computers (such as Adobe Acrobat reader, Flash plug-ins, and so forth).

**Technology is not cheap—there is a cost.**

The costs of acquiring, using, and maintaining the technology and the costs of the support and development staff must be weighed against the expected benefits. Also, does the organization have sufficient cash flow to invest in the heavy upfront costs for benefits that might not be realized for some time?

**Technology failure can occur at any point in the technology delivery chain.**

Technology is made up of many components, any one of which could fail unexpectedly during training delivery. What support will students have when this occurs? Who will make the fixes and how will they be trained? What is the backup plan for critical training rollouts?

**What must students do to set up and configure the technology?**

Will students be expected to obtain, install, and configure required hardware and software so that they can take the training? If so, what support will they have to do this? Will students have the skills and motivation to do this?

**How will instructors, designers, and developers be trained on the technology?**

Online virtual classrooms, for example, require trained instructors and support staff. Will they be available, and will you have the time and resources to train them? How will students be trained in using the virtual environment?

**Are you prepared to handle the additional complexity of planning, designing, developing, managing, and delivering technology-based training?**

Developing technology-based training requires the expertise of many people. Graphics must be professionally designed. Other media treatments and user interfaces must be carefully designed or scripted. Development tools must be configured and set up. Custom functionality must be programmed.

Developing technology-based training requires attention to thousands of details. Few people appreciate this fact until they have personally participated in the design and development of such training.

---

Here are two excellent books on designing web-based training and e-learning courses:

- *Designing Web-Based Training: How to Teach Anyone Anything Anywhere Anytime*, by William Horton, John Wiley and Sons, Inc., 2000, ISBN 0-471-35614-X.
- *e-Learning and the Science of Instruction: Proven Guidelines for Consumers and Designers of Multimedia Learning*, by Ruth C. Clark and Richard E. Mayer, John Wiley and Sons, Inc., 2003, ISBN 0-7879-6051-9.

# Chapter Summary— Determining the Instructional Delivery System

This chapter discussed how to determine which technology or method you will use to deliver training to students. This is the next step in the instructional design process. It is performed after you have completed the instructional and content analyses, structured the course, and written the instructional objectives (see the previous chapters in part 2 for a discussion of these topics).

You should now be able to

- define an instructional delivery system and provide several examples of different systems;
- explain why choosing a training delivery system requires judgment and the weighing of many factors; therefore, it cannot be determined by a mechanical process;
- list and explain audience considerations in choosing a training delivery system;
- list and explain organizational, logistical, and sponsor considerations in choosing a training delivery system;
- list and explain subject matter and learning outcome considerations in choosing a training delivery system;
- list and explain technology considerations in choosing a training delivery system;
- define blended learning solutions and explain when they should be considered;
- list and explain the advantages of a blended learning solution;
- list and explain the costs of a blended learning solution;
- list or draw the major components of IBM's 4-Tier Blended Learning Model and describe how the four tiers map to Benjamin Bloom's learning taxonomy;
- define Tier 1 delivery systems, explain when they should be used, and give several examples of them;

- define Tier 2 delivery systems, explain when they should be used, and give several examples of them;
- define Tier 3 delivery systems, explain when they should be used, and give several examples of them;
- define Tier 4 delivery systems, explain when they should be used, and give several examples of them;
- explain why technology does not automatically make training better;
- list and explain the key advantages of technology-based training; and
- list and explain considerations you should review when choosing technology-based training.

## Check Your Understanding

1. **True or false? An instructional delivery system is the set of technologies and methods by which you will develop the training.**

2. **True or false? Choosing an instructional delivery system is a complex decision but one that has been carefully worked out over the years and can be determined by following standard prescribed procedures.**

3. **Which of the following are audience considerations that should be considered in choosing a delivery system? (Select all that apply.)**
    A. Training development and delivery budget
    B. Complexity of the content
    C. How students are geographically distributed
    D. Availability of instructors for delivery
    E. Students' preferred learning style
    F. Hosting availability and cost
    G. Window of time available to students to take the training

H. Students' motivation to learn the content

   I. LMS integration requirements

   J. Where students will take the training

   K. Level of interactivity required to achieve mastery

4. **Classify each of the following factors that should be considered in choosing a delivery system into organizational, logistical, and sponsor considerations; subject matter and learning outcome considerations; or technology considerations:**

   A. Technical support personnel required

   B. Level of interactivity required to achieve mastery

   C. Maintenance requirements and course life span

   D. Types of learning objectives and outcomes

   E. Training development and delivery budget

   F. Students' access to the technology

   G. Complexity of the content

   H. Development window and training deadlines

   I. Accessibility and translation requirements

   J. Hosting availability and cost

5. **True or false? A *blended learning solution* is a training delivery system in which more than one training method or technology is used to deliver the training. Typically, at least one of the delivery methods is technology based.**

6. **Which of the following factors should you consider in deciding whether to use a blended learning solution? (Select all that apply.)**

   A. Do you have a large, geographically dispersed audience?

   B. Do different parts of the audience require different training outcomes?

C. Will the audience have trouble taking time away from their jobs for classroom training?

D. Are there major upfront units that teach largely conceptual (nonprocedural) enabling information?

E. Are blended learning solutions the latest trend in training delivery systems?

F. Would the training objectives best be taught using differing methods, each of which is matched to a specific type of objective?

G. Is a classroom too expensive or impractical?

7. **Which of the following are advantages of blended learning solutions? (Select all that apply.)**

    A. Technology-delivered portions of training ensure consistency of training.

    B. Training can be more economical to deliver.

    C. Technology-delivered components are often delivered on demand.

    D. Differing training needs of audience subgroups can be addressed.

    E. Blended learning solutions are by definition more instructionally effective.

    F. Training delivery methods are matched to the training delivery factors.

8. **True or false? The disadvantages of blended learning solutions include increased complexity, increased development effort, and possible student apprehension.**

9. **Match each tier in the IBM 4-Tier Blended Learning Model with its correct description.**

| Tier 4 | A. Performance support and reference |
|---|---|
| Tier 3 | B. Experience-based learning |
| Tier 2 | C. Collaborative learning |
| Tier 1 | D. Interactive learning |

*Creating Outstanding Instructional Designs*

10. **Classify each of the following descriptions into Tier 1, Tier 2, Tier 3, or Tier 4 learning.**

    A. Corresponds to the *Analysis* tier in Benjamin Bloom's learning taxonomy

    B. "Try it, play it, experience it"

    C. Learn from face-to-face (collocation) interaction

    D. Used when you are striving to achieve conceptual awareness and understanding

    E. "Read it, see it, hear it"

    F. Examples include online chat rooms, live virtual classroom environments, and interactive e-labs

    G. The general learning strategy is to learn from collaboration with others.

    H. Has two-way interaction between the student and the training application but no direct interaction between the student and an instructor or other students

    I. Corresponds to the *Synthesis* and *Evaluation* tiers in Benjamin Bloom's learning taxonomy

    J. Examples include computer-based training (CBT) and web-based training (WBT)

11. **True or false? The principles of learning and sound instructional design are the same, regardless of whether technology is used to deliver the training.**

12. **True or false? Although technology-delivered training can be more expensive to develop, the cost of delivery per student is often significantly less than non-technology-based training over a large number of students.**

13. **One of the considerations for designing and delivering technology-based training is how instructors, designers, and developers are _____ on the technology?**

## Answers

1. False. An instructional delivery system is the set of technologies and methods by which you will *deliver* the training to the students.

2. False. Choosing an instructional delivery system is not a mechanical process devoid of skill, experience, and judgment. It requires that you carefully weigh many factors.

3. C, E, G, H, and J

4. A, technology considerations; B, subject matter and learning outcome considerations; C, organizational, logistical, and sponsor considerations; D, subject matter and learning outcome considerations; E, organizational, logistical, and sponsor considerations; F, technology considerations; G, subject matter and learning outcome considerations; H, organizational, logistical, and sponsor considerations; I, organizational, logistical, and sponsor considerations; and J, technology considerations.

5. True

6. A, B, C, D, F, and G

7. A, B, C, D, and F

8. True

9. B, C, D, and A

10. A, Tier 3; B, Tier 2; C, Tier 4; D, Tier 1; E, Tier 1; F, Tier 3; G, Tier 3; H, Tier 2; I, Tier 4; and J, Tier 2

11. This statement is true. The rules of learning have not changed just because you change your delivery vehicle. All of the principles of learning and sound instructional design still apply, as do the procedures for designing and developing sound instruction.

12. True

13. The correct answer is "trained."

# CHAPTER 14
# Designing Practice Exercises and Other Instructional Events

This chapter presents the next step in the instructional design process: designing practice exercises and other instructional events. Instructional events, including practice with feedback, are one of the distinguishing characteristics of training. This chapter discusses how to decide where they should be included, what they should be, and how to design them.

## Where We Are at in the Instructional Design Process?

This chapter discusses step 7 in the instructional design process: Design practice exercises and other instructional events.

1. Gather requirements
2. Perform an instructional analysis on the job outcomes
3. Identify the enabling content

4. Structure the course
5. Write formal objectives
6. Determine the instructional delivery system
7. **Design practice exercises and other instructional events**
8. Design the prototype or example lesson
9. Create the formal design document

## Overview of Instructional Events

At this point in the design process, you have gathered training requirements, analyzed the job outcomes, determined the tasks and enabling content to teach, structured the content into modules and topics or units and lessons, written instructional objectives, and determined the delivery system for delivering the instruction.

You are now prepared to design the practice exercises and other instructional events and activities that will help students to gain the knowledge and skills they need to produce the desired job outcomes. As you learned in part 1 of this book, training is more than passive listening or reading on the part of students. It involves cognitive engagement, activity, and interaction. Otherwise, training would not be training. It would simply be a method of dispensing information to students.

Instructional events are learning strategies and activities that are built into the training that are specifically designed to facilitate and promote learning.

### Examples of instructional events and activities:

Presenting information is itself an instructional event, if it has been designed according to sound instructional design principles. Designing information presentations is one of the major themes of this book's companion book: *Instructional Development—Step by Step: Six Easy Steps for Developing Lean, Effective, and Motivational Instruction*. It will not be discussed in detail in this book.

Examples of other types of instructional events include

- answering questions,
- performing individual exercises,
- solving problems,
- taking quizzes and exams,
- participating in group discussions and exercises,
- interacting within a case study on a computer,
- using tools or new equipment,
- role-playing with fellow students,
- watching a video,
- viewing an animation or Flash sequence,
- playing an instructional game,
- watching demonstrations,
- observing expert performers,
- going through an online simulation,
- teaching others,
- completing a mentorship,
- making presentations,
- writing a paper,
- performing real work (usually, in a protected, "safe" environment), and
- interacting with a virtual world.

## Instructional Events Are Designed—Not Developed—During Instructional Design

The instructional designer does not create the actual materials for an instructional event during the design phase. Rather, the instructional designer writes the specifications that will be used by an instructional developer to develop the activity.

**Note:** What these specifications should contain is discussed at the end of this chapter.

You must perform three activities to specify instructional events:

- identify *where* instructional events are needed in the course
- determine *what* each event will be (its type, such as an exercise or quiz)
- *design* (write specifications for) the instructional event

Designing an instructional event is drafting the blueprints or constructing the skeleton of the event. It is specifying enough detail about the event so that an instructional developer can later develop the event's training materials and interactions.

## How to Determine Where Instructional Events Are Needed and What They Should Be

Determining where instructional events are needed in training is not an exact science. It requires much judgment and skill. Nevertheless, we will provide several guidelines in this chapter that can help you in making these decisions. Later, we will discuss a few specific instructional events in more detail. You will develop a better sense for where to include instructional events in a course as you follow these guidelines and become more knowledgeable and experienced at this task.

Perform the following steps to determine where instructional events are needed:

1. Systematically review each instructional segment (subtopic, topic, module, and course) using the guidelines that we present in this chapter to identify where instructional events should occur in that segment and what type of event it should be.

2. Document these events in the course structure document (the one created in step 4 of the instructional design process—see chapter 5) at the location they should occur. This will help you remember these events when you create your formal instructional design document.

## Factor #1: What Is the Level of Skill or the Depth of Knowledge That Is Required?

One of the first factors to consider in determining where instructional events are needed is the level of skill or the depth of knowledge that is specified in the instructional objectives for that segment.

For example, an objective might specify that students present an overview of the major steps for creating a quarterly report, or it might specify that students actually produce a quarterly report using a spreadsheet application. The first objective requires that students give a high-level verbal explanation as the prescribed behavior; the second objective requires that students actually perform a complex task and produce an actual work product. Obviously, deeper levels of skill and knowledge require more detailed and extensive training.

The latter, more in-depth objective in this example calls for more frequent instructional events—especially more practice with feedback—and special events, such as demonstrations or walk-throughs of the computer spreadsheet application. Practice exercises should test individual component subskills, and subsequent exercises should gradually integrate them into higher-level skills and should gradually increase in realism and faithfulness to actual job tasks. On the other hand, the former objective requiring only a verbal explanation of a process might need only a series of checkpoint questions or quizzes embedded at appropriate locations throughout the training.

# Factor #2: Does the Instructional Segment Teach Key Skills or Knowledge?

What are key skills and knowledge?

A key skill is one that meets any of the following criteria:

- It is used in many tasks (for example, calculating profit for many lines of business).
- It is responsible for producing much of the valued outputs (for example, closing a sale).
- It is a foundation skill on which other higher-level skills will be based (for example, listening to the client and understanding the client's concerns and needs is a foundational skill for selling a product or service).
- It has severe consequences if not performed correctly (safety, government penalties, lawsuits, defective products, returned products, and so forth).
- It must be performed with speed or urgency (shutting down a nuclear reactor in an emergency situation).


Key information is information that meets any of the following criteria:

- It is foundational information on which other important information is based.
- It is information that greatly facilitates, organizes, or simplifies the understanding of other information.
- It is information that must be understood to learn other key information.
- It is information that will be needed by students to produce important job outcomes.


Key information includes the key principles for the subject. Key skills include the key steps and performance guidance for the procedure.

Key information and skills merit a more careful and extensive treatment in your training, including a greater number of instructional events to acquire the knowledge and skills, store them into memory, and build students' confidence that they can recall and apply that knowledge or perform those skills.

## Factor #3: Are There Any Types of Learning That Require Special Instructional Activities to Acquire?

Some skills and knowledge are difficult to acquire without certain learning events. For example, teaching students nonverbal communication skills for sales presentations, including proper body language, is difficult to assess unless an instructor observes students giving a presentation in a role-play or in a real-life client presentation.

As another example, learning tasks that involve motor skills (the carrying out of very fine, coordinated motor movements, such as hand or body movements that often involve hand-eye coordination) typically require that practice include performing those movements on actual or simulated equipment or objects. Examples include performing surgery, operating a lathe, playing an instrument, or soldering a water pipe.

As another example, sometimes students must memorize certain information, such as call center classification codes, that are entered into a computer application when service representatives take calls. This situation calls for additional and special instructional events, such as more frequent practice sessions, drill-and-practice sessions, instructional games, and giving students memory mnemonics and organizing frameworks.

## Factor #4: What Is the Level of Complexity of the Skill or Knowledge That Is Taught in This Segment?

Complex skills and complex knowledge must be carefully broken down during instructional and content analyses to identify their component subtasks and steps or component knowledge. These component parts should each be provided with sufficient instructional events, including practice with feedback, to ensure their mastery so that a solid foundation is laid for building them into more complex knowledge and skills.

**How to identify complex tasks**

Complex tasks are tasks that involve making difficult or complex judgments as part of the task. This would include tasks that require

- making fine discriminations among several similar things (such as determining which of three marketing plans will lead to the greatest profit or deciding which of five job applicants who have similar qualifications to hire);
- the application of principles, rules, or policies that have many exceptions (the US tax code, for example, or corporate policies for handling customer complaints); and
- tasks that have a high number of easy- to medium-difficulty decisions scattered throughout the task—in this case, the task is complex because students must remember or understand a complex procedure flow.

Complex tasks call for special guidance, instruction, and practice to help students make complex discriminations or judgments and to understand exceptions to rules and policies. For example, the training might need an instructional activity that compares and contrasts several similar objects while pointing out the subtle differences on which the objects differ. Or the training might require that a detailed decision table be provided and discussed for how to make a particular decision in one of the procedure steps.

**Factor #5: How Long Have Students Been Learning Passively?**

Large blocks of information presentation—even well-designed information presentations—should be broken up with meaningful interactive instructional activities. This is important for a number of reasons:

### Why it is important to break up long periods of passive learning

- It provides variety, interest, and a change of pace for students. Without a change of stimulus, it is very easy for students to become bored or distracted. (In part 1 of this book, you learned that an unchanging stimulus is detrimental not only to perception but also to learning.)

- It provides the opportunity for students to practice what they have learned to firm up their understanding and their skills before too much additional material has been presented. (You learned in part 1 that short-term memory, where learning associations are actually made, is limited in capacity. Unless information is rehearsed and reinforced adequately at the time it is taught, the new information will crowd out existing information in short-term memory and the existing information in short-term memory will be lost.)

- It engages students' minds in more *active* cognitive learning processes—activities in which they have to actively apply the information in some kind of action—even if the action is as simple as answering a few meaningful questions.

- It helps to keep student motivation high. Training is better received when students frequently practice and apply what they are learning in active exercises and activities.

- It breaks up the material into smaller chunks.

## Factor #6: How Has the Material Been Chunked and Structured?

An instructional segment (such as a course, module, topic, or subtopic) has a beginning and an end. You should include certain instructional events at these beginning and end points.

### Beginning

The beginning of an instructional segment is where the segment should be introduced, overviewed, related to the previous material and to the larger course, and motivated. Prerequisite information should also be refreshed.

**End**

The end of an instructional segment is where the segment should be summarized and key information reviewed. It is also where end-of-segment exercises, quizzes, and other activities that are designed to practice, synthesize, and integrate all of the skills and knowledge of that segment are placed. Any additional instructional activities that are required to achieve that goal are provided at this point, such as group exercises, simulations, or team role-plays.

**End of two segments that need integration**

If two sequential instructional segments teach separate skills that must be integrated together to perform a higher-level skill, then provide additional practice exercises and integrative instruction at the end of the second segment (and later in the course, as required) to build and practice higher-level skills. Integrative events generally occur *between* instructional segments unless you need a dedicated instructional segment to teach how these skills are integrated, in which case the integrative exercises are part of that segment.

## Factor #7: What Are the Delivery System Constraints?

Your choice of delivery system can limit, constrain, or support the instructional events that you might choose to include. For example, web-based training delivery cannot provide expert observation and feedback by an instructor. A printed set of training manuals cannot by itself provide a computer simulation of the application that it is teaching. A satellite course delivered to remote locations that do not have expensive laboratory equipment and onsite instructors cannot provide monitored lab exercises.

These constraints and limitations are often the very reason why a blended learning solution is selected for delivery (for a discussion of blended learning solutions, see the previous chapter in this book). For example, a training curriculum might use web-based training to teach basic awareness and conceptual material and classroom instruction to teach skills and information that require student-teacher interaction, practice with expert feedback, or collaborative work with other students.

If a learning event is not supported by the delivery system, you will have to change to a delivery system that does support it, create a blended delivery and match instructional activities to the support delivery systems, or use a less-than-perfect substitute learning activity instead.

## Factor #8: What Are the Project and Organizational Constraints?

Designing and creating instructional events and activities requires time and resources. You should know the project budget and schedule before you choose your instructional activities. For example, you might want to include some online application simulations in your web-based training course, but they might not be feasible due to their development costs and the additional time it would take to design and develop them. You also might not have access to the specialized professionals who are needed to develop the activities.

In general, activities that use high-end media or the latest technology cost more to develop, take more time to develop, and require the expertise of skilled professionals, who might be in high demand. Training is developed and delivered in the real world; therefore, you will often be limited by real-world constraints.

## Course, Unit, and Topic Introductions

In the rest of this chapter, we will discuss some specific instructional events in more detail. Two of the most common types of instructional events are introductions and summaries. Every course, unit, and topic should be introduced. Introductions do more than just provide a transition to a new instructional segment. They

- tie the new topic or segment to what has been previously presented or overviewed,
- preview and overview information that is about to be presented,

- refresh any prerequisite skills or knowledge that is needed for this segment,
- develop students' motivation to learn the material by showing how the upcoming topic is relevant to their needs,
- provide advanced organizers and cognitive frameworks that will help students organize and remember the new material (for example, showing a graphic of the major steps of a process and displaying that graphic repeatedly at the beginning of each subsequent topic that discusses one of the steps), and
- provide the objectives.

The size of the introduction is determined by the size and complexity of the instructional segment (course, module, topic, or subtopic). It can range from a few sentences to an entire module.

Course introductions have some additional unique requirements.

**Tips and guidelines for designing course introductions**

- The course size and complexity determine how large the introduction is—from an entire module or topic in the course to one screen or short discussion.
- The course introduction should include things such as
  - course title and course code (if the course is part of a learning management system or curriculum) so that students can verify that they are taking the correct course;
  - a general (but short) description of the course;
  - course objectives;
  - course structure or agenda;
  - the time required to take the course;
  - prerequisites for the course;
  - where this course fits into a larger curriculum or certification path;
  - major course activities (from the student's point of view);
  - pass/fail criteria and reporting requirements;

- for classroom delivery, instructor and student introductions and classroom logistics, such as emergency procedures;
- for technology-based training, how to navigate, interact with, and know your location in the course;
- a description of the student materials (so that students can verify that they have all of the materials);
- a brief introduction to the topic of the course;
- motivational information, such as why the knowledge and skills that students are about to learn are valuable; and
- any additional information that students need to know about taking the course.

## Summaries and Reviews

Summaries and reviews are placed at the end of the instructional segments to which they apply. Summaries and reviews

- give students a moment to pause and reflect on what they have just learned,
- bolster students' motivation (by recognizing that they have mastered knowledge and skills that are important to them),
- are opportunities to summarize and review key information and procedures,
- provide a logical conclusion or transition point to wrap up or draw a topic to a close, and
- provide instructors and training materials a final opportunity to integrate and relate the material together at a higher level.

Major course segments, such as courses, modules, and sometimes topics, generally have summaries. Course summaries might be their own topics or modules, depending on how much you want to cover in the review and how much material is being reviewed. Choosing how detailed your summaries and reviews should be is a judgment call on your part.

## Quizzes, Exams (Tests), and Checkpoint Questions

Quizzes, exams, and tests are favorites of the academic world and typically consist of a series of questions (true/false, multiple choice, matching, fill-in-the-blank, and so forth) for students to answer. These are usually considered *conceptual tests*—they test students' understanding and recall of information.

*Performance tests* can also be designed in which students must either exhibit an overt performance, such as operating a machine, or provide evidence of the completion of a covert performance, such as providing the answer and mathematical logic for solving a calculus problem.

Quizzes and exams can be used for one of the following purposes:

- Assess the level of knowledge and skill of students for evaluation purposes—called *summative evaluation.* Examples of this purpose would be to assign grades or determine a pass/fail status.

- As a private learning activity for students to identify gaps in their understanding, to reinforce their learning, and to strengthen their memory and recall of the information—called *formative evaluation.* Examples of this purpose would be the use of checkpoint questions inserted periodically in web-based training to help students identify gaps in their understanding and reinforce their learning. These activities are private to the student—scores are *not* passed on to a monitoring authority, such as students' professors or supervisors.

## Creating Quizzes, Exams (Tests), and Checkpoint Questions

In creating quizzes, exams, tests, and checkpoint questions, you should

- create test items that match (test) the same skills that are called for in the objectives performed under the same conditions and evaluated using the same criteria. For example, if the objective calls for students to match the names of bones to numbered entries on a skeletal diagram, do not ask students to recall the names of the bones of the skeleton from memory;

- after you create each test item, check to be sure that it tests the same skills under the same conditions (tools, resources, job aids, and so forth) to the same criteria (not harder or easier) as the objective; and
- although academic instructors often create tests that require students to perform skills that they have not yet been taught (with the stated justification that they are "stretching" their thinking), this is not a valid purpose of a test.

How to create educationally sound quizzes, exams, and tests is out of the scope of this course.

---

For an in-depth discussion of creating quizzes, exams, and checkpoint questions, consult any college text on educational assessment, measurement, and evaluation.

For a simple and practical guide to measuring the results of instruction, refer to the book, *Measuring Instructional Results*, 3rd edition, by Robert F. Mager, The Center for Effective Performance, Atlanta, Georgia, 1997, available from the CEP bookstore at www.cepworldwide.com.

## Exercises

Exercises are any activities that are designed to practice either

- the behaviors that are prescribed in the objectives, or
- the behaviors that are component behaviors of the target behavior.

As you learned in part 1, practice must be accompanied by feedback to have a positive impact on learning.

Why should behaviors that are practiced in exercises and tested in exams match the behaviors (or component behaviors) that are prescribed by the objectives?

Matching the exercises and test questions in a course to the course objectives is paramount. If the objectives call for students to perform a task, then exercises that require students to memorize the steps of the task—while helpful—are insufficient. Exercises must ultimately practice the same skill that is specified in the objectives. If they do not, then how will you know that students have acquired the behaviors specified in the objectives?

Exercises can be big or small, depending on the need. An exercise designed to practice how to use the three pedals on a piano might be small compared to an exercise designed to rehearse an entire piano sonata. Integrative exercises that combine or integrate the component skills that were individually practiced previously are generally larger and more complex than exercises that practice lower-level component skills.

## Determining Where Exercises Are Needed

Exercises are generally required in the following places:

- at the end of major instructional modules and topics (units and lessons) that teach major skills and subskills
- at the end of instructional sequences or segments that integrate previously taught skills or subskills into higher-level skills
- at other appropriate locations within topics or lessons (see discussion below)

Within topics or lessons, exercises are usually required after key enabling subskills are taught and immediately following segments in which important discriminations, generalizations, and sequences are taught or where the recall of information needs to be practiced and strengthened.

**Note:** Discrimination is the skill of telling things apart. Generalization is the skill of applying to new instances. Sequence is the skill of listing things in their correct order.

## Using the Instructional and Content Analyses to Help Identify Where Exercises Are Needed

Instructional and content analyses produce a hierarchy of skills and enabling content. Major tasks are broken into successively smaller subtasks. At the lowest level, the subtasks are made up of behaviors (steps of the procedure) and enabling content.

Exercises should be provided that ultimately practice the performance of the entire major task and the application of the key enabling content. However, for complex tasks, each of the subtasks should also be exercised, unless students already know them. Integrative exercises should also be provided at appropriate points that require students to integrate (combine) the skills of two or more of the subtasks to perform a higher-level task.

The following table shows an example of how practice exercises should be provided at the different task levels of the instructional analysis:

| Job Outcome: System Running Normally After Failure | |
|---|---|
| **Job/Task Analysis** | **Corresponding Exercise** |
| 1. Determine if failure is hardware- or software-related | "Given a failed system, determine if the failure is due to hardware or software." |
| 1.1 Diagnose hardware problems | "Given a system with a hardware failure, diagnose the failure." |
| 1.1.1 Run diagnostics | "Run diagnostics and interpret the outcome on the following hardware …" |
| 1.1.2 Analyze log files | "Analyze and interpret the following log files to determine possible hardware failures." |
| 1. 2 Diagnose software problems | "Given a system with a software failure, diagnose the failure." |
| 1.2.1 Run SysDiag | "Run SysDiag and interpret the results for possible software failures." |
| 1.2.2. Analyze system logs | "Analyze the following system logs for possible software failures." |

Here is an example of how integrative exercises were included for a higher-level task:

**Job outcome:** Shoes with laces correctly tied

**Training objective:** Without any help, tie your shoes correctly

Subtasks that were identified during the analysis

- create a simple overhand knot
- form a loop

- create and push another loop through
- adjust the size of the final loops
- tighten the final knot

Where exercises were specified in the flow of the instruction:

Topic 1: Creating a simple overhand knot

**Exercise:** Creating a simple overhand knot

Topic 2: Forming a loop

**Exercise:** Forming a loop

**Integration exercise:** Creating a simple overhand knot and forming a loop

Topic 3: Pushing another loop through

**Exercise:** Pushing another loop through

**Integration exercise:** Creating a simple overhand knot, forming a loop, and pushing another loop through

Topic 4: Adjusting the size of the final loops

**Exercise:** Adjusting the size of the final loops

Topic 5: Tightening the final knot

**Exercise:** Tightening the final knot

**Integrative exercise:** Creating a simple overhand knot, forming a loop, pushing another loop through, and tightening the final knot

**Final exercise:** Tying tennis shoes, dress shoes, and other types of shoes (practice the same higher-level skill but in different contexts that are likely to be encountered in real life)

## Guidelines for Self-Paced Learning

As a general guideline, for self-paced learning, such as web-based training, computer media-based training (such as DVD or CD), self-instructional booklets, and so forth, include some type of meaningful instructional interaction or exercise every three to six screens or one to three pages. This guideline should be adjusted for influencing factors such as audience interest, motivation, skill set, attention span, complexity of the material, difficulty in mastering the skill, and so forth.

## How to Design Exercises

To design exercises, follow these steps:

1. **Identify and define the purpose of the exercise.**

   Identify the skill called for by the objective (for higher-level exercises) or by the lower-level subtask. Then write a purpose statement for the exercise that clearly describes what the exercise is designed to do so that instructional developers will have an unmistakably clear idea as to what the practice is intended to exercise and accomplish.

2. **Design activities that will practice the identical skills called for by the objective.**

   Determine the activity or activities that will exercise the skills that are specified in the instructional objective. Then check to make sure that in your activity you exercise these same skills using the same tools, aids, and environment that are called for in the objective.

3. **Design the appropriate level of guidance.**

   Guidance is providing steps, prompts, cues, or tips to students to follow or use while they are practicing. Determine how much guidance should be provided to "shape" the desired behavior throughout the exercise. To shape the desired behavior, provide more guidance at the beginning and less guidance at later repetitions of exercising the skill. Then design that level of guidance into the exercise by specifying the level of guidance for each exercise or exercise part.

4. **Design feedback mechanisms into the exercises.**

Determine and specify how students will receive feedback on their performance. For example, will an instructor provide it, will the delivery system technology provide it, or will it be apparent from real-life feedback? Also, feedback should be provided individually to students so that they can improve their own individual performance.

In providing feedback to students individually, make sure that the feedback is

- private,
- not humiliating,
- not embarrassing, and
- encouraging and positive in overall affect.

5. **Determine how much repetition of practice *within* the exercise to include.**

Sometimes designers fail to provide *repeated* practice of the *same* skill within an exercise. Repeated practice helps students to progressively improve their performance and to practice the skill until their performance meets the required standards.

For example, if you are teaching students how to shoot a ball from the free throw line, how many times should you have students practice shooting the ball from the free throw line?

Some of the factors you should consider are

- how many repetitions of practice are generally required to come up to full proficiency?
- is there a controlling party or mechanism that can individually vary the amount of practice for each student based on the student's speed of progression?
- how many varied conditions from the real world need to be included in the practice?
- do you have the budget for the additional practice?
- will students be required to perform the task from recall memory?

6. **Document the exercise specifications.**

The final step in designing exercises is to write the exercise specifications. These should generally include

- the name of the exercise;
- a statement of the purpose of the exercise;
- the expected duration of the exercise (expected time it will take students to complete the exercise);
- the description of each of the exercise activities and how feedback will be provided;
- the level of guidance to be given for each part of the exercise;
- specifications of the equipment and tools need to set up the exercise; and
- specifications of the equipment, tools, manuals, job aids, and so forth that students should have available to take the exercise.

**Example of exercise specifications:**

**Exercise Title**

HMC and SE Familiarization

## Exercise Duration

3 hours, 30 minutes

## Purpose

The purpose of this exercise is to provide students the opportunity to become familiar with the functions of the HMC and SE for the S/390 and zSeries computer systems.

## Specific Skills to be Exercised

Step-by-step instructions will be provided for students to follow to complete the following tasks:

- use the HMC to perform the tasks needed to monitor and control the CPC
- use the SE to perform the tasks needed to monitor and control the CPC
- log on and log off the HMC and SE
- navigate the View area, Work area, and Task area on the HMC and SE
- perform the steps necessary to set up scheduled operations
- create a backup ROC or DVD
- backup critical data to the ROC or DVD

## Exercise Feedback

The instructor will be present in the lab and will answer questions and assist students as needed to complete the exercise and verify final completion.

### **Special Requirements or Assumptions**

- Standard HMC lab configuration (as previously defined).
- This lab assumes that students have completed the previous night's homework assignment (How to use the hardware management console).

## Demonstrations

Demonstrations show students how to perform a task. Demonstrations are to tasks as examples are to concepts—they show how the procedure is performed for a specific instance. They therefore have great instructional value in teaching procedures.

In designing demonstrations, you should

- demonstrate at the level that you have just taught—not at a more difficult or less difficult level. For example, do not demo how to create a complex web page if you have only taught how to create a simple web page;
- give demonstrations *before* you have students practice the procedure. This allows students to model after the demonstration;
- highlight, point out, and emphasize the critical discriminations and generalizations that must be made in key steps when you give the demonstration;
- describe common pitfalls and mistakes that are typically made by novices; and
- provide warnings and cautions where appropriate.

## Documenting the Design of Instructional Activities

The design of an activity is a blueprint for its construction. It should include sufficient information for a training developer to write or create the actual activity.

Here are the entries that are typically included in the design of an instructional event or activity:

**Note:** Some elements might not be appropriate to a particular event.

- the name of the activity
- an overall summary or high-level description of the activity
- the purpose of the activity
- the structure of the activity (specific events and their sequence and format, such as "a numbered series of steps for students to follow")
- a detailed outline or description of the content of the activity, such as the specific functions or tasks to be exercised
- any templates that should be followed when developing the activity
- for events that employ questions, specifications for those questions, such as the number of questions, types of allowable questions, how many questions per instructional segment or topic, and how the questions will be administered, scored, and reported
- for instructor-led training, the design for this piece of the instructor exercise guide, if one is needed, that gives specific directions to the instructor on how to conduct the activity (for example, details on how to set up student group sessions, group presentations, and wrap-up class discussions)
- references to where the source material for the activity can be found

# Chapter Summary— Designing Practice Exercises and Other Instructional Events

This chapter presented the next step in the instructional design process: designing practice exercises and other instructional events. Instructional events, including practice with feedback, are one of the distinguishing characteristics of training. This chapter discussed how to decide where they should be included, what they should be, and how to design them.

You should now be able to

- define instructional events and activities and give several examples of them,
- describe the three main activities that are involved in identifying and designing instructional events,
- state and explain the two steps for determining where instructional events are needed and what they should be,
- describe how each of the following factors affects where instructional events are needed and what they should be
    - What is the level of skill or the depth of knowledge that is required?
    - Does the instructional segment teach key skills or knowledge?
    - Are there any types of learning that require special instructional activities to acquire?
    - What is the level of complexity of the skill or knowledge that is taught in this segment?
    - How long have students been learning passively?
    - How has the material been chunked and structured?
    - What are the delivery system constraints?
    - What are the project and organizational constraints?
- describe the purpose of beginning-of-segment introductions and list the elements that are typically included in a course introduction,
- explain the purpose of end-of-segment summaries,

- describe the difference between conceptual tests and performance tests,
- define formative and summative evaluation and describe how they differ,
- describe why it is important for test questions to match the objectives,
- define exercises and describe what they should practice,
- explain why the behaviors that are practiced in exercises and tested in exams should match the behaviors (or component behaviors) that are prescribed by the objectives,
- describe three general guidelines for determining where exercises are needed,
- describe how to use instructional and content analyses to help determine where exercises are needed,
- describe how and where integrative exercises should be used,
- state how often an instructional interaction or exercise should be included in self-paced training,
- in designing exercises
    - describe how to identify and define the purpose of the exercise,
    - describe how to design activities that practice the identical skills called for by the objective,
    - describe how to design the appropriate level of guidance,
    - describe how to design feedback mechanisms into the exercises,
    - describe how to determine how much repetition to include in the exercise, and
    - describe what should be included in the design specifications for exercises,
- describe how to design demonstrations, and
- list and explain the elements that are typically included in the design of an instructional event or activity.

## Check Your Understanding

1. **True or false? Instructional events are instances in which students ask instructors questions or request explanations of what was presented.**

2. **Which of the following descriptions are examples of instructional events? (Select all that apply.)**
    A. Answering questions
    B. Instructors preparing to teach the next day's material
    C. Interacting within a case study on a computer
    D. Role-playing with fellow students
    E. Teaching others
    F. Taking a lunch break

3. **Which of the following activities are required to specify instructional events for training? (Select all that apply.)**
    A. Identify where instructional events are needed in the course
    B. Determine the ideal class size for a classroom course
    C. Determine what each event will be (its type, such as an exercise or quiz)
    D. Design (write specifications for) the instructional event
    E. Determine students' entry-level skills and knowledge

4. **True or false? In determining instructional events, it is important to systematically review each instructional segment (subtopic, topic, module, and course) in light of a specific set of guidelines to determine where events should occur and what they should be.**

5. **True or false? Objectives that call for deeper levels of knowledge or skill generally require more practice and other instructional events in the training materials.**

6. **A ____ skill is a skill that meets any of the following criteria:**
   - It is used in many tasks.
   - It is responsible for producing much of the value.
   - It is a foundation skill on which other higher-level skills will be based.
   - It has severe consequences if not performed correctly.
   - It must be performed with speed or urgency.

7. **True or false? Some types of learning, such as fine motor skills, require special instructional activities to learn.**

8. **Which of the following descriptions identifies a task as a complex task? (Select all that apply.)**
   A. Tasks that are very long
   B. Tasks that require the application of principles, rules, or policies that have many exceptions
   C. Tasks that have a high number of easy- to medium-difficulty decisions scattered throughout the task
   D. Tasks that use a high amount of jargon or technical terms
   E. Tasks that require making fine discriminations among several similar things

9. **It is important to break up large blocks of passive information presentation with meaningful instructional events because: (Select all that apply.)**
   A. It breaks up the material into smaller chunks.
   B. It engages students' minds in more *active* cognitive learning processes.

C. It provides the opportunity for students to practice what they have learned to firm up their understanding and their skills before too much additional material has been presented.

D. It provides variety, interest, and a change of pace for students.

E. It helps to keep students' motivation high.

10. **True or false? The beginning and end of instructional segments (courses, modules, and topics) generally require certain specific instructional events.**

11. **True or false? If two sequential instructional segments teach separate skills that must be integrated together to perform a higher-level skill, then you should (1) provide additional practice exercises and integrative instruction at the end of the second segment (and later in the course, as required) to build and practice the higher-level skills, or (2) create a dedicated instructional segment to teach how these skills are integrated.**

12. **True or false? Decisions about instructional events and activities should be made independently of the instructional delivery system.**

13. **True or false? Project constraints such as budget and schedules might constrain your choice of instructional events that you can include in your training, especially for activities that use high-end media and technology.**

14. **Introductions to courses, modules, and topics are important because they: (Select all that apply.)**
    A. Tie the new topic or segment to what has been previously presented or overviewed.
    B. Preview and overview information that is about to be presented.
    C. Refresh any prerequisite skills or knowledge that is needed for this segment.
    D. Summarize what students learned in the previous instructional segment.
    E. Develop students' motivation to learn the material by showing how the upcoming topic is relevant to their needs.
    F. Provide advanced organizers and cognitive frameworks that will help students organize and remember the new material.

15. **True or false? Summaries often help bolster students' motivation.**

16. **True or false? *Formative* evaluation assesses the level of knowledge and skill of students for evaluation purposes, while *summative* evaluation is used to identify gaps in students' understanding, to reinforce their learning, and to strengthen their memory and recall of the information.**

17. **In creating tests, the skills and knowledge tested by the test item should match: (Select all that apply.)**
    A. The objective for a prior topic or lesson
    B. The skill (behavior) stated in the objective
    C. The conditions given in the objective
    D. Skills that have not yet been taught
    E. The criteria specified in the objective
    F. Related skills not given in the objective

18. **Indicate whether each of the following exercises matches its corresponding objective:**

   A. **Objective:** Without any aids and from memory, classify sailboats into their correct type.

   **Exercise:** Without using your book or any other source of help, classify the following sailboats into their correct type by writing the sailboat's type in the blank beside each sailboat.

   B. **Objective:** List the four main reasons web security is essential.

   **Exercise:** Write an essay on why web security is essential.

   C. **Objective:** Correctly identify the major components mounted inside the 9125 computer rack.

   **Exercise:** Explain the purpose of the major components mounted inside the 9215 computer rack.

   D. **Objective:** Define RAID disk arrays and distinguish them from non-RAID arrays.

   **Exercise:** Write the definition of RAID disk arrays, then identify which of the following arrays are RAID arrays.

19. **True or false? You should match the behaviors practiced in the exercises to the behaviors called for in the instructional objectives.**

20. **Exercises are generally needed: (Select all that apply.)**
   A. At the end of major instructional modules and topics (units and lessons) that teach major skills and subskills
   B. At the end of instructional sequences or segments that integrate previously taught skills or subskills into higher-level skills
   C. Wherever the subject matter experts think they should be placed

D. Within topics or lessons, after key enabling subskills are taught and immediately following segments in which important discriminations, generalizations, and sequences are taught

21. **True or false? Integrative exercises are exercises that require students to integrate (combine) the skills of two or more subtasks together to perform a higher-level task.**

22. **True or false? As a general guideline, for self-paced learning, such as web-based training, computer media-based training (such as DVD or CD), self-instructional booklets, and so forth, include some type of meaningful instructional interaction or exercise every eight to twelve screens or six to ten pages.**

23. **True or false? Exercise guidance is providing steps, prompts, cues, or tips to students to follow or use while they are practicing.**

24. **In providing individual feedback to students in exercises, make sure that the feedback: (Select all that apply.)**
    A. Is given in front of other students so that they can learn from that student's mistakes
    B. Is not humiliating
    C. Is encouraging and positive in overall affect
    D. Does not tell the student what he or she did wrong, but rather provides hints to stimulate the student's thinking
    E. Is not embarrassing
    F. Is private

25. **True or false? Tasks and procedures should not be practiced more than once in an exercise.**

26. **Which of the following items should be included in the design specifications for exercises? (Select all that apply.)**

    A. The purpose of the exercise

    B. The level of guidance to be given for each part of the exercise

    C. Specifications of the equipment and tools need to set up the exercise

    D. How long the exercise will take to develop during the development phase of the project

    E. Specifications of the equipment, tools, manuals, job aids, and so forth that students should have available to take the exercise

    F. The description of each of the exercise activities and how feedback will be provided

27. **True or false? In training, demonstrations are to tasks as examples are to concepts.**

28. **Information that should be documented in the design specifications for instructional events and activities include: (Select all that apply.)**

    A. The cost for developing the event or activity

    B. The structure of the activity

    C. The purpose of the activity

    D. A detailed outline or description of the content of the activity

    E. The name of the activity

    F. Any templates that should be followed when developing the activity

    G. An overall summary or high-level description of the activity

## Answers

1. False. Instructional events are learning strategies and activities that are built into the training that are specifically designed to facilitate and promote learning.
2. A, C, D, and E
3. A, C, and D
4. True
5. True
6. The correct answer is "key."
7. True
8. B, C, and E
9. A, B, C, D, and E
10. True
11. True
12. False. The choice of delivery system can limit or constrain the instructional events that you might choose to include.
13. True
14. A, B, C, E, and F
15. True. Summaries can help students to pause and recognize that they have mastered knowledge and skills that are important to them.
16. False. Exactly the opposite is the case. *Summative* evaluation assesses the level of knowledge and skill of students for evaluation purposes, while *formative* evaluation is used to identify gaps in students' understanding, to reinforce their learning, and to strengthen their memory and recall of the information.
17. B, C, and E
18. The exercises for objectives B and C do not match their objectives. The behavior exercised in exercise B—*writing an essay*—is different from the behavior called for by the objective—to simply *list* the four main reasons. The behavior exercised in exercise C—to explain the *purpose* of

the parts—is different from the behavior called for by the objective—to simply *identify* the parts.

19. True
20. A, B, and D
21. True
22. False. As a general guideline, for self-paced learning, such as web-based training, computer media-based training (such as DVD or CD), self-instructional booklets, and so forth, include some type of meaningful instructional interaction or exercise every *three to six screens* or *one to three pages*.
23. True
24. B, C, E, and F
25. False. Repeated practice helps students to progressively improve their performance and to practice the skill until their performance meets the required standards.
26. A, B, C, E, and F
27. True
28. B, C, D, E, F, and G

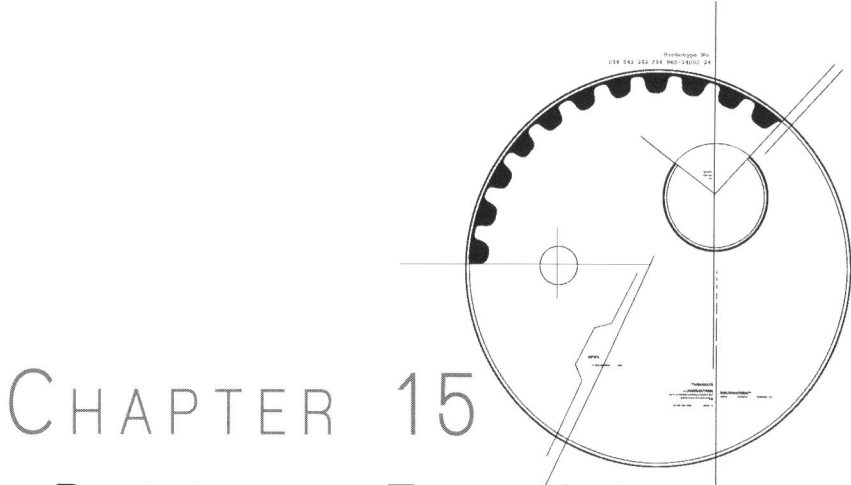

# CHAPTER 15
# Designing the Prototype or Example Lesson

This chapter explains how to design the training user interface for technology-based training or the example lesson for non-technology-based training along with their accompanying style guides. Designing a prototype or example lesson is the next step in the instructional design process after you have selected a training delivery system.

## Where We Are at in the Instructional Design Process

This chapter discusses step 8 in the instructional design process: Design the prototype or example lesson.

1. Gather requirements
2. Perform an instructional analysis on the job outcomes
3. Identify the enabling content
4. Structure the course
5. Write instructional objectives

6. Determine the instructional delivery system
7. Design practice exercises and other instructional events
8. **Design the prototype or example lesson**
9. Create the formal design document

## What Is a Prototype or Example Lesson?

After you have determined the instructional delivery system, the next step in the design process is to design and create a prototype or an example lesson. Which one you create depends on whether you are delivering technology-based training or non-technology-based training.

For technology-based training, you should develop a prototype, or working example, of what the course will look like and how students will interact with it when they take the training. The core task in designing a prototype is to design the user interface—the look-and-feel and the interactive and navigational methods that will be used in the training.

For non-technology-based training, such as self-study printed materials, you should create a sample lesson or topic. This involves designing the layouts and page designs of all of the different types of pages or presentation types in the course.

The prototype and the example lesson do not need to include actual course content (words, graphics, and so forth). Instead, "dummy" content—random words for text and placeholder images for graphics—is typically used in place of actual course content to depict course content. However, standardized phrases or images that will be used throughout the course should be included in the prototype, such as topic introductory phrases or standardized feedback to checkpoint questions.

## Create a Style Guide Along with Your Prototype or Example Lesson

Regardless of whether you are creating a prototype or an example lesson, you should develop a style guide that contains

- specifications for standard screen or page types and layouts,
- standardized text such as feedback for correct and incorrect answers or topic introductions,
- specific grammatical constructions to be used,
- usage rules for jargon and specific technical vocabulary or phrases, and
- specifications for any other elements that will help ensure consistency across the training materials.

Creating a style guide is especially important when the course is significant in size or when more than one developer will be creating course materials.

**Examples of issues that should be addressed in a style guide**

- Should you say "Click on the **Exit** button" or "Click the **Exit** button"?
- Should you use the phrase "pull down menu" or "drop down menu"?
- Should slide titles be written with an initial cap on the first word or with initial caps for all key words in the title?
- What should a topic introduction screen or page look like?
- What elements should each page type contain and how should they appear or be worded?
- How should feedback be phrased for correct and incorrect answers to questions?
- What font should be used?
- What should the size of the display window or text area be?

Your organization or company might also have a standard style guide that should be followed when creating your training or when designing web-delivered training pages.

In the rest of this chapter, we will discuss how to design a prototype for technology-delivered training, after which we will discuss how to design an example lesson for non-technology-based training.

## Characteristics of a Good User Interface

The user interface is what the end user sees, hears, and interacts with to take the training using the chosen delivery technology. For example, for web-based training, the user interface is everything that appears in the training window on the screen, including the different screen layouts, navigational buttons, graphics, interactive media elements, and so forth, along with the ways that students interact with the program using the keyboard, mouse, or other input devices.

In designing a user interface, you should strive to achieve a simple, easy-to-use, intuitive interface that does not require students to take a course just to learn *how* to take the training.

### Characteristics of a good user interface

- is intuitive, easy-to-learn, or walk-up-and-use
- is visually pleasing and well-designed
- is engaging and interactive
- has intuitive, easy-to-use navigational functions
- uses progress indicators to show you which parts of the course you have completed
- uses navigational indicators such as "breadcrumbs" to let students know where they are at in the course
- has excellent prompts and instructions

- provides friendly, supportive feedback and help
- provides graphics and media that support and enhance learning, rather than graphics that are used for "eye candy" or pizzazz
- uses interface elements, phrases, and words consistently throughout the course

## How to Design a User Interface

To create a user interface, complete the following twelve steps. We will discuss each step in the pages that follow.

1. Choose a delivery system (**Note:** this step has already been covered in a previous chapter in this part 2.)
2. Select the appropriate development tools
3. Determine the overall approach to the user interface
4. Decide on the course flow and students' freedom to deviate from that flow in the course
5. Select navigational methods
6. Decide on a method for students to maintain context within the course
7. If required by the client, design progress tracking and reporting capabilities
8. Determine and design all of the common screens and screen elements
9. Determine and write the feedback to be provided for interactions such as quizzes, self-check questions, tests, and so forth
10. Make sure that the course interface, content, and navigation are accessible to the disabled
11. Create and test the prototype
12. Create a style guide with specifications for common elements, style usage issues, and so forth

## Steps 1 and 2. Choose Your Delivery System and Select the Appropriate Development Tools

To develop technology-based training, you must first choose how the training will be delivered—a topic discussed in a previous chapter in part 2. Then you must identify and acquire an application or tool that will enable you to author training materials that can be delivered using that technology. For example, for web-based training, you need a tool that can author web pages if you do not want to write the materials directly in a web language such as html.

Some tools are used only to author the materials and rely on existing network or computer capabilities to deliver the training. For example, a tool might output an executable file that can be run directly on the computer's operating system or a Flash file that can run inside a browser that is Flash enabled.

Because it is laborious to create multiple copies of the different types of screens and user interactions from scratch, it is usually easier and more cost effective to purchase training authoring software that makes it easy, for example, to create modules and topics in a course structure, author interactive questions and quizzes, and create other course design elements. IBM, for example, offers *IBM Content Producer* for authoring web-based, CD-ROM-based, or computer-based training and *IBM Simulation Producer* for authoring simulations of Windows-based applications. Authoring software is constantly being revised and improved. Because a survey of such software is out of the scope of this book, please consult the book by the Hortons mentioned in the sidebar.

---

For additional information on how to select tools for authoring e-learning, consult sources such as *E-Learning Tools and Technologies*, William and Katherine Horton, Wiley Publishing, 2003, ISBN 0-471-44458-8.

## Step 3. Determine the Overall Approach to the User Interface

One of the first decisions you need to make in designing a training user interface is what the overall interface approach will be. As technology advances, new approaches to user interfaces are constantly being invented. Some of the current possibilities include

- standard menu driven (graphical or textual),
- exploratory (such as a simulated environment in which little direction is given),
- game,
- metaphor (such as an online interactive graphic of a personal organizer that represents a real-world personal organizer and calendar),
- job scenario or simulation,
- role-play,
- adventure,
- fantasy, and
- virtual world.

In choosing an overall approach, remember that more elaborate, media-rich, and resource-intensive interfaces, such as simulations, adventures, fantasies, and virtual worlds, generally require more development resources and specialized skills to design and create.

Also remember that learning is not automatically improved just because a more "exciting," media-rich, or expensive-to-develop interface design is selected. A motivated audience, for example, can learn just as effectively from a straightforward, inexpensive interface as from a more elaborate one.

## Step 4. Decide on the Course Flow and Students' Freedom to Deviate from That Flow

In determining course flow and students' freedom to deviate from that flow, many issues have to be decided:

- How will students proceed through the course? Will it be presented as one long sequence, as a layered approach (such as Modules, Topics, and Subtopics), or as a combination of the two?

- Will course flow be predetermined, and if so, will the recommended flow through the course be a suggested course flow or will it be strictly enforced? Similarly, how much freedom will students have to take course topics in a different order from that which is presented in the course map or menu? Will they have to "touch" (visit) every screen and complete every interaction before being allowed to move to the next screen?

- If course flow is strictly enforced, will students have the ability to selectively take parts of the course that they have already completed, say, for example, to refresh their memory at a later time on a particular topic?

In addressing these issues, you must also consider the course content. Some course content is strictly sequential in nature. For example, many math topics build on other math topics. If this is the case, then you might consider requiring that students follow a fixed sequence through the course. However, even in this scenario, it is probably best to allow students to take pretests and bypass topics they already know.

Except for unusual circumstances, it is generally better to give students a high degree of control over how they will take the course. You can then use postcourse performance or cognitive tests to verify acquisition of the required skills and knowledge.

## Step 5. Select Navigational Methods

To carry out this step, you must answer questions such as

- How will students navigate through the course—using buttons (Previous, Next, Main Menu, Unit Menu, Help, Exit, and so forth), keys, or some other manual means of navigation, or by some timed or automatic means, such as the completion of an audio narration or by students completing a certain interaction?
- For multimedia interactions, what level of control do you want to provide students (repeat, rewind, fast forward, stop, pause, and so forth)?
- Will students have the ability to bookmark their location in the course so that they can exit the course and later return directly to the bookmarked location?
- How will you indicate to students which parts of the course they have already completed?
- Will alternate, redundant means be provided for navigation, such as key equivalents for mouse clicks? Have you provided alternate navigational methods for those with disabilities?

## Step 6. Decide on a Method for Students to Maintain Context within the Course

How will students know where they are at in the course? This is a different issue from letting students know which parts of the course they have already completed. Context tells students where they are currently at in the course. It gives a sense of location within the course.

Just as people do not like driving around a city without knowing where they are at, where they are going, how they will navigate to their destination, and how far it is to their destination, students do not like to be lost in courses that do not indicate where they are at, how they can navigate to another part of the course, and how much farther it is to finish a topic or module.

One way this can be accomplished is by providing a text stream somewhere on the screen that contains location information (such as "Unit 1: Fractions, Topic 3: Lowest Common Denominator").

Within a topic, you might also want to let students know how many more screens they have to complete the topic by providing feedback such as "Screen 1 of 10" somewhere on the screen.

## Step 7. If Required by the Client, Design Progress Tracking and Reporting Capabilities

Clients vary in their desire to track student progress and course completion. Some clients want to know if students have navigated to every screen and completed every instructional interaction in the course. Other clients simply want to know if students have invoked every topic. Still other clients simply want to know if students have passed quizzes or course exams.

Sometimes a curriculum is set up so that students must successfully pass one course before they are allowed to enroll in another.

So how will all of this information be tracked and communicated to learning administrators? One way of addressing these needs is by creating training materials using a SCORM-compliant authoring application, such as *IBM Content Producer*. Such applications can automatically communicate this information to learning management systems that are also SCORM compliant.

In any case, developers and designers must give consideration for this need early in their selection of authoring tools and software; otherwise, they must hard code this type of intelligence directly into their training application—a costly proposition at best.

## Step 8. Determine and Design All of the Common Screens and Screen Elements

This step involves determining and designing the various types of screens that you will have in your course, such as

- splash or entry screen;
- content screens;
- overviews, reviews, summaries, and tracking screens;
- tests, quizzes, checkpoints, and feedback screens;
- exercises and case study screens;
- simulations, demonstrations, games, and interactive or collaboration screens; and
- course, unit, and topic completion screens.

As part of this task, you should design the common elements that will appear on most or all screens, such as

- backgrounds for content screens;
- navigational elements, such as menu screens or panes, breadcrumb trails, screen numbers, and so forth;
- banners, headers, footers, and peripheral elements;
- color scheme and typographical font and layout for various textual and graphical screen elements;
- design and placement of common graphical elements that will appear in various places through the course, such as a company logo or stylized course title; and
- design and layout of any other common screen elements.

## Step 9. Determine and Write the Feedback to Be Provided for Interactions

Training is not just the dispensing of information; real training provides students the opportunity to practice and test their skills and knowledge and receive feedback on their performance.

Such practice, however, is not very helpful and can actually make things worse unless instructive feedback is also provided to students to let them know what they did right and wrong. For example, piano students who practice a piece over and over again for several days without receiving any feedback from their teachers could simply ingrain into their brain wrong fingering, improper intonation, wrong musical interpretation, or incorrect notes, making it much more difficult to modify their behavior later when their teachers finally do provide feedback.

Instructive feedback should be provided for quizzes, self-check questions, exercises, activities, tests, and other practice exercises or testing activities. This feedback should be consistent in style, tone, and appearance and should be easily distinguished from other text or screen elements.

## Step 10. Make Sure That the Course Interface, Content, and Navigation Are Accessible to Students with Disabilities

Accessibility of online applications to those with disabilities is fast becoming required by law, by government entities, and by organizational edict. Designers and developers must become aware of and trained in how to make training accessible to those with disabilities.

A sampling of some of the issues that must be addressed for online accessibility include

- provide alternative text for graphics and images,
- provide sufficient contrast between screen elements such as text and background elements,

- provide written transcripts for audio presentations,
- make data tables readable to screen readers,
- provide keyboard shortcuts to mouse actions, and
- provide a logical tab order for the elements on the screen.

Many modern computer operating systems provide some capabilities to enlarge text, increase contrast, and provide keyboard substitutes for simultaneous keystrokes (such as "Press CTRL-ALT-DEL"). However, you must do much more than what the accessibility features of an operating system offer to comply with accessibility laws and requirements.

## Step 11. Create and Test the Prototype

The culmination of interface design is finalizing all of the design decisions into a flesh-and-blood prototype that contains mock-ups of the different screen types and interactions that will be used in the course, just the way that students will see them. This prototype should be a functioning online version that allows reviewers to navigate through the menu system, observe the tracking and context setting features, and in general experience the interface.

### Advantages of creating a working prototype

- It provides a proof of concept and demonstrates due diligence that the development team can create the design that was envisioned using the chosen development tools.
- It allows you to test the prototype with potential students from the target audience and ask questions on ease of use, the ability to maintain one's sense of location within the course, and the intuitiveness and desirability of various screen elements. Features meant to satisfy accessibility requirements can also be tested. This is true even if the prototype has "dummy" content in it instead of actual course content.
- It is an excellent means by which early client feedback can be obtained.

- Because it allows all of these types of feedback to be gathered early on in the project, many problems can be avoided and many improvements can be made to the interface.
- It is an excellent way to communicate visually the course design to other professional and technical staff members who are charged with creating the training materials.

If an actual working prototype cannot be created, a printed version of the prototype can be created that contains screen mock-ups and layouts. However, a paper prototype will be more difficult for others to visualize, especially for courses with layered information and many branch points.

## Step 12. Create a Style Guide

The final step in creating a training user interface is to document all of your layouts and design decisions in a style guide. The document should contain the detailed specifications for all interface design elements, such as

- style issues,
- grammatical constructions and jargon to avoid or use,
- usage issues,
- voice used in the text (first person plural, second person, third person, and so forth),
- dimensions and specifications for screens and screen elements, and
- descriptions of the functionality of all buttons and icons.

The style guide will help ensure that the course will have consistent presentations throughout the course. This is especially helpful when multiple developers are involved in creating course materials. It will also be used by the editor when editing the course to ensure that the grammar, style, spelling, and layout complies with the specifications set forth in the style guide.

## Interface Design Is an Iterative Process

This means that an initial design is sketched out, sent out for review, revised again, reviewed again, revised yet again, tested with potential students, revised yet again, and so forth until a professional, usable training interface is achieved.

This process can be likened to the process of creating a sculpture. The artist first creates a rough clay model, then analyzes it and makes refinements, then looks at it again, and so forth until the clay model is more or less perfect. Then the artist chisels the image in stone. If the artist is given unbiased reviews of the early clay models of the sculpture, he will avoid having to discard expensive pieces of half-chiseled marble after many more hours have been invested in the project.

In this analogy, the clay model is like the prototype. Work iteratively with the prototype until you get it right. Then develop the full course.

---

One excellent source for learning more about the *principles* of good user interface design is *Principles and Guidelines in Software User Interface Design*, Deborah J. Mayhew, Prentice Hall, 1992, ISBN 0-13-721929-6. For more recent books, search on the string "user interface design" in major online bookseller web sites.

---

## Designing Non-Technology-Delivered Training Prototypes (Such as Example Lessons)

Many of the same steps that we used to design technology-based user interfaces also apply to designing non-technology-based training interfaces, such as slides, instructor guides, or self-study workbooks. For example, you still need to

- identify an authoring tool, such as a word processor or slide show creation application;
- determine the overall approach to the training and course flow (such as a strictly linear sequence or one that allows for branching in the materials);
- determine a method for students to maintain context within the course (usually through header and footer information and chapter divider pages);
- decide how student progress will be tracked and reported (for example, if students will be required to take a teacher-monitored test or get on the web to take a web-administered test);
- determine and design common page types and page elements;
- write common feedback to be provided for quizzes, self-check questions, tests, and so forth;
- create and test the prototype; and
- create a style guide with specifications for common elements, style usage issues, and so forth.

## Principles of Layout and Design

Designing effective and pleasing layouts for hardcopy materials or projected materials is just as important as designing good online presentations. Principles of good visual design and layout apply to both technology-based and non-technology-based training. Although a thorough discussion of visual design and layout is beyond the scope of this book, we will list some of the basic elements of design and then provide a few references where you can learn more on this subject.

### Principles of good visual design and layout

- foreground/background
- balance
- symmetry

- unity
- density
- grouping
- proximity
- alignment
- repetition
- contrast
- simplicity
- appropriate use of color and type

For additional information on the principles of good visual design and layout, consult sources such as

- *The Non-Designer's Design Book: Design and Typographic Principles for the Visual Novice*, Robin Williams, Peachpit Press, Berkeley, California, 1994, ISBN 1-56609-159-4.
- *Instructional Message Design: Principles from the Behavioral Sciences,* by Malcolm Fleming and W. Howard Levie, Educational Technology Publications, Englewood Cliffs, New Jersey, 1978, ISBN 0-87778-104-4. Although this book is out of print, it very clearly teaches several of the above principles. Used copies should still be available from online booksellers or at your local library.

For an excellent book on designing graphics for training, consult *Graphics for Learning: Proven Guidelines for Planning, Designing, and Evaluating Visuals in Training Materials*, by Ruth Colvin Clark and Chopeta Lyons, Pfeiffer, New York, 2004, ISBN 0-7879-6994-X.

# Chapter Summary—
# Designing the Prototype or Example Lesson

This chapter explained how to design the training user interface for technology-based training or the example lesson for non-technology-based training along with their accompanying style guides. Designing a prototype or example lesson is the next step in the instructional design process after you have selected a training delivery system.

You should now be able to

- define a prototype and example lesson, describe when to create each, and explain if actual course content must be a part of a prototype or example lesson;
- define a style guide and describe the types of issues that should be addressed in a style guide;
- define the user interface and list the characteristics of a good user interface;
- list the twelve steps for designing a user interface;
- explain why development tools are necessary and what they must do;
- explain some of the major options that are available in choosing an overall approach to the user interface;
- explain the issues that must be addressed in deciding on the course flow and students' freedom to deviate from that flow;
- explain the issues that must be addressed in making navigational design decisions;
- explain why students need to maintain context when they are in a course and mechanisms for doing so;
- explain the issues associated with progress tracking and reporting;
- explain what it means to determine and design all of the common screens and screen elements;
- explain why instructive feedback should be provided to students for all learning interactions and the issues around providing that feedback;

- explain why training must be made accessible to those with disabilities, provide examples of user interface issues that must be addressed, and list a web site where more information about accessibility can be found;
- list the advantages of having a working prototype for online training;
- explain why a style guide is necessary;
- explain why interface design is an iterative process;
- list the steps in designing non-technology-based example lessons that are common with the steps for designing technology-based prototypes; and
- list the major principles of layout and design.

## Check Your Understanding

1. **True or false? The prototype or example lesson does *not* need to include actual course content.**

2. **Which of the following items belong in a style guide? (Select all that apply.)**

    A. Specifications for standard screen or page types and layouts

    B. The enabling content for the course

    C. Standardized text such as feedback for correct and incorrect answers or topic introductions

    D. A listing of the course prerequisites

    E. Specific grammatical constructions to be used

    F. Usage rules for jargon and specific technical vocabulary or phrases

    G. The course structure

3. **Which of the following descriptions are characteristics of a good user interface design? (Select all that apply.)**

    A. Uses complex navigational techniques

    B. Is intuitive, easy-to-learn, or walk-up-and-use

    C. Graphics and media are used to provide "eye candy" or pizzazz.

D. Uses progress indicators to show students which parts of the course they have completed

E. Uses navigational indicators such as "breadcrumbs" to let students know where they are at in the course

F. Uses the latest state-of-the-art user interface technology

G. Uses interface elements, phrases, and words consistently throughout the course

4. **True or false? *IBM Content Producer* and *IBM Simulation Producer* are examples of training development software.**

5. **True or false? In choosing an overall approach to the training user interface, media-rich and resource-intensive interfaces, such as simulations, adventures, fantasies, and virtual worlds, generally produce greater learning than traditional, simpler, or less media-rich user interfaces.**

6. **True or false? Course content should be considered in determining course flow and students' freedom to deviate from that flow.**

7. **Which of the following issues should be considered in choosing navigational methods in a training user interface? (Select all that apply.)**

A. Bookmarking

B. Course progress indicators

C. Redundant, alternate means of navigation

D. Navigational methods, such as buttons, timing, or activity completion

E. User controls for multimedia content

F. Test reporting capabilities

8. **True or false? Methods for helping students to maintain context in a course are different from methods for indicating course progress or completion.**

9. **True or false? The tracking of student progress in a course and the reporting of test results is made easier if both the training development software and the learning management system are SCORM compliant.**

10. **True or false? As part of the task of determining and designing all of the common screens, you should design the common elements that will appear on most or all screens.**

11. **True or false? Student feedback provided for quizzes, self-check questions, exercises, activities, tests, and other practice exercises or testing activities should be consistent in style, tone, and appearance and should be easily distinguished from other text or screen elements.**

12. **Which of the following are examples of actions that you must take to make your training accessible to those with disabilities? (Select all that apply.)**
    A. Provide a logical tab order for the elements on the screen.
    B. Provide keyboard shortcuts to mouse actions.
    C. Provide written transcripts for audio presentations.
    D. Provide alternative text for graphics and images.
    E. Provide sufficient contrast between screen elements such as text and background elements.
    F. Make data tables readable to screen readers.

13. **Which of the following are benefits of creating a *working* prototype of your training user interface? (Select all that apply.)**
    A. It can be used as a substitute for the instructional design document.
    B. It shows due diligence that the development team can create the design that was envisioned using the chosen development tools.
    C. It is an excellent means by which early client feedback can be obtained.
    D. It allows feedback about the interface to be gathered early on in the project, thus averting many potential problems and allowing for many improvements to be made to the interface.
    E. It allows you to test the prototype with potential students from the target audience.
    F. It provides a proof of concept.

14. **A style guide helps ensure ____ throughout the entire course.**

15. **True or false? Training user interface design is an iterative process of making successive refinements as initial designs and prototypes are created, reviewed, and tested.**

16. **True or false? Many of the steps in the procedure for designing a non-technology-based training prototype are the same or similar to the steps for designing a technology-based training prototype.**

17. **Which of the following are principles of good layout and design? (Select all that apply.)**
    A. Symmetry
    B. Unity
    C. Proximity
    D. Color wheel

E. Alignment

F. Repetition

G. Contrast

H. Indexing

I. Foreground/background

## Answers

1. True
2. A, C, E, and F
3. B, D, E, and G
4. True
5. False. Learning is not automatically improved just because a more "exciting," media-rich, or expensive-to-develop interface design is selected. A motivated audience, for example, can learn just as effectively from a straightforward, inexpensive interface as from a more elaborate one.
6. True. Some course content is strictly sequential in nature. For example, many math topics build on other math topics. If this is the case, then you might consider requiring that students follow a fixed sequence through the course. However, even in this scenario, it is probably best to allow students to take pretests and bypass topics they already know.
7. A, B, C, D, and E
8. True. Context tells students where they are currently at in the course. It gives a sense of location within the course. On the other hand, course progress or completion tells students which parts of the course they have already completed.
9. True
10. True
11. True
12. A, B, C, D, E, and F

13. B, C, D, E, and F
14. The correct answer is "consistency."
15. True
16. True
17. A, B, C, E, F, G, and I

# Chapter 16
# Creating the Formal Design Document

This chapter describes the instructional design document and the information it should contain. Creating the formal instructional design document is the last step in the instructional design process.

## Where We Are at in the Instructional Design Process

This chapter discusses step 9 in the instructional design process: Create the design document.

1. Gather requirements
2. Perform an instructional analysis on the job outcomes
3. Identify the enabling content
4. Structure the course
5. Write instructional objectives
6. Determine the instructional delivery system

7. Design practice exercises and other instructional events
8. Design the prototype or example lesson
9. **Create the formal design document**

## What Is an Instructional Design Document?

An instructional design document is a formal document that clearly details and communicates the training design. Together with the prototype and style guide, it specifies how to build the training. It is like a set of blueprints for a building.

The purpose of the instructional design document is to define, clarify, specify, and communicate the instructional design to

- sponsors (for approval);
- technical, media, and content developers (for training development);
- project managers (for sizing and costing, tracking, and verification of work completed); and
- other designers (for validation of the design).

### Typical entries in an instructional design document

- title page
- executive summary
- sign-off page
- overall business goal
- justification for training
- job outcomes targeted for training
- target audience
- course prerequisites and curriculum fit
- overall course description (including delivery mechanism)
- technology requirements

- course objectives
- course structure (modules and topics or units and lesson)
- course agenda (if instructor led)
- prototype, look-and-feel, or example lesson, or a reference to it
- course style guide or development specifications, or a reference to it
- module and topic and detailed descriptions
- evaluation and assessment procedures and criteria

We will look at each of these entries in more detail in the rest of this chapter.

## Title Page and Executive Summary

The *title page* is a dedicated page that contains the usual document titling information, such as the title, date of creation, author, author's title and organization, sponsoring business organization's name, and possibly a table showing the revision history or version history.

The *executive summary* section contains one or more paragraphs that summarize and describe the project, including

- why training is being developed (the business need),
- who the training is for,
- what students will be able to accomplish or produce back on their jobs as a result of the training,
- the overall features and design of the training,
- why the design is appropriate for the audience, and
- how the training fits into the larger curriculum.

The executive summary is intended to be read by managers, executives, and decision makers. It should therefore contain answers to the questions they will likely have in mind in reviewing this document. Don't assume that executives will read the design document from beginning to end. Write what you want executives to read in this section of the document, because it might be the only section that they read.

## Sign-Off Page, Overall Business Goal, and Justification for Training

The *sign-off page* is a dedicated page where sponsors and approvers sign off their approval of the design document. It is often placed upfront in the design document to make it easy to find. As typically used in a business, appropriate signatures on this page are a formal project management milestone and a baseline for future change control.

The *overall business goal* section summarizes the business plan points and the business goals that the training is expected to address. You should also explain how the business would be impacted if this need or goal were met.

The *justification for training* section explains why training is the right performance intervention and shows how training will address the business need or goal. If appropriate, it might also show the results of a cost-effectiveness or return on investment analysis for training that supports the decision to invest in training.

## Job Outcomes and Target Audience

The *job outcomes* section lists the overall job outcomes or accomplishments that students will be able to produce back on the job after they have taken the training. These are the same outcomes that were identified during instructional analysis and that appear in the first level or two of the hierarchical instructional analysis (see chapter 2 for a detailed discussion of job outcomes). Focusing on job outcomes as opposed to generic knowledge and skills clearly shows how training will address the business needs because job outcomes describe work products, results, or accomplishments that the business values.

The *target audience* section is a critical entry that describes in detail the target audience of the training, including the major audience subgroups and their characteristics. These characteristics should include

- demographics (including size, geographic distribution, age groupings);
- job title, job role, and job environment;
- existing job skills and knowledge (what students bring to the training);
- training history and preferences; and
- motivators and motivation level.

See chapter 2 for a detailed discussion of the target audience.

## Course Prerequisites and Curriculum Fit

This section shows how this course or curriculum fits into the larger curriculum or overall training road map for relevant job roles. This section also mentions if this course is part of a certification path.

In addition, this section lists course prerequisites—hard prerequisites that must be taken before students can enroll in this course, and soft prerequisites that are recommended but not required. Prerequisites can also include specific knowledge areas, the ability to produce certain work products, or other types of prerequisites.

Finally, this section lists the entry-level skills and knowledge that the course assumes that students will have when they begin the training.

## Overall Course Description and Technology Requirements

The *overall course description* section is a summary description of the course itself. It includes information such as

- course title,
- length of course (days or hours),
- type of course delivery (classroom, web-based, CD-ROM delivered, and so forth),
- overall course goal,
- total number of modules or units,
- general approach to the course design, and
- types of interaction (lectures, exercises, group work, labs, and so forth).

The *technology requirements* section describes the technology requirements for both developing the training and delivering the training, such as

- system requirements,
- network connection bandwidth and speed,
- browser requirements,
- plug-in requirements,
- other software requirements, and
- any special hardware requirements.

## Course Objectives, Course Structure, and Course Agenda

The *course objectives* section contains a list of the overall or high-level course objectives. Detailed objectives for each module and topic or unit and lesson are *not* provided here; rather, they are documented in a later section. The objectives given here should be broader and more general than the more specific objectives documented later for each module and topic.

The *course structure* section contains a succinct graphical or textual display of the structure of the course along with the titles of the course modules and topics or units and lessons. Again, details about each entry in the course structure are *not* provided here but are given in a later section. Rather, this section presents the course structure in a nutshell, much like a table of contents or main menu does.

The *course agenda* section shows the day-by-day and hour-by-hour course activities. It also shows the times when those activities begin and end. This section is relevant to training delivery methods that are delivered in fixed timeframes, such as in instructor-led training. The course agenda shows a chronological listing of course events—lectures, activities, group work, lab exercises, breaks, and so forth.

## Prototype or Example Lesson and the Style Guide

The *prototype or example lesson* section contains either a reference to a separate online working prototype for the course or several pages that detail the prototype in hardcopy format within the instructional design document itself. Prototypes were discussed more fully in chapter 8.

The *style guide* section contains either a reference to a separate style guide document for the course or several pages that detail the style guide in hardcopy format within the instructional design document itself. Larger projects usually have a separate style guide document. Style guides were discussed more fully in chapter 8.

## Module and Topic Detailed Descriptions

This section is typically the largest section of the instructional design document. It contains the detailed instructional design specifications for each of the modules, topics, and other instructional activities that are part of instruction of the course.

This section describes in detail the structure of each topic or lesson and the instructional activities that will be included in that topic. The information in this section will be used by the course developers to help them write or develop the actual course content. For each topic, for example, it should include the following information:

- topic objectives
- student seat time
- overall purpose of the topic (what this topic discusses and what students will learn)
- content overview or outline (this is usually the largest piece in this section)
- instructional activities employed in this topic and their design and description
- lesson plan (sequence of instructional events or flow through the topic)
- references (to where the source content for this unit or topic can be found)
- storyboards (if training is technology delivered and if storyboards are included by your organization in the instructional design document)

## Evaluation and Assessment Procedures and Criteria

This section describes the evaluation, assessment, and student tracking procedures and criteria that will be used in the course. Assessments are performed to see how well students received the training, achieved the course objectives, and transferred what they learned back to their jobs. This section also describes where in the course and after the course these assessments occur.

Many organizations use Donald Kirkpatrick's four levels of evaluation to describe a given assessment (for example, "A Level 2 evaluation will be performed at the end of the course."). The following table defines these levels.

| Kirkpatrick Level | Title | Level Description |
|---|---|---|
| Level 1 | Reaction | Course surveys or "smile" sheets administered immediately at the end of course to assess students' reactions and feelings about the course. |
| Level 2 | Learning | Instructional assessments or tests designed to measure what students learned in the course; usually administered at the end of major sections of the course, at the end of the course, or a short time later. |
| Level 3 | Transfer | Assessments designed to measure whether student learning was applied and used back on the job; usually administered a short time after training has ended, such as 30 days later. |
| Level 4 | Results | An analysis that looks at the business results that training was expected to change to see if bottom line business results were indeed impacted by the training; usually done a few weeks or months after the training to allow sufficient time for the results to occur and be detectable. |

## What *Not* to Include in the Instructional Design Document

The instructional design document is not intended to address all project or business-related concerns or issues related to managing or approving the training project. Rather, the design document, prototype, and style guide are like a set of blueprints for training.

As important as architectural blueprints and specifications are in the construction industry, they are not used alone; rather, they are supplemented by other construction documents, business contracts and agreements, and other administrative processes and procedures of the construction company.

What should *not* be included in the instructional design document? It should not contain

- project information, such as schedules, project staff and resources, formal business agreements between departments, and so forth;
- information meant to impress the reader with the deep knowledge or skill of the instructional designer;
- information designed to teach the reader about instructional design (for example, several pages of information on learning principles or instructional design techniques);
- other filler information, such as large appendices or information copied from other documents (bigger, fatter documents are usually harder to read and understand than small, more concise, focused documents);
- "flowery," wordy, or academic-sounding language; or
- any content meant to "pad" the document to make it more impressive or intimidating to others.

In short, adhere to the purposes given in this chapter for the instructional design document, and leave out any other information that does not directly support that purpose.

**The Effort Required to Create an Instructional Design Document**

If you have followed the instructional design process explained in this book and have completed the other design steps, the design document is just a formalization of information and design decisions that you have already made. For example, course modules and topics were identified during course structuring. Objectives were already written after course structuring. Outlines of content can be found in the combined instructional analysis and content analysis document.

Even with the information produced by the steps in our instructional design process, creating the instructional design document is still not a trivial exercise.

"Wordsmithing" the document alone can take several days, depending on the length and complexity of the training. Your organization will determine the level of formality and detail that they want included in this document.

The instructional design document is a communication vehicle. It by itself is not a "pure" instructional design activity—it is *not* an activity in which design decisions are being made. Rather, it is a reporting vehicle that documents the decisions and designs that were already made in the previous steps of the instructional design process. It also provides a level of business justification to the business sponsors and decision makers for undertaking the training.

## Is an Instructional Design Document Always Necessary?

Outstanding, instructionally sound training can be designed and created without an instructional design document (but not without following the steps in the design process!). This can occur in situations, for example, in which the training is fairly simple or routine, the instructional designer is developing the course as well as designing the course, or the level of trust between the sponsor and the instructional designer is high.

In this case, the instructional designer does not need to communicate the design formally to others. However, these situations are rare because the skills and input of others are often required to develop the training. Also, managers, sponsors, and executives like to document formal agreements, specifications, and decisions very explicitly. They also like to monitor closely the expenditure of budgets and resources and the progress of the design and development effort. Finally, they like to have a formal document that shows "proof" that the work was actually performed for audit trail and future questioning by others. Whether this administrative overhead is justified and needed is a management and business decision rather than an instructional design decision.

# Chapter Summary— Creating the Formal Design Document

This chapter described the instructional design document and the information it should contain. Creating the formal instructional design document is the last step in the instructional design process.

You should now be able to

- define an instructional design document and describe the information that it contains;
- describe the information you should include in the *title page* and *executive summary* sections of the design document;
- describe the information you should include in the *sign-off page*, *overall business goal*, and *justification for training* sections of the design document;
- describe the information you should include in the *job outcomes* and *target audience* sections of the design document;
- describe the information you should include in the *course prerequisites* and *curriculum fit* sections of the design document;
- describe the information you should include in the *overall course description* and *technology requirements* sections of the design document;
- describe the information you should include in the *course objectives, course structure,* and *course agenda* sections of the design document;
- describe the information you should include in the *prototype or example lesson* and the *style guide* sections of the design document;
- describe the information you should include in the *module and topic detailed descriptions* section of the design document;
- describe the information you should include in the *evaluation and assessment procedures and criteria* section of the design document;
- describe what not to include in the instructional design document; and
- describe the effort required to create an instructional design document and explain when one might not be required.

## Check Your Understanding

1. An ___ ___ ___ is a formal document that clearly details and communicates the training design.

2. True or false? The intended audience of the executive summary section of the instructional design document are managers, decision makers, and executives who are unlikely to read the entire document from beginning to end.

3. True or false? The *justification for training* section of an instructional design document explains why training is the right performance intervention and shows how training will address the business need or goal.

4. True or false? It is not necessary to describe the target audience in the instructional design document because that information was collected in the requirements gathering template.

5. True or false? Hard prerequisites are prerequisites that must be taken before students can enroll in a course; soft prerequisites are prerequisites that are recommended but not required.

6. True or false? The *overall course description* section of an instructional design document contains detailed information for each of the modules and topics of the course.

7. True or false? The course structure section of an instructional design document presents the course structure in a nutshell, much like a table of contents or main menu does.

8. **True or false? The prototype and style guide sections of an instructional design document might consist of a simple reference to an online prototype or external document, respectively.**

9. **True or false? The *module and topic detailed descriptions* section of the instructional design document is typically the largest section of the instructional design document.**

10. **True or false? A Level 3 evaluation in Patrick Kirkpatrick's evaluation taxonomy consists of instructional assessments or tests designed to measure what students learned in the course; they are usually administered at the end of major sections of the course, at the end of the course, or a short time later.**

11. **True or false? An instructional design document should include project information, such as project schedules, project staff and resources, formal business agreements between departments, and so forth.**

12. **True or false? There are circumstances in which an instructional design document is *not* necessary to create outstanding, instructionally sound training.**

## Answers

1. The correct answer is "instructional design document."
2. True
3. True
4. False
5. True

414   *Instructional Design — Step by Step*

6. False. This section contains a high-level summary of the course. Detailed descriptions of the modules and topics are provided in a later section.
7. True
8. True
9. True
10. False. The description given is for a Level 2 evaluation.
11. False
12. True. Outstanding, instructionally sound training can be designed and created without an instructional design document (but not without following the steps in the design process!). This can occur in situations, for example, in which the training is fairly simple or routine, the instructional designer is developing the course as well as designing the course, or the level of trust between the sponsor and the instructional designer is high.

# PART 3

## Instructional Design Tips and Traps

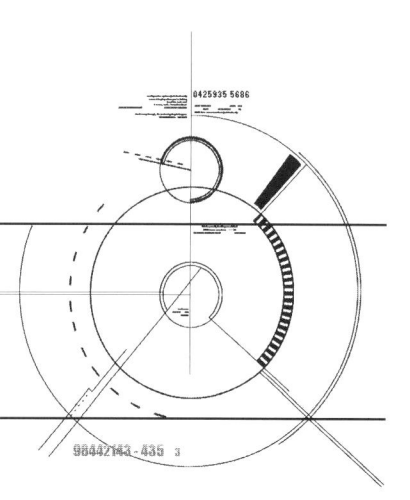

# Overview of Part 3

Part 3 discusses some specific instructional design tips and traps. It explains how to design software application end-user training—a common area of training in business, industry, and organizations today—and it lists twenty common training mistakes, how you can avoid them, and how you can correct them. These tips and traps should reinforce the concepts and techniques that you have already learned in this book.

After you complete part 3, you should be able to

- explain how learning computer applications differs from learning many other types of information;
- state several principles and design tips for designing software application training;
- list twenty common training mistakes; and
- for each common training mistake, explain what learning principles are being violated, how to remedy the mistake, and how to avoid making the mistake in the first place.

Part 3 is made up of three chapters.

## Why Another Part in This Book?

In part 1, you completed a brief overview of how humans learn—the biological and cognitive processes that humans must employ to learn. In part 2, you completed a short course in instructional design, learning the nine steps for performing instructional design along with a number of accompanying analysis techniques and design principles. With that, you should now be well grounded in the fundamentals of instructional design.

In the remainder of this book, we will discuss two specific areas. The first is computer application training. This chapter explains instructional design principles specific to training students to use computer applications. Because computers are so pervasive in the modern workplace and are the tool of choice in many professions, you will probably have to create training on computer applications at some point in your career as an instructional designer. Therefore, this topic merits special treatment.

The second area that we will discuss is a collection of twenty common training mistakes that are made by those who create and deliver training courses, be they professional instructional designers and developers, academic educators, full-time instructors, subject matter experts who are charged with putting together new training materials, or just someone who needs to teach something to others. Being aware of these potential pitfalls and traps will help you avoid making these mistakes yourself and will help you improve the quality of your training.

# CHAPTER 17
# Designing Computer Application Training

This chapter discusses the ways in which training students to use computer applications is different from other types of training and what you can do as an instruction designer to accommodate those differences. It also provides ten tips for designing computer application training and discusses instructional events that are especially important to include in computer application training.

## What Is Application Training?

Application training is training that is designed to teach students how to use a computer application to perform useful work.

Examples of applications that are typically used in the workplace include

- standard office applications, such as word processing, spreadsheets, databases, e-mail, presentations, project management, and so forth;
- specialized business applications in areas such as enterprise resource planning (ERP), customer relationship management (CRM), accounting,

finance, human resource (HR), computer-aided design (CAD), supply chain management (SCM), statistical analysis programs, and so forth;

- application development programs that are used by programmers and IT staff to create other applications, link applications together, access enterprise databases, provide security, and perform other computer tasks; and

- industrial and commercial applications that are used to operate, control, and monitor equipment or the status of real-life events.

## Why Learning Computer Applications Is Different: Abstractness

Learning computer applications is different from learning many other types of skills and content. Most of these differences are matters of degree more than matters of differing substance.

The first difference is that learning computer applications typically requires students to learn a considerable amount of abstract material—abstract objects, concepts, and functions that are invoked through arbitrary but predetermined means using keystrokes, mouse clicks, button clicks, and other methods of interaction. Until users create an accurate mental model of how the application works and how functions are accessed, organized, and applied, the application's use remains a mystery. "Walk-up-and-use" interface design has not yet been achieved, nor is it likely ever to be achieved for large, function-rich applications.

## Activity: Experience the Abstract Nature of Computer Procedures

This activity will help you experience for yourself the abstract and arbitrary nature of computer functions and procedures.

Follow these steps to complete this activity:

1. Set a timer for 1 minute.
2. Start the timer and look at procedure A (see below).

3. Try to memorize the instructions before the timer rings.
4. After the timer rings, write down as many of the steps of the procedure as you can remember.
5. Repeat the above steps for procedure B.

**Procedure A**

1. Move the borb to the fix box in the upper zylog sector.
2. Select the T5 twiddle bar next to the i-lap.
3. Hold down the W-zap key while entering *bapzap.*
4. Whizzle the fontzing button using a single klop.
5. Click the qwip control icon.
6. Wait until phistomorphis is complete.

**Procedure B**

1. Place the galvanized steel bucket on the ground.
2. Add a cup of sand.
3. Add a cup of pea gravel.
4. Add a cup of lime.
5. Add a cup of cement powder.
6. Add a cup of water.
7. Stir the entire mixture until fully mixed.
8. Pour the mixture into the forms.

**Why learning and remembering procedure A was harder than learning and remembering procedure B**

Procedure A consisted of instructions that involved abstract names and concepts that were sequenced in an apparently arbitrary way, while procedure B consisted of instructions that involved concrete objects that were sequenced in a more meaningful way. The objects being manipulated in procedure B were also more familiar and meaningful to you than those in procedure A.

## Implications of the abstract nature of computer procedures, concepts, and names

- Abstract concepts and procedures are more difficult to learn and remember.
- Training should help students create an accurate mental map of how the application works.
- Training should provide memory support interventions to help students remember the abstract information, such as repeated practice over time of key tasks.
- Training should also provide performance aids that reduce students' need to remember the information.

## Why Learning Computer Applications Is Different: Computers Are Digital, Not Analog

Interacting with computers is different from most real-life interaction. Computers are digital—bits are either on or off, a button is either pressed or it isn't, the correct key was either pressed or it wasn't, either all of the steps of the procedure were completed with 100 percent accuracy, or the function is not invoked. There are no shades of gray.

On the other hand, real life is mostly analog in nature. If you bake a cake at 326 degrees instead of 325 degrees, it still turns out just fine. If you clean most of the snow off your windshield, you can still drive your car. If you speak a little too loudly, the other person can still understand what you are saying. If you turn in an outstanding instructional design document that leaves out information about the learning preferences of the audience, it will still likely be signed off.

### Additional insights on the digital nature of computers

- They require 100 percent (or in some exceptional cases, nearly 100 percent) accuracy. Most things in life do not require perfect accuracy or performance.
- Approximate effort does not equal approximate results.

- They appear to be unforgiving; therefore, users can easily become frustrated or give up.
- It is easy for users to make a mistake and cause serious damage to important information or the actual loss of work or data; from the user's perspective, this creates fear before or during interaction with the computer and anger at the computer after such an event occurs.

**Strategies for addressing the digital nature of computers**

- Provide accurate, complete, explicit step-by-step instructions.
- Provide feedback for each step of the procedure so that students can verify that they are still on track; otherwise, students can unknowingly make a mistake, continue to invest significant time and effort in the procedure, and possibly even do negative things to their data or work product before they finally realize that they have made an error.
- Provide performance support aids, either hardcopy or online.
- Provide adequate problem-solving support for users so that they can figure out how to get back on track and fix any mistakes.
- If you have influence over the design of the application, provide a good online Help function and an Undo function.

## Why Learning Computer Applications Is Different: Applications Have an Overwhelming Number of Procedures

P®M3Major computer applications are often packed with dozens or even hundreds of individual functions and procedures. Each function or procedure consists of a series of steps that must be correctly performed in the proper sequence. To make matters worse, computer procedures often have one or more decision steps in their procedures.

A decision step is a step in the procedure that requires the user to choose from two or more options. For example, the procedure to restore a document that was being created after a word processing application unexpectedly and abruptly closed ("crashed") might display a list of temporary files that were last saved on disk and ask the user which file to restore. How would a user know which one contains the latest changes?

A modern, full-featured word processing application contains dozens if not hundreds of individual features and functions. To better understand the learning task that students face, ask yourself if you have ever had to remember a hundred different shopping lists at the same time, and if so, the degree that you could state the items in each list in perfect order. It is no wonder that users struggle to learn and remember the many features and functions of computer applications.

**The implications of computer applications having an overwhelming number of procedures**

- Information overload and therefore memory overload is a major concern.
- Memory aids, performance support, and job aids are desperately needed both during training and during job performance.
- Students need detailed step-by-step instructions or prompts for every procedure and additional support for making decisions that are part of procedures.
- When designed into the application, performance support systems (such as wizards or context-sensitive help) can help reduce the amount of information that is taught and that must be remembered.

**Why Learning Computer Applications Is Different:
Steps in a Procedure Seem Arbitrary to Users**

Performing a function consists of executing several seemingly arbitrary steps. Because the application's developer determined what those steps would be, not the laws of physics or the norms or experiences of real life, they often seem arbitrary.

To better understand this, carry out this activity:

1. Stand in an open room.
2. Step right.
3. Jump forward two steps.
4. Swing your arm in a circle.
5. Say the alphabet backwards.
6. Look behind you.
7. Count to 9.

After completing these steps, answer the following questions:

- How did carrying out the procedure feel to you?
- Did you feel ridiculous or embarrassed to be doing something that was so arbitrary and meaningless?
- Did these steps and their sequence seem arbitrary?
- Did they have any particular meaning?
- Are the individual steps of computer applications functions and procedures similarly arbitrary and meaningless to the novice user of the application?
- Can you understand how students feel when they have to follow, learn, and memorize similarly arbitrary and meaningless sequences of steps?

As another exercise, determine which list in the following table is more arbitrary, list A or list B:

| List A | List B |
|---|---|
| Seignorage | Oatmeal |
| Hysteresis | Oranges |
| Fiat money | Bananas |
| Consol | Cereal |
| Arbitrage | Toast |
| T-account | Eggs |
| Ricardian equivalence | Bacon |
| M3 | Cantaloupe |

The items in list A were taken from the glossary of a college textbook on banking and finance. They are not only abstract to readers unversed in university-level banking and finance concepts, they are an arbitrary collection of items. The items in list B are not only concrete, they are meaningful—they are all breakfast items.

Which list do you think would be easier to learn and remember?

## Additional Examples of the Arbitrary Nature of Computer Applications

As another example of the arbitrary nature of computer procedures, the steps to perform a function or procedure in one application might be entirely different from those to perform the same procedure in another application. For example, the steps for creating a header in one word processing program might be completely different from the steps to perform that same function in another word processing application.

Of course, some developers try to make their application procedures more meaningful by mimicking real life. For example, a developer might program the application so that the task of throwing a document into the trash is performed by dragging the file's document icon (which looks like a piece of paper) and releasing it when the cursor is on an icon that looks like a trash receptacle. When interaction methods and procedures model real life, the task becomes less arbitrary, more meaningful, and easier to learn and remember.

**Implications of computers using seemingly arbitrary sequences of steps in functions and procedures**

- Seemingly arbitrary actions and sequences lack meaning and thus impede learning and memory.
- Users need repeated practice exercises over time for each function to reinforce learning and increase recall. Many training programs only provide one instance of practice for each new function in the application; because of this, users fail to remember the function for very long.
- Students must find meaning in the way an application or task is designed, is conceptually laid out, or is used. Training provides a meaningful mental model that organizes and assigns meaning to the apparent arbitrary nature of the function or task. For example, explain the logic of why certain menu options were placed in the File menu option on the menu bar. As another example, show a concrete diagram of two documents that are being merged and visually show how the fields and data from the two documents are combined in the merged document.

## Method 1. Teach All Functions from A to Z

You can approach the design computer application training in at least three logical ways. The first approach is to teach all of the functions of the application individually, from A to Z.

**Description of Method 1**

- This approach teaches most or all of the functions that an application offers in an encyclopedic or systematic way.
- Simpler functions are often taught first, and more difficult or complex functions are taught later.
- Training that takes this approach might consist of several courses or an entire curriculum. The courses might have titles such as XYZ Application: Basic Level, XYZ Application: Intermediate Level, XYZ Application: Advanced Level.
- The perspective taken in training is that of the application and the functions it has to offer.
- This is a shotgun approach—it teaches students everything in the application to ensure that they know any of the functions they actually need back on the job.
- This approach is like training new carpenters on each tool in their toolboxes, including what each tool does and how to use it. It does not teach them how to do job tasks such as building new walls and roofs.

**Advantages**

- This approach is comprehensive and similar in nature to many user guides.
- The designer of the training does not have to worry about identifying how students will use the application back on the job.
- This approach assumes that students will be able to go back to their jobs and apply what was taught to real work.

**Disadvantages**

- Students will likely be overwhelmed.
- Students find it difficult to remember everything a few days or weeks later.
- Students often have trouble applying, generalizing, and sequencing multiple functions in the right order to produce real work results back on the job.

- This approach can be very costly to develop and deliver.
- Students might feel that much of the training is irrelevant; motivation, and hence learning, might suffer.

## Method 2. Teach the Application within the Context of Job Tasks

Another approach to teaching computer applications teaches the application in the context of performing job tasks.

### Description of Method 2

- This approach takes the perspective of the student rather than the application.
- Application functions are taught in the context of performing job tasks that are being performed in the students' workplaces.
- This is not a shotgun approach but a highly selective approach—functions that students do not need in their jobs are not taught.
- This approach is like teaching new carpenters how to build walls and roofs. Tools are taught as needed in the context of performing job tasks. This means that carpenters might not receive formal training on some of the tools in their toolboxes.

### Advantages

- Training is focused on helping students learn job tasks that produce valued outcomes.
- Students view the training as highly relevant; motivation, therefore, is typically very high.
- Students are able to generalize what they have learned in training to perform job tasks in the workplace.
- Training is typically less expensive to develop and deliver because only selective and key functions are taught.
- For all of these reasons, training is likely to have a higher return on investment.

**Disadvantages**

- The course designer must know (or find out) the job tasks in the students' workplaces that use this application.

- Training must teach all or a significant portion of the entire job task, not just the application functions.

- The instructional designer must perform more research upfront during requirements gathering to identify and document job tasks and where the application is used in performing those tasks.

- Training includes instruction on job tasks, not just application functions; this might increase the size of the training from just teaching selected application functions.

## Method 3. Teach the Application Using a Hybrid Approach

A third approach to teaching computer applications is a modified approach that combines the best of method 2 with the teaching of conceptual frameworks of how the application is designed and works.

### What Is a Conceptual Framework?

A conceptual framework is a conceptual, organizing map or scheme of how the application works and has been organized—such as how functions are grouped, common methods that are used in the application to invoke functions, and what you must understand conceptually behind the scenes to use certain functions intelligently.

For example, many application interfaces are structured with a main work area surrounded by menu bars, tool bars, and status bars from which the user can choose and interact. Many also support the clicking of the right mouse button to display a context -sensitive menu. Keyboard shortcuts are also supported in many applications.

Other conceptual frameworks might involve understanding the order in which work must be performed in the application, how functions were grouped, or how data flows through or becomes transformed by the application.

As another example of a framework, in word processing applications, the user must understand conceptually what mail merge does and the type of documents and data that are needed *before* doing a mail merge. A framework for mail merge presents and teaches these concepts, usually using instruction accompanied by conceptual graphics.

**Description of Method 3**

- This approach teaches the application using method 2—teach functionality in the context of job tasks—but only for key job tasks. In addition, it provides students a conceptual framework for understanding the application and its functions.
- This approach is like teaching new carpenters (1) how to perform key carpentry job tasks—things they will build back on the job, such as walls, floors, and roofs, and (2) key carpentry concepts and principles that will help them perform many other carpentry tasks that were not specifically taught. Carpenters will use general carpentry concepts and the principles they were taught and a little research on their own or the help of a mentor to perform other tasks and use other tools for which they were not specifically trained.

**Advantages**

- The problems of method 1 are avoided.
- The advantages of method 2 are enjoyed.
- The costs will likely be similar to or less than method 2.
- Students leave training having a framework by which to perform untaught functions.

**Disadvantages**

- You still have to know key job tasks and outcomes or at least common, generic tasks that can be easily generalized to the workplace.
- This approach requires that you understand the underlying conceptual framework of the application.

## Application Training Tip #1: Determine How Students Will Use the Application in Their Jobs

We will now discuss ten tips for designing and teaching computer applications. The first is that you as the instructional designer should make the effort to understand how students will be using the application in their jobs. More specifically, you should learn

- what job tasks will students perform using the application?
- which of these tasks are most critical? Most frequently performed? Most difficult? Most important to students?
- what work outputs, results, or accomplishments will they produce using the application?
- which of these work outputs are most critical or important?

Students see applications as tools—as a means to an end—not as ends themselves. Tools are simply one more thing that students must learn to produce what really matters—the real work for which they are rewarded in their jobs.

To have the most impact on the bottom line, training should focus on tasks that users perform in their jobs. Teaching application tool training in the context of meaningful job tasks has high relevance to students and results in higher transfer of learning to the workplace after the training is completed.

## Application Training Tip #2: Identify High Priority, Common, and Critical Tasks for Training

Students seldom have to know how to do *everything* that an application does. Even workers who use a major application every day, such as a word processor or spreadsheet program, probably do not know how to do *everything* that the application does. Those who were taught during their initial training how to perform every function of an application probably could not perform all of those functions a few weeks later from memory.

Except in rare and unusual circumstances (such as learning how to operate a nuclear power plant main computer console), application training should focus on the most important, critical, or common job tasks that require the use of the application. Students can learn how to perform other tasks from reference materials, online help, fellow coworkers, or additional specialized training courses.

## Application Training Tip #3: Translate Key Job Tasks into the Specific Steps That Must Be Performed in the Application

Students do not want to problem solve to learn how to use the application to perform their work. They expect instructional designers and trainers to do their homework and identify beforehand the tasks that students perform in their jobs so that training can give them step-by-step instructions on how to perform those tasks using the application. Do not force students to do the translation; do it yourself and present the translated steps in your training.

If you do not do this, students will be left on their own to problem solve and to determine which functions they need to use and the order to use them for every job task. As you learned in part 1, problem solving is at the top of the intellectual hierarchy. This means that it is one of the most difficult intellectual tasks to perform. Research shows that students typically perform it poorly without detailed structure and guidance.

The following story illustrates why it is important to translate job tasks into step-by-step instructions:

## The Tool Chest

Imagine that you have just purchased a $5,000 mechanic's tool chest and set of tools, complete with manual. "Now," you think, "I can make all of my minor car repairs myself. This tool chest has everything, from ratchets to rubber mallets to torque wrenches."

The manufacturer advertised that the tool chest contained all of the tools necessary to speedily complete any minor mechanical task on your car. In the store, the salesman made you feel good about investing your next two months' salary in such a wise investment.

When you arrive home, you carefully unpack your toolbox and admire the fine craftsmanship of each tool. You then set out to replace your broken fan belt. Realizing that you have less than an hour to do this before you are to meet your friend to go out, you feel a little pressured, but you take comfort in the thought of how quickly you will get the job done now that you have such a powerful set of new tools.

Confidently, you open the owner's manual. Inside you find complete instructions for using each tool—"How to Operate a Ratchet Wrench," "How to Use a Rubber Mallet," "How to Use a Torque Wrench" are some of the first you see.

"Ah ha," you say. "'How to Operate a Ratchet Wrench' appears first. Surely that must be what I need then." Looking into that section further, you discover detailed discussions about when to use and not to use a ratchet wrench, the different types of bolts and nuts on which a ratchet wrench can be used, and the maximum torque capacity of your ratchet wrench. You even find a quick step-by-step guide entitled "How to Use a Ratchet Wrench."

After further thought, you finally decide that you will indeed need to use a ratchet wrench because you have seen other mechanics replace a fan belt, and *they* loosened some bolts using a ratchet wrench.

Satisfied, you go on to the next section, discussing rubber mallets. "I wonder if I will have to use my rubber mallet to change the fan belt?" you ponder. Reading on, you discover that this section discusses things such as when rubber mallets should be used instead of steel hammers, explains what a rubber mallet looks like, and gives examples of how rubber mallets are used to repair a dented fender. You even find a quick step-by-step guide entitled "How to Use a Rubber Mallet." After scanning through the rest of this section, you finally decide that it will not be necessary to use your rubber mallet.

Stopping to look at the time, you realize that you only have a few minutes to meet your friend. A little disappointed, you walk inside and call a cab, realizing that you won't be going in *your* car.

## Sequel

The next day, you return your tool chest to the store for a refund. On your way out, you notice that the store next door is also selling tool sets. With some hesitancy, you make your way inside, where a salesman shows you a set of tools that are in every way equal to those that you just returned.

Wisely, you ask to see the owner's manual. This manual, you observe, is different from the one you tried to use the day before. It not only documents how to use each tool, it also contains a section with detailed step-by-step instructions on "How to Perform the Fifty Most Common Small-Repair Tasks on Your Car."

You quickly locate the section entitled "How to Change a Fan Belt" to see what is there. "Just what I need," you remark. "These instructions tell me *which* tools I need for this task, *when* I need to use them, and *how* to use them." Happily, you sign the bill of sale.

## Application Training Tip #4: Take the Perspective of the Student, Not the Application

Design and teach everything as if you were the student's mentor, telling the student step-by-step how to use the application to accomplish useful work. In other words, look at the training through the eyes and needs of students and design accordingly. Encyclopedic treatments of subject material tend to be extremely boring and overload students' brains very quickly. Remember that students see the tool as a means to an end, not as a topic of fascinating study.

To do this, use an active, second-person voice in your instructions (the "you" form). This will help you take the perspective of the student and be easier for students to follow. Passive constructions and third-party voice are more detached, sterile, and impersonal.

## Application Training Tip #5: Provide an Overview of the Application and Explain How to Access It

In the next several tips, we will discuss what you should teach about the application itself.

Training on applications should begin with an overview of the application: its purpose (why it was created), what it can do (key functions, in job terms, if possible), who will find it useful, when to use it, what it looks like (a few key, main, or typical screens), how it is used in your organization, and the benefits of using the application. This information gives students a concrete mental picture of the application, what it is, and what it can do. This should be kept at a high level; this is an introduction and overview of the application, not a comprehensive review.

Another thing to teach about the application is how to access it and make it ready to use: What are the system requirements, where can the application be obtained or accessed, how can you get permission to obtain or access it, and how is it installed and configured, if not already done?

# Application Training Tip #6: Provide a High-Level or Conceptual Overview of the User Interface

For example, provide a graphic or screenshot of the general physical layout of the user interface with callouts to fixed or dedicated areas of the interface that students will use, and describe what they do. Teach students the conceptual framework or model on which the application and interface are based. Explain where to find or expect information, tools, functions, and features; where the main work area is (if there is one); how the application data is processed; and what the flow of work tasks is in the application.

## Examples of three types of computer application conceptual frameworks

### User interface conceptual framework

- The major elements of the underlying user interface model
- **Example:** Any major business application; identify and notice its major visual and navigational components

### Business process conceptual framework

- The business process flow that the application supports and the business rules and policies that govern and support the process
- **Example:** The travel expense account (TEA) business process that a TEA application supports

### Work product conceptual framework

- The underlying concepts of the work product, such as the major components or sections, business rules associated with the work product, and so on
- **Example:** The parts of a standard document, such as the table of contents, headers, footers, text headings, index, and so forth

The purpose of providing a high-level conceptual framework of the user interface is to familiarize students with the main elements of the user interface, including key navigational features, how functions are grouped, and conceptual frameworks that help students understand what is happening to their data behind the scenes and how the application acts on data to perform useful work. This framework and the one described in the previous tip serve as advanced organizers or mental frameworks for students to learn more about the application (see part 1 for a more detailed discussion of why advanced organizers and mental frameworks improve learning).

## Application Training Tip #7: Provide Support for Decision Steps

Even when training materials provide detailed step-by-step instructions, students can fail to successfully complete a task if they do not understand how to perform one or more of the instructions. Training must teach the enabling content that is required for each step's instruction—the content that students must understand to carry out that step intelligently.

For example, an instruction might say "Select the file format for saving this graphic." How do students know which file format to use? If students do not come to the training with this knowledge, then they must be taught it as part of the training. Otherwise, they cannot intelligently perform the steps in the procedure. In this example, students would not be able to make the decision on which file format to use. Determining enabling content was discussed at length in part 2.

## Application Training Tip #8: Teach Functions or Tasks That Are Used Repeatedly

Some tasks or methods of interaction are used repeatedly throughout an application.

Some examples of repeated navigational and interface functions might be how to

- display and select functions from a menu bar,
- use a color palette dialog box,
- bring up a context-sensitive menu,
- use a tabbed properties box,
- undo an action, or
- undock, move, and position a toolbar.

Some examples of repeated tasks might be how to

- update a record,
- add a text comment,
- save a file, or
- enter credit card information.

These tasks and interactive methods merit special attention because they are used frequently, repeatedly, or in many other tasks.

## Application Training Tip #9: Discuss Major Quirks, Bugs, Pitfalls, Traps, and Common User Errors

If you were going to canoe down a river with class 3 and 4 rapids, you would probably appreciate having a guide to tell you what particular rocks and whirlpools to watch out for, which side of the river to stay on to clear certain rapids, and what to do if your canoe hangs on some hidden underwater rock outcroppings.

Similarly, students appreciate knowing about application pitfalls and bugs and how to handle the quirks of the system. Many major applications still have serious quirks, pitfalls, or bugs that can cause unexpected loss of data or work. Nothing is quite as frustrating as losing work that you have invested several hours to create, especially when that work is highly creative and would be very difficult to re-create.

### Application Training Tip #10: Provide Useful Tips and Best Practices

Provide students useful tips, cheat sheets, and best practices information. This is like the canoe guide giving instruction on how to best paddle the canoe, steer the canoe, and balance objects in the canoe. This might include, for example

- how to customize or optimize the application for students' jobs;
- keyboard shortcuts, macros, and other alternatives;
- job aids or cheat sheets that summarize procedures, functions, and navigational procedures;
- power user features;
- useful templates;
- productivity tips; and
- best practices learned from experience or research.

### Instructional Events That Are Especially Important for Application Training

Training is different from mere information because of its instructional design, which includes the learning events that are embedded in the instructional materials. Learning events are learning activities that support and promote the human biological and cognitive learning processes (see part 1), such as exercises, reviews, overviews, checkpoint questions, and so forth.

**Instructional events that are especially important for application training**

- demonstrations
- examples
- organizing diagrams, visuals, animations, or graphics with visual emphasis on the item under current discussion
- enabling information for how to intelligently make decisions
- practice (and lots of it) using the application to perform job tasks
- repetition of key concepts, procedures, conceptual frameworks, and exercises over time to enhance learning and prolong retention
- job aid training (training on how to use the provided job aids) so that students can successfully use the job aids back in the workplace
- simulations
- practice "sand boxes" (protected application environments containing dummy data in which students can practice application functions and tasks without altering actual client data or causing other negative effects)
- specific memory supports such as advanced organizers, frameworks, memory mnemonics, making material meaningful, and so forth (see part 1)
- performance support prompts to guide users through the procedure (this is usually integrated into the application itself as part of its Help function)

## So How Do I Design Application Training?

Application training is designed using the same instructional design process as other training. The preceding discussions and suggestions in this chapter do not negate any of the learning or instructional design principles that were taught in this book. They simply expand upon or provide more specific information on select topics as they pertain to application training.

You follow the same process to design application training as you do for any other training. Here, as a review, are the nine steps of the instructional design process (see part 2 for a detailed discussion of these steps):

1. Gather requirements
2. Perform an instructional analysis on the job outcomes
3. Identify the enabling content
4. Structure the course
5. Write instructional objectives
6. Determine the instructional delivery system
7. Design practice exercises and other instructional events
8. Design the prototype or example lesson
9. Create the formal design document

# Chapter Summary—
# Designing Computer Application Training

This chapter discussed the ways in which training students to use computer applications is different from other types of training and what you can do as an instruction designer to accommodate those differences. It also provides ten tips for designing computer application training and discusses instructional events that are especially important to include in computer application training.

You should now be able to

- define application training and list different categories of applications;
- explain why the abstract and arbitrary nature of computer procedures makes learning computer applications more challenging;
- describe the implications of the abstract nature of computer procedures, concepts, and names;
- explain why the digital nature of computers makes learning computer applications more challenging;
- describe strategies for addressing the digital nature of computers;
- explain why the large number of procedures in computer applications makes them more challenging to learn;
- describe the implications of computer applications having an overwhelming number of procedures;
- explain why the steps in application procedures often seem arbitrary to users;
- describe the implications of computers using seemingly arbitrary sequences of steps in functions and procedures;
- describe the approach to teaching computer applications that teaches all of the application's functions from A to Z and explain the advantages and disadvantages of this approach;
- describe the approach to teaching computer applications that teaches application functions within the context of performing job tasks and explain the advantages and disadvantages of this approach;

- describe the approach to teaching computer applications that combines the teaching of key student job tasks with the teaching of conceptual frameworks and explain the advantages and disadvantages of this approach;
- explain why it is important in teaching computer applications to determine how students will use the application in their jobs;
- explain why it is important in teaching computer applications to identify high-priority, common, and critical tasks for training;
- explain why it is important in teaching computer applications to translate key job tasks into the specific steps that must be performed in the application;
- explain why it is important in teaching computer applications to take the perspective of the student, not the application;
- explain why it is important in teaching computer applications to provide an overview of the application and explain how to access it;
- explain why it is important in teaching computer applications to provide a high-level or conceptual overview of the user interface;
- explain why it is important in teaching computer applications to provide support for decision steps;
- explain why it is important in teaching computer applications to teach functions or tasks that are used repeatedly;
- explain why it is important in teaching computer applications to discuss major quirks, bugs, pitfalls, traps, and common user errors;
- explain why it is important in teaching computer applications to provide useful tips and best practices;
- list and explain instructional events that are especially important for application training; and
- answer the question, "How Do I Design Application Training?"

## Check Your Understanding

1. **True or false? Examples of specialized business applications include applications for enterprise resource planning (ERP), customer relationship management (CRM), accounting, finance, human resource (HR), computer-aided design (CAD), supply chain management (SCM), and statistical analysis programs.**

2. **True or false? Learning computer applications typically requires students to learn a considerable amount of abstract and seemingly arbitrary material.**

3. **Which of the following statements are important implications of the abstract nature of computer procedures for application training? (Select all that apply.)**

    A. Training should help students create an accurate mental map of how the application works.

    B. Training should include a lot of noninstructional graphics that provide visual interest.

    C. Training should provide memory support interventions to help students remember the abstract information, such as repeated practice over time of key tasks.

    D. Abstract concepts and procedures are more difficult to learn and remember.

    E. Training should be written in a third-person, impartial voice.

    F. Training should provide performance aids that reduce students' need to remember the information.

4. **Which of the following statements are important implications of the digital nature of computer procedures for application training? (Select all that apply.)**

   A. Sound plays beautifully where used in the training.

   B. It is easy for users to make a mistake and cause serious damage to important information or the actual loss of work or data.

   C. Approximate effort does not equal approximate results.

   D. Training materials can be reproduced with perfect accuracy from a master copy.

   E. They appear to be unforgiving; therefore, users can easily become frustrated or give up.

   F. They require 100% (or in some exceptional cases, nearly 100%) accuracy.

5. **Which of the following statements are important implications of the overwhelming number of procedures in computer applications for application training? (Select all that apply.)**

   A. When designed into the application, performance support systems (such as wizards or context-sensitive help) can help reduce the amount of information that is taught and that must be remembered.

   B. Memory aids, performance support, and job aids are desperately needed both during training and during job performance.

   C. The number of training days or hours must be increased to accommodate the training of all the functions.

   D. Students need detailed step-by-step instructions or prompts for every procedure and additional support for making decisions that are part of procedures.

   E. Information overload and therefore memory overload is a major concern.

6. **True or false? Steps in a procedure can seem arbitrary because the application's developer determined what those steps would be, not the laws of physics or the norms or experiences of real life.**

7. **Which of the following statements are important implications for application training of computers using seemingly arbitrary sequences of steps in functions and procedures? (Select all that apply.)**

   A. Provide a variety of learning activities to improve motivation and reduce boredom.

   B. Seemingly arbitrary actions and sequences lack meaning and thus impede learning and memory.

   C. Help students find meaning in the way an application or task is designed, is conceptually laid out, or is used.

   D. Provide a meaningful mental model that organizes and assigns meaning to the apparent arbitrary nature of the function or task.

   E. Provide repeated practice exercises over time for a function to reinforce its steps and increase recall.

8. **True or false? One advantage of the method 1 approach to training computer applications, in which all of the applications functions (A through Z) are taught, is that the designer of the training does not have to worry about identifying how students will use the application back on the job.**

9. **True or false? The method 2 approach to training computer applications, in which functions are taught in the context of job tasks, takes the viewpoint of the application, not the student.**

10. **True or false? Method 3, the hybrid approach to teaching computer applications, consists of teaching key job tasks and teaching conceptual frameworks of how the application is designed and works.**

11. **True or false? Students typically see applications as tools—as a means to an end—not as ends themselves or as one more thing that they must learn to produce what really matters.**

12. **True or false? Those who use a major application every day such as a word processor or spreadsheet program eventually learn how to do *everything* that the application does.**

13. **True or false? In training computer applications, you should translate key job tasks into the specific steps that students must perform in the application.**

14. **True or false? In computer application training, you should use an active, second-person voice in your instructions (the "you" form).**

15. **An overview for computer application training should include which of the following topics? (Select all that apply.)**
    A. The benefits of using the application
    B. Its purpose (why it was created)
    C. How it is used in your organization
    D. What it can do (key functions, in job terms, if possible)
    E. What it looks like (a few key, main, or typical screens)
    F. A preview of each and every function
    G. Who will find it useful

16. **True or false? In teaching computer applications, it is helpful to teach students the conceptual framework or model on which the application and interface are based.**

17. **True or false? In teaching computer procedures in computer application training, it is sufficient to provide detailed step-by-step instructions.**

18. **True or false? Computer application training should include teaching tasks or interactive methods that are used frequently, repeatedly, or in many other tasks.**

19. **True or false? Because many major computer applications still have serious quirks, pitfalls, or bugs that can cause unexpected loss of data or work, computer application training should discuss major quirks, bugs, pitfalls, traps, and common user errors.**

20. **When you provide useful tips and best practices information in your computer application training, you should consider including which of the following topics? (Select all that apply.)**

    A. Useful templates

    B. Productivity tips

    C. How to customize or optimize the application for students' jobs

    D. Keyboard shortcuts, macros, or other alternatives

    E. Job aids or cheat sheets that summarize procedures, functions, and navigational procedures

    F. Power user features

    G. Best practices learned from experience or research

21. **In designing computer application training, which of the following instructional events are especially important to include? (Select all that apply.)**

    A. Group discussions

    B. Demonstrations

    C. Examples

*Instructional Design Tips and Traps*    451

D. Decision support for decision steps in procedures
E. Repeated practice using the application to perform job tasks
F. Simulations and "sand boxes"
G. Job aids
H. Organizing frameworks

22. **True or false? Designing computer application training follows the same basic instructional design steps as designing other forms of training.**

## Answers

1. True
2. True
3. A, C, D, and F
4. B, C, E, and F
5. A, B, D, and E
6. True
7. B, C, D, and E
8. True
9. False. It actually takes the viewpoint of the student.
10. True
11. True
12. False
13. True
14. True
15. A, B, C, D, E, and G
16. True
17. False. Students can fail to successfully complete a task if they do not understand how to perform one or more of the instructions. The training

fails to teach the enabling content that is required for each step's instruction—the content that students must understand to carry out that step intelligently. This is especially true of decision steps in the procedure when the instructions do not provide any decision-making support.

18. True
19. True
20. A, B, C, D, E, F, and G
21. B, C, D, E, F, G, and H
22. True

# Chapter 18
# Twenty Common Training Mistakes, Part 1

The next two chapters present twenty common training mistakes. Although these mistakes are more frequently made by those who do not have an educational background, they are sometimes made even by education professionals and full-time instructors. Being aware of these mistakes and pitfalls will help you avoid them in your own training. In this chapter, we will discuss ten of these common mistakes, in no particular order or priority, and we will discuss ten others in the next chapter.

## Sound Instructional Design Is Becoming Increasingly Challenging

Is designing and developing training becoming increasing more complex and challenging or less complex and challenging?

**Issues that you should consider before you answer this question**

- Are more people with different specialties involved in creating training today than in the past?
- Are training development schedules being lengthened or squeezed?
- Is training typically developed in an environment in which insufficient resources are available?
- When business pressures sway decision makers to demand "quick-and-dirty training"—for example, to ask subject matter experts to throw together courses—are learning and instructional design principles more likely or less likely to be violated?
- Is developing technology-based training more complex and resource intensive than non-technology-based training?
- Is choosing blended learning (using a mix of technology- and non-technology-based delivery systems in the same course or curriculum) becoming more common or less common?
- Are organizations moving toward a model of training that emphasizes the simple presentation of information with the responsibility for learning residing completely with the employee?
- If training is becoming more complex to design and develop, are there more opportunities to make design oversights and mistakes?

The need for sound instructional design is greater today than ever. This is due to several factors, including

- more technology-based training is being developed today. New and sophisticated technologies for training also continue to become available. A wide number of professionals with differing expertise are required to produce high-tech training,
- budgets and resources are being scrutinized more closely than ever before. Business processes are being refined, more closely monitored, and better controlled. Managers are expecting employees to produce more with fewer resources. This includes the training department staff as well,

- schedules are being continually compressed to meet various business pressures, demands, and executive expectations, and
- training is becoming increasingly important to keep workers skilled in an increasingly complex world. This has increased the demand for training considerably.

Amidst all these pressures, instructional designers and developers must not forget to follow the principles of sound instructional design and development. If they do, the twenty training mistakes we are about to discuss will become even more common than they are today. For each mistake, we will describe the mistake, state related design principles, discuss how to avoid the mistake, and explain how to remedy the mistake.

## Mistake #1: Creating a Book or Talking Head Instead of Training

As we have discussed throughout this book, training is not just the dispensing of information in book-like or lecture format.

### Description

**Definition:** Creating training that is
- a seemingly endless string of speech or text, or
- a continuous display or discussion of information without any significant instructional events.

**Examples**
- many academic lectures in universities
- "slide show" presentations given in corporate "training" sessions
- technology-based or web-based training that presents only content with little or no interaction

**Related design principles**

- Valid training is based on specific instructional strategies and contains many instructional events that were determined from the performance, knowledge, and attitudinal outcomes and objectives. These objectives were derived from the instructional and content analyses.

- Training is not
  - the simple presentation or display of detailed information from a live or simulated "talking head,"
  - asking an expert to do a "content dump" in front of a class, in print, or over the web, and
  - just presenting information—after all, manuals, books, and documents do that.

**How to avoid this mistake**

- Follow the correct instructional design process from the start.
- Avoid thinking that information equals training.
- Recognize that, as in any worthwhile endeavor, there is no free lunch; therefore, use your resource dollars for training only where training is truly required and where it will provide a good return on investment.

**How to remedy this mistake**

- This mistake is easily identified, even by those who are not education professionals.
- Remedy requires rework, perhaps even starting over again to follow sound instructional design.

## Mistake #2: Providing Too Few Examples

For students who are trying to learn, examples are worth their weight in gold. How many times have you said to yourself during training, "I wish I could see an example of that" or "I wonder if my understanding is correct"?

## Description

**Definition:** Presenting new concepts, definitions, procedures, processes, classifications, principles, and other information with few or no examples

**Example:** Any place in the training materials or discussion where students ask for or wish that examples were provided to illustrate a concept, idea, or procedure

## Related design principles

- People learn by example.
- Examples assist learning by
  - making concrete what is often abstract in students' minds, and
  - allowing students to correct or confirm their understanding.
- Examples and nonexamples are required when teaching concepts.
- Examples do not cost much to provide, but they are powerful in their effect on learning.

## How to avoid this mistake

- Provide examples … and then provide more examples.
- When presenting a new concept, procedure, principle, definition, classification, or structure, provide one or more examples.
- Err on the side of providing too many examples—provide at least one example for each new key concept, procedure, or idea.
- Recognize that demonstrations are examples of procedural tasks.
- Graphical illustrations can be used to show examples too.

## How to remedy this mistake

- Review the materials to see how often examples are provided.
- If the materials need additional examples, identify where they are needed and then provide them.

# Mistake #3: Creating Information Overload

As you learned in part 1, learning is biological, not just intellectual. Bottlenecks exist in our biological and cognitive ability to perceive, process, and remember information. Exceeding the capacity of these bottlenecks overloads the human system, resulting in failed learning, fatigue, and diminished learning capacity.

## Description

**Definition:** Presenting information too quickly to be assimilated and processed by human cognitive processes.

Information overload often

- leads not only to a failure to learn, but to the premature fatiguing of the biological and mental learning apparatus, making it even more challenging for learning to occur, and
- is accompanied by too much or unnecessary detail.

**Example:** An "information dump" or "fire hose" approach to training almost invariably leads to information overload with students.

## Related design principles

- The human mind is not a *tabula rasa* (blank slate or tablet) on which an instructor or training course writes simply by presenting information; it takes much more time and effort on the part of both the instructor and the student for anything to be permanently written on that tablet.
- This approach presumes that a "one-exposure-to-information" approach to learning is adequate; it is, in fact, inadequate. This approach is called "single-trial learning" by educational researchers.
- An overload can occur at any point in human information processing; for example, in sensation and perception, in short term memory, and in the encoding and storage of information into long-term memory.
- Short-term memory is probably the most common bottleneck. Memory mediation techniques must be used to handle this bottleneck (see

*Mistake #20: Failing to Help Students Remember Information* in the next chapter).

- Storage into long-term memory requires work, active mental processing, and, in most cases, repeated exposure to or repeated rehearsal of the information.

**How to avoid this mistake**

- Train to memory only when students must perform job tasks from memory in their workplace.
- Eliminate all unnecessary and extraneous information (see *Mistake #19: Failing to Make Instruction Lean* in the next chapter).
- Maintain a training pace that does not exceed students' capacity to process and learn the information.
- Simplify and emphasize key information and place related information in the background.
- Repeat or rehearse key information over time.
- Relate new information to what students already know.
- Apply learning and memory facilitation and mediation techniques such as chunking, spaced review and practice, meaningful associations, mnemonic devices, elaboration, reviews and summaries, organizing structures, context, concreteness, vivid visualizations, overviews, analogies, metaphors, graphics, mental models, information layering, simplification, and examples.

**How to remedy this mistake**

- Assess the materials for information overload and then selectively apply the techniques listed above in the section, *How to avoid this mistake*.
- Serious cases of information overload usually indicate that little or no instructional design was ever performed; in this case, you will have to perform significant rework, perhaps even starting over again to follow the instructional design process.

# Mistake #4: Providing Insufficient or Inappropriate Practice and Feedback

As we discussed in part 1, practice is a key step in the learning process, but practice without feedback does little to improve performance and can actually reinforce incorrect actions. Practice is any activity in which students are allowed to apply their skills and knowledge. Practice helps students know what they really know and know what they do not know ("I guess I didn't understand that as well as I thought"). It not only builds skills, it also builds students' confidence in performing those skills.

## Description

**Definition:** Not providing enough practice exercises with feedback to raise performance to the desired target outcomes described in the objectives or not matching the behaviors practiced to those specified in the objectives

## Examples

- Not providing any practice with feedback during training.
- Not matching the actions required in the practice to the behaviors given in the instructional objectives. For example, if the training objectives call for actual performance of tasks that are trained, then exercises that only test memory of the steps of the procedure are not adequate by themselves.
- Military training for how to operate a 50mm cannon does not rely solely on a few checkpoint questions. Actual performance of the task is exercised as well.

## Related design principles

- Practice exercises should be
  - matched to the behaviors given in the instructional objectives,
  - sufficient in number to reach the target skill levels, and
  - phased—gradually increased in complexity and realism to real-world tasks and integrated with the subskills that were taught.

- If you remove practice with feedback from training, it ceases to be training. For example, reading a book on how to play tennis might be helpful, but it is no substitute for actual one-on-one instruction, observation, and feedback out on the tennis court.

**How to avoid this mistake**

- Make practice exercises match the objectives that are taught.
- Provide enough appropriate practice with feedback to ensure that students can perform the desired exit tasks.
- By following the instructional design process, appropriately matched practice with feedback will be an integral part of the training.

**How to remedy this mistake**

- Assess existing practice exercises to see if they conform to the guidelines listed above in the section, *How to avoid this mistake.*
- Identify where additional practice exercises are needed and create them.
- If no instructional objectives are provided, you will not know what behaviors should be practiced in the practice exercises and to what level or degree; in this case, you might need to perform some instructional design to focus the course and identify the objectives.

## Mistake #5: Expecting Students to Remember Everything by Recall

Part 1 taught that recall memory—remembering detailed information completely from memory without any cues, prompts, or hints—is more difficult than recognition memory. For example, describing a person's face that you only saw a couple of times is more difficult than recognizing that face among six other faces. Yet many training programs assume that students will recall everything that was ever presented or discussed simply because it was presented once.

**Description**

**Definition:** Expecting students to remember everything that is presented in training henceforth and forevermore, with just one exposure to the information

**Example:** The training materials expect students to remember acronyms, definitions, and concepts that were presented some time earlier in the training or in the course materials.

**Related design principles**

- Students, unlike computers, have biological limitations that generally preclude them from remembering large streams of continuous information.
- Training students to perform tasks from pure recall memory is more expensive and time-consuming to create, deliver, and take as a student than training students to perform tasks using only recognition memory, such as training them to use job aids, reference materials, or printed procedure cards.

**How to avoid this mistake**

- Do not teach to recall memory unless it is absolutely necessary.
- Ask yourself, "Does on-the-job performance require training to recall memory because of issues such as speed of performance, social acceptability, and the environment?" For example, it might be unacceptable for a sales agent to pull out a cheat sheet when answering a client's objections to closing a sale.
- Do not assume that training should always have as its goal that students remember everything by recall memory.

### How to remedy this mistake

- Review the materials and identify the critical information that students must remember using recall memory. For the other material, train students to perform tasks using job aids, performance aids, and reference material.
- Eliminate discussions or materials that provide unnecessary levels of detail in the training. Provide students instead with references to other sources of detailed information.
- Serious violation of this principle might require that you start over to follow the instructional design process.

## Mistake #6: Assuming Students Know Information They Do Not Know

Students are frustrated when the training presents new information, assuming that they already know certain concepts, technical terms, acronyms, or other information that they do not know. They soon find themselves unable to understand the new information because they do not understand the enabling content that an understanding of the new information requires.

### Description

**Definition:** Making either of the following assumptions when teaching new information that depends on an understanding of prerequisite information

- assuming that students already know certain concepts, technical terms, acronyms, principles, procedures, policies, facts, and so forth that they do not know
- assuming that students possess certain skills that they do not possess

**Example:** Assuming that students know how to add, subtract, multiply, and divide when you teach them how to find the square root of a number when, in fact, students do not possess those skills

**Related design principles**

- Knowledge builds on other knowledge.
- Prerequisite ideas and concepts must be taught and understood before students can understand new information that builds on them.
- A missing link in a properly sequenced chain of ideas can halt students' progressive understanding of those ideas.
- This mistake can occur when you fail to
  - perform requirements gathering to understand the skills and knowledge that students bring with them to the training;
  - perform instructional analysis to identify required entry skills;
  - explain a new concept, term, or acronym when it is first used;
  - pilot the training to identify unclear information; or
  - investigate and review for yourself any required prerequisite courses to ensure that they indeed teach the assumed entry-level skills and knowledge for your course.

**How to avoid this mistake**

- Perform requirements gathering and instructional analysis and design to identify all required prerequisite skills and knowledge (see part 2), and then sequence and teach information in proper order and carefully document and validate assumed entry-level skills and knowledge against the audience information you collected during requirements gathering.
- Don't make assumptions about what students already know unless you can prove those assumptions.
- Pilot the training to uncover missing explanations that were overlooked.
- Provide ways for students to give specific feedback on your training.

**How to remedy this mistake**

- Aside from an occasional oversight, serious cases of making incorrect assumptions about students' entry-level skills and knowledge indicate that requirements gathering, instructional analysis, and content analysis were not performed (see part 2). In this case, you will have to perform significant rework, perhaps even starting over again with instructional design.

# Mistake #7: Failing to Provide All of the Enabling Content

Another common mistake is failing to identify and teach *all* of the enabling content that is required to learn a new topic or skill. Enabling content is *all* of the skills and knowledge that are necessary to understand new information or to carry out a step in a procedure.

## Example of enabling content for a step in a procedure

Consider the instruction, "Place the gyrogimball in the center of the precision bearing chamber and lock it down with the U-turn bolts." To carry out this instruction, you must know all of the following enabling information:

- what a gyrogimball, precision bearing chamber, and U-turn bolts are; how to visually identify them; how to orient them when assembling them with other parts; and how to safely handle them to protect both yourself and the parts
- how to center the gyrogimball in the center of the precision bearing chamber
- how to lock the gyrogimball down with the U-turn bolts, including how to use any tools that are required to lock it down

Failure to teach any one of these enabling skills and knowledge that students do not already understand will impede their ability to learn and carry out this instruction correctly.

## Description

**Definition:** Failing to identify and teach all of the enabling content that is required to learn a new topic or skill.

**Example:** In teaching Newton's second law of physics, "force equals mass times acceleration," failing to define and explain what mass, force, and acceleration are and failing to validate that students understand equations and know how to multiply.

- It is easy to overlook some of the necessary enabling content unless a systematic content analysis was performed during instructional design (see part 2).
- If a systematic content analysis was not performed, then teaching all of the required enabling content is a hit-or-miss proposition, and training will suffer accordingly.

**Related design principles**

- *All* of the enabling content must be taught at the point it is needed (or somewhere prior to that point) for successful, effective, and complete learning to occur. If it is taught earlier than the point at which it is needed, then you probably need to refresh that information in students' minds (see *Mistake #11: Failing to Refresh Prerequisite Information Immediately before New Information* in the next chapter).

**How to avoid this mistake**

- Systematic instructional and content analyses are the only thorough way to identify all of the enabling content.
  - SME instructors and training developers are often so familiar with the subject matter that they forget what it takes for a novice to understand the information or develop new skills for the first time.
  - A casual approach to identifying enabling information and skills will result in flawed instruction and hampered learning.

**How to remedy this mistake**

- Performing thorough and complete instructional and content analyses is the only way to ensure that all of the enabling content is identified.

# Mistake #8: Providing Too Little Repetition

Students often wish that instructors would restate the definitions of key concepts or acronyms, especially the second and possibly the third times they are used. This is particularly important if some time has elapsed or a great deal of other material has been taught since they were first taught. Students need more than one exposure to information and more than one practice to firmly embed a concept or procedure in their minds.

## Description

**Definition:** Never revisiting, reviewing, or refreshing information that was previously taught, especially key information.

**Example:** Defining several accounting acronyms once in topic 1 and expecting students to remember them when they get to topic 5.

Factors that discourage sponsors and decision makers over training from agreeing to any repetition of information within the training include

- constrained training budgets,
- tight schedules,
- scarce resources for design and development, and
- desire for minimum student seat time (the time students spend taking training away from their real jobs).

These sponsors often view any repetition of information as an unnecessary redundancy, as evidence of sloppy design, or as an indication of a lack of confidence in students' learning abilities and self-study habits.

## Related design principles

- Spaced review (repetition) of key ideas and concepts strengthens learning and storage and retrieval of information into long-term memory.
- Repetition does not require that you repeat entire lessons or presentations at the same level of detail; rather, key information should be the focus of repetition.

- Refreshing prerequisite information right before you present new information is a key training strategy.

**How to avoid this mistake**

- Do not be afraid to provide deliberate repetition of key information (for example, "As you recall, a widget is a ...") at critical points in the training.
- Refresh the information at increasingly higher levels of detail at each review.
- Provide drill-and-practice programs with built-in "spaced reviews" (periodic reviews over time) for learning large amounts of detailed information that must be stored in long-term memory.

**How to remedy this mistake**

- Review the materials or audit the training to see if key information and procedures are reviewed, refreshed, and revisited at critical points in the training.
- Provide reviews in the training for key information that was not refreshed or rehearsed.

## Mistake #9: Failing to Chunk Information into Bite-Sized Pieces

Training should break big bodies of information and complex concepts, principles, procedures, and processes into smaller bite-sized instructional chunks that students can understand individually. As the instruction progresses, more complex ideas or procedures can be built using these individual chunks. You truly cannot eat an elephant in one bite.

### Description

**Definition:** Presenting large amounts of information or complex ideas or procedures all at once without breaking it up visually, conceptually, and instructionally into smaller "bite-sized chunks"

**Examples**

- a training course with few subdivisions (modules, units, topics, subtopics)
- continuous or lengthy text unbroken by labels or headings
- an instruction sheet for assembling a complex child's outdoor play set that shows a single drawing with all of the parts visually "exploded"
- trying to teach a complex procedure "all at once" without breaking it down into major activities, steps, and substeps

**Related design principles**

- Chunking is a well-established principle of perception, learning, and memory.
- Masses of unbroken information are not only intimidating, they are more difficult to understand, remember, and reference at a later time.
- Student motivation is visibly affected when they are mentally clobbered with a large mass of nonchunked information.
- A well-chosen chunking scheme forms a framework that assists learning and retention.

**How to avoid this mistake**

- Make the requirement to chunk information into smaller pieces a requirement of the project in your style guide or training design document.
- Perform instructional and content analysis as part of instructional design—these techniques automatically break higher-level procedures and information into lower-level procedures and information.
- One way of chunking information is to structure it into increasing layers or levels of detail (see *Mistake #10: Failing to Layer Information* in this chapter).

### How to remedy this mistake

- Scan through your materials for large or lengthy unbroken blocks of information. Identify large or complex concepts and procedures. Make sure that they have been adequately broken down.
- Repackage unchunked information using a logical and appropriate chunking scheme.

## Mistake #10: Failing to Layer Information

Unlayered information fails to hide increasing levels of detail from students. All of the details of the information are presented at the same level of emphasis in the presentation. From a student's point of view, taking training that is not layered is like reading a large book that contains a single stream of text. It is very difficult to sort out high-level information from low-level information or key information from non-key information.

### Description

**Definition:** Presenting all the complexity and details of the information in the same way without hiding increasing levels of detail from students.

**Example:** Imagine what it would be like to move to a new city and be required to learn a detailed city map containing hundreds of streets. A layered approach, in which you learned only the main and key side streets in the beginning and learned increasing levels of city streets in subsequent training, would be much more effective.

### Related design principles

- Elaboration is a key learning and teaching principle.
- Start with a simple, high-level conceptual overview or organizing framework and then provide increasing levels of detail in subsequent discussions.
- As you elaborate and provide additional levels of detail, make it clear how the more detailed layers of information fit into the big picture.

**How to avoid this mistake**

- Present key or simplified information first while "hiding" or reserving more detailed information for subsequent discussions.
- Use techniques of layering such as a hierarchical course structure of modules, topics, and subtopics; a hierarchical heading structure for text; descriptive titles; graphical overviews; conceptual and organizing frameworks; callout or sidebar text boxes; and pointers or links to additional information.

**How to remedy this mistake**

- Review the materials or audit the training to see how well these principles were applied.
- Restructure the training to incorporate elaboration.

# Chapter Summary—
# Twenty Common Training Mistakes, Part 1

This chapter and the next present twenty common training mistakes. Although these mistakes are more frequently made by those who do not have an educational background, they are sometimes made even by education professionals and full-time instructors. Being aware of these mistakes and pitfalls will help you avoid them in your own training. In this chapter, we discussed ten of these common mistakes, in no particular order or priority, and we will discuss ten others in the next chapter.

You should now be able to

- describe why following the principles and techniques of sound instructional design is becoming increasingly important; and
- for each of the following ten common training mistakes, define and describe the mistake, state the design principles that are being violated, explain how to avoid the mistake, and describe what to do to remedy the mistake:
  - creating a book or talking head instead of training
  - providing too few examples
  - creating information overload
  - providing insufficient or inappropriate practice and feedback
  - expecting students to remember everything by recall
  - assuming students know information they do not know
  - failing to provide all of the enabling content
  - providing too little repetition
  - failing to chunk information into bite-sized pieces
  - failing to layer information

**Check Your Understanding**

1. **True or false? Designing and developing computer training is becoming easier and less complex than it was in the past, due in part to modern courseware authoring software.**

2. **True or false? Good training can consist of a strategy as simple as the straightforward presentation of detailed information from a live or simulated "talking head."**

3. **Why is providing examples in instruction important? (Select all that apply.)**
   A. People learn by example.
   B. To students, examples are prized entities.
   C. Examples assist learning by making concrete what is often abstract in students' minds.
   D. Examples are a way to transition from one idea to the next.
   E. Examples assist learning by allowing students to correct or confirm their understanding.

4. **___ ___ is presenting information too quickly to be assimilated and processed by human cognitive processes and is often the result of an "information dump" or "fire hose" approach to training.**

5. **True or false? Providing insufficient or inappropriate practice and feedback is *not* providing enough practice exercises with feedback to raise performance to the desired target outcomes described in the objectives or not matching the behaviors practiced to those specified in the objectives.**

6. **Practice exercises should be: (Select all that apply.)**
   A. Matched to the behaviors given in the instructional objectives.
   B. Sufficient in number to reach the target skill levels.
   C. Slightly greater in complexity and scope than what was just taught to "stretch" students' thinking and build their problem-solving skills.

D. Phased—gradually increased in complexity and realism to real-world tasks and integrated with the subskills that were taught.

E. Always placed at the end of an instructional unit, topic, or lesson.

7. **True or false? The training mistake of expecting students to remember everything by recall is expecting students to remember everything that is presented in the training with just one exposure to the information.**

8. **Which of the following failures can lead to making faulty assumptions about what students already know when they take the training? (Select all that apply.)**
    A. Failing to structure the course in a logical fashion
    B. Failing to perform requirements gathering to understand the skills and knowledge that students bring with them to the training
    C. Failing to perform instructional analysis to identify required entry skills
    D. Failing to investigate and review for yourself any required prerequisite courses to ensure that they indeed teach the assumed entry-level skills and knowledge for your course
    E. Failing to collect information about the IT system requirements for technology-based training during requirements gathering

9. **True or false? Enabling content is all of the skills and knowledge that are necessary to understand new information or to carry out a step in a procedure.**

10. **True or false? Systematic instructional and content analyses are the only thorough way to identify *all* of the enabling content.**

11. **True or false? Repetition of key content should be avoided because of constrained training budgets, tight schedules, scarce resources for design and development, and a desire to minimize student seat time.**

12. **Why is the "chunking" of information important in instruction and training? (Select all that apply.)**
    A. Chunking is a well-established principle of perception, learning, and memory.
    B. Masses of unbroken information are not only intimidating, but more difficult to understand, remember, and reference at a later time.
    C. Chunking creates leaner instruction and is therefore cheaper to develop.
    D. Student motivation is visibly affected when students are mentally clobbered with a large mass of nonchunked information.
    E. A well-chosen chunking scheme forms a framework that assists learning and retention.

13. **True or false? Unlayered information hides increasing levels of detail from students.**

14. **____ is an instructional strategy in which information is taught by starting with a simple, high-level conceptual overview or organizing framework and then providing increasing levels of detail in subsequent discussions.**

## Answers

1. False. More people with different specialties are involved in creating training today than in the past, training development schedules are being squeezed, training is often developed in an environment in which limited resources are available, business pressures often sway decision makers to demand "quick-and-dirty training," and technology-based training is becoming mainstream and is more complex and resource intensive to develop.

2. False. Valid training is based on specific *instructional strategies* and contains many *instructional events* that were determined from the performance, knowledge, and attitudinal outcomes and objectives. It is more than simply presenting information while students passively listen, read, or watch. Creating a book or talking head instead of training is one of the twenty common training mistakes.

3. A, B, C, and E

4. The correct answer is "Information overload."

5. True

6. A, B, and D

7. True

8. B, C, and D

9. True

10. True

11. False. These are reasons often given to justify the failure to repeat and refresh key information. Spaced review (repetition) of key ideas and concepts strengthens learning and storage and retrieval of information into long-term memory.

12. A, B, D, and E

13. False. Layered information hides increasing levels of detail from students.

14. The correct answer is "Elaboration."

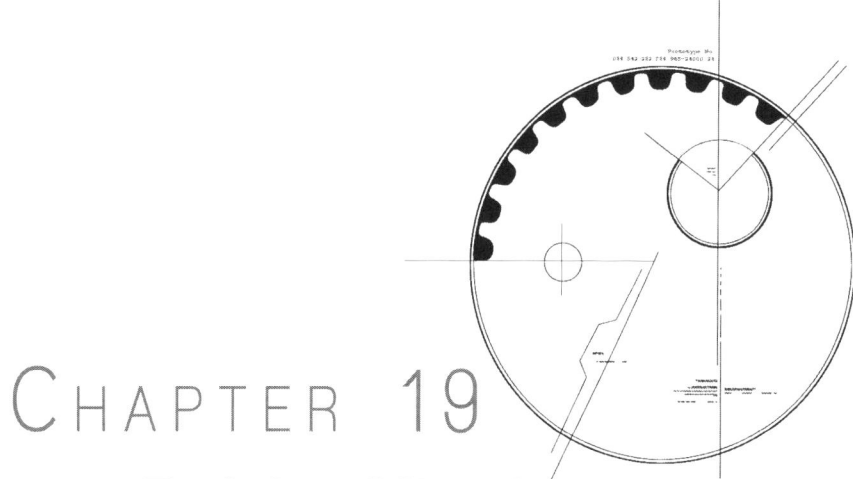

# CHAPTER 19
# Twenty Common Training Mistakes, Part 2

This chapter and the previous one together present twenty common training mistakes. Although these mistakes are more frequently made by those who do not have an educational background, they are sometimes made even by education professionals and full-time instructors. Being aware of these mistakes and pitfalls will help you avoid them in your own training. In this chapter, we will discuss the final ten common training mistakes, in no particular order or priority. We also provide a rating sheet that can be used to evaluate existing training programs based on these mistakes.

## Mistake #11: Failing to Refresh Prerequisite Information Immediately before New Information

Good math teachers refresh and review key information from the previous day's class before they teach new information; they know that math concepts and procedures typically build on and presume an understanding of previous concepts and procedures.

Instructors often assume that what they taught students a day or two ago is still fresh in their minds. Course materials can make the same mistake—for example, assuming that information taught in module 1, topic 1 will be remembered in module 3, topic 7.

## Description

**Definition:** Assuming that students remember everything that was ever presented to them, even material that was presented several days previously or several lessons prior in the training.

**Example:** Starting a new topic on the TCP/IP network protocol without refreshing students' memories of what a network protocol is.

Unfortunately, the suggestion to refresh prerequisite information right before it is needed is often seen as an unjustified luxury or is criticized as being repetitive or redundant. Those that do so believe in "one-trial" learning—that is, one exposure to information is all that is needed for students to learn and remember the information.

## Related design principles

- New knowledge must be associated with other knowledge in short-term memory for learning to occur. Unless the prerequisite information can be retrieved and thereby placed into short-term memory, the new associations cannot be made and learning will not occur.
- Training for hierarchically related knowledge (such as math, the sciences, and engineering) is especially prone to this mistake.

## How to avoid this mistake

- Whenever new information is introduced—from a single idea to an entirely new module—ask yourself what prerequisite information is required, whether it is still fresh in students' memories, and if not, what needs to be refreshed and at what level it needs to be refreshed. Then provide for refreshing this information.

**Note:** Prerequisite information consists of enabling content and assumed entry-level skills and knowledge. These are identified through audience analysis and instructional and content analyses (see part 2).

### How to remedy this mistake

- Review the training to see if prerequisite information is reviewed or refreshed at the point where it is needed, especially when the prerequisite information was taught some time earlier in the training. Then add the activities to refresh this information where it is needed.

## Mistake #12: Failing to Relate New Information to What Students Already Know

Knowledge not only builds on other knowledge, it also expands out in a network-like fashion as new associations are made to existing associations in the minds of students.

Students want to know how the new information they are about to learn relates to the information they have just learned or to information they already know. This is important not only to support the cognitive learning process, but to student motivation as well. If students do not perceive the new material as relevant (important for them to acquire), then they will likely fail to pay attention or engage with the training as extensively and actively as they would have otherwise done.

### Description

**Definition:** Failing to help students understand new information by relating it to what they already know

**Example:** Relating the abstract concept of a computer file to a concrete object—an office file cabinet with drawers and folders

*Instructional Design Tips and Traps* 481

**Related design principles**

- In training, move from the known to the unknown.
- Relate new information to known or similar information.
- Impose organizing structures on the information that add meaning to it.
- Use analogies, metaphors, similes, and anecdotes where appropriate to make abstract concepts more familiar and concrete.

**How to avoid this mistake**

- Relate new information to known information; if necessary, use analogies, metaphors, similes, and anecdotes to relate abstract information to concrete or familiar information.
- Use familiar organizing structures to organize information, such as hierarchy, part-whole, set-subset, timelines, charts, and tables.
- Provide plenty of examples.

**How to remedy this mistake**

- Review the materials or audit the training to see if this mistake was made.
- Add activities in the training to refresh prerequisite information where they are needed.

**Mistake #13: Failing to Highlight and Emphasize Key Information**

Bombarding students' minds with large amounts of amorphous information numbs their brains and leaves them unable to distinguish what information they must learn and remember from information that is more detailed or auxiliary and noncritical.

## Description

**Definition:** Failing to distinguish key information from more detailed or less important information.

**Note:** Key information is information that meets one of the following criteria:

- is foundational information on which other important information is based
- is information that greatly facilitates, organizes, or simplifies the understanding of other information
- is information that must be understood to learn other important information
- is information that will be needed by students to produce important job outcomes

Key information includes the important principles for a subject area and the key steps and performance guidance for a procedure.

This mistake is typically one of the negative results of taking an "information dump" or "fire hose" approach to training.

## Related design principles

- Not all information is equal—some information is key information.
- Emphasize key information—make it stand out both visually and cognitively.
- Give key information more extensive treatment and coverage in both the presentations and the exercises.
- Do not leave the task of identifying key information to students.

## How to avoid this mistake

- To determine key information, perform proper instructional and content analyses.
- You can also take into consideration feedback from subject matter experts (SMEs) and students who have recently gone through training.

- Use the foreground/background principle of perception to place key information in the foreground (see part 1 for references to books on this topic).
- Make key information stand out visually, semantically, structurally, and organizationally.

**How to remedy this mistake**

- Use the techniques listed above in the section, *How to avoid this mistake,* to identify key information. Then make it stand out.

## Mistake #14: Failing to Provide and Maintain Context

Maintaining context is not just letting students know where they are at in the agenda, where they have navigated to in an online course, or how far they have progressed in the training. It also involves telling students contextual information that shows them how the information about to be discussed relates to the bigger picture or to a previously presented conceptual framework.

**Description**

**Definition:** This mistake is failing to
- provide an overall conceptual or organizing framework upfront and referring back to it throughout the course or instructional unit;
- relate new information to information that was already presented; or
- let students know where they are in the course, where they have navigated to in a course, or how far they have progressed in the training.

**Examples**
- shifting from one topic to another without providing students with any sense of where they are at, why this new topic is being presented, and how it fits into the unit and course
- failing to provide linking and transitional information

**Related design principles**

- When designing and developing training, address the question: "How does what I am about to discuss or present relate to what was just presented or previously presented?"
- Context is how new information relates to the most recently presented information and to the larger, overall framework given earlier or upfront.
- Providing contextual information when new information is introduced
  - aids comprehension,
  - relates new information to an organizational scheme that enhances memory,
  - relates the unknown (the new information) to the known (what students already know),
  - supports elaboration, and
  - demonstrates relevance and increases student motivation.

**How to avoid this mistake**

- Tell students how the new information relates to what was just presented using transitional units, topics, slides, pages, paragraphs, and sentences, as appropriate.
- Never leave students wondering where they are at in a course or why new information is being presented.
- Provide navigational cues, breadcrumbs, trail markers, icons, or other indicators of the student's location in the course.

**How to remedy this mistake**

- Look for abrupt changes of subject material that lack transition and context-setting information.
- Assess how easy it is for students to know where they are at in the course.
- Apply the techniques listed above in the section, *How to avoid this mistake*.

# Mistake #15: Failing to Provide Support for the Transfer of Skills to the Job

Why can students take training for a generic computer application—say, for a spreadsheet program—that teaches them how to perform the individual functions of the application and then return to their jobs and be unable to produce real work products using the application, such as a current-quarter sales projection? The answer involves transfer of learning to the workplace—a tricky area for students unless the training was designed to support it.

## Description

**Definition:** Teaching concepts, principles, facts, and so forth without
- doing so in the context of producing real work,
- showing how they can be applied to the real world, or
- providing practice with feedback and integrated practice with feedback that pulls together what was taught into increasingly realistic and complex real-world tasks.

**Example:** Training statisticians by teaching individual statistical techniques across several courses but failing to teach students how to analyze real-life situations to determine an appropriate statistical technique or experimental design

## Related design principles

- Transferring or applying knowledge to the real world must be explicitly shaped; otherwise, it is unlikely to be very successful.
- Research shows that people believe they are better at transferring (applying) knowledge to the real world than they really are.
- The real world is full of complexity and variation.
- Provide exercises in training that eventually integrate the individual to performing real-life job tasks or subtasks.

**How to avoid this mistake**

- Use requirements gathering and instructional analysis to identify students' job outcomes and the major activities and tasks that produce those outcomes (see part 2).

- Practice individual subskills first and then integrate those skills into higher-level skills in later practice while gradually increasing the realism and complexity of the exercises.

- Provide examples, case studies, demonstrations, and other instructional events that show how the information can be applied to real-world situations.

**How to remedy this mistake**

- Conduct interviews or surveys with students who have recently taken the training and have returned to their jobs. Have them identify the specific job tasks and subtasks that they could not perform, despite their previous participation in the training.

- Analyze those job tasks and subtasks to break them into their component parts for training and apply the techniques listed above in the section, *How to avoid this mistake.*

## Mistake #16: Failing to Structure or Sequence the Information Logically

This mistake is easy to understand but is more common than you might expect.

### Description

**Definition:** Failing to structure the training so that prerequisite topics and information are taught before teaching other information that depends on these prerequisites

**Example:** Structuring a course so that the topic on using circular saws is taught after the topic on framing walls, thus violating the logical prerequisite order of these two skills

**Related design principles**

- Structure the course so that prerequisite topics and information are taught before the information that relies on them in the following manner:
  - Teach prerequisite information right before the new information, unless there are special instructional design reasons to teach it earlier.
  - If several places in the course require the same prerequisite information, organize it and teach it as a separate unit, topic, or module somewhere before the first place in the course where it is needed.

**How to avoid this mistake**

- Perform instructional and content analyses to determine prerequisite relationships and therefore the proper sequencing of content.
- Pilot test your training to help you identify topics or information that is out of order.

**How to remedy this mistake**

- Information that has been hastily thrown together or that has been cut-and-pasted from other sources typically has sequencing problems.
- Be especially careful of SME-designed courses and "information dump" presentations—they can suffer from the same problems too.
- Human inspection, especially by a SME, typically does not identify all prerequisite relationships.
- Correct sequencing is based on instructional and content analyses. If these have not been performed, then you might have to perform considerable rework.

# Mistake #17: Failing to Provide Adequate Interactivity and a Variety of Activities

Training is more than the presentation of information. Properly determined instructional events not only make training more effective, they also provide a variety of interactions and a change of pace for students.

## Description

**Definition:** Presenting training material that provides little or no *meaningful* interaction or that contains instruction using the same stimulus for long periods of time

- Such training fails to engage learners and does not accommodate their biological limitations or fatigue limits.
- Meaningful interaction engages students' cognitive learning processes.

## Examples

- In web-based training, clicking different parts of a graphic to display additional information is a form of student interaction, but it does not in-and-of-itself have any instructional value, other than, perhaps, providing a mechanism for layering the information. It is not the kind of interaction that engages students' cognitive learning processes.
- Failing to provide meaningful checkpoint questions, group exercises, labs, role-plays, games, simulations, and other instructional events that support the learning objectives.

## Related design principles

- The human brain is a living, biological organ prone to fatigue, especially if it is subjected to an unchanging stimulus.
  - **Example:** Experiments done in human sensation have shown that visual perception *requires* changing stimuli. If the small, imperceptible movements of the eye are counteracted so that the visual image falls on exactly the same place on the retina of the eye, the person soon becomes temporarily blind.

- Long periods of "passive learning" on the part of students are detrimental to attention, motivation, and learning.
- Students' cognitive learning mechanisms must be engaged, not simply stimulated with a constant stimulus.

**How to avoid this mistake**

- Provide *meaningful* interaction and a variety of learning stimuli during training, such as reading, listening, answering questions, solving problems, working exercises, doing group work, engaging in a case study on a computer, using tools or equipment, having discussions with fellow students, watching videos, viewing animations, playing games, seeing demonstrations, observing role models, participating in simulations, teaching others, being mentored, making presentations, and performing real work.
- Reduce fatigue through frequent breaks, interaction, changes in pace, individual and group exercises, and a variety of appropriate learning activities.
- For classroom instruction, keeping students in training for ten or twelve hours a day is not much more productive than keeping them focused for six to eight hours. Remember, learning is biological, not just intellectual.

**How to remedy this mistake**

- For classroom instruction, monitor students to see if they are actively engaged and interested in the materials and are participating in discussions. If students are falling asleep or are disengaged, then revisit the materials to determine how to make them more engaging. Apply the techniques listed above in the section, *How to avoid this mistake.*

## Mistake #18: Failing to Take the Viewpoint of the Student

Training should be centered on students, not on the instructor or on the training materials. Training should be focused on what students need to learn to produce valued work products and job outcomes, not on personal opinions by the instructor or others about what they think students ought to know.

The educational model of students sitting quietly at the feet of an oracle or guru who dispenses a constant stream of knowledge and wisdom is rarely appropriate for training. Students should be actively engaged with instructors, other students, and training materials and participating in a variety of learning events and types of interaction to maximize learning. Training is not about reverencing gurus, it is about helping students learn.

## Description

### Definition

- failing to conduct performance and audience analysis to determine what students need and tailoring the course to those needs
- failing to design the training from the perspective of the student—for example, taking a subject matter-based approach to training
- failing to address students directly in the training and use an active, second-person voice (the "you" form) in the text and narration
- failing to provide adequate support for learning, such as expecting students to learn difficult material that was not prepared using sound instructional design principles

### Examples

- Teaching the functions of a computer office application from A to Z but failing to teach students how to perform their job tasks using the application.
- A movie director directs movies with an eye to how they will be experienced from the perspective of moviegoers. Training should do the same for students.

## Related design principles

- Determine actual student attributes and needs through audience and instructional analyses. Then, design and create a course that will be experienced by students, not just taken by students.

- It is not enough to know the general audience. You must know your students and their specific needs and then cater to those needs.
- Taking the perspective of the student will increase student motivation by making training more relevant to students.

**How to avoid this mistake**

- Conduct audience and instructional analyses to determine specific on-the-job outcomes and tasks and identify audience needs.
- Structure the course to reflect the high-level tasks identified in the instructional analysis and to reflect a job-task orientation.
- Ask students after training if they felt like the course
  - was created just for them (tailored to their needs),
  - was like having a mentor by their side, or
  - was friendly.

**How to remedy this mistake**

- Courses that were assembled from large chunks of existing reference material typically suffer from this problem.
- Good instructional design is the only real way to avoid a dry, subject matter-based course that fails to take the perspective of the student.
- For minor infractions, perform the techniques listed above in the section, *How to avoid this mistake.*

## Mistake #19: Failing to Make Instruction Lean

Including unnecessary material in training bloats training and increases costs by expanding development time, delivery time, and student seat time. Moreover, when unnecessary material is interspersed with key information, students find it difficult to distinguish key information from information they do not need to know. Finally, bloated training taxes students' limited cognitive processes and increases the likelihood of mental and biological fatigue.

## Description

**Definition:** Failing to follow the steps in the instructional design process, resulting in training that is bloated and filled with unnecessary and irrelevant material and activities.

## Examples

- various parties to design and development throwing in their favorite topics or material that they believe is important
- giving students all of the information you can find on a topic so that you do not have to perform instructional analysis or sort out what is really needed
- having a "More is better" mentality when it comes to including content in the course

Bloated training shows a lack of discipline on the part of the course designer or developer to follow sound instructional design principles and techniques.

## Related design principles

- Training should be lean; it should only contain material and activities that are essential to helping students produce valued work outcomes and to achieving the training objectives.
- Students appreciate lean training that is produced by sound instructional design. It shows that the instructional designer and course developer respect students' time and took the trouble to understand their needs. Students see this kind of training as highly relevant.
- "More is often worse, not better," for a variety of reasons, including information overload, failure to teach information in the context of job tasks, and failure to focus on and emphasize key information.

## How to avoid this mistake

- Outstanding movies include only what is required in each scene to evoke certain emotions or communicate certain ideas. Likewise, your training should include only what is necessary (as dictated by the instructional and content analyses) for students to produce the valued job outcomes.

- Lean training is the result of conducting instructional and content analyses to identify all required information for the course, all the way down to the individual concept, fact, principle, and step level.
- If you cannot show that a piece of information is required somewhere in the instructional analysis to perform one or more activities, tasks, subtasks, or steps, then leave it out of the course.
- If the training teaches pure ideas (it has no performance objectives), then perform a content analysis and design the course from that analysis.

**How to remedy this mistake**

- Students often can sense when training is bloated. They will feel that much of the material is not relevant to their needs, because it does not help them perform tasks that produce the desired job outcomes.
- If a course is not obviously bloated, how can you tell if it contains unnecessary information? Only a comparison of existing course content to the content identified in instructional and content analyses can objectively tell you if noncritical or unnecessary content is included in a course. Otherwise, it is one person's opinion against another's.

## Mistake #20: Failing to Help Students Remember Information

Instructional designers add value by designing training that helps students learn. Some educators feel that their responsibilities are adequately discharged when they simply present information to students—generally in the form of an "information dump" or a series of lectures—leaving students on their own to make sense of it, learn it, and remember it.

### Why an information dump is not appropriate for training

The philosophy of simply dispensing information is embraced in many formal academic settings. Educators often justify this approach by saying that requiring students to provide their own learning events more fully engages their intellectual processes. These educators generally provide only a few carefully selected learning events, such as requiring that students answer a few questions, take a pop quiz, or write a short paper to help stimulate their thinking.

However, relying on students to provide their own instructional events to learn the material has many pitfalls and is a risky training proposition for the following reasons:

- Many students do not possess adequate cognitive strategies to assemble information into more complex ideas without explicit guidance.
- Students often do not have adequate time and resources to do the additional research that is necessary to fill in missing concepts or gaps in their understanding.
- Adequate organizing frameworks are often deliberately withheld from students to make learning more challenging; this creates yet another stumbling block to learning.
- Some students will never arrive at the desire insights and conclusions, no matter how hard they try to deduce them or generalize them from the information that was presented. They simply do not have the sophisticated cognitive strategies to do so.
- Adequate practice with feedback is usually not provided; instead, the focus is on evaluating students' abilities at fixed intervals, such as at the end of chapters, quarters, or semesters.
- The educators themselves often benefit when some students fail to learn: Courses are easier for educators to develop when they do not have to design and create adequate instructional events. Students who perform poorly provide a nice distribution of scores by which these educators can assign grades. It should be obvious that any educational system that is charged with helping students learn but in fact benefits when they do not learn is self-serving.
- The focus of instruction for both instructors and students is on "How can I make an A in this course?" rather than on how instructors can design, create, and provide learning events that facilitate and support the learning process so that all of the students can learn the material.

## Description

**Definition:** Presenting large amounts of information that you expect students to remember without providing sufficient (or any) support for helping students to process and store that information into long-term memory

**Examples:** Lectures that simply dispense information without providing sufficient instructional interaction and learning events designed to help students learn and remember the material

## Related design principles

- Do not train to recall memory unless absolutely necessary.
- When you must train to recall memory, use techniques that facilitate cognitive processing and the storage of information into long-term memory (see part 1).
- Know the fundamental principles of memory and how to apply them to facilitate recall.

## How to avoid this mistake

- Capitalize on the fundamental principles of memory:
  - *spaced review:* rehearse critical information repeatedly over time
  - *meaning:* make information meaningful
  - *organization:* organize and structure information in meaningful ways
  - *chunking:* break masses of information into smaller, meaningful chunks
  - *concreteness:* choose the concrete over the abstract
  - *sequence:* place important information first or last in a sequence
  - *visualization:* create vivid visualizations of the information
  - *attention:* make sure attention is obtained and maintained
  - *interference:* recode information to reduce interference from similar information
  - *association and elaboration:* relate the unknown to the familiar
  - *contiguity:* place items to be associated near each other in time and space

- *mnemonic aids:* provide acronyms, rhymes, or other mnemonic techniques
- *advanced organizers and mental models:* use overviews, analogies, graphics, metaphors, and mental models

**How to remedy this mistake**

- Identify key information and determine if students are given any support to help them remember this information.
- For key information, apply the techniques listed above in the section, *How to avoid this mistake.*

## Rating Existing Training Materials Using the *Twenty Common Mistakes Rating Sheet*

The following rating sheet can be used to assess an existing training course on the twenty common training mistakes that we have just discussed. Although these ratings are subjective and depend on the instructional design expertise of the rater, they can help provide an overall picture of where the training has violated the principles discussed in this and the previous chapters.

You might find it helpful to review this checklist both before and during instructional design and development as a reminder to avoid these mistakes in your own training.

## Twenty Common Mistakes Rating Sheet

**Instructions:** For each pair of descriptors, mark an "x" in the blank that most accurately represents the attributes of the training

**The Training ...**

| | | |
|---|---|---|
| 1. Is a book or a "talking head" | ____ ____ ____ ____ | Is real training with meaningful and appropriate instructional interaction |
| 2. Has too few examples | ____ ____ ____ ____ | Has an adequate number of examples |
| 3. Induces information overload | ____ ____ ____ ____ | Manages learning to avoid information overload |
| 4. Has insufficient or inappropriate practice with feedback | ____ ____ ____ ____ | Has sufficient and appropriate practice with feedback |
| 5. Expects students to remember everything using recall memory | ____ ____ ____ ____ | Expects students to remember only information that must be recalled from memory on the job |
| 6. Assumes students know information they do not know | ____ ____ ____ ____ | Does not assume students know information they do not know |
| 7. Fails to provide all of the enabling content | ____ ____ ____ ____ | Provides all of the enabling content required for learning |
| 8. Provides too little repetition | ____ ____ ____ ____ | Provides sufficient repetition to reinforce learning |
| 9. Fails to chunk information into bite-sized pieces | ____ ____ ____ ____ | Chunks information into bite-sized pieces |
| 10. Fails to layer information | ____ ____ ____ ____ | Layers information appropriately |

| | | |
|---|---|---|
| 11. Fails to refresh prerequisite information immediately before presenting new information | ____ ____ ____ ____ | Refreshes prerequisite information immediately before presenting new information |
| 12. Fails to relate new information to what students already know | ____ ____ ____ ____ | Relates new information to what students already know |
| 13. Fails to highlight and emphasize key information | ____ ____ ____ ____ | Highlights and emphasizes key information |
| 14. Fails to provide and maintain context | ____ ____ ____ ____ | Provides and maintains context |
| 15. Fails to provide support for the transfer of skills to the job | ____ ____ ____ ____ | Provides support for the transfer of skills to the job |
| 16. Fails to structure or sequence the information logically | ____ ____ ____ ____ | Structures or sequences the information logically |
| 17. Fails to provide adequate interactivity by using a variety of learning activities | ____ ____ ____ ____ | Provides adequate interactivity by using a variety of learning activities |
| 18. Fails to take the viewpoint of the student | ____ ____ ____ ____ | Takes the viewpoint of the student |
| 19. Fails to make instruction lean | ____ ____ ____ ____ | Provides lean instruction (only essential information is taught to achieve the outcomes) |
| 20. Fails to help students remember information | ____ ____ ____ ____ | Helps students remember information (provides memory support) |

# Chapter Summary—
# Twenty Common Training Mistakes, Part 2

This chapter and the previous one together presented twenty common training mistakes. Although these mistakes are more frequently made by those who do not have an educational background, they are sometimes made even by education professionals and full-time instructors. Being aware of these mistakes and pitfalls will help you avoid them in your own training. In this chapter, we discussed the final ten common training mistakes, in no particular order or priority. We also provided a rating sheet that can be used to evaluate existing training programs based on these mistakes.

You should now be able to

- for each of the following ten common training mistakes, define and describe the mistake, state the design principles that are being violated, explain how to avoid the mistake, and describe what to do to remedy the mistake:
  - failing to refresh prerequisite information immediately before new information
  - failing to relate new information to what students already know
  - failing to highlight and emphasize key information
  - failing to provide and maintain context
  - failing to provide support for the transfer of skills to the job
  - failing to structure or sequence the information logically
  - failing to provide adequate interactivity and a variety of activities
  - failing to take the viewpoint of the student
  - failing to make instruction lean
  - failing to help students remember information
- describe when to use the *Twenty Common Mistakes Rating Sheet* and explain how to use it.

## Check Your Understanding

1. **True or false? Refreshing prerequisite information immediately before new information is important because new knowledge must be associated with other knowledge in short-term memory for learning to occur.**

2. **Techniques for moving from the known to the unknown in teaching new information include: (Select all that apply.)**
   A. Relate new information to known or similar information.
   B. Impose organizing structures on the information that add meaning to it.
   C. Provide reviews at the end of instructional units and topics.
   D. Use analogies, metaphors, similes, and anecdotes where appropriate to make abstract concepts more familiar and concrete.
   E. Tell students that the new information is not tied or related to anything they already know.

3. **Key information is information that meets any one of which of the following criteria? (Select all that apply.)**
   A. It is foundational information on which other important information is based.
   B. It is information that is usually included in appendices and external reference documents.
   C. It is information that greatly facilitates, organizes, or simplifies the understanding of other information.
   D. It is information that must be understood to learn other important information.
   E. It is information that will be needed by students to produce important job outcomes.

4. **True or false? Failing to provide and maintain context in training is failing to do any of the following:**

- Provide an overall conceptual or organizing framework upfront and referring back to it throughout the course or instruction unit.
- Relate new information to information that was already presented.
- Inform students where they are in the course, where they have navigated to in a course, or how far they have progressed in the training.

5. **True or false? Transfer of knowledge to the real world must be explicitly shaped during training; otherwise, it is unlikely to be successful.**

6. **True or false? Teach prerequisite information right before the new information, unless there are special instructional design reasons to do otherwise.**

7. **True or false? Instructional interaction in training is any interaction that students have with the instructor or the materials—for example, in web-based training, clicking buttons to make information appear or to navigate to the next screen.**

8. **True or false? The educational model of students sitting quietly at the feet of an oracle or guru who dispenses a constant stream of knowledge and wisdom is rarely appropriate for training.**

9. **Which of the following actions are ways in which training can fail to take the viewpoint of the student? (Select all that apply.)**
   A. Failing to take a subject matter approach to training
   B. Failing to conduct performance and audience analysis to determine what students need

C. Failing to address students directly in the training and use an active, second-person voice (the "you" form) in the text and narration

D. Failing to provide adequate support for learning, such as expecting students to learn difficult material that was not prepared using sound instructional design principles

10. **True or false? Failing to make instruction lean is the result of failing to fit the instruction into the budget and timeline that were given by the sponsors of training.**

11. **True or false? Principles of memory that you can apply to help students remember information include spaced review, meaning, organization, chunking, concreteness, sequence, visualization, attention, interference, association, elaboration, contiguity, mnemonic aids, advanced organizers, and mental models.**

12. **True or false? The *Twenty Common Mistakes Rating Sheet* can be used (1) to assess existing training to get an overall picture of where these mistakes might have been made and (2) as an aid to refresh your memory about important design principles both before and during instructional design and development to help you avoid these mistakes in your training.**

## Answers

1. True. Unless the prerequisite information can be retrieved and thereby placed into short-term memory, the new associations cannot be made, and learning will not occur.
2. A, B, and D
3. A, C, D, and E
4. True
5. True

6. True
7. False. Interaction must be *meaningful* to have instructional value. Meaningful interaction engages students' cognitive learning processes. It consists of instructional activities and events that have been designed to enhance and support the learning process. It can include activities such as answering questions, solving problems, working exercises, doing group work, engaging in a case study on a computer, using tools or equipment, having discussions with fellow students, watching videos, viewing animations, playing games, seeing demonstrations, observing role models, participating in simulations, teaching others, being mentored, making presentations, and performing real work.
8. True
9. B, C, and D
10. False. Lean training is the result of conducting instructional and content analyses to identify all required information for the course—all the way down to the individual concept, fact, principle, and step level—and then teaching only that content.
11. True
12. True

# Summary

Congratulations! You have now completed the instructional part of this book. You should now be able to

- list and explain the fundamental principles of human learning;
- describe the overall cognitive learning process, identify where bottlenecks can occur in that process, and explain how to overcome those bottlenecks;
- design effective, lean, and motivational technology-based and non-technology-based training courses and materials by following the nine steps in the instructional design process;
- design blended learning solutions; and
- list twenty common training mistakes; for each mistake, describe the mistake, state the learning principles that were violated, explain how to avoid the mistake, and describe what to do to remedy the mistake.

You should now be better prepared to create effective, lean, and motivational training.

## What You Should Have Learned

In part 1, you learned

- that learning is biological, not just intellectual;
- the biological requirements for learning;
- the cognitive process by which humans learn, the limitations of that process, and how to address those limitations, especially those of short-term memory capacity and encoding information into long-term memory; and
- several key principles of learning and teaching.

In part 2, you learned

- the nine steps for performing instructional design, beginning with gathering requirements and ending with creating the formal instructional design document; and
- why each step in this process is necessary, how to perform it, and why this process is the fastest, most efficient way to design effective, lean, and motivational training.

In part 3, you learned

- how to design training that teaches computer applications; and
- twenty common training mistakes, how to avoid them, and how to correct them.

If you do not feel confident in your understanding of any of this material, please review the content in those sections.

## Applying Instructional Design in an Imperfect World

Before concluding this book, let us answer the commonly asked question, "How can I apply the instructional design process to an imperfect world?"

It would be great if you had unlimited time and resources to design and develop your training. Unfortunately, the real world is seldom so kind. More often than not, you have limited access to subject matter experts, tight schedules, poor source material, or clients who do not understand the need to perform "front-end analysis" or to perform instructional design at all before creating training materials.

So what is a person to do?

## Suggestions on How To Apply Instructional Design in an Imperfect World:

First, make an effort now, and over the long term, to educate your clients on the value of instructional design—how it is the fastest, least expensive way to produce effective, lean, and motivational training. Help them to see the strong return on investment that typically results and the costs and consequences of producing poor-quality training. Help them to understand that, although everyone has created some kind of training in their lifetime, this fact alone does not make them an expert on how training should be designed for maximum learning with minimum effort.

Help them to understand that training is not an art form—it is an engineering endeavor. Remind them that engineers require significant front-end time and resources to gather real-life data, analyze that data, and design solutions before they pour a bridge's first pier or lay a skyscraper's first beam. Instructional designers need to do likewise before they create a course's first screen, web page, or slide.

The second suggestion is to recognize that you will be constrained by the limitations of resources, time, budget, and organizational politics that are imposed on you by the sponsors of your training. How you deal with these constraints is a personal decision that only you can make. The decision you make might in part depend on whether you are an independent training consultant or are working as an employee of the sponsoring organization, as illustrated here:

- If you are an independent training consultant, you probably have more freedom to push back or to go on to another client when you judge that the quality of the training is being sacrificed beyond what you are willing to tolerate. You have your professional reputation to consider and safeguard and probably do not want to tarnish that reputation by knowingly producing poor-quality training.
- If you are an employee of the sponsoring organization, then you might consider making a reasonable effort to educate your decision makers on the specific risks that they are taking and the potential consequences that can arise by circumventing sound instructional design practices. If you do this, be sure that you carefully and factually document your efforts (for example, in a follow-up e-mail) so that your actions become part of the historical record that you can refer back to if the training is deemed a failure or unsatisfactory. Nonetheless, whether you put your neck on the line and question the decisions of those higher in authority is a personal decision that only you can make.

Regardless of whether you work independently or not, if poor training could result in consequences that could legally endanger you or the company, consult legal advice and counsel from those who are professionally qualified to give such advice. If legal issues are not a factor, then you must judge what you should do under the circumstances, recognizing that the goal of perfection is not often attained in the business world. Instructional designers sometimes just have to do the best with what they are given.

## Your Next Steps

This book discussed the fundamental concepts, processes, procedures, principles, and techniques of sound instructional design. It was designed by following the same principles that it teaches. Hopefully, you found it easy to understand, logically sequenced, and relevant to your own personal needs. This book presented many activities, examples, and questions with feedback to help you learn this information.

However, this book can only take you so far. Having been grounded in the fundamentals of instructional design, your next step is to apply your knowledge and skills to the real world. Hopefully, you will do this under the tutelage of an experienced instructional designer who has a deep understanding of this process. By doing so, you can continue to learn and refine your abilities through further practice with feedback on actual projects.

The follow-on and companion activity to instructional design is *instructional development*. Instructional development is the set of activities that are required to create the instructional materials that were specified and prescribed by the instructional design document—the blueprints of the training. It is the construction phase of the training project. In instructional development, the course materials are "fleshed out" into their final verbiage and form, based on the course and topic objectives.

Instructional development requires knowledge of such things as how to sequence the instruction, how to identify different types of information, and how to design and write instructional prose, graphics, and treatments accordingly.

---

For a how-to manual on instructional development, see my companion book, *Instructional Development—Step by Step: Six Easy Steps for Developing Lean, Effective, and Motivational Instruction.* Bloomington, IN: iUniverse, 2013.

# Appendix A:
# Example Printout of a Template for Microsoft Word that Has Been Created Especially for Instructional Analysis

## This is a title

### 1. This is a heading 1
This is Heading 1 body text
#### 1.1 This is a heading 2
This is Heading 2 body text
##### 1.1.1 This is a heading 3
This is Heading 3 body text
###### 1.1.1.1 This is a heading 4
This is Heading 4 body text
**1.1.1.1.1 This is a heading 5**
This is Heading 5 body text
**1.1.1.1.1.1 This is a heading 6**
This is Heading 6 body text
**1.1.1.1.1.1.1 This is a heading 7**
This is Heading 7 body text
**1.1.1.1.1.1.1.1 This is a heading 8**
This is Heading 8 body text
**1.1.1.1.1.1.1.1.1 This is a heading 9**
This is Heading 9 body text

This is body text

**IMPORTANT!** Switch to **Outline** view (click **View**, **Outline**) before using the outline functions below.

Shortcut keys for assigning Heading 1 through Heading 9 styles:

Heading 1    Ctrl+Alt+Shift+F1
Heading 2    Ctrl+Alt+Shift+F2
Heading 3    Ctrl+Alt+Shift+F3
Heading 4    Ctrl+Alt+Shift+F4
Heading 5    Ctrl+Alt+Shift+F5
Heading 6    Ctrl+Alt+Shift+F6
Heading 7    Ctrl+Alt+Shift+F7
Heading 8    Ctrl+Alt+Shift+F8
Heading 9    Ctrl+Alt+Shift+F9

Shortcut keys for promoting, demoting, moving up, or moving down a heading:

Promote    Alt+Shift+Left Arrow OR Shift+Tab
Demote    Alt+Shift+Right Arrow OR Tab
Move Up    Alt+Shift+Up Arrow
Move Down    Alt+Shift+Down Arrow

Dragging the symbols in front of the paragraphs left or right or up or down will also promote, demote, move up, and move down a heading. Another method is to click the **Promote**, **Demote**, **Move Up**, and **Move Down** buttons on the **Outlining** toolbar when the cursor is located within a heading.

**NOTE:** Subordinate body text will move with its parent heading. Also, text within a collapsed entry will move with its corresponding parent heading. Selecting (highlighting) multiple lines of text before promoting, demoting, moving up, or moving down will move all paragraphs that include the selected text.

# Appendix B:
# Example of an Instructional Analysis

## Working SS/6000Z SP Network After Networking Problems and Changes

### 1 Understand the customer's request
#### 1.1 Ask the customer the following questions:
  1.1.1 How would you describe the problem you are having?
  1.1.2 Is this a new network?
    1.1.2.1 Has the network ever worked?
  1.1.3 Have there been any recent network changes?
    1.1.3.1 Have there been any new network hardware additions, subtractions, or relocations?
    1.1.3.2 Have there been any configuration changes in IP addressing, network software, and network-related APARs?
  1.1.4 Have you already performed any problem determination?
    1.1.4.1 Have you checked cables?
    1.1.4.2 Have you checked that the network is properly cabled to network components?
    1.1.4.3 Have you done any sniffer traces?
    1.1.4.4 Have you checked the adapter configurations?
  1.1.5 Do you know what is causing the problem?
    1.1.5.1 Why do you think that is the problem?
  1.1.6 Does the problem only affect a single node or does it affect multiple nodes?
  1.1.7 Has anyone else worked on the problem?
  1.1.8 Is the problem intermittent or solid?
  1.1.9 What do you want me to do?

# 2 Gather information specific to the network type
## 2.1 Ask the customer what type of network he has
2.1.1 If the customer has token ring network
- 2.1.1.1 How big is the ring?
  - 2.1.1.1.1 Are you running a multiple MAU (or CAU or token ring hub) network?
- 2.1.1.2 What type of cabling are you using?
  - 2.1.1.2.1 If Type 1
    - 2.1.1.2.1.1 Probably indicates a hub or CAU network
  - 2.1.1.2.2 If Type 5
    - 2.1.1.2.2.1 Probably indicates a MAU network
- 2.1.1.3 Does your network have a beaconing condition?
  - 2.1.1.3.1 Yes, the network has a beaconing condition
    - 2.1.1.3.1.1 Does the customer have the appropriate cabling diagrams to help determine where the break is?
      - 2.1.1.3.1.1.1 Yes, the customer has the appropriate cabling diagrams
        - 2.1.1.3.1.1.1.1 Check the cabling at the appropriate locations in the network
      - 2.1.1.3.1.1.2 No, the customer does not have the appropriate cabling diagrams
        - 2.1.1.3.1.1.2.1 Refer to the token ring problem determination guide
  - 2.1.1.3.2 No, the network does not have a beaconing condition
    - 2.1.1.3.2.1 Is the problem affecting a single node or multiple nodes?
      - 2.1.1.3.2.1.1 Problem is affecting a single node
        - 2.1.1.3.2.1.1.1 Perform single-node problem determination (see below)
      - 2.1.1.3.2.1.2 Problem is affecting multiple nodes
        - 2.1.1.3.2.1.2.1 Perform multiple-node problem determination (see below)

2.1.2 Customer has Ethernet network
- 2.1.2.1 Determine the type of Ethernet cabling and topology
  - 2.1.2.1.1 Ask the customer if they have a thin net or UTP cabling and topology
    - 2.1.2.1.1.1 If the customer has thin net
      - 2.1.2.1.1.1.1 Topology is a bus
    - 2.1.2.1.1.2 If the customer has UTP
      - 2.1.2.1.1.2.1 Topology is a star
- 2.1.2.2 Ask the customer if he is having a performance problem
  - 2.1.2.2.1 If the customer is having a performance problem (a large number of collisions)
    - 2.1.2.2.1.1 Limit scope of hardware problem determination and consider having the customer bring in a systems performance consultant
  - 2.1.2.2.2 If the customer is not having a performance problem
    - 2.1.2.2.2.1 Is the problem affecting a single node or multiple nodes?
      - 2.1.2.2.2.1.1 If problem is affecting a single node
        - 2.1.2.2.2.1.1.1 Perform single-node problem determination (see below)
      - 2.1.2.2.2.1.2 If problem is affecting multiple nodes
        - 2.1.2.2.2.1.2.1 Perform multiple-node problem determination (see below)

2.1.3 Customer has GDDI or ZTM network

2.1.3.1 Is the problem affecting a single node or multiple nodes?
　2.1.3.1.1 If problem is affecting a single node
　　2.1.3.1.1.1 Perform single-node problem determination (see below)
　2.1.3.1.2 If problem is affecting multiple nodes
　　2.1.3.1.2.1 Perform multiple-node problem determination (see below)

# 3 Diagnose problems that only affect a single node
## 3.1 Check the error log for errors on the failing adapter
3.1.1 If there are errors
　3.1.1.1 Follow the problem determination procedures in the maintenance documentation
3.1.2 If there are no errors
　3.1.2.1 Continue with the next task

## 3.2 Use the mcnft command to determine if the adapter is properly configured?
3.2.1 If adapter is not properly configured
　3.2.1.1 Run advanced diagnostics to verify that the adapter is properly functioning
3.2.2 If adapter is properly configured
　3.2.2.1 Continue with the next task

## 3.3 Use ping to verify that the local adapter is functioning
3.3.1 If local adapter is functioning
　3.3.1.1 Use DMIT to verify and correct as needed the configuration options (verify with the customer the IP address, netmask, hardware config as appropriate)
　3.3.1.2 Continue with the next task
3.3.2 If local adapter is not functioning
　3.3.2.1 Run advanced diagnostics to verify that the adapter is properly functioning
　　3.3.2.1.1 Follow the procedures in the maintenance documentation

## 3.4 Verify the cabling from the adapter to the network component
3.4.1 Verify that the adapter has been physically connected to the appropriate network component
3.4.2 Verify the physical integrity of the cable

## 3.5 Run advanced diagnostics on the adapter to verify that the network drivers are functioning
3.5.1 If drivers are not functioning
　3.5.1.1 Replace the adapter card
3.5.2 If drivers are functioning
　3.5.2.1 Continue with the next task

## 3.6 Use ping with the host name to verify that you can communicate with several of the other hosts on the same network

3.6.1 If ping returns with "unknown host" response
- 3.6.1.1 Diagnose name resolution problem
  - 3.6.1.1.1 Verify that the host name is listed in the /etc/hosts file on the local host
  - 3.6.1.1.2 Verify that the IP address of the Domain Name server is listed in the /etc/resolv.conf file on the local host
  - 3.6.1.1.3 Verify that the Name Server is functioning

3.6.2 If ping returns with "network is unreachable"
- 3.6.2.1 Diagnose routing problem
  - 3.6.2.1.1 Ask the customer to verify that the IP address and subnet mask of the local host are correct
  - 3.6.2.1.2 Ask the customer to verify that all hosts on the local network are using the same subnet mask
  - 3.6.2.1.3 Ask the customer to verify that the default (gateway) router IP address is correct
  - 3.6.2.1.4 If problem is not resolved, call the next level of support

3.6.3 If ping returns with no response
- 3.6.3.1 Ask the customer to verify that the IP address and subnet mask of the local host are correct
- 3.6.3.2 Ask the customer to verify that all hosts on the local network are using the same subnet mask
- 3.6.3.3 Ask the customer to verify that the default (gateway) router IP address is correct
- 3.6.3.4 If problem is not resolved, call the next level of support

3.6.4 If ping returns with a good response
- 3.6.4.1 Continue with the next task

## 3.7 Use ping with the IP address to verify that you can communicate with several of the other hosts on the same network

3.7.1 You can communicate with at least one other host on the same network
- 3.7.1.1 You cannot communicate with at least one of the other hosts
  - 3.7.1.1.1 Ask the customer to verify that the IP address and subnet mask of the local host are correct
  - 3.7.1.1.2 Ask the customer to verify that all hosts on the local network are using the same subnet mask
  - 3.7.1.1.3 Ask the customer to verify that the default (gateway) router IP address is correct
  - 3.7.1.1.4 If problem is not resolved, call the next level of support
- 3.7.1.2 You can communicate with all of the other hosts on the network
  - 3.7.1.2.1 Continue with the next task

3.7.2 You cannot communicate with any of the other hosts on the same network

3.7.2.1 Ask the customer to verify that the IP address and subnet mask of the local host are correct

3.7.2.2 Ask the customer to verify that all hosts on the local network are using the same subnet mask

3.7.2.3 Ask the customer to verify that the default (gateway) router IP address is correct

3.7.2.4 If problem is not resolved, call the next level of support

## 3.8 If the network is a WAN or consists of multiple networks, use ping to verify that you can communicate with a host on another network

3.8.1 Ask the customer to verify that the default (gateway) router IP address is correct

3.8.2 Ask the customer to verify that the routing tables in the local host and the default router are correct

3.8.3 Call the next level of support

3.8.3.1 If problem is resolved, you are finished

3.8.3.2 If the problem is not resolved and you are confident that the hardware covered under the maintenance agreement is properly functioning, advise the customer that the problem resides with components not covered by the maintenance agreement

# 4 Diagnose problems that affect multiple nodes (on the same or different networks)

## 4.1 Are all the failing nodes on the same network (as indicated by the customer)?

4.1.1 No, the failing nodes are on different networks (as indicated by the customer)

4.1.1.1 Diagnose each failing node using the single node approach (see above)

4.1.2 Yes, all failing nodes are on the same network (as indicated by the customer)

4.1.2.1 Are all the nodes on this network failing (as indicated by the customer)?

4.1.2.1.1 Yes, all nodes on this network are failing (as indicated by the customer)

4.1.2.1.1.1 Check configuration at each node

4.1.2.1.1.1.1 Use DMIT to verify and correct as needed the configuration options (verify with the customer the IP address, netmask, hardware config as appropriate)

4.1.2.1.1.1.2 Continue with the next task

4.1.2.1.1.2 Remove nodes from the network to isolate the problem while checking the cables for physical integrity and damage

4.1.2.1.1.2.1 If network is telephone twisted pair on an Ethernet hub

4.1.2.1.1.2.1.1 Disconnect nodes one by one until the network works

4.1.2.1.1.2.1.2 Step A: Connect additional nodes one by one until network fails
4.1.2.1.1.2.1.3 Identify that node as a failing node
4.1.2.1.1.2.1.4 Disconnect the failing node
4.1.2.1.1.2.1.5 Repeat the above steps from Step A until all nodes have been tested and identified as failing or not failing
4.1.2.1.1.2.2 If network is 10BaseT
4.1.2.1.1.2.2.1 Divide the network into two smaller networks and test each one
4.1.2.1.1.2.3 If network is Token Ring
4.1.2.1.1.2.3.1 Twisted Pair Hub/MAU
4.1.2.1.1.2.3.1.1 Disconnect each one in turn and test the remaining network
4.1.2.1.1.2.3.2 Multiple MAUs
4.1.2.1.1.2.3.2.1 Isolate the MAUs one by one and test remaining network
4.1.2.1.1.2.4 If network is ZTM
4.1.2.1.1.2.4.1 Remove each in turn from the ZTM switch and test remaining network
4.1.2.1.1.2.5 If network is GDDI
4.1.2.1.1.2.5.1 Remove from the GDDI loop and test remaining network
4.1.2.1.1.2.6 Did you identify which node(s) are failing?
4.1.2.1.1.2.6.1 Yes, failing nodes were identified
4.1.2.1.1.2.6.1.1 Diagnose using single node diagnostic procedure
4.1.2.1.1.2.6.2 No, failing nodes were not identified
4.1.2.1.1.2.6.2.1 Continue with the next task
4.1.2.1.1.2.7 Check other network components on the local network
4.1.2.1.1.2.7.1 If all of the network components are covered under the maintenance agreement
4.1.2.1.1.2.7.1.1 Call the next level of support
4.1.2.1.1.2.7.2 If some of the network components are not covered under the maintenance agreement and you are confident that the covered components are not at fault
4.1.2.1.1.2.7.2.1 Ask the customer to perform problem determination on the noncovered components
4.1.2.1.2 No, fewer than all the nodes on this network are failing (as indicated by the customer)
4.1.2.1.2.1 Check configuration at each node
4.1.2.1.2.1.1 Use DMIT to verify and correct as needed the configuration options (verify with the customer the IP address, netmask, hardware config as appropriate)
4.1.2.1.2.2 Verify that each host has been physically connected to the appropriate network component
4.1.2.1.2.3 Verify the physical integrity of the cables
4.1.2.1.2.4 Check other network components on the same network

4.1.2.1.2.4.1 If all of the network components are covered under the maintenance agreement
   4.1.2.1.2.4.1.1 Call the next level of support
4.1.2.1.2.4.2 If some of the network components are not covered under the maintenance agreement and you are confident that the covered components are not at fault
   4.1.2.1.2.4.2.1 Ask the customer to perform problem determination on the noncovered components

# Appendix C: Example of Using a Structured-English Outline to Capture Complex Logic

## 1 Take a call
### 1.1 Make yourself available to take calls
    1.1.1 Do one of the following:
        1.1.1.1 Press *AutIn* on the telephone
            1.1.1.1.1 Result: The *AutIn* green light shines
        1.1.1.2 Click *Avail* in SDPhone
            1.1.1.2.1 Result: The *AutIn* green light shines

### 1.2 Listen for an incoming call
    1.2.1 When a call arrives, you will hear a beep and a whisper
        1.2.1.1 Examples of whispers:
            1.2.1.1.1 "Software"
            1.2.1.1.2 "AIX"
            1.2.1.1.3 "Rational"
            1.2.1.1.4 "Return caller"

### 1.3 Introduce yourself and ask if this is a new or existing call
    1.3.1 Say, "My name is [your first and last name]. Is this for a new or existing call?"

### 1.4 Is this for a new or existing call?
    1.4.1 How to decide if it is new or existing, if the caller does not know:
        1.4.1.1 If the caller is calling on an issue or request that he or she has previously made to ABC SERVICE CENTER, a PMR should have already been created, so it is an existing call
        1.4.1.2 If the caller is calling with a new request that he or she has *not* previously made to ABC SERVICE CENTER, then it is a new call
            1.4.1.2.1 The new request could be for anything, such as:
            1.4.1.2.2 Service for a software product
            1.4.1.2.3 A request for TSR
            1.4.1.2.4 A request to talk to a duty manager
    1.4.2 Case A: New Call
        1.4.2.1 Ask the caller, "May I have your customer number or serial number?"

1.4.2.2 Did the caller provide one or both of the following: a customer number or serial number?
1.4.2.3 Case A: Yes
1.4.2.3.1 Record on paper or in MS Notepad the information
1.4.2.3.2 Continue the procedure
1.4.2.4 Case B: No
1.4.2.4.1 Record on paper or in MS Notepad that the customer could not provide a customer number or serial number
1.4.3 Case B: Existing Call
1.4.3.1 Ask the caller, "May I have your PMR number and branch?"
1.4.3.2 Verify the PMR number with the customer
1.4.3.2.1 Example: Say "Thank you, that's PMR xxxxxx, branch xxx?"
1.4.3.3 Record on paper or in MS Notepad the information

# 2 Is this a new or existing call?

# 3 Case A: New call

## 3.1 Did the caller provide the customer number, serial number, both, or neither?

## 3.2 Case A: Customer number

3.2.1 [label 120] Type the customer number in the *Customer Number* field in the *Caller Verification* screen in CCMS Call Center

## 3.3 Case B: Serial number

3.3.1 [label 1006] Type the last five digits of the serial number in the *Serial* field in the *Caller Verification* screen in CCMS Call Center

## 3.4 Case C: Both customer number and serial number

3.4.1 Is this failing product likely to be serial number entitled?
3.4.1.1 How to decide
3.4.1.1.1 Base operating system products are likely to be serial number entitled; most middleware products are not
3.4.2 Case A: Yes
3.4.2.1 Type the last five digits of the serial number in the Serial field in the *Caller Verification* screen in CCMS Call Center
3.4.3 Case B: No
3.4.3.1 Type the customer number in the *Customer Number* field in the *Caller Verification* screen in CCMS Call Center

## 3.5 Case D: Neither

3.5.1 Identify the caller's issue if you haven't already done so
3.5.1.1 If you have not done so, ask the caller for the failing product and the version and release
3.5.1.1.1 Ask, "What product are you needing assistance with today?"

3.5.1.1.2 Ask, "What is the version and release of the product?"
    3.5.1.1.2.1 Verify the information with the customer
        3.5.1.1.2.1.1 Examples:
            3.5.1.1.2.1.1.1 "Thank you, [Mr., Miss] [last name], was that xyz?"
            3.5.1.1.2.1.1.2 "Xyz?"
    3.5.1.1.3 Record the caller's response on paper or in MS Notepad
3.5.1.2 If you have not done so, ask, "What is the operating system and its version and release?"
    3.5.1.2.1 Record the caller's response on paper or in MS Notepad
    3.5.1.2.2 Verify the information with the customer
    3.5.1.2.3 Is the failing product a zSeries or middleware product running on the zSeries operating system?
    3.5.1.2.4 Case A: Yes
        3.5.1.2.4.1 Ask the caller, "Is this a usage or defect issue?"
            3.5.1.2.4.1.1 Verify the information with the customer
    3.5.1.2.5 Case B: No
        3.5.1.2.5.1 Verify the information with the caller
        3.5.1.2.5.2 Continue the procedure
    3.5.1.2.6 Record the caller's response on paper or in MS Notepad
3.5.1.3 Is this a zSeries product or a product that runs on the zSeries platform?
3.5.1.4 Case A: Yes
    3.5.1.4.1 Ask, "Is this a usage or defect issue?"
    3.5.1.4.2 Record the caller's response on paper or in MS Notepad
3.5.1.5 Case B: No
    3.5.1.5.1 Continue the procedure
3.5.1.6 If you have not done so, ask, "May I have a brief description of your problem or question?"
    3.5.1.6.1 Record the caller's response on paper or in MS Notepad
    3.5.1.6.2 Verify the information with the customer

3.5.2 Determine if the failing product is automatically entitled for free support under a default service package other than the Registration Discrepancy service package
    3.5.2.1 How to determine if the failing product is entitled to free support
        3.5.2.1.1 All of the following have free telephone support
            3.5.2.1.1.1 For zSeries defect issues:
                3.5.2.1.1.1.1 All zSeries defect issues, including Catia on zSeries
                      3.5.2.1.1.1.1.1 Record on paper or in MS Notepad the following: Select the *US ES* entitlement center (EC) and select the *Defect* service package
                3.5.2.1.1.1.2 *Any* Shop zSeries issues
                      3.5.2.1.1.1.2.1 Record on paper or in MS Notepad the following: Select the *US ES* entitlement center (EC) and select the *Service Support for Shop zSeries* service package
                3.5.2.1.1.1.3 All usage support issues for Candle Omegamon products running on zSeries

3.5.2.1.1.1.3.1 Record on paper or in MS Notepad the following: Select the *US ES* entitlement center (EC) and select the Candle/Omegamon/Command CTR Usage SUPT service package

3.5.2.1.1.2 For AS400 issues:
3.5.2.1.1.2.1 All 5250 Emulation without Client Access
3.5.2.1.1.2.1.1 Record on paper or in MS Notepad the following: Select the *US AS/400* entitlement center (EC) and select the *Non-Entitled Products* service package
3.5.2.1.1.2.2 Performance Management 400 (PM400)
3.5.2.1.1.2.2.1 Record on paper or in MS Notepad the following: Select the *US AS/400* entitlement center (EC) and select the *AS/400 PM/400 – Service Agent Option* service package
3.5.2.1.1.2.3 Performance Edge
3.5.2.1.1.2.3.1 Record on paper or in MS Notepad the following: Select the *US AS/400* entitlement center (EC) and select the *AS/400 PM/400 – Service Agent Option* service package
3.5.2.1.1.2.4 Service Director
3.5.2.1.1.2.4.1 Record on paper or in MS Notepad the following: Select the *US AS/400* entitlement center (EC) and select the *AS/400 PM/400 – Service Agent Option* service package
3.5.2.1.1.2.5 License Keys (failures/problems)
3.5.2.1.1.2.5.1 Record on paper or in MS Notepad the following: Select the *US AS/400* entitlement center (EC) and select the *Non-Entitled Products* service package

3.5.2.1.1.3 For AIX issues:
3.5.2.1.1.3.1 Catia version 4
3.5.2.1.1.3.1.1 Record on paper or in MS Notepad the following: Select the *US AIX* entitlement center (EC) and select the *Catia V4/V5 Non-Entitled Default* service package

3.5.2.1.1.4 For PC (xSeries) issues:
3.5.2.1.1.4.1 Catia version 4
3.5.2.1.1.4.1.1 Record on paper or in MS Notepad the following: Select the *US PC* entitlement center (EC) and select the Catia *V4/V5 Non-Entitled Default* service package

3.5.2.1.1.5 For RSS Store Systems issues:
3.5.2.1.1.5.1 All RSS Store Systems *driver* support issues
3.5.2.1.1.5.1.1 Record on paper or in MS Notepad the following: Select the *Store Systems* entitlement center (EC) and select the *RSS Free Driver Support* service package

3.5.3 Is the failing product automatically entitled for free support?

3.5.4 Case A: Yes
3.5.4.1 Record on paper or in MS Notepad that the customer is entitled to free support for the failing product
3.5.4.1.1 Note: You will need this information later in this procedure when you are asked if the customer is entitled to free support

3.5.4.2 Goto [label 008] [Go to the first part of the logic for a registration discrepancy; then branch out of registration discrepancy to finish the procedure]

3.5.5 Case B: No

3.5.5.1 Record on paper or in MS Notepad that the customer is *not* entitled to free support for the failing product

3.5.5.1.1 Note: You will need this information later in this procedure when you are asked if the customer is entitled to free support

3.5.5.2 Identify the caller's issue if you haven't already done so

3.5.5.2.1 If you have not done so, ask the caller for the failing product (version and release)

3.5.5.2.1.1 Ask, "What product are you needing assistance with today?"

3.5.5.2.1.1.1 Verify the information with the customer

3.5.5.2.1.1.1.1 Examples:

3.5.5.2.1.1.1.1.1 "Thank you, [Mr., Miss] [last name], was that xyz?"

3.5.5.2.1.1.1.1.2 "Xyz?"

3.5.5.2.2 If you have not done so, ask, "What is the version and release of the product?"

3.5.5.2.2.1 Record the caller's response on paper or in MS Notepad

3.5.5.2.2.2 Verify the information with the customer

3.5.5.2.3 If you have not done so, ask, "What is the operating system and its version and release?"

3.5.5.2.3.1 Record the caller's response on paper or in MS Notepad

3.5.5.2.3.2 Verify the information with the customer

3.5.5.2.3.3 Is the failing product a zSeries or middleware product running on the zSeries operating system?

3.5.5.2.3.4 Case A: Yes

3.5.5.2.3.4.1 Ask the caller, "Is this a usage or defect issue?"

3.5.5.2.3.4.1.1 Verify the information with the customer

3.5.5.2.3.5 Case B: No

3.5.5.2.3.5.1 Verify the information with the caller

3.5.5.2.3.5.2 Continue the procedure

3.5.5.2.3.6 Record the caller's response on paper or in MS Notepad

3.5.5.2.4 If you have not done so, ask, "May I have a brief description of your problem or question?"

3.5.5.2.4.1 Record the caller's response on paper or in MS Notepad

3.5.5.2.4.2 Verify the information with the customer

3.5.5.3 If you have not already asked, ask "May I have your company name?"

3.5.5.4 Record on paper or in MS Notepad the information

3.5.5.5 Goto [label 008] [Create a registration discrepancy]

## 3.6 Verify that US *HW/NUMA* is selected in the *Ent. Centers* list

3.6.1 Note: CCMS Call Center should have been previously configured so that all ECs are searched when you select US *HW/NUMA* in the *Ent. Centers* list

## 3.7 Click *Search* (or press *Enter*)

3.7.1 Results:

3.7.1.1 The system searches all entitlement centers for customer contracts

3.7.1.2 Those entitlement centers that are associated with that customer number are listed in the *EC Search Results* list at the bottom of the screen

## 3.8 [label 100] Do any ECs appear in the EC Results list?
## 3.9 Case A: Yes
  3.9.1 Is this a new or existing call?
  3.9.2 Case A: New call
    3.9.2.1 Identify the caller's issue if you haven't already done so
      3.9.2.1.1 If you have not done so, ask the caller for the failing product and the version and release
        3.9.2.1.1.1 Ask, "What product are you needing assistance with today?"
        3.9.2.1.1.2 Ask, "What is the version and release of the product?"
          3.9.2.1.1.2.1 Verify the information with the customer
            3.9.2.1.1.2.1.1 Examples:
              3.9.2.1.1.2.1.1.1 "Thank you, [Mr., Miss] [last name], was that xyz?"
            3.9.2.1.1.2.1.1.2 "Xyz?"
        3.9.2.1.1.3 Record the caller's response on paper or in MS Notepad
      3.9.2.1.2 If you have not done so, ask, "What is the operating system and its version and release?"
        3.9.2.1.2.1 Record the caller's response on paper or in MS Notepad
        3.9.2.1.2.2 Verify the information with the customer
        3.9.2.1.2.3 Is the failing product a zSeries or middleware product running on the zSeries operating system?
        3.9.2.1.2.4 Case A: Yes
          3.9.2.1.2.4.1 Ask the caller, "Is this a usage or defect issue?"
            3.9.2.1.2.4.1.1 Verify the information with the customer
        3.9.2.1.2.5 Case B: No
          3.9.2.1.2.5.1 Verify the information with the caller
          3.9.2.1.2.5.2 Continue the procedure
        3.9.2.1.2.6 Record the caller's response on paper or in MS Notepad
      3.9.2.1.3 If you have not done so, ask, "May I have a brief description of your problem or question?"
        3.9.2.1.3.1 Record the caller's response on paper or in MS Notepad
        3.9.2.1.3.2 Verify the information with the customer
  3.9.3 Case B: Existing call
    3.9.3.1 Continue the procedure

## 3.10 Case B: No
  3.10.1 What appeared: the *CCM Call Center Information* message window or a list of names in the *Name* list?
  3.10.2 Case A: The *CCM Call Center Information* message window
    3.10.2.1 Results: The *CCM Call Center Information* message window appears with the message "No hits were found for your search on any entitlement center"
    3.10.2.2 Click *Dismiss*
      3.10.2.2.1 Result: The *CCM Call Center Information* message window closes
  3.10.3 Case B: A list of names in the Name list

3.10.3.1 Continue the procedure
### 3.10.4 Is this a new or existing call?
### 3.10.5 Case A: New call
3.10.5.1 If you have not already done so, identify the caller's issue
3.10.5.1.1 If you have not done so, ask the caller "What product are you needing assistance with today?"
3.10.5.1.1.1 Verify the information with the customer
3.10.5.1.1.1.1 Examples:
3.10.5.1.1.1.1.1 "Thank you, [Mr., Miss] [last name], was that xyz?"
3.10.5.1.1.1.1.2 "Xyz?"
3.10.5.1.2 If you have not done so, ask, "What is the version and release of the product?"
3.10.5.1.2.1 Record the caller's response on paper or in MS Notepad
3.10.5.1.2.2 Verify the information with the customer
3.10.5.1.3 If you have not done so, ask, "What is the operating system and its version and release?"
3.10.5.1.3.1 Record the caller's response on paper or in MS Notepad
3.10.5.1.3.2 Verify the information with the customer
3.10.5.1.3.3 Is the failing product a zSeries or middleware product running on the zSeries operating system?
3.10.5.1.3.4 Case A: Yes
3.10.5.1.3.4.1 Ask the caller, "Is this a usage or defect issue?"
3.10.5.1.3.4.1.1 Verify the information with the customer
3.10.5.1.3.5 Case B: No
3.10.5.1.3.5.1 Verify the information with the caller
3.10.5.1.3.5.2 Continue the procedure
3.10.5.1.3.6 Record the caller's response on paper or in MS Notepad
3.10.5.1.4 If you have not done so, ask, "May I have a brief description of your problem or question?"
3.10.5.1.4.1 Record the caller's response on paper or in MS Notepad
3.10.5.1.4.2 Verify the information with the customer
### 3.10.6 Case B: Existing call
3.10.6.1 Continue the procedure
### 3.10.7 Did a list of callers appear in the *Name* list at the bottom of the window?
### 3.10.8 Case A: Yes
3.10.8.1 If you have not already done so, ask for the failing product information and problem description
3.10.8.1.1 Ask the caller for the failing product (version and release)
3.10.8.1.1.1 Ask, "What product are you needing assistance with today?"
3.10.8.1.1.1.1 Verify the information with the customer
3.10.8.1.1.1.1.1 Examples:
3.10.8.1.1.1.1.1.1 "Thank you, [Mr., Miss] [last name], was that xyz?"
3.10.8.1.1.1.1.2 "Xyz?"
3.10.8.1.2 Ask, "What is the version and release of the product?"
3.10.8.1.2.1 Record the caller's response on paper or in MS Notepad

3.10.8.1.2.2 Verify the information with the customer
3.10.8.1.3 Ask, "What is the operating system and its version and release?"
3.10.8.1.3.1 Record the caller's response on paper or in MS Notepad
3.10.8.1.3.2 Verify the information with the customer
3.10.8.1.3.3 Is the failing product a zSeries or middleware product running on the zSeries operating system?
3.10.8.1.3.4 Case A: Yes
3.10.8.1.3.4.1 Ask the caller, "Is this a usage or defect issue?"
3.10.8.1.3.4.1.1 Verify the information with the customer
3.10.8.1.3.5 Case B: No
3.10.8.1.3.5.1 Verify the information with the caller
3.10.8.1.3.5.2 Continue the procedure
3.10.8.1.3.6 Record the caller's response on paper or in MS Notepad
3.10.8.1.4 Ask, "May I have a brief description of your problem or question?"
3.10.8.1.4.1 Record the caller's response on paper or in MS Notepad
3.10.8.1.4.2 Verify the information with the customer
3.10.8.2 Determine which EC to search for entitlement based on the operating system and failing product
3.10.8.2.1 Note: In the steps that follow, do not entitle the PMR as a registration discrepancy before you apply the following strategy to search all applicable Entitlement Centers (ECs) based on the failing product and operating system that was given by the caller
3.10.8.2.2 If the caller's issue relates to an operating system
3.10.8.2.2.1 Search the EC for that operating system
3.10.8.2.3 If the caller's issue relates to middleware
3.10.8.2.3.1 Search the *Passport Advantage* EC first, then search the appropriate operating system EC
3.10.8.2.4 Search the following ECs, if they are listed in the *EC Search Results* list, in the following order:
3.10.8.2.4.1 *Passport EC*
3.10.8.2.4.2 *HW/NUMA EC*
3.10.8.2.4.3 *Store Systems EC*
3.10.8.2.5 Search any remaining ECs that you have not already searched
3.10.8.3 Is the appropriate EC already highlighted in the *Ent. Centers* list?
3.10.8.4 Case A: Yes
3.10.8.4.1 Goto [label 304]
3.10.8.5 Case B: No
3.10.8.5.1 Are your searching by customer number or serial number?
3.10.8.5.2 Case A: Customer number
3.10.8.5.2.1 Goto [label 908] [ask if it is serial number entitled and continue in the code at the very top]
3.10.8.5.3 Case B: Serial number
3.10.8.5.3.1 Ask the caller, "May I have your customer number?"
3.10.8.5.3.2 Did the caller provide a customer number?
3.10.8.5.3.3 Case A: Yes
3.10.8.5.3.3.1 Verify the customer number with the caller

3.10.8.5.3.3.2 Record on paper or in MS Notepad the customer number that the caller provided *and* the customer number that is in the *Customer Number* field on the *Caller Verification* window
    3.10.8.5.3.3.2.1 Notes:
        3.10.8.5.3.3.2.1.1 You will need to search both of these customer numbers for valid contracts
        3.10.8.5.3.3.2.1.2 Search first using the customer number that the caller provided
3.10.8.5.3.4 Case B: No
  3.10.8.5.3.4.1 Record on paper or in MS Notepad the customer number that is in the *Customer Number* field on the *Caller Verification* window
3.10.8.5.3.5 Click *Clear* in the *Caller Verification* window
  3.10.8.5.3.5.1 Results:
    3.10.8.5.3.5.1.1 All fields in the *Caller Verification* window are cleared
    3.10.8.5.3.5.1.2 The US *HW/NUMA* EC is highlighted in the *Ent Centers* list
3.10.8.5.3.6 Type the customer number in the *Customer Number* field
3.10.8.5.3.7 Click *Search*
  3.10.8.5.3.7.1 Result: The ECs associated with that customer number appear in the *EC Search Results* list
3.10.8.5.3.8 Goto [label 100] [jump up to the code a few lines earlier to ask if any ECs came up]
3.10.9 Case B: No
  3.10.9.1 Are you searching by customer number or serial number?
  3.10.9.2 Case A: Customer number
    3.10.9.2.1 Have you already tried to display the *ECs* for this customer number in CCMS?
      3.10.9.2.1.1 Notes:
        3.10.9.2.1.1.1 This question is asking if any ECs appeared in the *EC Search Results* list when you entered the customer number and clicked *Search*
        3.10.9.2.1.1.2 If no ECs appear when you entered and searched on the customer number, answer "Yes" to this question
    3.10.9.2.2 Case A: Yes
      3.10.9.2.2.1 Have you already searched *for ECs* using all of the serial numbers provided or associated with the call?
        3.10.9.2.2.1.1 Note: This question is asking if any ECs appeared in the *EC Search Results* list when you entered the serial number and clicked *Search*
      3.10.9.2.2.2 Case A: Yes
        3.10.9.2.2.2.1 Goto [label 2007] [Check the denied parties list in the code just below]
      3.10.9.2.2.3 Case B: No
        3.10.9.2.2.3.1 Do you have a serial number to search on?
        3.10.9.2.2.3.2 Case A: Yes
          3.10.9.2.2.3.2.1 Note: In the following steps, you will search by serial number
          3.10.9.2.2.3.2.2 Click *Clear*
            3.10.9.2.2.3.2.2.1 Results: All fields in the *Caller Verification* are cleared

3.10.9.2.2.3.2.3 Goto [label 1006] [Search by serial number in the code just above]
  3.10.9.2.2.3.3 Case B: No
    3.10.9.2.2.3.3.1 If you have not already done so, ask "Do you have a serial number for this product?"
    3.10.9.2.2.3.3.2 Did the caller provide a serial number?
    3.10.9.2.2.3.3.3 Case A: Yes
      3.10.9.2.2.3.3.3.1 Note: In the steps that follow, you will search for entitlement using the serial number provided because no ECs were associated with that customer number
      3.10.9.2.2.3.3.3.2 Record on paper or in MS Notepad the serial number provided
      3.10.9.2.2.3.3.3.3 Click *Clear*
      3.10.9.2.2.3.3.3.4 Result: All fields in the *Caller Verification* window are cleared
      3.10.9.2.2.3.3.3.5 Goto [label 1006] [Type in serial number in code just above to search by serial number]
  3.10.9.2.3 Case B: No
    3.10.9.2.3.1.1.1.1 Goto [label 2007] [Check the Denied Parties List]
3.10.9.2.4 Case B: No
  3.10.9.2.4.1 Note: In the following steps, you will search by customer number
  3.10.9.2.4.2 Do you have a customer number for this call?
  3.10.9.2.4.3 Case A: Yes
    3.10.9.2.4.3.1 Click *Clear*
      3.10.9.2.4.3.1.1 Result: All fields in the *Caller Verification* window are cleared
    3.10.9.2.4.3.2 Goto [label 120] [Type in customer number in code just above to search by customer number]
  3.10.9.2.4.4 Case B: No
    3.10.9.2.4.4.1 If you have not already done so, ask "Do you have a customer number for this product?"
    3.10.9.2.4.4.2 Did the caller provide a customer number?
    3.10.9.2.4.4.3 Case A: Yes
      3.10.9.2.4.4.3.1 Note: In the steps that follow, you will search for entitlement using the customer number provided because no ECs were associated with that serial number
      3.10.9.2.4.4.3.2 Record on paper or in MS Notepad the customer number provided
      3.10.9.2.4.4.3.3 Click *Clear*
        3.10.9.2.4.4.3.3.1 Result: All fields in the *Caller Verification* window are cleared
      3.10.9.2.4.4.3.4 Goto [label 120] [Type in customer number in code just above to search by customer number]
3.10.9.2.5 Case B: No
  3.10.9.2.5.1.1.1 Goto [label 2007] [Check the denied parties list in the code just below]

3.10.9.3 Case B: Serial number
  3.10.9.3.1 Have you already searched *for ECs* using this serial number?
    3.10.9.3.1.1 Note: This question is asking if any ECs appeared in the *EC Search Results* list when you entered the serial number and clicked *Search*
  3.10.9.3.2 Case A: Yes
    3.10.9.3.2.1 Have you already searched *for ECs* using all of the customer numbers associated with the call?
      3.10.9.3.2.1.1 This question is asking if any ECs appeared in the *EC Search Results* list when you entered the customer number and clicked *Search*
    3.10.9.3.2.2 Case A: Yes
      3.10.9.3.2.2.1 Goto [label 2007] [Check the denied parties list in the code just below]
    3.10.9.3.2.3 Case B: No
      3.10.9.3.2.3.1 Do you have a customer number to search on?
      3.10.9.3.2.3.2 Case A: Yes
        3.10.9.3.2.3.2.1 Note: In the following steps, you will search by customer number
        3.10.9.3.2.3.2.2 Click *Clear*
          3.10.9.3.2.3.2.2.1 Results: All fields in the *Caller Verification* window are cleared
        3.10.9.3.2.3.2.3 Goto [label 120] [Search by customer number in the code just above]
      3.10.9.3.2.3.3 Case B: No
        3.10.9.3.2.3.3.1 If you have not already done so, ask "Do you have a customer number?"
        3.10.9.3.2.3.3.2 Did the caller provide a customer number?
        3.10.9.3.2.3.3.3 Case A: Yes
          3.10.9.3.2.3.3.3.1 Click *Clear*
          3.10.9.3.2.3.3.3.2 Result: The fields in the *Caller Verification* window are cleared
          3.10.9.3.2.3.3.3.3 Goto [label 120]
        3.10.9.3.2.3.3.4 Case B: No
          3.10.9.3.2.3.3.4.1 Goto [label 2007]
  3.10.9.3.3 Case B: No
    3.10.9.3.3.1 Note: In the following steps, you will search by serial number
    3.10.9.3.3.2 Do you have a serial number for this call?
    3.10.9.3.3.3 Case A: Yes
      3.10.9.3.3.3.1 Click *Clear*
        3.10.9.3.3.3.1.1 Result: All fields in the *Caller Verification* window are cleared
      3.10.9.3.3.3.2 Goto [label 1006] [Type in serial number in code just above to search by serial number]
    3.10.9.3.3.4 Case B: No
      3.10.9.3.3.4.1 If you have not already done so, ask "Do you have a serial number for this product?"
      3.10.9.3.3.4.2 Did the caller provide a serial number?

3.10.9.3.3.4.3 Case A: Yes

3.10.9.3.3.4.3.1 Note: In the steps that follow, you will search for entitlement using the serial number provided because no ECs were associated with that customer number

3.10.9.3.3.4.3.2 Record on paper or in MS Notepad the serial number provided

3.10.9.3.3.4.3.3 Click *Clear*

3.10.9.3.3.4.3.3.1 Result: All fields in the *Caller Verification* window are cleared

3.10.9.3.3.4.3.4 Goto [label 1006] [Type in serial number in code just above to search by serial number]

3.10.9.3.4 Case B: No

3.10.9.3.4.1.1.1 [label 2007] Note: In the following steps, you will check the Denied Parties List to see if the company name or the caller's name is listed

3.10.9.3.4.1.1.2 Click the Lotus Notes icon in your Windows task bar

3.10.9.3.4.1.1.2.1 Result: Lotus Notes opens

3.10.9.3.4.1.1.3 Double click the *Denied Parties List* database in your Lotus Notes desktop

3.10.9.3.4.1.1.3.1 Result: The *Denied Parties List* database opens

3.10.9.3.4.1.1.4 Click Search DPL on the left side of the window

3.10.9.3.4.1.1.4.1 Result: The Search the *Denied Parties List* window appears

3.10.9.3.4.1.1.5 If you have not already done so, ask the caller, "May I have your name and your company name?"

3.10.9.3.4.1.1.6 Record on paper or in MS Notepad the caller's information

3.10.9.3.4.1.1.7 Do you want to search by the company name or by the caller's name?

3.10.9.3.4.1.1.7.1 Note: You should search by both the company name and the caller's name to see if either is on the list

3.10.9.3.4.1.1.8 Case A: Company name

3.10.9.3.4.1.1.8.1 [label 889988] Type the company name in the *Search for* field

3.10.9.3.4.1.1.8.2 Example: Search on "Marriott" for Marriott International

3.10.9.3.4.1.1.8.3 Click *Search*

3.10.9.3.4.1.1.8.4 Result: A list of denied parties matching the search criteria is displayed

3.10.9.3.4.1.1.8.5 Do you also want to search by the caller's name?

3.10.9.3.4.1.1.8.6 Case A: Yes

3.10.9.3.4.1.1.8.7 Click the close icon (x) in the upper right corner of the *DPL Search Results* tab page

3.10.9.3.4.1.1.8.8 Click *Search DPL* on the left side of the window

3.10.9.3.4.1.1.8.9 Goto [label 998899]

3.10.9.3.4.1.1.8.10 Case B: No

3.10.9.3.4.1.1.8.11 Continue the procedure

3.10.9.3.4.1.1.9 Case B: Caller's name

3.10.9.3.4.1.1.9.1 [label 998899] Note: When searching on a name, search on the portion that is most likely to find a hit

3.10.9.3.4.1.1.9.2 Type the caller's name in the *Search for* field

3.10.9.3.4.1.1.9.3 Click *Search*

3.10.9.3.4.1.1.9.4 Result: A list of denied parties matching the search criteria is displayed

3.10.9.3.4.1.1.9.5 Do you also want to search by the company name?

3.10.9.3.4.1.1.9.6 Case A: Yes

3.10.9.3.4.1.1.9.7 Click the close icon (x) in the upper right corner of the *DPL Search Results* tab page

3.10.9.3.4.1.1.9.8 Click *Search DPL* on the left side of the window

3.10.9.3.4.1.1.9.9 Goto [label 889988]

3.10.9.3.4.1.1.9.10 Case B: No

3.10.9.3.4.1.1.9.11 Continue the procedure

3.10.9.3.4.1.1.10 Did you find a likely match?

3.10.9.3.4.1.1.11 Case A: Yes

3.10.9.3.4.1.1.11.1 Is the likely match in the same country as either the company or the caller?

3.10.9.3.4.1.1.11.2 Case A: Yes

3.10.9.3.4.1.1.11.3 Double click the likely entry in the list

3.10.9.3.4.1.1.11.4 Result: Detailed information for the company or the individual appears

3.10.9.3.4.1.1.11.5 Read the information about the company or caller

3.10.9.3.4.1.1.11.6 Case B: No

3.10.9.3.4.1.1.11.7 Continue the procedure

3.10.9.3.4.1.1.11.8 Click the close icon (x) in the DPL Record Active

3.10.9.3.4.1.1.11.9 Click the close icon (x) in the DPL Search Results Tab

3.10.9.3.4.1.1.11.10 Click the close icon (x) in the Denied Parties List Search Tab

3.10.9.3.4.1.1.12 Case B: No

3.10.9.3.4.1.1.12.1 Continue the procedure

3.10.9.3.4.1.1.12.2 Click the close icon (x) in the DPL Search Results Tab

3.10.9.3.4.1.1.12.3 Click the close icon (x) in the Denied Parties List Search Tab

3.10.9.3.4.1.1.13 Click the minimize icon (-) in the upper right corner of Lotus Notes

3.10.9.3.4.1.1.13.1 Result: Lotus Notes minimized to the icon in the Windows task bar

3.10.9.3.4.1.1.14 Is the company name or the caller's name on the Denied Parties List?

3.10.9.3.4.1.1.15 Case A: Yes

3.10.9.3.4.1.1.15.1 Note: Do not create a PMR

3.10.9.3.4.1.1.15.2 Click the close icon (x) in any open windows for this PMR

3.10.9.3.4.1.1.15.3 Is the failing product a Lotus product?

3.10.9.3.4.1.1.15.4 Case A: Yes
3.10.9.3.4.1.1.15.5 Say, "To better assist you, I will now transfer you to the Lotus Console Team to discuss your support options"
3.10.9.3.4.1.1.15.6 Note: In the following steps, you will warm transfer the call to Lotus Console Team.
3.10.9.3.4.1.1.15.7 Press *Transfer* on the telephone or click *Transfer* in SDPhone
3.10.9.3.4.1.1.15.8 Dial the Lotus Console Team number.
3.10.9.3.4.1.1.15.9 When the Lotus Console Team member answers, say "My name is [your name]. I have a customer who is listed in the Denied Parties List."
3.10.9.3.4.1.1.15.10 When the Lotus Console Team member agrees to transfer caller over to him or her, press *Conference* on the telephone or click *Conf* in SDPhone
3.10.9.3.4.1.1.15.11 End of procedure: Handle a new or existing call
3.10.9.3.4.1.1.15.12 Case B: No
3.10.9.3.4.1.1.15.13 Say, "To better assist you, I will now transfer you to the software Entitlement Team (CET) to discuss your support options"
3.10.9.3.4.1.1.15.14 Note: In the following steps, you will warm transfer the call to Software CET: Extension 74161, option 0
3.10.9.3.4.1.1.15.15 Press *Transfer* on the telephone or click *Transfer* in SDPhone
3.10.9.3.4.1.1.15.16 Dial the Software CET number (Extension 74161, option 0)
3.10.9.3.4.1.1.15.17 When the Software CET team member answers, say "My name is [your name]. I have a customer who is listed in the Denied Parties List."
3.10.9.3.4.1.1.15.18 When the Software CET team member agrees to transfer caller over to him or her, press *Yes* to transfer the caller in SDPhone
3.10.9.3.4.1.1.15.19 End of procedure: Handle a new or existing call
3.10.9.3.4.1.1.16 Case B: No
3.10.9.3.4.1.1.16.1 Goto [label 008] [Create a registration discrepancy]

# 4 Case B: Existing Call
## 4.1 [Logic continues from here.]

# Appendix D: Example of a Content Analysis

## 1 Fundamental network concepts
### 1.1 Networking concepts
   1.1.1 Definition of a network
      1.1.1.1 Collection of interconnected hosts that share information
         1.1.1.1.1 Systems interconnected with wires or fibers
         1.1.1.1.2 Wires and fibers are attached to system adapter cards and other network components (hubs, routers, and switches)
         1.1.1.1.3 Signals are transmitted through the wires using specific hardware and software protocols (data packaging and signaling standards)
         1.1.1.1.4 Data moves through the physical network using these network protocols
   1.1.2 Network control
      1.1.2.1 Why network control is necessary
      1.1.2.2 Types of network control
         1.1.2.2.1 Hierarchical network (e.g., RTLL, CSAM, BRL/TRU)
            1.1.2.2.1.1 One central host that controls the entire network
            1.1.2.2.1.2 One host (system) within the network controls all data flow across the network
            1.1.2.2.1.3 Requires adapter cards
         1.1.2.2.2 Peer-to-peer network (TCP/IP, BDL, ZAQ201, ZPPN)
            1.1.2.2.2.1 All the hosts in the network are equal (peers to each other) and equally control the network
            1.1.2.2.2.2 No central controlling host required; each peer has its own network control program
            1.1.2.2.2.3 Network control program must be running in each peer
            1.1.2.2.2.4 SS/6000Z SPs are peer-to-peer
            1.1.2.2.2.5 Requires adapter cards
         1.1.2.2.3 Net-centric network (e.g., GGL, frame relay)
            1.1.2.2.3.1 Does not require a host
            1.1.2.2.3.2 No network operating system
            1.1.2.2.3.3 Any host can be attached to this type of network
            1.1.2.2.3.4 Requires some kind of box to attach to the network (e.g., 9125, router)
   1.1.3 Network cabling [how to recognize cable type and connector]
      1.1.3.1 Why you need to know about network cables

- 1.1.3.1.1 Each topology specifies valid cable types
- 1.1.3.1.2 To check the physical integrity of the cable and connector
- 1.1.3.2 Types of network cables
  - 1.1.3.2.1 Type 1
    - 1.1.3.2.1.1 Best wire but bulky and expensive
    - 1.1.3.2.1.2 Black box connector (like the old token ring)
  - 1.1.3.2.2 Type 5 (STP: Shielded Twisted Pair)
    - 1.1.3.2.2.1 Next best wire but fairly expensive
    - 1.1.3.2.2.2 RJ-45 connector
  - 1.1.3.2.3 UTP: Unshielded twisted pair
    - 1.1.3.2.3.1 Cheap but susceptible to noise
    - 1.1.3.2.3.2 RJ-45 connector
  - 1.1.3.2.4 Coax
    - 1.1.3.2.4.1 Strong and shielded but uncommon (used mainly for thin net)
    - 1.1.3.2.4.2 Requires termination
      - 1.1.3.2.4.2.1 Termination requires 50 Ohm terminators
    - 1.1.3.2.4.3 BNC
  - 1.1.3.2.5 Fiber
    - 1.1.3.2.5.1 Fastest and most expensive but most reliable
    - 1.1.3.2.5.2 Two kinds
      - 1.1.3.2.5.2.1 Multi-mode
        - 1.1.3.2.5.2.1.1 Bigger fiber but slower speed
        - 1.1.3.2.5.2.1.2 Usually an LED driver
      - 1.1.3.2.5.2.2 Single-mode
        - 1.1.3.2.5.2.2.1 Thinner but faster speeds
        - 1.1.3.2.5.2.2.2 Laser (avoid looking at the fiber to prevent eye damage)
    - 1.1.3.2.5.3 ST-ST connection?
- 1.1.4 Network topologies
  - 1.1.4.1 Network topologies
    - 1.1.4.1.1 Ring (e.g., cash register store loop)
      - 1.1.4.1.1.1 Shielded twisted-pair cabling
      - 1.1.4.1.1.2 Rules [get from LAN concepts Redbook]
        - 1.1.4.1.1.2.1 Distance
        - 1.1.4.1.1.2.2 Number of connections
        - 1.1.4.1.1.2.3 Number of hosts per segment
    - 1.1.4.1.2 Bus (e.g., Ethernet)
      - 1.1.4.1.2.1 Coax cabling
      - 1.1.4.1.2.2 T-connectors
      - 1.1.4.1.2.3 Terminators
      - 1.1.4.1.2.4 Rules [get from LAN concepts Redbook]
        - 1.1.4.1.2.4.1 Distance
        - 1.1.4.1.2.4.2 Number of connections
        - 1.1.4.1.2.4.3 Number of hosts per segment
    - 1.1.4.1.3 Star (e.g., twisted-pair Ethernet with hub or twisted-pair token ring with hub)
      - 1.1.4.1.3.1 Shielded or unshielded twisted pair cabling

1.1.4.1.3.2 Hub
1.1.4.1.3.3 Rules [get from LAN concepts Redbook]
1.1.4.1.3.3.1 Distance
1.1.4.1.3.3.2 Number of connections
1.1.4.1.3.3.3 Number of hosts per segment
1.1.4.1.4 Star-ring (e.g., token ring)
1.1.4.1.4.1 Type 1 cable, Type 5 cable, or shielded twisted-pair cabling
1.1.4.1.4.2 One or more MAUs and/or CAUs
1.1.4.1.4.2.1 Access ports
1.1.4.1.4.2.2 Ring in and ring out (interconnect MAUs or CAUs)
1.1.4.1.4.3 Rules [get from LAN concepts Redbook]
1.1.4.1.4.3.1 Distance
1.1.4.1.4.3.2 Number of connections
1.1.4.1.4.3.3 Number of hosts per segment
1.1.4.1.4.3.4 Speed
1.1.4.1.5 Exercise: Validating customer LAN configurations
1.1.5 ISO model
1.1.5.1 The ISO model and how it functions
1.1.5.1.1 What is the ISO model?
1.1.5.1.1.1 Was an attempt to standardize the network industry to allow interoperability of networking hardware
1.1.5.1.2 Why understand the ISO model?
1.1.5.1.2.1 To understand how the network protocols (such as TCP/IP) function (see below for detailed discussion of network protocols)
1.1.5.1.2.2 To understand how routers and bridges function
1.1.5.1.3 ISO model has 7 layers
1.1.5.1.3.1 Level 1: Physical Layer
1.1.5.1.3.1.1 Physical network interface
1.1.5.1.3.1.2 Has the bit encoding and synchronization
1.1.5.1.3.1.3 Has the electrical and mechanical specifications (e.g., the ISO model specifies that token ring use the standard 802.5 electrical and physical specification)
1.1.5.1.3.2 Level 2: Data link layer
1.1.5.1.3.2.1 Station-to-station information transfer
1.1.5.1.3.2.2 Error detection with optional error recovery
1.1.5.1.3.3 Level 3: Network layer
1.1.5.1.3.3.1 Network addressing and routing
1.1.5.1.3.3.2 Optional flow control
1.1.5.1.3.4 Level 4: Transport layer
1.1.5.1.3.4.1 N to N information transport
1.1.5.1.3.4.2 The interface between thc lower communication layers and the upper communication layers
1.1.5.1.3.5 Level 5: Session layer
1.1.5.1.3.5.1 Synchronization of data exchange
1.1.5.1.3.5.2 Regulates the send and receive of data flow
1.1.5.1.3.6 Level 6: Presentation layer

    1.1.5.1.3.6.1 Presentation of data in a manner that can be understood by both sender and receiver
   1.1.5.1.3.7 Level 7: Application layer
    1.1.5.1.3.7.1 The interface between the communication functions and the actual application
    1.1.5.1.3.7.2 Has direct end-user services such as FTP, mail, telnet, and SNMP
  1.1.5.1.4 How the 7 layers communicate with each other
   1.1.5.1.4.1 Ports
   1.1.5.1.4.1.1
   1.1.5.1.4.2 Sockets
   1.1.5.1.4.2.1
  1.1.5.1.5 Examples of how each layer of the ISO model can be implemented in practice (e.g., Level 1 can be handled through a token ring or an Ethernet adapter card) [IBM wall chart is available showing layers and how they can be implemented]
  1.1.5.1.6 How data flows (up and down through the layers) from end-user to end-user through a network that uses the ISO model (end-to-end communication)
 1.1.5.2 Software suites that use the ISO model
  1.1.5.2.1 Definition: A software suite is ISO compliant software that defines how data is physically and logically moved across the network to preserve the data's integrity
  1.1.5.2.2 Each software suite implements the ISO model (all 7 layers)
  1.1.5.2.3 TCP/IP
   1.1.5.2.3.1 How TCP/IP functions in the ISO model
    1.1.5.2.3.1.1 Layers 1 & 2 are the IP part (physical transport)
     1.1.5.2.3.1.1.1 IP is considered a connectionless protocol
      1.1.5.2.3.1.1.1.1 No data or error recovery (data recovery and error recovery is left to higher network layers)
      1.1.5.2.3.1.1.1.2 Does not care what physical layer is used (e.g., token ring or Ethernet)
      1.1.5.2.3.1.1.1.3 Packets can be received in random order and are reassembled in proper order at the transport level
     1.1.5.2.3.1.1.2 IP packets
     1.1.5.2.3.1.1.3 IP addressing
     1.1.5.2.3.1.1.4 Subnet masking
     1.1.5.2.3.1.1.5 Routing and routing tables
    1.1.5.2.3.1.2 Layers 3 through 7 are the software component parts (FTP, UDP, SNMP, mail, telnet, etc.)
  1.1.5.2.4 Other software suites
 1.1.6 Types of networks
  1.1.6.1 LANS
   1.1.6.1.1 Definition of LAN (Local Area Network)
    1.1.6.1.1.1 Geographically small network made up of one or more network topologies (including two or more of the same topology)

1.1.6.1.1.2 Simple (one topography only) to complex (many different topographies interconnected on the same LAN)
1.1.6.1.2 Segments
 1.1.6.1.2.1 Smallest physical unit of a network that makes up a network in-and-of itself
 1.1.6.1.2.2 Has one topology
 1.1.6.1.2.3 Segments can be interconnected through bridges and routers to form more complex LANs
1.1.6.1.3 Bridges
 1.1.6.1.3.1 A network component that is used to connect both similar and dissimilar LAN segments together to form a larger network
 1.1.6.1.3.2 Are relatively "dumb" network components that pass all network traffic passively
 1.1.6.1.3.3 Function only in the physical layer (layers 1 and 2 in the ISO model)
 1.1.6.1.3.4 Two kinds of bridging
  1.1.6.1.3.4.1 Transparent bridging
   1.1.6.1.3.4.1.1
  1.1.6.1.3.4.2 Source route bridging
   1.1.6.1.3.4.2.1
 1.1.6.1.3.5 ARP/RARP Tables
  1.1.6.1.3.5.1 Takes the network address (e.g., IP address) and maps it to a MAC address
   1.1.6.1.3.5.1.1 Media Access Control (MAC) address
    1.1.6.1.3.5.1.1.1 Physical address of the adapter card
1.1.6.1.4 Routers
 1.1.6.1.4.1 Are more intelligent network components
 1.1.6.1.4.2 Function from the physical layer (layers 1 and 2) through the transmission layer (layer 3)
 1.1.6.1.4.3 Have knowledge of the entire network through dynamic routing tables (see IP discussion for detail on routing tables)
  1.1.6.1.4.3.1 Can intelligently forward data on to its destination
 1.1.6.1.4.4 Have more filtering capability (e.g., can screen out traffic that is not destined for a given network)
 1.1.6.1.4.5 Have their own operating system
  1.1.6.1.4.5.1 RIP
   1.1.6.1.4.5.1.1 An older technology
   1.1.6.1.4.5.1.2 Susceptible to network slowdowns because it does not handle network traffic efficiently
  1.1.6.1.4.5.2 OFPF (Open Fastest Path First)
   1.1.6.1.4.5.2.1 Better, newer technology
   1.1.6.1.4.5.2.2 Determined through routing tables
1.1.6.1.5 Backbones
 1.1.6.1.5.1 A segment that is only used to connect other segments together
 1.1.6.1.5.2 Does not have a host connection
 1.1.6.1.5.3 Interconnected to other segments through a bridge or router

1.1.6.1.6 Types of LANs
　1.1.6.1.6.1 Token ring
　　1.1.6.1.6.1.1 Topology
　　　1.1.6.1.6.1.1.1 Star hub
　　　1.1.6.1.6.1.1.2 Star ring
　　1.1.6.1.6.1.2 Physical layer protocol
　　　1.1.6.1.6.1.2.1 Token ring goes through five phases when getting on the ring
　　　　1.1.6.1.6.1.2.1.1 Phase 1: Test the adapter card
　　　　1.1.6.1.6.1.2.1.2 Phase 2: Sends the phantom 5 voltage to the MAU or the CAU to open the relay
　　　　1.1.6.1.6.1.2.1.3 Phase 3: Determine if anyone else is out on the ring
　　　　1.1.6.1.6.1.2.1.4 Phase 4: Determine the active monitor (lowest MAC address)
　　　　1.1.6.1.6.1.2.1.5 Phase 5: Rebuild the network and determine who nearest upstream neighbor is

[The content analysis continues from here.]

# Bibliography

Brookfield, Stephen D. *Understanding and Facilitating Adult Learning: A Comprehensive Analysis of Principles and Effective Practices*. New York: Jossey-Bass, 1991.

Clark, Ruth C, and Richard E. Mayer. *e-Learning and the Science of Instruction: Proven Guidelines for Consumers and Designers of Multimedia Learning*. New York: John Wiley and Sons, 2003.

Clark, Ruth C., and Chopeta Lyons. *Graphics for Learning: Proven Guidelines for Planning, Designing, and Evaluating Visuals in Training Materials*. New York: Pfeiffer, 2004.

Fleming, Malcolm, and W. Howard Levie. *Instructional Message Design: Principles from the Behavioral Sciences*. Englewood Cliffs, New Jersey: Educational Technology Publications, 1978.

Gagne, Robert M. *The Conditions of Learning*, 3rd ed. New York: Holt, Rinehart, and Winston, 1975.

Higbee, Kenneth L. *Your Memory: How It Works and How to Improve It*, 2nd ed. New York: Marlow and Company, 2001.

Hoffman, John S. *Instructional Development—Step by Step: Six Easy Steps for Developing Lean, Effective, and Motivational Instruction*. Bloomington, IN: iUniverse, 2013.

Horn, Robert E. *Mapping Hypertext: The Analysis, Organization, and Display of Knowledge for the Next Generation of On-Line Text and Graphics*. Waltham, Massachusetts: Information Mapping, 1990.

Horton, William. *Designing Web-Based Training: How to Teach Anyone Anything Anywhere Anytime.* New York: John Wiley and Sons, 2000.

Horton, William, and Katherine Horton. *E-Learning Tools and Technologies.* New York: John Wiley and Sons, 2003.

Mager, Robert F. *Measuring Instructional Results,* 3rd ed. Atlanta, Georgia: The Center for Effective Performance, 1997.

Mager, Robert F. *Preparing Instructional Objectives*, 3rd ed. Atlanta, Georgia: The Center for Effective Performance, 1997.

Mager, Robert F., and Peter Pipe. *Analyzing Performance Problems, or You Really Oughta Wanna*, 3rd ed. Atlanta, Georgia: The Center for Effective Performance, 1997.

Mayhew, Deborah J. *Principles and Guidelines in Software User Interface Design*. New York: Prentice Hall, 1992.

Medsker, Karen L., and Robert M. Gagne. *The Conditions of Learning: Training Applications.* Belmont, California: Wadsworth Publishing, 1995.

Williams, Robin. *The Non-Designer's Design Book: Design and Typographic Principles for the Visual Novice.* San Francisco, California: Peachpit Press, 1994.

Wilson, Arthur L. and Elisabeth R. Hayes. *Handbook of Adult and Continuing Education*. New York: Jossey-Bass, 2000.

# Index

## A

action step. *See* procedure, action step
adult learners  71
adult learning principles  83
advanced organizers  24
analysis (Bloom)  56
animation, used to gain attention  18
application (Bloom)  56
association  26
attention
  bottlenecks to  16
  gaining  16, 18, 26
  maintaining  20, 26
attitude
  as part of Gagne's taxonomy  53
  as part of SKA taxonomy  47
audience. *See* training requirements
audience analysis. *See* training requirements

## B

background. *See* sensory perception, background
best practices  442
blended learning. *See also* instructional delivery system
  advantages of  322
  definition of  140, 320
  disadvantages of  323
  IBM 4-Tier Blended Learning Model. *See* IBM 4-Tier Blended Learning Model
  when to consider  321
Bloom, Benjamin  55
bottlenecks to learning. *See* learning, bottlenecks to
brain
  different from a computer  11
Brookfield, Stephen D.  72

## C

case statement (in structured-English outlines). *See* structured-English outlines, case statement
channel capacity  95
  ways to manage  95
cheat sheets. *See* job aids
checkpoint question. *See* exam
chunking  26, 95, 349, 470
Clark, Ruth C.  ix, 330, 333, 393
classification
  as a type of information (Horn)  61
  of information into its type  62
closure. *See* sensory perception, closure
cognition. *See also* learning
  bottlenecks to higher-level  17

cognitive encoding techniques  10
cognitive framework  432. *See* also cognition, mental models
cognitive strategy (Gagne)  52
higher-level  16, 24
layering information. *See* information layering
mental models  77, 79, 96, 432
multi-channel multi-sensory stimuli  23
ways to influence  24
cognitive framework. *See* cognition, cognitive framework
cognitive strategy. *See* cognition, cognitive strategy
color
  in sensory perception. *See* sensory perception, color
  used to gain attention  18
  used to maintain attention  20
comprehension (Bloom)  56
computer application training  421
  definition of  421
  how it differs from other learning  422
  how to design  434
  instructional events for  443
  requires teaching abstract information  422
  requires teaching arbitrary steps  426
  requires teaching numerous procedures  425
  three approaches to  429
concept
  as a type of information (Horn)  59
  concept (Gagne)  52
  defined concept (Gagne)  51
conceptual framework  439. *See* also cognition, cognitive framework
concreteness  26
content analysis  131, 133
  how to perform  254
  tips for analyzing steps  255
  used to identify enabling content  250
  what is needed to perform  254
context, maintaining  484

continue the procedure statement (in structured-English outlines). *See* structured-English outlines, continue the procedure statement
continuity. *See* sensory perception, continuity
contours. *See* sensory perception, contours
course prerequisites  405

# D

decision step. *See* procedure, decision step
delivery system. *See* instructional delivery system
demonstrations  364
design document. *See* instructional design document
discriminations (Gagne)  52

# E

eloboration  26
enabling content  122, 247. *See* also content analysis
  analyzing nonprocedural  133
  can be any type of information  258
  conceptual view of  131
  definition of  131, 248
  deleting  252
  examples of  131, 133, 249, 251, 256, 270–271
  failing to provide all  467
  format of  259
  how to identify  131, 247, 250
  necessity for  248
  systematic identification of  134
  teaching as a whole  272
  tied to specific behaviors  249
  used repeatedly  256
  what to do if SME wants to include content that is not  250

end of procedure statement (in structured-English outlines). *See* structured-English outlines, end of procedure statement

evaluation (Bloom)  57

events of instruction (Gagne)  94

exam
  conceptual test  354
  how to create  354
  performance test  354
  purposes of  354
  question types  354

examples  76, 102
  guidelines for providing  103
  importance of  458

excitement
  sense of, used to gain attention  18

exercises. *See* practice

## F

fact (Horn)  60

fading. *See* memory, retention and extinction

familiarity. *See* sensory perception, familiarity

Fleming, Malcom  23, 393

foreground. *See* sensory perception, foreground

framework, mental. *See* cognition, mental models

front-end analysis. *See* training requirements

fuzzy verbs  290

## G

Gagne, Robert  50, 54

Gestalt  22

Gilbert, Thomas F.  158

goto statement (in structured-English outlines). *See* structured-English outlines, goto statement

grouping. *See* sensory perception, grouping

## H

Hayes, Elisabeth R.  72

Higbee, Kenneth L.  32

horizon. *See* sensory perception, horizon

Horn, Robert  ix, 58, 63

Horton, Katherine  382

Horton, William  333, 382

## I

IBM 4-Tier Blended Learning Model  325
  mapped to Bloom's taxonomy  326
  Tier 1 - Performance Support and Reference  326
  Tier 2 - Interactive Learning  327
  Tier 3 - Collaborative Learning  328
  Tier 4 - Experience-Based Learning  329

if-then-else statement. *See* structured-English outlines, if-then-else statement

information
  how to classify into its type  62
  key  80, 103, 481–482
  sequencing  487. *See also* structuring the course

information dump  95, 494

information layering  472

information overload  460

information types. *See* taxonomies, learning, information types (Horn)

instructional analysis  122, 126, 191
  analyzing complex procedures. *See* procedure, analyzing complex
  conceptual view of  126, 170, 193
  examples of  193, 204
  how to perform  127, 194, 201
  importance of using knowledgeable SMEs for  202
  necessity for  129

performing without SME availability  128
requires judgment and skill  194
templates for  199
tools for performing  195
validating SME information  201
what to do with undefined processes  203
word processor use in  197, 199
working with SMEs during  199, 250
instructional delivery system  122, 139, 309, 311
  choosing  173, 311, 314, 317, 319, 331
  definition of  123, 140, 310
  determining constraints for  172
  examples of  140
  fads in  330
  impact on choosing instructional events  350
  strengths of technology delivery  331
instructional design  116. *See also* training; learning
  analytical nature of  118
  blended learning. *See* blended learning
  definition of  116
  delivery system. *See* instructional delivery system
  for computer application training. *See* computer application training
  identifying enabling content. *See* enabling content
  importance of  455
  introductions. *See* introductions
  layout and design principles. *See* layout and design principles
  making false assumptions during  465
  need for  117
  nine steps of  122
  overview of  118, 121
  performing in an imperfect world  507
  quiz. *See* exam
  skills and attitudes necessary to do  119
  structuring the course. *See* structuring the course
  summaries. *See* summaries

  target audience. *See* training requirements
  test. *See* exam
  training requirements. *See* training requirements
instructional design document  123, 143, 401
  course agenda  406
  course description  406
  course fit into curriculum. *See* course prerequisites
  course objectives  406
  course prerequisites. *See* course prerequisites
  course structure  406
  definition of  143, 402
  effort required for  410
  evaluation and assessment procedures and criteria  408
  example lesson  407
  executive summary  403
  job outcomes  404
  justification for training  404
  module and topic descriptions  407
  not always necessary  411
  overall business goal  404
  prototype  407
  purpose of  402
  sign-off page  404
  style guide  407
  target audience  404
  technology requirements  406
  title page  403
  typical entries in  144, 402
  what not to include  409
instructional development  509
instructional events  122, 141, 341
  definition of  141, 342
  designing  142, 342, 344
  documenting  364
  examples of  141, 342
  factors to consider in choosing  345
  for computer application training  443
  not developed during instructional design  343

instructional lesson. *See* lesson; structuring the course
instructional modules. *See* structuring the course
instructional objectives  79, 122, 138, 283
  are not capability statements  291
  conditions component of  292
  criteria component of  293
  definition of  138, 284
  editing  294
  examples of  287
  how to write  289
  performance component of  290
  relationship to course content, exercises, and tests  296
  three components of  287
  three types of  284
  uses of  138
  using verbs from Bloom's taxonomy in  290
  validating  294
  writing  122
  written at many different levels  288
  written for communication  299
  written late in the design process  139, 285
instructional strategies  100
  concrete to abstract  101
  example of for a concept  100
  example of for a procedure  100
  known to unknown  101–102
  simple to complex  101
instructional topics. *See* structuring the course
instructional units. *See* structuring the course
intellectual skills (Gagne)  33, 50
interactivity  489. *See* also instructional events
interference  26
introductions  351
  designing  352

## J

job aids  76
job analysis. *See* instructional analysis
job outcomes  178. *See* also training requirements
  characteristics of  162–163
  definition of  161
  evaluating statements of  166
  examples of  168, 358
  identifying  162, 172
  incorporating performance standards in  167
  types of  166
  what they are not  164
  why not begin with skills instead of?  162
job skills  74. *See* also job outcomes

## K

Kirkpatrick, Donald  408
knowledge
  as part of SKA taxonomy  47
  key. *See* information, key
  knowledge (Bloom)  55

## L

label statement (in structured-English outlines). *See* structured-English outlines, label statement
layering. *See* information layering
layout and design principles  392
lean instruction. *See* training, lean
learned capabilities  50
learning. *See* also training
  adult learning principles. see adult learning principles
  analogies  76
  biological requirements for  14
  bottlenecks to  5, 10, 17, 24
  cognitive encoding techniques. *See* cognition, cognitive encoding techniques

cognitive model of  37
context  79
cramming  8
examples. *See*  examples
exercises. *See*  exercises
firehose approach to  9
human  4
information dump  117
is biological, not just intellectual  7
memory. *See*  memory
motivation  19, 72, 75, 77, 83
needs analysis. *See*  instructional analysis
occurs when new neural interconnections are made  7
one-trial  8
pace. *See*  training, pace
practice. *See*  practice
relevance. *See*  learning, motivation
repitition  10
sensory perception. *See*  sensory perception
should be tailored to student's needs  74
simulations. *See*  training, simulations
stimulus  21
taxonomies. *See*  taxonomies, learning
transfer to the real world  77
lesson  122, 142, 377
  designing  122, 142
  designing prototype  378, 391
  style guide  379
levels of evaluation (Kirkpatrick)  408
Levie, Howard  23
Lyons, Chopeta  393

## M

Mager, Robert  ix, 158–160, 287, 299, 355
meaning  26
Medsker, Karen  54
memory
  bottlenecks to  17, 24
  chunking. *See*  chunking
  facilitating  26
  limitations of  25
  long-term  25
  methods for aiding  494
  recall  28, 32, 463
  recognition  28, 32, 463
  retention and extinction  8
  retrieval from long-term  28
  short-term  11, 25
motion
  used to gain attention  17
motivation. *See*  learning, motivation
motor skills (Gagne)  33, 53
multi-channel, multi-sensory stimuli  23

## N

needs
  satisfaction of used to gain attention  18
needs analysis  73. *See also*  instructional analysis
neural interconnections  7
  fade over time unless reinforced  9
  how to strengthen  10, 33
note statement (in structured-English outlines). *See*  structured-English outlines, note statement
novelty
  used to gain attention  17

## O

objectives. *See*  instructional objectives
organization  22, 25
overviews  79, 96

## P

performance gap. *See*  instructional analysis
performance test. *See*  exam
Pipe, Peter  159

practice  xiii, 24, 81–82, 103, 122, 141, 356, 462
  bottlenecks to  17
  can make things worse  35
  definition of  141
  designing  360
  determining where needed  357
  environment for  81
  feedback for  34, 361, 462
  in self-paced learning  360
  repetition of  361, 469
  required for learning  34
  requires feedback  16, 36, 388
  should match behaviors in objectives  356
  spaced review  26, 103
  specifications  362
prerequisite information  479
  refreshing  24
principle (Horn)  60
procedure
  action step  217
  analyzing complex  215
  as a type of information (Horn)  58
  conceptual view of complex  215
  decision step  217, 440
  identifying complex  348
  indented outline representation for  220
  limitation of flowchart representation for  219
  structured-English outline. See structured-English outline
  teaching complex  237
process (Horn)  59
prototype. See lesson, designing prototype

## Q

quiz. See exam

## R

result statement (in structured-English outlines). See structured-English outlines, result statement
Roy G. Biv  25
rule
  higher-order rule (Gagne)  51
  rule (Gagne)  51

## S

sensory perception  16, 23
  background  22
  bottlenecks to  16
  chunking  22
  closure  22
  color  22
  continuity  22
  contours  22
  familiarity  22
  foreground  22
  Gestalt  22
  grouping  22
  horizon  22
  organization  22
  stimulus position  22
  typography  22
sequence  26
skill
  as part of SKA taxonomy  46
  not a substitute for job outcome. See job outcomes
SMEs (subject-matter experts). See instructional analysis, working with SMEs during
sound, used to gain attention  18
stimulus. See also learning, stimulus
  change of used to gain attention  17
  multi-sensory  23
  position of. See sensory perception, stimulus position
structure, as a type of information (Horn)  61
structured-English outlines  222

case statement  224–226
continue the procedure statement  227
end of procedure statement  232
goto statement  222, 225
if-then-else statement  226
label statement  223
note statement  234
result statement  233
subroutine statement  229
structuring the course  75, 122, 135, 267, 487
   conceptual view of  136
   definition of  268
   examples of  136, 268
   how to perform  135
   identifying and grouping common enabling information  270
   mapping activities and tasks to course units  273
   necessity for  137
   overview of  269
   refining the course structure  276
   why structure should be based on analysis  277
style guide. *See* lesson, style guide
subject-matter experts (SMEs). *See* instructional analysis, working with SMEs during
subroutine statement (in structured-English outlines). *See* structured-English outlines, subroutine statement
summaries  353
synthesis (Bloom)  57

# T

tabula rasa  460
talking head training  457
target audience. *See* training requirements
task analysis. *See* instructional analysis
taxonomies, learning

Bloom's Learning Taxonomy, Cognitive Domain  57
Horn's Information Types  99
teaching, key principles of  105
television advertisements  19
test. *See* exam
Tool Chest, The  436
training. *See* also learning
   ad hoc approach to  117
   analysis. *See* instructional analysis
   audience. *See* training requirements
   blended learning. *See* blended learning
   breaking up long-periods of passive  349
   building confidence  82
   case studies  76
   delivery system. *See* instructional delivery system
   demonstrations  76
   enabling skills and content  97
   environment  78
   examples. *See* examples
   exercises. *See* practice
   fire hose approach to  117
   introductions. *See* introductions
   layout and design principles. *See* layout and design principles
   lean  492
   lesson. *See* lesson
   making false assumptions  465
   mistakes. *See* twenty common training mistakes rating sheet
   module. *See* structuring the course
   motivation  xiv
   needs analysis. *See* needs analysis
   objectives. *See* instructional objectives
   overviews. *See* overviews
   pace  81–82
   practice. *See* practice
   prerequisite information  97
   prerequisites. *See* course prerequisites
   quiz. *See* exam
   rating. *See* twenty common training mistakes rating sheet

should be tailored to meet the student's needs  xiv, 83
should include only necessary content  74
should take the viewpoint of the student  490
simulations  77
strategies. *See* instructional strategies
structuring. *See* structuring the course
style and tone  104
summaries. *See* summaries
talking head  457
target audience. *See* training requirements
test. *See* exam
topic. *See* structuring the course
unit. *See* structuring the course
usually requires the teaching of multiple types of information  62
what it should feel like  xiv
training analysis. *See* instructional analysis
training audience. *See* training requirements
training design document. *See* instructional design document
training requirements  123, 157. *See also* content analysis; instructional analysis
　audience analysis  161, 176, 405
　definition of  123
　describing the target audience  161
　determining delivery system constraints  173
　gathering general project-related information  174
　how gathered  125
　identifying job outomes  172
　necessity for  124
　overview of  156
　questions to be addressed by  125
　template for  126, 181
transfer of skills to the job  486
twenty common training mistakes rating sheet  497

typography. *See* sensory perception, typography

# U

user interface  380
　accessibility of  388
　authoring tools  382
　characterisics of a good  380
　common screens  387
　determining overall approach  383
　how to design  381
　layout and design. *See* layout and design principles
　maintaining context  385
　navigation  385
　progress tracking and reporting  386
　prototype for  389
　requires interative design  391
　student path through  384
　style guide for  390

# V

verbal information (Gagne)  53
visualization  26

# W

Williams, Robin  393
Wilson, Arthur L.  72
Winchester Mystery House  117
word processor. *See* instructional analysis, word processor use in

Printed in Great Britain
by Amazon